Locality, Province and Nation

Essays on Indian Politics 1870 to 1940

Locality, Province and Nation
Essays on Indian Politics

1870 to 1940

Reprinted from Modern Asian Studies 1973

EDITED BY

JOHN GALLAGHER, GORDON JOHNSON
& ANIL SEAL

CAMBRIDGE
AT THE UNIVERSITY PRESS
1973

Published by the Syndics of the Cambridge University Press
Bentley House, 200 Euston Road, London NW1 2DB
American Branch: 32 East 57th Street, New York, N.Y. 10022

© Cambridge University Press 1973

Library of Congress Catalogue Card Number: 73–78322

ISBN: 0 521 09811 4

Printed in Great Britain by
Alden & Mowbray Ltd.
at the Alden Press, Oxford

Contents

Maps

The research in this volume has been generously supported by the Social Science Research Council's Modern Indian History Project; the Master and Fellows of Trinity College, and the Faculty Board of Oriental Studies, Cambridge, have made grants towards the cost of publication. The articles are reprinted from *Modern Asian Studies*, volume 7, part 3 (July 1973).

Imperialism and Nationalism in India

ANIL SEAL

AMONG the dominant themes of world history during the nineteenth and twentieth centuries have been the imperialism of the west and the nationalism of its colonial subjects. Nowhere were these themes developed more spectacularly than in South Asia; its history quite naturally came to be viewed as a gigantic clash between these two large forces. The subject then was held together by a set of assumptions about the imperialism of the British and the reactions of the Indians against it. That imperialism, so it was thought, had engineered great effects on the territories where it ruled. Those who held the power could make the policy, and they could see that it became the practice. Sometimes that policy might be formulated ineptly or might fall on stony ground or even smash against the hard facts of colonial life. But for good or ill, imperial policy seemed to be the main force affecting colonial conditions. It emerged from an identifiable source, the official mind of Whitehall or the contrivances of pro-consuls; and so the study of policy-making made a framework for investigations into colonial history.

These assumptions were convenient, but historians of colony after colony have knocked them down. The emphasis has shifted from the elegant exchanges between London and colonial capitals to the brutal clashes between colonial politicians struggling at the more humdrum levels where the pickings lay. No longer will it do to exalt the work of Mr Mothercountry, cobbling together constitutions for dependencies, above the inescapable constraints inside them. The old assumption that direct imperial power was strong has been replaced by the new doctrine that it was hobbled at every turn. It depended on local allies. Local conditions might buckle its policies. Often it did not know what it was doing. Assumptions about the irresistible power of imperialism were always slippery notions;[1] now they are refuted notions. Once the study of policy-making lay in the mainstream; now it has retreated into

---

[1] Perhaps the most devoted advocate of imperial power was Curzon, but bitter experience led him to conclude that 'The Government of India is a mighty and miraculous machine for doing nothing'. Curzon to Hamilton, 9 April 1902. Curzon Papers, Mss Eur F 111/161, India Office Library.

backwaters. The effect upon the study of modern Indian history is plain. Historians have switched their attention from imperial fiats to Indian facts, from the rambling generalizations of the Raj to the concreteness of local studies, from large imprecision to minute exactitude. In so doing, they have demolished part of the framework of the subject.

At the same time they have cracked the other casing which helped to hold it together. However tentative its beginnings, nationalism in India used to be seen as a general movement which voiced the interests of large sections of the Indian people. Just as imperial policies were thought to lead to imperial practice, so nationalist programmes were thought to emerge from national movements. But much the same findings which have been fatal to the old views about imperialism have also destroyed the view that nationalism was a force working generally inside a nation. As its provincial, and then its local roots have been laid bare, what looked like an all-India movement appears as nothing of the sort. Programmes proclaimed from above were at odds with the way politicians worked lower down. What held true in one part of India was not true in another. It is no longer credible to write about a movement grounded in common aims, led by men with similar backgrounds, and recruited from widening groups with compatible interests. That movement now looks more like a ramshackle coalition throughout its long career. Its unity seems a figment. Its power appears as hollow as that of the imperial authority it was supposedly challenging. Its history was the rivalry between Indian and Indian, its relationship with imperialism that of the mutual clinging of two unsteady men of straw. Consequently, it now seems impossible to organize modern Indian history around the old notions of imperialism and nationalism. But their disappearance has had awkward results.

Having failed to discover unities in the politics of all-India, historians cut their losses by turning to the study of the regions, whether defined as the old provinces of British India or as areas with a common language. There they hoped to find unities to help them regulate these new fields of study: caste seemed to explain much about the politics of Bengal and Madras, as did religious allegiance in the Punjab, kinship in the United Provinces and language in Orissa or the Karnatak. In turning to the regions, and to the solidarities within them, these scholars were in fact falling back on positions prepared long ago by the British administrators. Over and over again the Old India Hands had stressed that India was not a nation but a congeries of countries,[2] each of which

---

[2] According to Sir John Strachey, '. . . the first and most essential thing to learn about India—[is] that there is not, and never was an India, or even any country of

contained large groups of people who were held together by bonds such as caste and kin, community and language, and who could be classed under these tidy heads for the convenience of the administrators. Here were sets of ready-made uniformities around which the historian of the region could crystallize his explanations. For a time it seemed as though the truisms of the Raj were to become the dogmas of the historians.[3] But the roots of politics turned out to lie lower still. Other workers have dug below the province and the region, into the district, the municipality, even the village. Mining at such deep levels had led to the caving-in of beliefs that there were regional uniformities cementing Indian politics. What seems to have decided political choices in the localities was the race for influence, status and resources. In the pursuit of these aims, patrons regimented their clients into factions which jockeyed for position. Rather than partnerships between fellows, these were usually associations of bigwigs and followers. In other words they were vertical alliances, not horizontal alliances. Local struggles were seldom marked by the alliance of landlord with landlord, peasant with peasant, educated with educated, Muslim with Muslim and Brahmin with Brahmin. More frequently, Hindus worked with Muslims, Brahmins were hand in glove with non-Brahmins; and notables organized their dependents as supporters, commissioned professional men as spokesmen and turned government servants into aides. In the everyday decisions of life as they were taken in many localities, the social dockets devised by the administrator and adopted by the historian had little meaning.

As knowledge has increased, so has confusion. Politics at the base seem different in kind from politics in the province or in the nation. Whatever forces may have brought men into partnership at these higher levels, they can hardly have been the same as those which made men work together in the neighbourhoods. However persuasive the slogans from the top, they can have made little impact upon the unabashed scramblers for advantage at the bottom. Indeed there seems no necessary reason why the politics of these localities should have become enmeshed with the larger processes at all. It is not obvious why bosses

India, possessing according to European ideas, any sort of unity. . . .' It is interesting that this classic apology for British rule stressed its centralizing and unifying impact, but denied that 'such bonds of union can in any way lead towards the growth of a single Indian nationality'. John Strachey, *India* (London, 1888), pp. 5, 8.

[3] The officials of the Raj provided many of the data upon which studies of the political arithmetic of the regions are based, and administrative practice rested on their categories. That is another reason why their arguments have powerfully influenced the new wave among historians of India.

in Tanjore or Belgaum should have sought allies in Madras or Bombay, still less in all-India circles. But there is no denying that such linkages existed, and that they came to exert a vast influence over the country's politics. The Indian Association and the Unionist party each spanned a province; the Hindu Mahasabha, the anti-untouchability league, the movements for sanatanadharma and cow-protection worked across several provinces; the Home Rule Leagues, the National Liberal Federation, the Indian National Social Conference, the all-India Scheduled Castes Federation, the Khilafat Party and the Muslim Conference claimed to be national bodies; while the Congress and the Muslim League were undeniably all-India organizations. Non-cooperation, civil disobedience, and the movements for Quit India and for Pakistan were not the products of the village green. It would be a sterile historiography which resigned itself to declaring that these were the products of linkages whose nature is unknown. The result would be the disintegration of the subject.

One of the main tasks in its reintegration must be to identify the forces which drove Indian politics upwards and outwards from the oddities of the locality, or downwards from the hollow generalities of all-India, which bonded their political activities together, and which determined the nature of the relations between them. This work of reconstruction must also find an explanation for the extraordinary volatility and discontinuity of political behaviour in so much of India, as well as for the palpable gap between what politicians claimed to represent and what they really stood for. The priorities of politicians, the roles they played, the principles they claimed to support, seem to have varied as they moved between one arena and another; in each and every sphere, the alliances they made showed extreme shifts and turns. Members of the Justice Party in the nineteen-twenties were the Congressmen of the nineteen-thirties. Cooperators became non-cooperators. The gaolbirds of civil disobedience came out for council entry. Congress Muslims turned round and supported Pakistan. These are large problems, and they call for large solutions. It is not good enough for the historian to set up an explanation of the workings of politics at one level and then cast around for a few supporting examples at another, higher or lower, conveniently forgetting that most of these cases actually cut across the grain of his argument. In the analysis of a political system which worked at different levels, models appropriate for one of them cannot simply be transposed to the others. Local, provincial and national politics worked as they did because they were interconnected; it is the connections which must be elucidated. The problem is central to the history of all colonial nationalisms in modern times. Formed out of disparate aspirations and grievances, they were somehow generalized into unities stronger than their own contradictions. In the Indian context, the problem takes this form. A great deal of local Indian politics (although, as we shall see, not all) was organized into factions by the influence of the strong upon the weak, and into systems apparently insulated from each other. Lateral connections and solidarities which might have united them were few. Yet they came to be linked with other systems, thereby producing large movements. What was the nature of those linkages?

Several explanations have been suggested. One line of argument has stressed the enduring importance of traditional forces throughout all the changes in modern India. Webs of kinship and of clan, solidarities of community and ritual might be seen as conserving or regenerating supra-local unities. Another argument asserts that the development of the economy drove the localities into larger and larger systems of production and exchange. Admittedly there was no national economy: development was far too patchy for that. But in some parts of India the increase in cash crops, the growth of trading communities and the development of the professions stimulated both town and country, encouraging the spread of social groups, whether they were rich peasants in the Andhra delta, traders along the Ganges, the western-educated in Calcutta or businessmen in Bombay. There is merit in both arguments. Certainly there were cases in most regions where the emergence of larger groupings can best be explained by linkages which were the result of traditional or economic forces. It is still more suggestive that some of these groupings tended to stick together through thick and thin, an atypical trait which was to give them great importance in Indian politics. However, these cases of horizontal connection cannot explain how linkages were forged between the host of factions that did not possess solidarities of this sort. Yet it was precisely these factions that were the stuff of most Indian politics. On the unsteady base of local squabbles for spoils rested the larger political systems of India: the Justice and Unionist parties, and the Congress itself, were largely built out of this rubble. Both types of politics need to be explained, but the arguments mentioned so far can apply only to the loyalties of horizontal connection and not to the vast mass of political systems which lacked them. In order to provide a more general explanation, we propose an alternative approach.

This entails reopening the study of government, although not along the old lines. The argument that the rule of strangers in India goaded their subjects into organizing against it is not our concern. The suggestion that government prepared its own destruction by fostering an intellectual elite is not relevant.[4] The fact that the power of imperialism was far from irresistible can readily be admitted. What is important about the role of government is the structure which the British created for ruling their Indian empire. However much they may have relied on Indian collaborators, their government was organized for the power and profit of their imperial system throughout the world. In the pursuit of this aim, they needed to treat their Indian possessions as a whole. Though they were the successors of nawabs and maharajahs galore, they were in India not as partitioners but as unifiers. Essentially, the Indian empire was meant to be indivisible.[5] Hence it was ruled through a chain of command stretching from London to the districts and townships of India; hence too, the government of India held sway over all-India, so that even the pettiest official intervention in a locality issued from a general authority. These administrative lines formed a grid which at first rested loosely upon the base. Later it was pressed down more firmly by the heavier intervention of the Raj in local matters and by the growth of representative institutions. Indians needed to treat with the Raj, and increasingly they came to do so by exploiting its structure of control and the forms in which its commands were cast. This called for a political structure of their own which could match the administrative and representative structure of the Raj, and was in time to inherit its functions. In this way we may help to explain the nature of the linkages which were to bind together the very different activities of Indians in arenas large and small.

II

We shall begin by looking afresh at the interplay between imperialism and Indian political society. It is our hypothesis that the structure of imperial government can provide a clue to the way Indian politics developed. This structure in India cannot be explained by Indian considerations alone. It is obvious that the development of the Raj moved widdershins to the tendencies prevalent in the British empire as

[4] Graduates and professional men in the presidencies undoubtedly had a large part to play in the politics of province and nation. But they were not quite as important as they once appeared. Some of the suggestions in Anil Seal, *The Emergence of Indian Nationalism* (Cambridge, 1968), have dropped through the trapdoor of historiography.

[5] Of course the presidencies liked to recall their separate historical pasts. So did the princes. But the Supreme Goverment eroded these little local vanities.

a whole. When the British were relying upon the techniques of informal empire to better their world position, their Indian possessions stood out as a huge exception, as a formal empire on the grand scale. At the very time they were slackening control over many of their colonies, they were tightening London's hold over India. Incongruities of this sort continued into the twentieth century, when the administrative diversities in the new African colonies contrasted with the uniformities of the Raj, and when imperial control over defence and foreign policy, splintered throughout much of the empire, remained as firm as ever in India. Most of the essential aspects of the connection between Britain and India remained substantially unchanged until 1947. Why should this have been so? The reasons for these incongruities lie in the permanent importance of India to the position of Britain in the world and the permanent difficulties of maintaining the British position in India.

India's worth was clear to Pitt and Dundas; the establishment of British power in India was matched by her growing importance as a base for further expansion in the Indian Ocean and the Yellow Sea. During the nineteenth century India became a good customer for British manufactures; she was to become a useful supplier of raw materials, a crucial element in the British balance of payments and a field for large capital investment. But the balance sheets of imperialism do not reveal the full importance of the Raj to the British Empire. Imperialism is a system of formal or informal expansion, driven by impulses of profit and of power, each of which feeds on the other. India's growing foreign trade helped to push the influence of the British deeper into west and east Asia alike. Her growing military power underwrote the informal influence they were developing in those regions, as well as the formal empire which they built in Burma, Malaya and East Africa. India became the second centre for the extension of British power and influence in the world; and when she dropped this role after 1947, the British empire did not take long to disappear.

Throughout the century and a half of British rule, the Raj was being worked in the service of interests far larger than India herself, since they bore upon the British position in the world. That is why the control of the Raj as a system of profit and power had to lie in London. And that is why London's control over India had to be matched by the increasingly tight grip of the Governor-General over his subordinate administrations. These imperial aims combined with the circumstances in India itself to determine the structure of government and the nature of its administration. The British wanted to pull resources out of India, not to put their own into India. Therefore the administrative and mili-

tary system had to pay for itself with Indian revenues. At the top, this
called for a skilled bureaucracy capable of handling large issues bearing
upon the economy and the army. But at lower levels this control had
to be looser. There, imperial ends had to be satisfied by more modest
programmes. The chief source of Indian revenue lay in land, and it had
to be collected from millions of payers. In the localities the main tasks
were to secure the cheap and regular collection of revenue and to see to
it that the districts remained quiet. But these tasks were beyond the
unaided capacity of the British administrators on the spot.[6] British
agents were costly. Happily, Indian collaborators were not, and for
much of the business of extracting tribute and keeping the peace, the
British were content to follow the precepts of Clive and Cornwallis by
relying on the help of influential Indians prepared to work with the
regime. It was in the administration of the localities that the vital
economies in ruling had to be made. There, governance had to be
pursued by simpler arrangements, such as the frontier methods of Nikel
Seyn in the Punjab or the lonely patrols of Cross Beames in the wilds of
Orissa, or by enlisting the cooperation of zemindars, mirasidars, talukdars, and urban rais.

By accepting such men as their local collaborators, the British were in
fact striking a political bargain. Its terms were that they could depend
on the collection of revenue, provided that they did not ask too officious-
ly who paid it; and that they might take public order for granted,
provided that they themselves did not play too obtrusive a part in
enforcing it. The British built the framework; the Indians fitted into
it. Local bargains of this sort were of great advantage to the British
because they reduced Indian politics to the level of haggles between the
Raj and small pockets of its subjects, a system which kept them satis-
factorily divided. These were solid gains, but they had to be paid for.
In return, the British had to acquiesce in an arrangement where strong
local intermediaries could block them from meddling in the affairs of
those who owned land, or controlling the others who tilled it. This
meant in practice that the British were winking at the existence of a
legal underworld where the private justice of faction settled conflicts
with the blows of lathis, or where, at the best, the strong could get their
own way in the courts. In the mythology of empire, the age of Elphin-
stone, Munro and Thomason seems one of heroic social engineering;
but under the pinnacles of their Raj lay a ground-floor reality where
Indians battled with Indians, sometimes for the favours of the district
officer, sometimes to do each other down without reference to him and

[6] White settlers, once prohibited, later were never more than a handful.

his book of rules. At these levels, it might be the British who governed, but it was Indians who ruled.

This is not to suggest that at any period the Raj was merely a night-watchman and receiver of tribute;[7] or that its systems of collaboration simply meant confirming things as they were. Even under John Company, government ratified, or upset, social and economic arrangements which extended far beyond the localities. In this rupturing of the autonomy of regions and localities lies one of the chief innovations of British rule. The Raj defined the forms and established the categories even in matters where its subjects were allowed a free hand. Already in this period Indian response had to take note of British regulation. After 1843 men from Sind, Gujarat, Maharashtra and the Karnatak had to vie with each other for the favours of an administration run from Bombay city. Once men had been classed as zemindars or ryots in the settlements, they had to accept these classifications when they treated with government.

But the irruption of government into the regions and localities went much further in the second half of the nineteenth century. As imperial interests expanded, so did their demands upon India. Indian revenues had to pay for an army liable to defend British interests outside India;[8] they had to meet the growing overheads of administration; they had to guarantee loans for the railways. These demands were harder to meet. In 1858 the Crown inherited from the Company a regime crippled by poverty, and until the end of the century the reorganized government was never to escape from financial weakness. A costly dash in and out of Afghanistan, a fall in silver or a bad monsoon could tip Indian finances into deficit. Crises were likelier than windfalls. Direct taxes yielded little.[9] Locked in these fetters, the Raj had to create more resources and

[7] Many of the land settlements of the Raj were also designed to stimulate agrarian improvement; its canals brought new land under cultivation; its improvements to transport linked cities which it had done so much to create. It sent Indians to school, partly to train cheap clerks for its offices, but also to create economic men. But to judge the Raj as an immensely powerful system of government makes sense only in terms of policy-making. In practice, many of its efforts were buckled by the hard facts of Indian society.

[8] About a third of the total expenditure of the Indian government in the four decades before World War I was on its army. Statistical tables on government's finances (and on many other aspects of Indian society and economy) are being prepared, with the help of C. Emery, by the modern Indian history project at Cambridge, financed by a grant from the Social Sciences Research Council. It is hoped to publish these results soon.

[9] Expanding its revenues was a difficult task for a government which relied upon so regressive a system of taxation. Income tax was obstructed by Indian interests, customs duties were kept low by imperial interests, opium was threatened by humani-

take its cut. Tribute from the lease of franchises to local notables was no longer enough to meet the bill. Loose controls by London of Calcutta, by Calcutta of its provinces, by provincial capitals of the districts had all to be tightened. Raising revenues meant a greater administrative intervention in the affairs of Indian society, going deeper than the previous system had done. But such an intervention was exposed to the perennial dilemma of the Raj. If the administrative cost of intervening was not to overtake the returns and the security of the state not to be put at risk, Indian collaboration would have to be much extended. So the Raj mitigated its administrative drive by devising new methods of winning the cooperation of a larger number of Indians. Systems of nomination, representation and election were all means of enlisting Indians to work for imperial ends.

The Government of India Act of 1858 had created a Secretary of State whose powers stretched far beyond those of his predecessor, the President of the Board of Control. He was in continuous touch with policy-making; before long he had won 'abundant power in one way or another of enforcing his views';[10] and he could demand due obedience from all British authorities in India. Thus the constitutional principle became established that '. . . the final control and direction of affairs of India rest with the Home Government, and not with the authorities . . . in India itself'.[11] Even the Acts of 1919 and 1935 kept London in command of the centre, and until 1947 the vital attributes of sovereignty remained there.[12] London did what it pleased with India's army; it took her to war, and it brought her to peace; London alone could alter her constitution. It was London that took the decisions about the siphoning-off of Indian revenues, the pace of Indian development, and the deployment of Indian power; and these controls were kept intact until London decided to divide and quit.

Not only did the nature of imperial aims call for London's control

tarian interests. Until the beginning of the twentieth century, government finances continued to be propped up by the peasants, since receipts from land revenue were greater than receipts from all other taxes put together.

[10] Sir Charles Wood quoted in R. J. Moore, *Sir Charles Wood's Indian Policy 1853–66* (Manchester, 1966), p. 39.

[11] A. C. Banerjee, *Indian Constitutional Documents 1757–1947* (Calcutta, 1961, third edition), II, 319.

[12] Control over defence and foreign policy was not even mentioned in the Montagu–Chelmsford report; the Government of India Act of 1935 stated that this control was to remain in British hands (26 Geo. V, c. 2, section 11). London also kept the true underpinnings of profit. It was from London that Indian loans came; London manipulated the exchange rate of the rupee as it saw fit and knocked India off the gold standard when that suited its purpose. Even the granting of tariff autonomy to India meant less in practice than in publicity.

over India; it also called for control over its subordinate administrations to keep them in line with British purposes. The Charter Act of 1833, which brought the Supreme Government into being, had also granted the Governor-General in Council control over the entire revenues of all the territories in British India. Point by point, the government in Calcutta hammered home these advantages, strengthening its manager- ial services, framing a central budget, and regulating finances so that the provinces had to live on whatever doles the centre saw fit to allow them. One by one, the old freedoms of the Presidencies were mopped up by Calcutta. In 1893 the Bombay and Madras military commands were abolished; during the early twentieth century the central government gradually wrested from the provinces their control over relations with the princely states. It became the orthodoxy of constitutional lawyers that, whatever the rights and the duties of the provinces in running their affairs, yet '... in all of them the Government of India exercise an unquestioned right of entry...'[13] During the nineteenth century the provinces had been degraded into mere agents of the centre. In the twentieth century administrative necessity might demand decentraliza- tion and political pressures might call for devolution, but even the Acts of 1919 and 1935 were not permitted by the rulers of India to threaten central control over matters that crucially affected imperial purposes in India.[14] In terms of formal constitutional history these Acts may have altered the working arrangements of the Raj; but in terms of power they were simply changes in the methods by which the British pursued their essential aims.

But managers need agents, and in the Indian empire these had to be the provincial administrations. The general principles of legislation and administration were laid down from above, but the execution of both had to be undertaken in the provinces. In the later nineteenth century London and Calcutta decided that more needed to be done with their Indian empire: tenancy legislation, new laws about contract and trans- fer of land, public works, irrigation, public health, forest conservancy, famine codes, takkavi loans, education both primary and secondary, all

---

[13] *Report on Indian Constitutional Reforms* (Calcutta, 1918), para. 49, p. 33.

[14] After 1919 the provinces had assured monies of their own; but the central government took a firmer grip than before in auditing their accounts. Again, the provincial governments administered the Criminal Investigation Departments founded between 1905 and 1907; but important intelligence work was always left to officers from the central CID after 1919, and the reforms of 1935 led to the appointment in the province of a Central Intelligence Officer who was responsible to the Intelligence Bureau in New Delhi. Sir Percival Griffiths, *To Guard My People. The History of the Indian Police* (London, 1971), pp. 342–54.

came to be in the day's work for this improving government. Much of the legislation was framed in the provinces. Most of the actual work was done in the provinces. Provincial secretariats and district officers had new duties piled upon them. The local arms of all the central departments, whether forestry or agriculture, commerce or industry, excise or education, were jerked into a new activity. The hordes of petty officials who had been government servants more in name than in deed, now had to respond more efficiently to orders from above.

But these developments had to be paid for. Since government needed to squeeze the last rupee out of its territories, this in turn could only mean more thorough intervention on its part. In pulling up the slack at the base of the system, the Raj called upon its provinces and their agents to meddle more actively below. The easy-going collaboration which had guided affairs in so many localities was no longer adequate for those purposes. Hence there were bound to be big upsets in old franchises. But here was the rub. Even under the old system, there had been plenty of upsets. After the rising of 1857, the British became preoccupied with the stability of their rule, more sensitive to Indian pressures, more alert to Indian opinion. They were well aware that they had to soothe discontents and, wherever possible, deflect them against other Indians. The new situation complicated that task: the heavier the intervention, the higher the risk.

Between the pressures of imperial demands and of Indian discontents, the Raj negotiated uneasily. In obedience to the former, there had to be more rule-making and general instructions from headquarters, and the power of the bureaucracies had to smack harder upon Indian society. On the other hand, these new intrusions into old immunities were balanced by the development of a system of representation, designed to make administrative pressures more acceptable, the rule-making process less arbitrary, and the recruitment of Indian assistants at the levels where they were needed less difficult. This system was set to work particularly at the points of execution rather than of command.

To begin with, there were strong pragmatic grounds for granting Indians a limited say in the conduct of local affairs.[15] These were not in the main the reasons that appealed to Ripon in his famous resolution, nor have they been emphasized by historians who see local self-government as the first stage in the political education of Indians. As Lawrence

[15] But leading Indian politicians, concerned to change the structure of the Legislative Councils, quickly lost interest in local self-government when they saw that it was to begin and end in the localities; only when it came to be tied more firmly to the structure of rule above, did their interest in the municipalities and rural boards revive.

and Mayo were acutely aware, financial stringency made good sense of changes which successfully loaded the new municipalities with police and conservancy charges. When municipal and local boards were formed in most of the provinces after 1882, economy was again the clue. These local institutions also aided the Raj in its search for resources. Their powers were small, but the sums they raised and disbursed steadily increased. They had another useful role to play. They enabled government to associate interests in the localities more widely, and balance them more finely, than had the old rule of thumb methods of the Collector.[16]

Beyond these pragmatic considerations, the widening of the representative system carried political advantages of a different sort. It brought more Indians into consultation about the management of their affairs; yet it kept them at work inside a framework which safeguarded British interests. In other words, the new system was casting wider nets to find collaborators. Conversations in the dak bungalow or on the Collector's verandah were no longer a satisfactory means for selecting them. Nomination based on the representation of interests was one way of finding them; elections found even more. Both methods worked to keep them in equipoise. In this way, representation became one of the vehicles for driving deeper into local society.

But these modest representative bodies were to become important for another reason. Once the British extended municipal and district boards into most of the provinces, they went on to use them for purposes beyond the limited spheres of local taxation and administration. The British found them convenient as a way of adding, first a representative, and later an elective, veneer to the superior councils which they were now developing. After the India Councils Act of 1861, provincial legislative councils were set up in Madras, Bombay and Bengal; the North-western Provinces obtained a council in 1886, and the Punjab in 1897. The Act of 1892 increased the number of nominated members on these councils; but it also admitted the elective principle by the back door, since nominations might now be recommended by specific Indian organizations. In practice, this came to mean that district boards and municipalities, together with landlords, chambers of commerce and universities, nominated a few members. In 1909 the Morley–Minto reforms extended the links between higher and lower councils and

---

[16] Thus, for example, the membership of the rural boards in the Central Provinces was intended to represent the interests of landlords and traders; during the eighteen-eighties some towns in the Punjab began to reserve seats for communities. Much the same process can be seen in the municipalities of the United Provinces before 1916.

enlarged the role of local men. Twelve of the twenty-seven members of the Legislative Council of the Governor-General were to be chosen by the non-official members of the provincial councils; and in each of the provincial councils a number of members were to be elected by the municipalities and district boards. At the same time, special interests such as landlords, Muslims and businessmen had the right to elect members to both provincial councils and the council of the Governor-General.

Throughout this evolution two processes were at work. First, it is evident that Government was now balancing interests by separating them into categories of its own defining. Who were 'the Mohammadan Community in the Presidency of Bengal' or the 'Landholders in the United Provinces', each of whom was to elect one member to the Governor-General's Council? Neither of these bland categories made any sense at the local level in Bengal and the United Provinces; both of them ignored the different interests and rivalries among those groups whom the British bundled together in a phrase.

In the second place, the spread of representation had now produced a legislative system which extended from the lowest to the highest level in India. In one sense the system formed a sort of representative pyramid. In most provinces the sub-district boards acted as electoral colleges for part of the membership of district boards. Together with the municipalities, these boards elected members to the provincial councils, which in turn elected members to the imperial council. But in a wider sense the British had now constructed a representative and legislative structure which complemented their administrative structure. Together these two systems created bonds between the localities and the higher arenas of politics and administration.

While the reforms of 1919 upset the pyramid, they greatly strengthened these bonds. Local bodies no longer elected to provincial councils, but they were bolted much more firmly into provincial politics. As part of the bargain of dyarchy, local self-government became the responsibility of ministers who were appointed from among non-official members. They used their influence over local affairs to reward their friends and punish their critics. But there was another side to the coin. Members of local boards and of provincial councils alike were now elected on a much wider franchise. Hence a wider range of local interests had to be cajoled. Members of the new provincial councils found that their constituents were much more disposed to re-elect them when the lives of these voters had been sweetened by tit-bits flung to them by the ministers. Charity in the locality now began in the province.

The hierarchy of British rule through Indian collaboration survived the reforms of 1935. The centre still kept a firm grip over sovereign authority, reserving important powers over the provinces and giving its Indian collaborators little say in these safeguards; by granting the provinces the substance of self-government, by widening the electorate, the British ensured that their provincial successors had also to take account of far larger numbers of Indians who had the vote. While shooting Niagara, the British saw to it that their central powers remained intact and that India was still ruled by an interconnected system of government. The federal provisions of the 1935 Act never came into operation. The uncertainty that flowed from this, together with the outbreak of war, meant that this Act was only a temporary settlement. The proposals from the Viceroy, the missions from London, and the talks at Delhi were preludes for transfer of power at the centre which the Raj had guarded so jealously for so long.

As preparations to concession, whether interim or final, the British stuck to their old strategy of thrusting their subjects into broad categories and divisions. The Hindus, Muslims, Sikhs and Depressed Classes defined by the Communal Award of 1932 were the penultimate classifications in a policy which ended in Partition. By the federal arrangements of 1935 an even more improbable category, the Indian Princes, was brought into the game. This was part and parcel of a process which can be seen both in the administrative and the representative systems of the Raj in India. As government intervened more, as its regulations became more uniform, its rules more Olympian, the categories which defined Indian diversity had to become more and more abstract and rough-hewn. What remained true from first to last was that Indians could not afford to ignore them in their political response.

III

In this section, the emphasis will lie on the forces which brought together the politics of small and larger arenas in India. By scrutinizing linkages, perhaps some of the puzzles of modern Indian history will be resolved: Why have good arguments about the nature of politics at one level lost cogency when applied to another? Why have Indian politicians played such apparently inconsistent roles in different spheres? Why have they claimed to stand for one interest when in fact they were pursuing another? How have the politics of constitutionalism and agitation been connected? What has governed the timing of outbursts of activity and of relapses into quiescence?

A straightforward hypothesis provides a way into the problem. Government was intervening in the local affairs of its subjects. These interventions took place inside a system of rule stretching from London to the Indian village. Government was pressing upon the uneven and disjointed societies of its subjects; they reacted, and their reactions differed. Indian diversity ensured endless variations in their response to government pressure, normally uniform, but they all had to devise systems of politics which enabled them to react at the points where that pressure was applied. In responding to government Indians had to be adaptable, and here one pliancy met another. However much it may have blustered to the contrary, the Raj was designed to respond to some pressures from its subjects, who were thus encouraged to organize to treat with it. Some saw advantage in doing so. Others saw it as necessary insurance against disadvantages. Either way, their efforts to exploit the network of government constitute one of the forces linking the arenas of Indian politics.

But the argument must go beyond this simple hypothesis. Government intervention might be on the increase; but it never gained exclusive possession of the lives of its subjects. Indians stood firmly by their own essentials, whether these were matters of ritual, family feuds or local standing. The Raj, plastic in many matters but unbending in some, maintained its reserved topics. So too did its subjects.[17] Neither side cared much about the other's.[18] Hence many of the Indian responses to government's initiatives were for limited purposes and at limited periods.

There is another qualification to the hypothesis. It would be convenient if Indian political action had been simply a response to British initiative; but it would be too convenient to be true. Admittedly, there were parts of the country with few interests beyond those of the locality; and here kinship spun small webs, buying and selling were done in tiny marts, and religious horizons seldom lay beyond the nearby temple or mosque. In the arid Madras Deccan, for example, common interests

---

[17] One consequence of the reforms was the growing intervention by Indians in matters where the Raj had always feared to tread: the Hindu Religious Endowments Act of 1926 was not a measure that the Madras Government would have passed before devolution.

[18] Of course, when the British retreated upon the centre, their concern with the details of the religious and social prejudices of their subjects became more remote than ever, while Indian interest in the powers which the British retained became much keener.

were narrow, and government institutions provided the chief impulse for bringing village and firkar into wider systems. But other regions had more powerful solidarities. Whatever moved the rich peasants such as the jotedars of Midnapore, the patidars of Gujarat and the ryots of the Andhra deltas, the Agarwal enthusiasts who traded along the Ganges, or the Khilafatists of Hindustan, it was not merely a desire to parley with their rulers. Granted, they could not ignore the Raj, since it had helped to widen the opportunities for trade and to heighten the resentments of Muslims. But they possessed a community of interest which did not simply arise from the behest of the Raj. Cases such as these make it clear that the bald hypothesis with which we began cannot provide a total explanation of the problem of linkages.

Early in the nineteenth century Indian politicians were already anxious to negotiate with London. That is evidence of the logic of the interconnection. Over high policy, such as the constitution or fiscal issues or the employment of covenanted civilians, it was not Calcutta which could satisfy them, but only the ultimate authority. From the time of Rammohan Roy's passage to England, every reconsideration of India's constitution by parliament led to a rush of Indian petitions to Westminster, and the setting-up of organizations to back them. The Bombay Association, the Deccan Sabha, and the Madras Native Association owed their existence to the Charter revision of 1853. In the eighteen-eighties, hopes for constitutional crumbs created several new associations in the presidency capitals and then in 1885 joined them together into the Indian National Congress. At first this mendicancy by the nation led to little more than annual festivals, where provincial delegates met, orated and dispersed.

Their provincial organizations might seem hollow, with nothing to lose but their prospectuses; but they had an operational part to play. As officials and legislatures in the provinces took more of the decisions and made more of the rules, butting into local sanctuaries, shuffling the standing of men and their share of the booty, they gave district bosses reasons for negotiating with the administration at heights to which they had not previously been minded to climb. It was through the provinces that government intervened; hence it was through provincial politics that local men hoped to influence it. Searching for credentials, coteries in the capitals sought supporters up country; needing a forum, mofussil men sometimes turned to the magniloquently named bodies in the cities.

The Raj itself had cut the steps which these petitioners had to mount; it had also defined the tests they had to pass. Its administration had

c

carved its peoples into large administrative blocks;[19] and it had set up a system of representing them. In effect Indians were now being invited to voice the interests of others, if they could show credentials as the spokesmen of a block. This amounted to a licence, almost a command, to form associations intelligible to government. For the ambitious politician the entrance fee was to assert or pretend affinities with those who had been bundled into the same category.[20] Some of these associations were small, claiming to speak for parochial interests; but others, such as the National Muhammadan Association of Calcutta and the British Indian Association of Bengal, bravely claimed wider constituencies.

As the British extended their representative systems, the growth of these associations became self-sustaining. As a promoter successfully asserted his claim to speak with government, he might hope for nomination to the higher councils, for greater influence over the regulations and useful contacts among the bureaucrats at the top. But the promoter's gain was likely to mean his competitor's loss; and the best hope for the loser was to adopt the same tactics as the winner for whom they worked so well. The result was often an organizational tit-for-tat where the forming of one association provoked the forming of a rival. At least this might prevent one's case from going by default; it might cast doubt on the credibility of his opponents; and at best it might pluck from them the coveted accolade of official recognition. But competitiveness led to more than that. Rivalry forced opponents to search for supporters at lower levels. The Indian Association did so in Bengal, and so did Tilak in Bombay, when he wooed city labourers for his Home Rule League. It compelled defeated groups to look for allies at their own level elsewhere, as the Ghose brothers, Bipin Chandra Pal and Aurobindo were doing when they approached Tilak in Poona during the swadeshi and boycott agitations. It might compel them to seek help at higher levels, as the Hindu zealots had in mind when they formed an all-India Hindu Mahasabha in 1909. Associations looking

[19] It suited the administrative convenience of the British to deem that throughout India, a landlord was a landlord and that a Muslim was a Muslim. Deeming is always dangerous, and many historians have been misled by this example of it. Sir Herbert Risley was responsible for much of the category-making behind the Morley–Minto reforms; but we need not suppose that such a distinguished ethnographer, with thousands of castes to his credit, believed that Indians could really be shut into such large boxes.

[20] In the towns and villages, men of different religions, castes and occupations worked promiscuously together, heedless of the categories of the census and legislation. Indians had to don new caps to fit the rules. Cornwallis's zemindars and Munro's ryots had done much the same.

for support above, below, and at their side proliferated greatly. Now, they required politicians whose profession was to act as intermediaries and spokesmen, men at home with the governmental grid and the matching structure of politics, able to shuttle between arenas. Sometimes they had no base of their own, and this very freedom from the webs of local interest gave them a role that went beyond the localities. The careers of Dadabhai, Gokhale, the Ali brothers, the Nehrus, Jinnah and Gandhi himself show the increasing importance of the profession of politics.[21] Associations, like cricket, were British innovations, and, like cricket, became an Indian craze.

This explanation has been baldly stated because the purpose of an introduction is to introduce and the range of cases is immense. But the visit to India of the Secretary of State at the end of 1917 provided striking illustrations of the process that had been at work. As soon as Montagu arrived, deputations and memoranda cascaded upon him. 222 associations addressed representations to him. They were just the tip. Many other groups would have approached him had they not been turned away. Still others left their cases in the hands of larger bodies.[22] The 112 deputations which won an audience with Montagu had clearly been organized in terms of the categories devised by the British. Nineteen claimed to represent landowners; eleven, businessmen; twenty-three, Muslims; five, high-caste Hindus and eight, the 'depressed classes'. Again, the fact that ninety-four of them limited their membership to one or other of the British provinces, shows how truly the lines for Indian political organization traced the administrative boundaries of the Raj.[23] That many of these classifications existed only in the thinking of the Raj is plain from the rivalries which now came into the open. Forty-four representations in all had been received from Muslim bodies; they showed divisions so glaring as to cast doubt on the existence of a Muslim community at all. In the Punjab the provincial branch of the Muslim League, having seceded from the all-India body in protest

[21] These are examples of political brokers (and in due course managers) at the top; they had innumerable counterparts, who performed much the same function at lower levels: Rafi Ahmed Kidwai of the United Provinces, Rangaswami Iyengar and Satyamurti in Madras, and Anugraha Narayan Sinha in Bihar are middlemen of this sort.

[22] 'Addresses presented in India to . . . the Viceroy and . . . the Secretary of State for India', *Parliamentary Papers*, 1918, XVIII, 469–587.

[23] Their membership also illustrates that a politician might be forced to play many roles. As Montagu's advisers recognized, 'One individual might, and often did, appear as a member of several deputations, which represented, for instance, his religious community, his social class or professional interest, and his individual political views'. *Ibid.*, 472.

against the Congress-League scheme, now led a cat-and-dog existence with the new provincial body which had been improvised to take its place. There was also the Punjab Muslim Association, which had been founded by landlords and claimed to speak for 'humbler agriculturists, the great bulk of the population of this province'24—a memorable example of how categories could be profitably confused. But for a community to split, it did not have to be large. The Ahmadiya sect of dissident Muslims might have seemed small enough to see the virtues of unity; but while their chief spokesman rejected the Congress-League scheme for demanding too much, its 'immediate adoption' was demanded by the Ahmadiya Anjuman Ishaat-i-Islam, a 'body of about 50 persons established at Lahore'.25 In the United Provinces, again, Muslim opinion was sharply divided. Here the provincial branch of the League supported the joint scheme, while the UP Muslim Defence Association rejected it. Less concerned with constitutional formulae, the ulema of the provinces held more antique views. At the Deoband seminary the maulvis called for an alim on every council, while the Majlis Muid-ul-Islam of Lucknow simply demanded that the Jewish Secretary of State should bring India under the rule of the true principles of the Koran.

The exploitation of community for political rivalry was matched by the exploitation of the caste categories of the census. Montagu met several deputations which each claimed to speak for all the forty million non-Brahmins of the Madras Presidency. They split along the usual lines, the Madras Presidency Association supporting the Congress-League scheme, the others repudiating it. But another deputation, from the Adi Dravida Jana Sabha, raised the spectre of six million untouchables in the south, harassed by Brahmins and non-Brahmins alike, for whom the only hope lay in special representation. This indeed was the prize the southern politicians yearned for, especially those whom Montagu was spared from seeing. The alleged unity of the non-Brahmins could not hold firm against such a prospect: Nadukottai Chetties, Tiyyas, Nadars, Marawars, Lingayats, Visva Brahmins,26 Adi Andhras and Panchamas all called for it.27 Orthodox Brahmins, Jains,

24 *Ibid.*, 478.

25 *Ibid.*, 479, 486.

26 These pretentious pot-makers, the Visva Brahmins, managed to split into five separate associations, with three distinct demands.

27 Solomon's problem was child's play compared to Montagu's; the Governor of Madras, who had to work the minister's solutions by balancing these claims inside dyarchy, bitterly complained: 'Oh, this communal business. I am being bombarded by all sorts of sub-castes of the non-Brahmins for special representation and as I

Buddhists and Christians all joined in the rush, and in all some thirty-eight groups in Madras demanded special consideration and special rights. Madras was the extreme example of the general trend throughout India. In every province, at every level and inside every category, political associations were formed as the expression of claim and counter-claim, of group and counter-group, of competitors vying for the favour of the Raj by playing politics couched in its own formulae.

The Secretary of State made his way to these rancorous caravanserais in the period before his new constitution devolved powers to the provinces and gave Indians a share of them. Until then many local politicians did not keep a continuous line open to the province. Associations were, of course, one of the ways of doing so, but they were not enough to ensure success in the everyday affairs of localities. There, the old arts were still the best. No amount of bombinating in the British Indian Association could by itself give a zemindar control over his neighbourhood; the man who walked tall in the Sarvajanik Sabha might be without a shred of power in Poona; there were earthier and surer ways of pursuing interests. These associations were such imperfect indications of men's real priorities in the localities that we cannot assert that their expansion completely explains the growing linkages in Indian politics apparent in Montagu's time.

Yet nearly all localities were being pulled into larger worlds. Two political forces drew them upwards, the one constitutional, the other agitational. The pressure of provincial bureaucracies upon the little sanctuaries continued to grow, and to interfere more with their lives. The Madras government, for example, raised its revenues from eight crores of rupees to twenty-four between 1880 and 1920. Some part was redistributed within the province. To share these golden showers, the men in the localities had to surrender some of their isolation. The twin instruments of nomination and election made it easier to influence provincial decisions after 1909. The Act of 1919 greatly extended representation, and it also gave a smattering of power in the provinces themselves to Indian politicians, not least the power of spending money in their localities. This brought a heightened reality into elections; and, as we have seen, it made the politicians both of the centre and of the locality more dependent on each other.

But another motor for driving local affairs up to higher arenas was

believe there are some 250 of these, I am not likely to satisfy many in a council of 127. You're a nice fellow to have given me this job!' Willingdon to Montagu, 20 February 1920. Willingdon Papers, India Office Library. David Washbrook dug out this gem.

provided by the development of Indian politics. The forming of the Home Rule Leagues and the alliance between the Congress and the Muslim League in 1916 were portents of agitations which could now be set in motion by bodies claiming to stand for all-India interests. By 1920, these agitations were dominating politics.[28] Gandhi shouldered aside the old Congress hands who had previously claimed to speak for the movement. His own agitation, fortified by his alliance with the Khilafatists, emerged as the non-cooperation campaign of 1920–22. In practice the campaign was a series of interconnected district battles, fought by men from the localities. The hillmen of Kumaon, the coolies of Assam, the headmen of Oudh, the turbulent peasantries of Midnapore and Guntur, Kaira and Bhagalpur, were all using what were allegedly national issues to express their local complaints. Local grievances were chronic and narrow, but they put the stuffing into campaigns which were intermittent and wide. It was not possible for the localities to reject the linkages of agitation. For the provincial and national leaderships to press the British at the top, they had to cause the base to fulminate, and so they did all they could to bring the localities into the movement. Many localities welcomed a wider agitation as a means of paying off old scores against the administration and those who sided with it. But in any case, had they ignored the movement, they would have risked losing all influence upon what was clearly a growing power in their province.

Some of the supporters from the localities made awkward allies for the leadership. National and provincial campaigners with large interests to watch had to be more prudent than men whose local grievances were not assuaged by all-India strategies. When Gandhi wanted to cool his campaign in 1922, the men of Bardoli and Guntur were spoiling for a fight; his efforts to observe the armistice in 1931 meant nothing to the peasants of Rae Bareli or Bara Banki. But these difficulties in controlling agitation were balanced by its success in bringing ever more local politicians into the ambit of the provinces.

During the quiescent period between 1922 and 1928, many of these agitational links snapped, and provincial parties almost closed down shop in the districts. But it was business as usual in the political exchanges of the provincial capitals, where jobbers organized factions to enter and break the councils, or to work them. It mattered little to these

[28] Constitutional politics and agitation rode in unsteady tandem throughout this period. The defeat of the constitutionalists in 1920 was more tactical than strategic. By December 1920 when the Nagpur Congress met, the first elections under the reforms had come and gone. By the time of the next elections in 1923, the Swaraj party was in the front seat, and Gandhi was back-pedalling from gaol.

groupings whether they retained formal allegiance to the Congress or not; they did so only when it suited their convenience, and when it did not, they left the Congress to their rivals. They stepped nimbly in and out of the all-India organizations, like so many cabs for hire. From local torpor and national insignificance, Indian politics were rescued by constitutional changes. The Award had settled the share of the communities. By extending the electorate, the imperial croupier had summoned more players to his table. By transferring political power to politicians in the provinces, he made them the main agencies of intervention in the localities. Now there was no help for it. Local men were forced into connections with those who claimed to represent the big battalions and would control their destinies in the future. At last the localities were soldered to the provinces.

But the agitations and negotiations which led to the Act of 1935 had also given a new importance to organizations claiming to represent all-India interests. Gandhi returned to take control of civil disobedience; Congress spoke with one voice at the Second Round Table Conference. Once power in the provinces was up for bids, interests outside the Congress also needed their national spokesmen. So the Muslims reorganized under Jinnah in 1934–5, and groups with even shakier all-India connections, such as the Depressed Classes, found it necessary to have a negotiator of their own. All these spokesmen grew in stature by being recognized, even if reluctantly, by Delhi and London, as the plenipotentiaries of constituents in the provinces. But just as the Raj had to counter-balance provincial devolution by strengthening its centre, so Indian politicians at the centre had to confront an analogous problem, since provinces controlled by Indians might go their own way. The only safeguard open to the leaders of Congress and League against provincial autonomy was to construct central controls strong enough to tie their provincial satraps to them. In this difficult task they were helped by two trends. Although the 1935 Act was intended by the British to contain Indian politics within the provinces, they could not be checked at that level. Some factions, such as those led by Pant in the United Provinces, Rajagopalachari in Madras and Kher in Bombay, cheerfully glutted themselves with power in the provinces between 1937 and 1939. But plenty of others had no power to enjoy. Hence the Congress High Command could arbitrate between the 'ins' and 'outs' of the provinces, and in the Central Provinces went to the length of breaking a ministry.[29] Provincial leaders whose hopes had been permanently blasted by the

[29] Once war came, Vallabhbhai ordered all the Congress ministers to quit office. Reluctantly they obeyed.

Communal Award had every reason to cling to their centre. In this way, the adhesion of the Muslims of the United Provinces helped to keep the League alive during the two lean years before the war.

The other trend strengthening the centres was the steady raising of the constitutional stakes. The offers of Linlithgow in 1940 and of Cripps in 1942 promised an immediate share in the central government and a post-dated cheque for its control after the war. These were matters beyond the provincial politicians. They could whip their own dogs, but no one else's. Only men claiming to take all the nation's interests into account, and having the all-India organizations to back these claims, could work at such altitudes. In the deadly end-game played with Wavell, the Cabinet Mission and Mountbatten, these politicians claimed to be custodians of all the sets of interests crammed into the Pandora's boxes of the Congress and the League. Now there was everything to play for: the prize was the mastery of the subcontinent. Those who competed for it had to provide a firm leadership to their followers. The size of the stake let Jinnah break at last the independence of the Muslim bosses in the Punjab. Just as the agitations of the twenties and thirties had swung the localities behind the provincial leaderships, so the crisis of the last days of the Raj swung the provinces behind the national leaderships. The parallel went further. Just as civil disobedience had been complicated by *enragés* who went further than their leaders had wished, now on the eve of independence there were pressures from below which reduced the leaders' freedom of manœuvre. Jinnah was hoist with his own petard of Pakistan, and Nehru was harassed by the Sikhs and the Hindu Mahasabha. But in the outcome, Nehru, Jinnah and Vallabhbhai Patel settled the fate of the provinces over their heads, and all but one of them[30] marched obediently into one or other of the new nations of India and Pakistan. At last the province had been soldered to the centre.

* * *

These interpretations arise from two main arguments. Simply put, Indian politics were an interconnected system working at several levels; and government had much to do with the linking of those levels. When these arguments are applied to modern Indian history, some of its conundrums look less intractable. In the first place, we need not be dismayed if some of the hard facts which have been revealed at the base of the system seem to run counter to the ways in which politics worked at

[30] The North-West Frontier Province.

other points. Once Indian politicians were pressed into treating with government and their fellow subjects at several levels, they played several roles, each of which might seem to make nonsense of the others. But those who varied their tunes between bucolic patter and urban suavity were not brazen impostors. To make use of the system, they had no choice but to play those contradictory roles. In catching them out at their tricks and dwelling on their inconsistencies, historians are simply playing a game at which the administrators used to excel. But to demonstrate that Indian politicians were not always what they claimed to be is not to describe what they were. Moral judgment is easy; functional analysis is hard. Perhaps our approach will help to make the one more difficult and the other less arduous.

Secondly, the part played by ideology in the growth of Indian politics can now be re-assessed. Those who have convinced themselves that India is the home of spiritual values have found them everywhere in her politics; others have seen nothing but *homo homini lupus*. The truth seems to lie in between. Whatever held together the gimcrack coalitions of province and nation, it was not passion for a common doctrine. It was lower down that ideology was important. Illustrating the wit and wisdom of Mohamed Ali would be unprofitable as well as painful; but there is no gainsaying the Hindu zealotry in the localities of Hindustan, or the Muslim resentments against it which lent that adventurer an improbable fame. Ideology provides a good tool for fine carving, but it does not make big buildings.

We can make some inroads into a third question. Many historians have argued that the timing of Indian agitation was governed by the imminence of British concession. The point is a simple one; it was made by Simon; and it is demonstrated by the landmarks of constitutional change from 1853 until 1947. Yet at the lower levels these simplicities melt into a more revealing complexity. There, government intervention helped to create the agitations over cow protection in 1893, the partition of Bengal in 1905, the canal colonies of the Punjab in 1907, the municipalities of the United Provinces before 1916, the coolies of Assam in 1921–22, the rights of village officers in the Kistna and Godaveri deltas in 1922, and the agrarian grievances of Gujarat, Oudh and Andhra during the Depression. Agitations of this sort fed into the larger movements, helping to start and sustain them, often surviving them and remaining at hand for the next all-India campaign.

This conclusion alters our ideas about the nature of these large campaigns. Many local grievances dragged on, whether the leaderships were militant or not. When the malcontents of the neighbourhood aligned themselves with the provincial and national campaigns which arose from time to time, they hoped to exploit these issues for their own causes. The small issues, which historians used to neglect, moved on different clocks from the large issues on which study has been concentrated. Small discontents existed before they were caught up by the agglutinative tendencies of larger campaigns and they went on simmering after the large agitations had cooled. Many localities had their irreconcilables, men whose interests could not be patted smoothly into the prudences of provincial politics, and who turned into permanent 'outs'. This held good at higher levels too. After their position had been exploded by the Communal Award and by the silent consent to it of the all-India Congress, Bengalis, who had hitherto been among its leaders, now became malcontents at the national level, willing to make common cause with the mavericks of other provinces. Subhas's Forward Bloc looked backwards to the old triangle of Lal, Bal and Pal, to the Home Rule Leagues or the Hindu Mahasabha of Bhai Parmanand. All of them were coalitions of 'outs'.

In turn, this helps to explain the relations between the constitutional and the agitational sides of Indian politics. For many historians, Indian politics kept on making clean breaks from one to the other; the smooth formulations which Sapru penned at Albert Road in Allahabad went unheard every time the trouble-makers escaped from their cages. This was not the way matters went. As we have seen, the roots of political activity in the localities twisted in many directions. Local grievances always looked for the best outlets. We cannot make a simple distinction between the constitutionalists, who scampered from board to council, and the agitators from less accommodating areas who shunned such opportunism. Local studies reveal that there was much interaction between them. Even the most uncooperative areas had to work through government institutions; even the dacoits could not disregard them.[31] Gandhi freely allowed satyagrahis to hold posts in local government, and the president of the Ahmedabad municipality in the mid-twenties was a not unknown agitator named Vallabhbhai Patel. The converse was true as well. Constitutionalists readily became agitators when local conditions forced them to do so. The law-abiding municipality of Nagpur organized one satyagraha over flags, and the time-servers of Jubbulpore were swept into another over forests. Many local men were dual-purpose politicians, switching their bets between constitutionalism and agitation according to the temper of their sup-

---

[31] Many villages hired their chowkidars from the criminal tribes, following the old adage.

porters and the calculation of their interest. These ambiguities were shared by men at all levels.

These conclusions suggest that some of the difficulties in Indian history can be met by putting new life into old factors, and that the subject can be reintegrated by seeing the roles of imperialism and nationalism in a different light. Imperialism built a system which interlocked its rule in locality, province and nation; nationalism emerged as a matching structure of politics. The study of local situations, the components of these larger wholes, cannot by itself identify a bedrock reality. The Raj had smashed the autonomy of localities; the historian of British rule cannot put it together again. Indian politics have to be studied at each and every level; none of them can be a complete field of study on its own. Each of them reveals only that part of social action which did not depend upon interconnection. As that part became caught up by the linking forces of Indian history, it steadily shrank.

In no colonial situation can government's part be ignored. We have suggested that much of the crucial work of connecting one level with another came from its impulses. This hypothesis can explain many of the problems of linkage. Others still elude us. We need more facts about such bonds as kinship patterns, urban ties, professional and educational interests. All that can be said at present about arguments built upon them is that they are probably significant, possibly crucial, but certainly not general. In the meantime, the range of cases which can be explained by looking at imperialism and nationalism in the new way suggests that their importance has been too hastily marked down. Perhaps this volume will do something to bring them back into their own.

Patrons and Politics in Northern India

C. A. BAYLY

1. Introduction

FOR many Hindu residents of the great cities of northern India in the mid-nineteenth century, the most powerful figures in the community were members of the wealthy families of indigenous bankers and traders which controlled credit and dispensed patronage for the religious life of their localities. Just as in the smallest bazaar great power lay in the hands of the petty moneylender, so in the cities which remained clusters of bazaars and residential blocs, the banking and trading oligarchies determined the limits of commercial activity with their credit notes, and helped to supply the community through their secondary trades in cloth, grain and sugar.

In general, the landowners and urban commercial magnates who made up the class of local notables were content to preserve their parochial power through the mediation of the district authorities, and at first kept aloof from the new politics of rally and pressure group whether in support of or in opposition to the government. But in the Hindi-speaking areas of north India, a significant number of members of powerful mercantile families played an active part in the early Congress and in related organizations. Contemporary observers generally adhered to the official view of the Congress as a product of déraciné Young India, but some were clearly aware of and puzzled by the number of threads which led back from the new politics into the labyrinth of old city notabilities. A member of the Viceroy's executive council thought the Congress in 1889 'more influentially supported' than other officials were prepared to concede.[1] Shortly after the Congress session in Allahabad in 1888, Sir Auckland Colvin, Lieutenant-Governor of the North-Western Provinces remarked on the

---

[1] Marginal note by (?) (Sir) Antony MacDonnell to a minute claiming that the Congress was a preserve of lawyers and schoolteachers, Home Department Public (Unrecorded, Confidential) Proceedings, December 1889, 1–3, printed in Papers Connected with the 'Report of the Councils Committee', II, Minto Papers M 1050, National Library of Scotland, Edinburgh.

predominance of professional people among supporters of the Congress. But he also noted that 'the class which is more inclined than any other to identify with the claims of the literary and law class is the trading section of the community, especially the retail trader caste [sic] of the large towns'.[2] In Punjab, the English journal *Tribune* reported the widespread appearance of 'independent merchants' at early political meetings.[3] Throughout its first phase also, some officials directly linked the new secular nationalism with aspects of contemporary Hindu revivalism, especially the great cow-protection movement of 1882–93, which were known to be widely supported, particularly among the urban commercial magnates.[4] Few commentators went on to analyze the nature of the political linkages between Congress and associated interest groups. But there was a widespread assumption that, directly or indirectly, Congress represented more than a cartel of dissident journalists and lawyers largely divorced from the rest of Indian society.

In fact, even if the nature of the early Congress is to be deduced solely from the annual delegates' lists, and within the rough categories they employ, a much wider splay of interests seems to have been represented. It has been calculated that between 1885 and 1901, public meetings and societies in the North-Western Provinces and Oudh delegated to Congress sessions 'Brahmins' 551 times, and 'Kayasths' 294 times. But they also elected 'Khattris', 'Agarwals' and other members of the mercantile castes at least 404 times,[5] and well over half of these were classed as 'bankers' or 'traders'. Nor were these men simply small capitalists drawn into the political movement by their legal advisers. In most Hindustani cities, the mercantile élite produced one or two individuals of great local and even provincial importance in the

[2] Note by Sir Auckland Colvin on provincial councils, 11 June 1889, Home Public A August 1892, 237–52, National Archives of India, New Delhi [NAI].

[3] E.g. *Tribune*, 10 December 1881, meeting at Rawalpindi in favour of English education; *Tribune*, 10 May 1884, report on a meeting of congratulation for Lord Ripon attended by 'educated natives and independent traders'; *Tribune*, 21 March 1885, Lahore Indian Association, includes Lala Jia Ram, banker, treasurer of Bank of Bengal, Lahore, among other commercial people; *Tribune*, 12 September 1888, Congress meeting Peshawar attended by five local bankers; *Tribune* 17 August 1889, obituary of Rai Balak Ram, banker, Jullunder. Several of these men were active patrons and organizers of Punjabi political movements: they were not mere figureheads.

[4] E.g. Sir Charles Crosthwaite, Actg. Lieutenant-Governor, NWP and Oudh, to Landsdowne, 18 September 1893, and enclosure 1, Lansdowne Papers, Mss Eur D 558/23, 31, India Office Library, London [IOL].

[5] Based on J. L. Hill, 'Congress and Representative Institutions in the United Provinces, 1886–1901' (Duke University, Ph.D. thesis, 1967), p. 324, table 3, microfilm copy, Cambridge University.

new politics. In Benares, the city's commercial aristocracy, the Naupati bankers, gave rise to a succession of active Congressmen, who, though educated and sophisticated beyond their background, continued to adhere to many of the social preconceptions and to work within the community bodies of the Agarwal tradesmen. Chief among them were Bhagwan Das,[6] Rai Krishnaji,[7] Shiva Prasad Gupta[8] and Sri Prakasha. In Allahabad, pre-eminently a city of the new professional man, Lala Ram Charan Das, a Khattri banker, became treasurer of the provincial Congress committee,[9] while wealthy commercial people patronised political and social activities initiated by Madan Mohan Malaviya's wing of the Congress until Independence. In Cawnpore, an expanding commercial centre, Lalas Bishambhar Nath and Baijnath dominated the Congress committee and related bodies as office holders and patrons until at least 1920.[10] Throughout the cities of the west of the provinces, a sprinkling of rich landowning bankers supported public activities and became embroiled in the conflicts of the new municipalities, while generally preserving their links with the British authorities.[11]

As a relatively literate[12] section of Hindustani society, less dependent on the patronage of government than landowners, and possessed of

---

[6] *Agrawal Jati ka Itihasa* (Agarwal History Office, Bhanpura Indore State, 1938) II, 376–80. Bhagwan Das, member of the Shah family, father of Sri Prakasha. They were theosophists and nationalists.

[7] A descendent of the great banker and government servant Raja Patni Mul, he was responsible for the revival of the family's commercial fortune. Interview with Rai Kishen Das, Benares Hindu University, May 1972.

[8] *Agrawal Jati*, II, 167–8; Home Reforms B March 1921, 34–100, p. 499, NAI.

[9] *Advocate* (Lucknow) 20 January 1907, United Provinces Native Newspaper Reports [UPNNR] for 1907.

[10] R. A. Gordon, 'The Hindu Mahasabha and the Indian National Congress, 1916–26', unpublished Ms, South Asian Studies Centre, Cambridge University, p. 28, fn. 1.

[11] F. C. R. Robinson, below.

[12] *1891 Census, NWP & Oudh Report*, XXVI, part I, 262.

Male literacy among selected mercantile communities, etc.

Caste	Learning	English	Other languages	Illiterate	Total
Khattri	9.890	5.302	33.132	51.676	100
Bania	3.560	0.300	22.660	73.480	100
Kalwar	2.330	0.070	14.440	83.160	100
Teli	0.219	0.009	2.090	97.610	100
Brahmin	2.527	0.227	15.192	82.054	100
Kayasth	11.949	2.052	47.019	38.980	100

supra-local links, rich commercial men might have been expected to contribute something to the developing nationalist movement. Yet the relationship had more significance. The Congress' monied patrons provided cash, support and a link with the politics of the localities. But they also helped to confirm Congress in upper India in its socially conservative character. At the same time, they directly or indirectly helped to strengthen the forces of Hindu cultural revivalism within the emerging nationalist movement at the expense of the broader, cross-communal tradition represented by the Urdu speaking élite of lawyers and government servants in the North-Western Provinces. This essay examines the motives which propelled some commercial and banking magnates into the new politics of ascriptive associations and approaches the question of the nature of political change in India from the local standpoint.

2. Bankers in Northern India

The word banker used in this article is a rough translation of the term *mahajan*.[13] It implies a series of economic and social relations based on the manipulation of credit. The economic resources of men called *mahajans* varied greatly from banking house to banking house and from region to region. These differences were important because they determined the nature and extent of the influence which a man could deploy in society. One important line of distinction was between those who were broadly urban and those who were broadly rural bankers. Raja Motichand of Benares[14] and the Seths of Jubbulpore, members of whose families were active in the Congress and political associations in the 1920s and 1930s, were examples of rural moneylenders who acquired great influence in town politics. But generally, rurally-based business houses became assimilated into the life-style and ultimately

[13] L. C. Jain, *Indigenous Banking in India* (London, 1929), and C. N. Cooke, *The Rise, Progress and Present Condition of Banking in India* (Calcutta, 1863); a valuable discussion of late eighteenth-century banking practice is to be found in K. P. Mishra, 'The Administration and Economy of the Banaras Region, 1738–1795' (London University, Ph.D. thesis, 1970). The generalizations in the preliminary section of this essay derive from enquiries and extracts from *bahi khatas* (bankers' books) of the second half of the nineteenth century, made in Benares, Allahabad and Delhi, January to September 1972. A fuller discussion will appear elsewhere, but wherever possible I have acknowledged the help of the descendents of the *mahajani* families. The detailed work on Allahabad was completed during 1967–69.

[14] See, e.g., N. Madhava Rau, *Encyclopedia of North and Central India* (Madras, 1933–34), VII, 2–3.

into the sectional associations of the landholding class. It was usually bankers with strong urban interests who became involved in Hindu revivalist and nationalist activities.

Another line of distinction between bankers was in the structure of their clientèle. At one extreme were families like the Rastogis of Lucknow[15] or the Hundiwallas of Benares[16] who specialized in short-term loans to artisans and the poorer sections of the urban population. Depending on high interest rates, rapid turnover of capital, and a degree of coercion in realization, these enterprises could be extremely lucrative. But they severely limited the social influence of such families, which had less contact with the notables of local society, while the sometimes unseemly association of this type of business degraded its practitioners in the eyes of their own communities. At the other end of the scale were old and prestigious 'court' banking firms which had to some extent absorbed the style of life of the nobility of the declining Moghul regional capitals.[17] Families like these were essentially high-class urban moneylenders. For them banking was less an economically profitable activity, or the provision of a range of services for the local business community, than a form of low-profit investment, similar perhaps to the purchase of jewellery, or later, of government paper.[18] The continuance of these businesses reflected less their importance as income than their importance in maintaining the social prestige of their principals through association with the aristocracy, and the owners often combined *mahajani* interests with sinecures at a raja's court or with landholding. The stake of such families in the *status quo* would tend to preclude them from any independent political role either in local or in regional politics.

Between these two poles stood the majority of prominent city *mahajans*. These men were likely to run a credit-note (*hundi*) business

15 *Report of the United Provinces Provincial Banking Enquiry Committee, 1929-30* (Allahabad, 1930), II, *Evidence*, 58 (M. L. Shah).

16 Interview with Sri Radhe Mohan Hundiwallah, Suriya, Varanasi, August 1972.

17 In Benares, this had been the fate of the great banking houses associated with the Rajas of the city, notably the Khattri family of Lala Kashmiri Mul and the Oswal family of Lala Bachraj. By the mid-nineteenth century their descendents were little more than court pensioners. Other families made a successful leap into landholding, e.g., the Dubes of Jaunpur or the Chaddhas of Allahabad.

18 A house such as that of Harrakh Chand-Gopal Chand of Benares, for instance, seems by the end of the nineteenth century, to have fallen into a pattern characterized by low turnover of capital, investment of large sums in 'solid' magnates (e.g. the Raja of Bettiah) and relatively low profits by comparison with a flourishing *hundi* business like that of the Benares Shahs or the Allahabad Tandons. *Rokarh Khatas*, St. 1943-45, 1961-62 (A.D. 1886-87 and 1904-05), by courtesy of Sri Kumud Chandra, Dr Giresh Chandra, Chaukambha.

over a wide area, as well as moneylending locally and taking deposits from zamindars, commercial men and widows. The *hundi* businesses were run as services for the dominant local trades. Thus in Benares, bankers were closely concerned with the financing of pilgrimages, on the one hand, and with the trade in Banarsi sarees and silk piece goods on the other. In Allahabad, by contrast, in the second half of the nineteenth century, the emphasis appears to have been on the servicing of local firms who traded in agricultural cash crops. Linseed, castor oil, indigo and mild drugs appear to have been important locally.[19] In the west of the North-Western Provinces, the boom in the grain trade at the end of the century profited the area's large class of Agarwal and Khattri bankers.[20] Again, some of the most prestigious men in Delhi ran banking facilities for importers who introduced English piece goods through Calcutta to this reviving regional capital.[21]

Though the *mahajan* families remained highly conservative in their banking practices during the nineteenth century, they displayed a high degree of fluidity in regard to their secondary economic functions. Some bankers, particularly Khattris and Oswals, had originated as jewellers;[22] others, especially Mehra Khattris, as cloth traders. Several Agarwal families had originally been connected with the riverborne grain trade. These businesses were often maintained even after they had become peripheral sources of income. Other bankers moved into new or lucrative trades or services on the basis of their credit control. Sugar, indigo, opium, *ganja* and *bhang* (two mild drugs) provided valuable sidelines. In large and developing centres, such as Allahabad or Cawnpore, bankers moved into property ownership not only in the old cities but in the new residential areas.[23] Most generally, prominent commercial groups were associated with the finance and support of the local authorities, as government treasurers, court treasurers

[19] Tandon *Khatas* ('Manohar Das Kandheya-Lal'?) St. 1950–51 (1892–93), etc., by courtesy of Sri Beni Prasad Tandon, Harimohan Das Tandon and Lalji Tandon, Ranimandi.

[20] For the economic development of the west, see, T. Prasad, *The Organisation of the Wheat Trade in the North-Western Region of the United Provinces* (Allahabad, 1932), p. 6; A. C. Chatterjee, *Notes on the Industries of the United Provinces* (Allahabad, 1908), p. 3. For its political results see F. C. R. Robinson, below.

[21] E.g. the great firm of Chunna Mal Saligram. Interview with Sri Krishna Prasad, Chandni Chowk, August 1972.

[22] I am indebted to Sri Satyapal, National Archives of India, for preliminary enquiries in Delhi; cf. interview with Sri Devi Narain, *vakil*, Varanasi, May 1972.

[23] Title deeds in possession of the Tandon family in Ranimandi Allahabad, show that many such properties were acquired as lapsed security or in sales for debt. The Chunna Mals acquired Muslim properties in Chandni Chowk, Delhi, especially after 1857.

or official contractors. The reason for this diversification was the limited commercial wealth of Hindustan and also the extreme suspicion with which the *mahajan* viewed extensive investment in any one economic function. This had the contradictory results of bringing *mahajan* families into direct economic and patronal relationship with large sections of the urban population, yet of prohibiting their development of long-term interests and resources in any single aspect of the cities' economy. House property, of minimal value before 1900, and land rights, however valuable on paper, seem often to have been regarded as embarrassing accumulations of lapsed collateral security.

The geographical organization of trading networks in upper India is also significant when we come to consider the developing public patronage of bankers towards the end of the century. A feature of the old 'high prestige' urban banks was the manner in which they continued to work within the boundaries of the now defunct Moghul provinces (*subahs*). Thus the Raj of Benares, the Kingdom of Oudh and the provinces of Kara, Allahabad and Farrukhabad continued to support self-contained banking and credit systems. But two other regional networks were imposed on these systems. The first was supplied by the eastward emigration at the end of the eighteenth century of large numbers of Agarwal, Khattri and Arora families from central and east Punjab.[24] Many were connected with Moghul courts and Muslim landowners, and among Khattris they formed a separate body of 'western' Khattris distinct from other caste fellows who had migrated into the Ganges valley at an earlier date. The commercial interests of such families continued to incline towards the west, up the Doab river system towards Delhi and Lahore. Marriage patterns initially followed and reinforced these links.

Another inter-regional network was provided by Bengalis moving up country with the East India Company as its commissariat contractors or paymasters. This westward facing link was reinforced by the development of Hindustani Agarwala interests in Calcutta[25] and later by the spread back into the Ganges valley of Calcutta-based Marwari

[24] H. R. Nevill, *District Gazetteers of the United Provinces of Agra and Oudh*, XXIII, *Allahabad* (Allahabad, 1911), 59–61; *Agrawal Jati*, II, *passim*; the ritual differences between 'Western' and 'Eastern' Khattris are set out in a number of obscure publications, e.g. *Khattri Jati ka Itihas* (Khattri Mahasabha, Moradabad, c. 1957), but are well known to all old Khattri families.

[25] E.g. one of the main branches of the Shah family, the descendents of Manohar Das Shah, established themselves at Calcutta in the 1780s. J. P. Sah, *Sah Vanshavali*, (Varanasi, 1956), *passim*. For other non-Marwari Agarwal families in Calcutta, see *Agrawal Jati*, II, *passim*.

enterprises.[26] The Bengal connection became politically important in the 1880s, for instance, when Calcutta associations were beginning to establish up-country connections. In 1878 Surendranath Banerjea, touring on behalf of the Bengal Indian Association, elicited speeches and garlands from Bengali lawyers at every major town in northern India, yet it was Nil Kumar Mitter, a commissariat contractor with interests in Calcutta, Allahabad and Benares, who arranged the tour.[27] Ten years later, Nil Kumar's son, Charu Chunder Mitter, combined with the Khattri bankers of Allahabad to help organize and finance the Congress of 1888.[28] Similarly, during the 'extremist' movement of 1906–10, some western UP Arora commercial families and their connections were implicated in the activities of Lala Lajpat Rai's party which was attempting to spread advanced nationalist activities from the Punjab.[29] Throughout the period, commercial-cum-marriage networks were used in the propagation of Hindu political and literary movements.

3. Bankers, Politics and Revivalism

Bankers in Hindustan in the mid-nineteenth century had many of the attributes which could make them powerful figures in both local and regional politics. They had wealth, extensive credit control and access to supra-local social networks. But in view of the extreme caution of these family businesses, it cannot be considered inevitable that they should have involved themselves in local political associations, let alone in regional pressure groups. What forces had in their case forged the links between the politics of informal local consultation and those of the Congress and the Hindu associations, of rally, publicity and agitation? The close connection of the *mahajans* with the functions of local government suggests that the answer could lie in the distortion of that relationship by the forces of administrative change. This would be in accordance with many recent interpretations of Indian political change which stress the leading role of government and the importance

---

[26] 'Jit Mul Kalu Mul', indigo and sugar merchants, Allahabad, Tandon *Rokarh*, 1892–93; 'Abhaya Ram Chunni Lal', grain merchants, Benares, 'Bhartendu *Rokarh*', 1904–05. Other Marwari families had migrated earlier into the area, direct from Rajasthan, e.g. the Juggilal Kamlapat family. *Northern India Patrika, UP Supplement* 11 April, 1972.

[27] S. Banerjea, *A Nation in Making* (London, 1925), p. 41.

[28] *Tribune*, 24 March 1888, 31 October 1888.

[29] Notes of Commissioner, Meerut Division, Home Poll D August 1907, 4, NAI.

of new arenas in municipal boards and local legislative councils.[30] An acceptable hypothesis would be that new bureaucratic initiatives had disillusioned some of government's local supporters and forced them into temporary opposition. In this interpretation, Congress itself, numerically dominated by the professional classes, acted as a kind of regional and all-India *vakil* or representative for the commercial interests in local society, as it did from time to time for other interests.

Now clearly, there are examples of this type of political dynamic. During the later 1880s, government feeling itself under increasing financial pressure, reintroduced the income tax and allowed considerable increases in the licence tax in the cities. There is no doubt that the Congress protest against these new fields of taxation elicited considerable support from the monied classes. A delegation of notables met the Viceroy after the 1887 Congress session and one of them was an Allahabad moneylender who specifically asked 'when the income tax would be taken off'.[31] The realization of the tax was also impeded in several cities by a campaign of objections in which the mercantile oligarchies played a considerable part,[32] and Congress lecturers made much play with the iniquities of taxation.[33] At various times in the next two generations government made specific assaults on the interests of Hindustan's monied classes, and their protests were often channeled through the local or provincial organs of Congress. The controversy over the Punjab Land Alienation Act, for instance, drew into the Congress session of 1900 large numbers of bankers from the North-Western Provinces, as well as their Punjabi connections.[34] Congress leaders and newspapers also opposed the Bundelkhand Encumbered

[30] E.g. my own article, *Modern Asian Studies*, 5, 4, 1971, 289–311, which set up an over-mechanical model; also F. C. R. Robinson, *ibid*, 313–336; and the important work of C. Baker and D. Washbrook, Cambridge University Ph.D. theses, 1972 and 1973.

[31] *Tribune* (Lahore), 10 August 1889; extract from a (?) publication of Sir Edward Watkin (untraced); the commercial notable in question must have been either Ram Charan Das, banker, or Charu Chunder Mitter, contractor.

[32] *Report on the Working of the Income Tax Act II of 1886, in the North-Western Provinces and Oudh for the year ending 31 March 1887* (Allahabad, 1887), p. 12.

[33] Note the tendency of lecturers to compound material and religious grievances; one itinerant sadhu 'solicited signatures to Congress petitions to parliament for the reform of the legislative councils under the pretext that the measures would lead to the stoppage of kine-killing and the abolition of the Income-Tax'. Note on cow-protection, Judicial and Public Papers, 367, No. 257, 1894, IOL.

[34] 99 Khattris from the NWP alone attended the Lahore session of the Congress; this massive leap in numbers was clearly a gesture of solidarity with their Punjabi brethren.

Estates Act[35] which threatened the interests of the Allahabad, Benares and Jubbulpore bankers in precisely the same fashion.[36] On these and other occasions, the Congress discharged its role as advocate for the interests of dissident groups, which it consistently pursued in its early years.

But a 'challenge and response' theory to account for the involvement of local commercial interests in the new ascriptive associations is not entirely satisfactory. In the first place, it is difficult to show that the political or commercial interests of the banking families were substantially or continually threatened by government action between 1860 and 1885, when many of the relationships which were later incorporated into the nationalist movement originated. Next, it is not clear that members of the *mahajan* class would inevitably have moved into any new arenas where caches of material patronage had been deposited by a decentralizing government, particularly when informal contacts with collector, police chief or other municipal commissioners could still protect a man's interests quite effectively. Finally, many organizations, which look superficially like pressure groups forming around the distribution of material resources in local government, are, on closer scrutiny, more concerned with symbolic or ideological issues.

The commercial magnates had, by and large, prospered since the 1840s in contrast to government service families who had found themselves under increasing pressure from new departures in education and general administrative change. Both urban and rural property had come their way from declining landed and service families before 1857,[37] and the process was accelerated by government confiscation after the Revolt.[38] Equally, it was during this period that the *mahajans* worked out a satisfactory system of relationships with the government. Relations had not always been amicable. Before 1830 there had been considerable friction on matters such as the exchange rate between various styles of coinage then current, the rate of discount on government bills, and on the intervention of British courts in 'the ancient

---

[35] E.g. Malaviya's speech to the local legislative council, *Speeches and Writings of Pandit Madan Mohan Malaviya* (G. Natesan, Madras, 1919?), introduction, p. 4.

[36] It put brakes on the transfer of land from 'agricultural' to 'non-agricultural' castes. Allahabad and Benares bankers scaled down their operations in Bundelkhand. *Banking Committee Report*, II, 129 (L. C. Jain).

[37] F. C. R. Robinson, below.

[38] Basta 36 of 1861, Judicial collection, rewards and confiscations 1858, Records of the Commissioner of Allahabad [CA]; and Rebellion in the eastern districts, rewards and punishments, 225 of 1858 Judicial, Benares Commissioners Records, Uttar Pradesh State Archives, Allahabad [UPSA]; also *District Gazetteers*.

custom of the bankers'.[39] By 1860, however, the standardization of the currency, the establishment of the Bank of Bengal, and an efficient system of government revenue stamps, had removed many of the root causes of this friction. In the courts it had become customary to appoint 'respectable *mahajans*' to examine the books of their peers in debt or property cases, and thus save them the embarrassment of risking their credit by bringing their books to court.[40]

The efforts at administrative devolution initiated by the British government in the 1870s and 1880s generally tended to enhance rather than detract from the local position of bankers and commercial men. It may be that power was often thrust upon them; but the benches of honorary magistrates founded in the cities during these years gave many prominent bankers a degree of judicial power over people who were already their clients in business and their dependents in caste associations. Initially also, the departures in municipal government released by the Acts of 1872 and 1883 in the North-Western Provinces reinforced rather than weakened the connections of the banking *raises*.[41] In almost all the cities one or more of the factional groups working within the municipal boards were based on, or derived their power from, the kin of a powerful banking family. In Delhi the firm of Chunna Mal Saligram had two family members and several connections on a board of under twelve members in the 1870s.[42] In Benares, members of the Naupati banking fraternity, prominent since the days of the Rajas of Benares, perpetuated their influence within the municipality.[43]

Moreover, as many of the functions of local government were modernized in the first generation after the Mutiny, commercial families moved into an even closer relationship with the authorities. The Raj had inherited the extreme financial timidity of the East India Company. The desire to protect shareholders from the financial

[39] For one such dispute, see, e.g., answer to petition of the 'shroffs' of Benares regarding regulation XVI of 1824 concerning rates on stamp paper etc., Sec. to Governor-General in Council, to Agent to G-G., Benares, 3 November 1824, Benares Collectorate Records Vol. 17, 473–92, UPSA.

[40] *North-Western Provinces Zilla Court Decisions* (monthly, Agra and Allahabad 1848–63). Commercial cases requiring scrutiny of books were referred to a *panchayat* of three respectable mercantile men, named by the parties themselves, under provisions of Clause 2, Section 3, Regulation VI of 1832.

[41] F. C. R. Robinson, below.

[42] Interview with Sri Krishna Prasad, Chandni Chowk, August 1972.

[43] List of municipal commissioners, Benares, 1879, President, Municipal Committee, Benares, to Commissioner, Benares, 9 July 1881, 112 Judicial of 1881, Benares Commissioners Records, UPSA.

results of defalcation and corruption which were a constant theme during the early days of British rule had given rise to a complex system of sureties and guarantees for the proper management of the farms or financial organs of government. Security demanded in land, urban property or government promissory notes was so large that functions like district, court and military treasuries were effectively made the monopoly of the few monied interests which could bear them financially. Before the Mutiny, Tori Ram of Agra had been government treasurer for no less than eleven districts.[44] But despite government's expressed wish to break up cartels after 1857, we find the function remained in a very few hands. The government treasurers of Cawnpore and Allahabad, as well as most of the army contractors in those cities, were branches of a single family.[45] The treasurer of Mirzapur was an old manager (*gomashta*) of their business.[46] The treasurers of Agra, Moradabad and Shahjahanpur were also related, and connected with some of government's clients in Benares.

Many of the associations and relationships between patron and publicist which later became part of the fabric of the early Congress movement predated any direct assault by the government on the interests of their monied supporters in the localities. Many important organizations such as literary societies and religious associations which were only indirectly connected with government policy, can be seen as elements in the more general political growth of Hindustan. These relationships and the organizations which perpetuated them had more connection with the maintenance and improvement of religious status than with simple questions of political and monetary resources. The paramountcy of acts of religious charity in the social lives of the Hindu commercial classes, for instance, is quite plain in the very documents which chart most obviously their material interests. Their business books or *bahi khatas* and their personal account books or *kharach khatas* start with inventories of temple furniture; patronal deities had their own accounts; large sums of money were passed in and out of charitable bequests. But more than this, these books suggest a reappraisal of the social and consequently of the political aims of the monied classes of the towns. It is obvious that Hindustani bankers wished to make money

---

[44] *District Gazetteer* [*DG*] *Allahabad*, p. 60.

[45] Family History of Cawnpore and Allahabad branches of the family, and family tree in possession of Sri Beni Prasad Tandon, Allahabad; cf. *DG Allahabad*, pp. 59–60, and Benares Commissioners Records, 49 Revenue of 1879, 'pay of the Treasurer of Mirzapur collectorate', recommendations of Sheo Prasad, son of Tunti Mul, UPSA.

[46] Petition of Sheo Prasad and Tulsi Ram, *ibid*; They attempted to gain control of the office themselves by claiming that the ex-*gomashta* had insufficient security.

and to increase their social influence, but to what end, and against what gauges of social status did they test themselves? The sums that they had at their disposal were after all very considerable in the subsistence economy of nineteenth-century northern India. My impression is that few firms had more than five lakhs of Rupees invested in banking itself during the years 1850–80; but with subsidiary trades and offices included, joint families of 'respectable' city bankers could earn between Rs 20,000 and Rs 80,000 per annum.[47] This was the income of the top half dozen lawyers of the Allahabad High Court during these years, or of a medium-range landowner. But it is crucial that the institutional and social overheads of the *mahajans* were negligible by comparison with either a lawyer's or landholder's. Except for those who had worked closely with the Moghul Courts, the life-style of the Agarwal and Khattri bankers, at least until the last decade of the century, was very meagre. Some families had moved rather earlier into forms of sumptuary expenditure, but the dominant impression is one of great financial stringency. The major bankers of Allahabad lived until the 1880s as joint families in several small mud houses in the central market area.[48] Benares bankers were no more opulent. In connection with the difficulties of levying a *chaukidari* rate on the basis of house value or conspicuous expenditure, the officiating magistrate of Benares wrote in 1860,

Rai Narain Dass is generally allowed to be one of the richest bankers in this city. The house in which he resides in Phatuk Rangeel Das hardly covers a greater area of ground than one of the city thannas [police posts] whereas Raja Deo Narayan Singh who is not possessed of perhaps $\frac{1}{10}$th of the wealth of the former occupies with his house and residence, outhouses, stables and garden an area of probably 10 acres or more of land.[49]

[47] Estimated income of 'bankers' and 'bankers and landowners' in Allahabad and Cawnpore Durbar Lists, 1892, Records of Commissioner, Allahabad Division, basta 10, 57 General Administration Department [GAD] of 1892, CA; cf. 'honorary magistrates, Jaunpur', 164 GAD of 1883, Benares Commissioners Records, UPSA, estimates income of district's largest banker at Rs 30,000 p.a.; cf. *NWP Income Tax Report, 1886–87*, Appendix A.

[48] Until about 1870 Manohar Das, under whom the firm 'Gappoo Mal Kandheya Lal' made its greatest growth, lived with his whole family in a tiled *kacha* house on the South side of Ranimandi; they then moved into a larger one, which is still in use, but by no means opulent; Ram Charan Das built a large 'nawabi' style mansion at Ram Bagh in the early 1890s; a relative, Bisheshwar Das, built a large town house in Ranimandi after 1900. But this was long after the family acquired wealth and local status; within the main branch of the family, the emphasis on austerity continued. Interview with members of the Tandon family, 6 April 1972.

[49] Offg. Magistrate, Benares, to Commissioner, Benares, 5 December 1859, 25 Judicial of 1866, Benares Commissioners Records, UPSA.

In the typical *mahajani* family, food remained strictly vegetarian and servants were few; residents of *mohullas* banded together to fund night watchmen,[50] which obviated the need for the huge bands of clubmen and toughs which absorbed so much of the income of the landowners, and made them so much more exposed figures in local society.

The degree to which banking magnates were prepared to spend money and acquire ranges of vulnerable political interests was also limited by the very rigid conceptions of 'credit' which they maintained. 'Credit' was a banker's most important possession, for with it he could mobilize, in an emergency, three or four times his own assets from his peers. *Mahajani* anecdotes until recently in circulation[51] point out again and again the bankers' fear of loss of 'credit', if they were unable to meet unexpected credit notes whose terms required payment before sunset (*darshani hundis*). Expensive litigation over land or property was to be avoided; a banker must concentrate on *mahajani* and eschew politics. Jingles and rhymes whereby the *mahajani* alphabet was taught stressed the need to divide capital again and again; to bury some, to invest some in jewellery and other securities and only then to employ a minimum sum in active banking or trading. Even in the mid-nineteenth century, the communal memory of the upper Indian banker remained in the dangerous last days of the Moghul Empire, and the spectre of financial ruin reinforced the parsimonious habits of the commercial castes.

It was pre-eminently in the sphere of religious patronage that the big urban bankers found themselves as social as well as economic focuses for the activities of the community, for the two roles might have remained distinct. Here the greater part of their social energy and optional patronage was directed. The family accounts of one branch[52] of the great Shah concern of Benares for the years 1870–77 make it plain that when the immediate needs of the members' frugal eating and clothing habits and few servants had been satisfied, by far the most important category of social expenditure was connected with religion. Items for the service of temples, for the feeding of Brahmins

[50] 'Introduction of Act 20 of 1856 into Benares', Offg. Magistrate, Benares, to Commissioner, Benares, 9 May 1860, 25 Judicial of 1856, Benares Commissioners Records, UPSA.

[51] Interviews, May 1972, with Sri Ram Krishna, Shivala, Varanasi and Sri Beni Prasad Tandon, Ranimandi, Allahabad, February–August, 1972.

[52] This was the joint family represented in the 1870s and 80s by Babus Bisheshwar Prasad, Raghunath Prasad, Baijnath Prasad and Hanuman Das. *Sah Vanshavali*, appendix (family tree); I am very grateful to its present representative, Sri Shiva Prasad Shah, for allowing me the use of *bahis* in his possession.

and *pandas*, for Ganges bathing, for cattle and for outlay on the many religious festivals occur again and again.[53] Equally, the foundation of temples, bathing places, community shrines (*sanghats*) and religious trusts seems to have absorbed a very high percentage of the assets of major bankers such as the Tandons of Allahabad, once the ongoing expenses of their firms had been met. Sumptuary expenditure outside the religious sphere was at this time limited, by comparison with that of the landowner. Yet conspicuous religious expenditure was not merely an indulgence but a necessary element in the maintenance of family and community status. Family and community status reflected on marriage prospects, which in turn influenced the commercial credit of the family businesses.

Between 1830 and 1890, the volume and direction of religious activity within the Hindi speaking area of northern India took important new directions. Some of the manifestations of this revivalism originated in the changed educational and employment policies of government. But other elements were largely autonomous reactions either to broader forces of 'westernization', such as the printing press and the missionaries, or to the changing balance of power in Hindustani cities. The rapid collapse of the service and landholding élites of Muslim rule, especially in the cities of the old Benares province,[54] was matched by the growing wealth of the Hindu commercial classes. This was reflected before

[53] *Kharach Bahi*, Bysak Sudi 12, St. 1930-Cheyt Budi 15, 1937, (1870–77). Not all items of expenditure were specified, which makes quantification difficult. But some comparisons (from the first nine months of the *bahi*) are instructive, as these highlight the *relatively* high rate of religious and ritual expenditure by comparison with the cost of running the joint family. Household servants' wages (*Charkri Khata*) were Rs. 4 per month; one month's *puja* at one of the several temples was Rs 3 1½ as., at another Rs 4; milk for 28 days for the family, Rs 2 1½ as.; *puja* to Ganesh, apparently a household deity, for the same period, was Rs 3 2 pie. *puja* Rs 4 was spent on a *tilak* ceremony for a connection; Rs 8 was the cost of two *dhotis*; sums of 2 as. were regularly spent on Ganges bathing, given to sadhus or in charity to Brahmins; the labour for constructing a bed was 1 a., flour for chappatis for a week (?) was also 1 a. Much larger sums were expended during the many religious festivals. The only substantial outgoings from the expense book were generally connected with the purchase of jewellery, a form of investment rather than a luxury. Most significant perhaps, the accounts suggest the relatively large volume of social contact afforded by acts of religious charity, compared with the circumscribed life otherwise led by a *mahajani* family, (Sri Matthura Das read the *mahajani*).

[54] The decline of the power of Muslim landed-groups in the cities of the Benares province, and their environs, can be traced to the patronage exercised by the Hindu rulers of Benares after they replaced the erstwhile Muslim subadars. While this was essentially family rather than 'communal' patronage, it is significant that Sheo Lal Dube, the archetypal new Hindu magnate, instigated the first recorded move to have Muslim cow-slaughter banned in the city limits. Proceedings of Resident of Benares 33, II, 23 July, 19 August, 1790, UPSA.

1857 in symbolic conflicts over temple and mosque lands and in stirrings in places of religious importance such as Benares,[55] Allahabad[56] and Ajodhia.[57] A growing sense of social and political security encouraged the revival of Hindu claims and challenges which had lain dormant for several generations.

Hindu revivalism in upper India is generally associated with the impact of the Arya Samaj and the Sanatan Dharma Sabhas and dates from the second half of the nineteenth century. But it seems likely that the styles of relationship and ideologies incorporated within these movements originated earlier. Between 1760 and 1830 the Mahrattas poured wealth into Benares, Allahabad and Hardwar, constructing large numbers of religious buildings and feeing a whole new generation of priests in these centres. Similarly, the drift into Hindustan of commercial groups from Punjab and Rajasthan from the 1780s was probably significant. Sikhism appears to have had a strong but unobtrusive effect on traditional urban Hinduism. Most of the Khattri and Arora bankers who established themselves in the cities accepted the Sikh gurus as 'sants'[58] and supported *sanghats* which in their more institutionalized form and emphasis on community differed from the family–priest relationships of 'traditional Hinduism'. During the same period the wealth of the Gosain religious groups multiplied considerably, while the peculiar religiosity and puritanism of the Jain sects were imported by families of jewellers and bankers who drifted into the region. The Jain commercial people in particular provided many of the most fervent supporters of cow-protection movements in the second half of the century.[59]

The urban commercial classes had already begun to support a

---

[55] E.g. Agent to the Governor-General, Benares, to acting secretary to government, 23 October 1809, Agent to G-G., outgoing correspondence, UPSA. There were several other instances of clashes over the Gyanbaffee mosque before 1857.

[56] Magistrate, Allahabad, to Commissioner, Allahabad Division, 28 October 1885, basta 208, 351 Judicial of 1885, CA.

[57] Ram Gopal Pandey, *Jai Janma Bhumi, Shri Ram Janma Bhumi* (Ajodhia, 1970); a popular pamphlet tracing attempts by Hindus to recapture sacred lands in the area.

[58] *Khattri Itihas* (Lahore, ?, n.d.), and *Khattri Jati ka Itihas* (Moradabad, c. 1957). The Khattri and Arora communities in several UP towns claim knowledge of *sanghats* dating from before 1850; evidence of the organization of Khattri 'Sikhs' in Benares before 1800 is to be found in Proceedings of the Resident, Benares, Vol 52, 6 January 1792, case of Bedamo v. Bhowanny Singh, UPSA.

[59] The results were sometimes political. Upper India 'Jains and Marwaris' were thought to have given financial support to the extremist boycott of British goods in 1910–11 because politicians agreed to include cow-protection in their platform. UP police report, 10 January 1911, Home Poll B February 1911, 1–5, NAI.

range of little-known departures in Hindu belief which emphasized the book, the vernacular, and the sermon, some time before Swami Dayananda's first ministry. Around the book, the vernacular, and the sermon, developed many of the relationships which were later incorporated into the general background of Indian nationalism in the Ganges valley, and in these relationships the city bankers played a general role of patron. Benares banking families supported scriptural-based revivalist movements twenty years before the foundation of the Sanatan Dharma Sabhas.[60] Members of the Jagat Seth family (Jain Oswals), who sought refuge in Benares after the collapse of their Bengal commercial empire, were closely connected with the development of Hindi literature in the city.[61] In the 1860s and 70s, the connection between high-status urban commercial people and the literary revival became plain. Bhartendu Harish Chandra and Jagganath Das Ratnakar, two of the foremost Hindi literateurs of the period, were both from Agarwal banking families and both continued *mahajani* to some extent.[62] In Allahabad, the Tandon and the Bhalla bankers[63] were responsible for the foundation of the Bharti Bhawan vernacular library, but rich bankers there had previously been responsible for the finance and distribution of religious tracts in Sanskrit.[64] Towards the west, the same sort of relationships could be seen within the connections of the Lakshman Das family of Muttra[65] and the Nihal Chand family of Muzaffarnagar.[66] Organizations such as the Hindi Sahitya Samellan[67]

[60] E.g. the support of members of the Dulhinji *mahajan* family for the religious sect *Pustimarg Sampraday*, *Agrawal Jati*, II, 293, 94. Another early revivalist movement closely connected with urban mercantile circles was the *Radha Swami* Sect, whose first *guru* was Tulsi Ram, an Agra banker. J. N. Farquhar, *Modern Religious Movements in India* (first Indian edition, 1967), p. 163. Swami Dayananda's father also seems to have been a banker.

[61] G. A. Grierson, *The Modern Vernacular Literature of Hindustan* (Calcutta, 1889), p. 99.

[62] *Agrawal Jati*, II, 29–31; brief family history of the Bhartendu Family in possession of Sri Kumud Chandra, Chaukambha, Varanasi; Grierson, *op. cit.*, pp. 124–6.

[63] *Bharti Bhawan Pustakalya ka Satara Varshiya Jayanti Granth* (Allahabad, 1956), pp. 77–9.

[64] See, e.g., *Hindi Pradip*, 1 April 1878 (banker not specified); *DG Allahabad*, p. 60.

[65] Lala Srinivasa Das, *gomashta* of the firm of Lakshman Das in Delhi was author of one of the earliest Hindi novels, *Pariksha Guru*. I am indebted to Mr A. S. Kalsi of the Oriental Faculty, Cambridge University, for this information.

[66] E.g. *Tribune* (Lahore), 21 October 1891, refers to the publication of religious tracts with Nagri translations by Rai Nihal Chand.

[67] The Allahabad Hindi Sahitya Samellan was founded about 1911, but many of its prominent members, including Balkrishna Bhatt, Mahabir Prasad Dwivedi and Madan Mohan Malaviya had been connected with the Bharti Bhawan Library since the 1880s.

and the Nagri Pracharini Sabha,[68] which later formalized these earlier links, became incorporated into the political structure of northern India. Sometimes they acted as focuses for interest groups; sometimes, moving towards quasi-political goals themselves, they influenced the Congress leaders in the direction they took on wider political issues.

More significant yet was the support given by commercial wealth to local societies and organizations which arose prior to, but later became electorates for, the early Congress. These organizations were generally devoted to public improvement and philanthropy, but within a specifically Hindu context. In Allahabad, the Hindu Samaj and the People's Association represented alliances between urban monied interests and their connections among professional men. The president of the Meerut Association, founded in 1881, was 'so popular amongst the raises and residents of the station that since his appointment as permanent president almost all the bankers and landholders of the station have joined the Association and they all take deep interest in matters connected with it'.[69] In Benares, the Kashi Sujan Sabha founded about 1880[70] for the improvement of pilgrimage and other facilities, contained several members of the Shah family and other bankers.[71] The Sabha returned prominent commercial and professional men to the 1888 Congress. After 1910 it was resuscitated to become the local power base for the nationalist politicians Rai Krishnaji and Bhagwan Das who were themselves Agarwal business magnates.[72] Even mercantile caste associations *per se* were directly involved in the early phase of Congress. A Khattri Conference presided over by a local banker was held concurrently with the Congress of 1888,[73] while the so-called 'Khetry Hitkary Community' (Khattri Improvement Society) of Agra delegated its president to the session.[74] In Lucknow, the nationalist leader, Ganga Prasad Varma and three of his mercantile caste fellows were selected as representatives of the 'Khetrio and Saraswati Sobha'.[75] It is important to remark that though government policy sometimes transformed these relationships into more formal

---

[68] E.g. Shyam Sunder Das, founder of the Sabha, and several associated writers were Khattris; prominent city bankers supported the organization. I am indebted for this information to Mr C. King of the University of Wisconsin.

[69] *Tribune*, 20 October 1888; annual report of the Meerut Association, 1882–83.

[70] Address of the Kashi Sujan Sabha, GAD 1917, 553, Uttar Pradesh Secretariat Records, Lucknow.

[71] *Leader*, 6 May 1910.   [72] *Ibid.*, 24 June 1917.

[73] *Hindustan* (Kalakankar, Partabgarh, Hindi–English), 11 December 1888, UPNNR 1888.

[74] *Report of the Indian National Congress [INC] 1888* (Calcutta, 1889), p. 129.

[75] *INC 1888*, pp. 119–20.

organization, they originated from independent drives within Hindu society. Thus the creation of the central Hindu Samaj at Allahabad in 1884 was clearly connected, among other things, with the per-ambulation of the Education Commission of 1883 and the fillip which it gave to the Hindi interest all over the Provinces. But the commercial magnates and Brahmin publicists who founded the earlier local Hindu Samaj in 1880 were carrying on an older tradition of association as supporters or protectors of the 'monastic' foundations and bathing priests which congregated there. Equally the lines of ritual mobility connecting the great pilgrimage centres of the province continued to provide an important network for the propagation of religious and cultural movements.

That it was possible for a complex and supra-local political organi-zation concerned with religion and status to spring up was made clear by the great cow-protection movement that disturbed northern India between 1882 and 1894. Here, the participation of mercantile wealth can be traced in detail in the funding of the *gaushala* (cow shed) organization which was thrown up by the movement. The agitation was seen by one observer as 'a platform on which all classes of Hindu society could unite, however much at variance on other subjects'; its main supporters were 'the great trading and banking classes, who are bigoted Hindus . . .'[76] along with some classes of landowners. The importance of the movement lay in its patrons as much as in its publi-cists, and in the bazaars of the towns as much as in the countryside. Even the petty moneylender was involved in the system of *chituki* or levy on produce sold in village shops which then went to swell cow funds. The whole movement can in fact be regarded as a controlled experiment for other forms of political activity, since bankers and title holders were not, at first, called on to make a choice between their relationship with government and the patronage of Hindu interests which their position as *rais*, or notable, demanded of them.

The detailed material presented in this essay is designed to suggest that in the infra-structure of new political relations in late nineteenth-century north India, two forms of relationship can be seen between patron and publicist, as also between various levels of political activity. One was the relationship between patron and publicist designed to protect material interests, or to promote them within new political

---

[76] Note on the organization of the *gauraksha* [sic] *sabha*, Judicial and Public Papers, 1894, Vol. 367, 257, IOL. The Jains and Marwaris of Cawnpore were prominent in later outbreaks of the movement, 'Note on the Anti-Cow-Killing Agitation in the U.P., 1913–16', Home Poll D November 1916, NAI.

arenas—the *vakil* relationship. The other concerned the protection or enhancement of particular conceptions of status conceived within the bounds of revived Hinduism—the *dharmik* relationship. It is difficult to separate them and unwise to emphasize one to the exclusion of the other. Just as religious catch-cries were sometimes used in battles between political factions which centred on the disposition of objective political resources, so conflicts of a purely subjective nature, such as those over music before mosques and the sale of beef on the streets, could also make and break political alliances. Indeed, some organizations, which at first sight seem paradigms of 'modern' and rationally directed pressure groups, are found on closer inspection to have been sectional interests concerned to capture not so much material resources as added religious status.

But because of the paramountcy of religious symbolism in their conceptions of social status, the general drift of religious protest and organization could also sometimes cause the urban notable to break his natural patronage connection with the local authorities and move into a position of dissidence. In Benares, this had happened in the 1850s when some powerful bankers, for long among the most whole-hearted aids of government, were suspected of 'disloyalty' in the course of a religious dispute.[77] It was to happen again on a wider scale and in a more significant context during the 1880s and 90s, when some commercial magnates were drawn into nationalist activity through their Hindu interests. We have taken the case of Allahabad to illustrate the variety of relations in local society which could make this possible.

4. Allahabad Connections, Religion and Politics
1880–1920

(A) THE TANDONS, A DOMINANT CONNECTION

When Lala Ram Charan Das died in August 1917, his commemoration meeting was presided over by Madan Mohan Malaviya, who extolled the dead man's courage in defying the local government of the time to

---

[77] The cry of 'religion in danger' was raised regarding eating facilities in the Benares jail. The bankers, appealed to by the populace, said that 'it was a matter of religion and that they would not be backward'. F. B. Gubbins, Magistrate of Benares, to E. A. Reade, Superintendant of Police, 7 August 1852, in *UP State Records Series, Selections from the English Records, Banaras Affairs (1811–1858)*, II, 168–9, 174.

finance the pavilion and arrangements for the Indian National Congress session which had been held at Allahabad in 1888.[78] Ram Charan Das was the wealthiest of the local magnates to give his support to political and religious organizations in the city, and he was for some years a particularly close associate of Malaviya and his group. Besides serving on three reception committees of the Congress, and becoming treasurer of its provincial branch in 1907,[79] Ram Charan Das had been intimately involved with all the various movements for the educational and political uplift of the Hindu community which had been the particular preserve of the Malaviya family. He was treasurer of the Allahabad Hindu Boarding House Committee in 1903,[80] and gave Rs 75,000 to the institution that it foreshadowed, the Benares Hindu University.[81] Ram Charan Das and his relatives were also consistently active in the mainstream of Hindu political associations in the UP. They took part in the Prayag Hindu Samaj of the 1880s, attended and helped to organize the Allahabad Hindu Mahasamellan of 1906, convened by Malaviya and Sri Krishna Joshi[82] to clarify the Hindu movement's aims.[83] Indeed, they were inconspicuously involved in all the conferences, societies and movements which culminated in the United Provinces Hindu Sabha of 1915, and, ultimately, in the All-India Hindu Mahasabha itself. The *Leader*, Allahabad's English daily, also owed much to the patronage of Ram Charan Das, for he was the first to undertake to purchase shares in 'Newpapers Limited', the company founded to print it, when Malaviya and Sapru were canvassing the idea in 1909.[84] The newspaper later wrote of these negotiations, 'Pandit Malaviya always consulted him [R. C. Das] whenever any new undertaking was projected, whether it related to the formation of

---

[78] *Leader* (Allahabad), 11 August 1917.

[79] *Advocate* (Lucknow), 20 January 1907, UPNNR 1907.

[80] *Indian People* (Allahabad), 15 November 1906. The drive to found a hall of residence for Hindu students at Allahabad University was suggested by Malaviya as early as 1889. It received support from Sir Antony MacDonnell (Lieutenant-Governor 1896–1902) after whom it was named.

[81] *Allahabad Hindu University Society Progress Report, 1914* (Allahabad, 1914), p. 49.

[82] Prominent Hindu revivalist of the 1880s; class fellow of Madan Mohan Malaviya and coadjutor of his in the Sanatan Dharma Sabha (orthodox religious association).

[83] Circular from Malaviya and Sri Krishna Joshi, *Pioneer* (Allahabad), 24 September 1905. The Mahasamellan was essentially an attempt to capture the educated but orthodox Hindu revivalists alienated by the more reactionary Bharat Dharm Mahamandal (All-India Central Religious Association).

[84] The Board of the *Leader* included most of Allahabad's lawyer politicians such as Motilal Nehru, Tej Bahadur Sapru and Satish Chandra Bannerjee, but also Ram Charan Das, his relation, Lala Shimbhu Nath and an Agarwala banker.

E

an association, or the holding of a sitting of the Indian National Congress'.[85]

Allahabad itself has many memorials to the Tandons' munificence. There is the clocktower built at their expense for the municipality in which they wielded influence for so long. Two ghats (bathing places) on the rivers Ganges and Jumna, the Minto Park, and a number of educational institutions including the City Anglo-Vernacular School and the Khattri Pathshala, received support from Ram Charan Das and his immediate family. Yet this role as patron of religious and philanthropic charity was only one aspect of his real influence. Ram Charan Das' relationship with the district and provincial authorities was equally close. He was a darbari and an honorary magistrate for Allahabad City, treasurer for the Allahabad Bank, and, as government treasurer for the locality and treasurer to the High Court,[86] a full member of the district administrative staff.[87] His influence was recognized and enhanced by the attention of British officials, and when the Lieutenant-Governor in person consented to open the Lala's new ghat at Ram Bhag in 1906, the event symbolized not only an access of piety among the Hindus of Allahabad, but also the close connection of local influence and patronage with the requirements of administration.[88]

Ram Charan Das' involvement with Malaviya and other Hindu publicists seems to have sprung naturally from the family's position as a major Hindu patron in the city.[89] He was head of the 'Hathi Ram' religious party in the Chauk[90] and a prominent member of the Prayag Hindu Samaj, a revivalist association connected with the arrangements for the Magh Mela religious fair, which later became an elective body for the 1888 Congress. He was also the major local donor to Swami Ala Ram's cow-shed fund,[91] the collections for which were hardly distinguishable from Congress meetings between 1888 and 1892.

But the largely personal relationship between Ram Charan Das and Malaviya was merely the most striking example of a wider set of

[85] *Leader 'Jubilee Number'*, 1935, p. 12.

[86] *UP Gazette*, 6 February 1909, part V, p. 23.

[87] Darbaris for Allahabad District, Records of the Commissioner, Allahabad Division, Post-Mutiny Records basta 10, file 57 of 1892. See Appendix.

[88] *Indian People* (Allahabad), 8 November 1906.

[89] Tandon family tradition has it that Malaviya used to 'sit with' or pay court to Ram Charan Das while he was still attending his religious seminary. Interview with Sri Hari Mohan Das Tandon, April 1972.

[90] *Leader*, 17 October 1910.

[91] *Hindi Pradip* (Allahabad, Hindi), 17 September 1888, UPPNR 1888.

connections, part religious, part economic, which linked the commercial notables of the old *mohullas* with the Malavi Brahmins. This
was partly the result of their adjoining living areas in the Allahabad
chauk. The Tandons themselves were a closely-knit banking and
commercial community. Apart from their interest in the Allahabad
Bank,[92] the main branch of the family owned the banking and cloth-
trading firm, 'Gapoo Mal Kandheya Lal Ltd.', while Ram Charan
Das' brother, Munni Lal, and his sons, Bisheshwar Das and Misri
Lal, owned the firm 'Manohar Das Munni Lal'; another brother,
Chunni Lal started a third firm 'Manohar Das Chunni Lal', which
was managed by his son, Lala Shimbhu Nath.[93] As an indication of
their wealth, the total assets, partitioned[94] by Lala Manohar Das
before his death in 1894, seem to have amounted to about Rs 16 lakhs,
while Ram Charan Das' annual income in 1892 was calculated at
Rs 60–90,000 and must have increased considerably before his death.[95]
Most members of the family were also medium-sized landholders
in the district. Ram Charan Das paid Rs 14,706 land revenue on estates
in the Phulpur region, and worked the indigo factories which his father
Manohar Das had received from government in 1858. Bisheshwar Das
and Misri Lal paid Rs 4,152 for lands in the immediate vicinity of
the city, and held properties on a small scale throughout the district,
as did Shimbhu Nath.[96] Tandons were also general merchants in
the Chauk and one Rai Debi Prasad, a more distant relative,[97] was
the most prominent contractor locally. When their assets as urban
property owners are taken into account, it is clear that the Tandons
must have been easily the most wealthy group of families in Allahabad,
though it would appear that Ram Charan Das himself was less wealthy
than Raja Motichand of Benares, for instance, who is said to have had

[92] They were treasurers for all branches of the Allahabad Bank.
[93] *DG Allahabad*, p. 59.
[94] The partition entry is to be found in the *rokarh* book of the firm 'Manohar Das Kandheya Lal' (perhaps a firm created solely for the partition year), for Sambat 1950–51 (A.D. 1892–93) under the date Magh Sudi 11 (c. 2 January 1893). Rs 7,80,286 were divided among three branches and Rs 2,00,000 were put aside for clearance of liabilities. The branches further received more than Rs 1,00,000 each in government notes. Manohar Das also created religious and family trusts to the tune of about five *lakhs* of rupees (for this see an Ms. family history written by Sri Manmohan Das Tandon about 1935 at Ranimandi). For another estimate of some of the assets before partition (Rs 11,60,096), see *Leader*, 23 March 1911, Allahabad Civil Suit, 268 of 1910.
[95] Wise investment, for instance, had increased Manohar Das' bequest (for charity) by 33 per cent between 1894 and 1908. *Indian People*, 8 November 1906.
[96] *DG Allahabad*, pp. 218–9.
[97] Tandon Family Tree, Ranimandi.

an income of Rs 4,00,000 p.a. in 1908.[98] The Tandon clan was not held to be ritually the highest in the Khattri community, but with 77 enumerated members in 1896, it was the largest sub-group in Allahabad.[99]

The accumulation of these various resources by the Tandon family and the metamorphosis of the connection reflected, above all, its response to the commercial and political requirements of government. Evolution went through several stages; first (c. 1800–30) a period of riverine trading in grain and cloth, and diversification into indigenous banking; second (c. 1830–57) a period of contracting for the arsenal, moneychanging and entrepreneurial activities for government. The third phase (c. 1857–90) saw investment in landed property or house-ownership and a shift away from the *hundi* business to a closer association with joint-stock banking.[100] Finally, the last phase (1890–1935) saw the ending of the connection's dominance of urban politics, partition, and a growing emphasis on the exploitation of landed estates. From the political point of view, it was the third phase that was critical because the connection, fostering the growth of revivalist associations, contributed through its association with local publicists to early nationalist activity.

Tandons and other major commercial families lived in the Rani Ki Mandi-Mirganj area in the centre of Allahabad near the spot where Manohar Das' Clocktower was later constructed, while Malavis lived close by, in the old service area of Ahiyapur. In the fifteenth or sixteenth century the Malavis were said to have emigrated from their native region of Indore after a caste dispute and settled in Allahabad and Mirzapur as pandits and business men.[101] By the later nineteenth century many Malavi Brahmins had forsaken their priestly calling and 'many of them live by secular occupations such as trading, doing clerk's work and general service, and they are in fact more of a trading than a priestly caste'.[102] Malaviya's own brothers were a case in point. One was a railway contractor, another a trader in the Chauk, and another a clerk in the Board of revenue.[103] Tandons, as local moneylenders and cloth and grain retailers, must have been associated with them

[98] Home Reforms B March 1921, 34–99, p. 499, NAI.

[99] W. Crooke, *Tribes and Castes of the North-Western Provinces and Oudh* (Calcutta, 1896), III, 274.

[100] *Indian People*, 13 February 1908. Ram Charan Das was personally responsible for the phenomenal growth of the Allahabad Bank, the most successful in upper India. By 1908 it had a working capital of 4½ crores and a dividend of 18 per cent; on the board he was associated at first with Congress activists such as Rampal Singh.

[101] S. R. Chaturvedi, *Pandit Madan Mohan Malaviya* (Benares, 1936), p. 7.

[102] Crooke, *op. cit.*, III, 452.   [103] Chaturvedi, *op. cit.*, p. 11.

occupationally, and indeed, here was probably an instance where economic ties, and ties of religious patronage, combined to create a political connection.

The Malavis' proximity in living quarters with the Khattris had one fruit in the Bharti Bhawan Library, a vernacular institution, situated in an alley off the main cloth and grain market, which was constructed through the munificence of Brij Mohan Das Bhalla, another major banker,[104] and the Tandons.[105] The organizers of this library included several members of the Malaviya community, such as Madan Mohan himself, a relative by marriage, Dr Lakshmi Narayan Vyasa, who was first president of the Allahabad Hindu Samaj,[106] and Balkrishna Bhatta, a noted Hindi writer, editor of the *Hindi Pradip*, and later adherent of the extremist party.[107] The library, opened in 1886, was originally devoted to the propagation of Hindi and Sanskrit literature and stood in the same relation to the later Allahabad Hindi Sahitya Sammellan as did the MacDonnell Hindu Boarding House to the Benares Hindu University, and the Hindu Samaj of the 1880s to the UP Hindu Sabha of 1916. For the group of protagonists in each case was widened, but remained at core the same, and the major Allahabad patrons in each case were the Tandons and other commercial men. The guide lines of Malaviya's career, and indeed, of the whole Hindu political movement in this part of Hindustan, were laid in the Allahabad Chauk in the 1880s, particularly in co-operation with its Khattri magnates.[108]

Common living areas also naturally gave Tandons and Malavis common interests in municipal affairs, especially since Ward IV (South Kotwali) had one of the largest concentrations of poor Muslims in the city.[109]

[104] *Ibid*, p. 35; *Leader*, 14 May 1913. The secretary of the library in the 1910s was Bihari Lal and Manmohan Das was responsible for upkeep and repairs.

[105] *Bharti Bhawan Jayanti Granth*, p. 79.

[106] Lakshmi Narayan Vyasa. Educated Sanskrit Pathshala Allahabad, Benares College 1846–47. Later deputy Inspector of Schools NWP, President of Samaj until his death about 1894.

[107] Balkrishna Bhatta 'is not regarded as a man of great status, but is known to be a Sanskrit scholar and is respected as such'. Editor of *Hindi Pradip*, later Professor of Sanskrit at the Kayastha Pathshala where he became involved in the revolutionary movements of the 1900s associated with the journal *Swarajya*. Educated Sanskrit Pathshala and High School, Allahabad, but failed university entrance. Report on the Vernacular Press of Upper India, 1890, Home Public B September 1891, 129–35 NAI; *Leader*, 23 July 1914, etc.

[108] Bhowani Prasad Bhalla, another Khattri banker prominent in caste associations, also appeared regularly at Congress meetings and in political connections.

[109] *Pioneer*, 20 October 1884, registered voters in the old city; Ward III, European, 39; Hindu, 507; Muslim, 250; Bengali, 94. Ward IV, European, 4; Hindu, 504; Muslim, 208; Bengali, 43.

Malavi males in Allahabad in 1914 numbered 150,[110] and under the relatively liberal Allahabad municipal franchise of rental value Rs 72 per year, they had a significant voting power. But apart from the need to preserve religious and monopolize conservancy arrangements, this ward was important to the merchant community because it was the power base of the Tandons, who consistently led the assault on the European traders of the Civil Lines who appropriated most of the available municipal funds for their own purposes in the early days. In fact, when the early over-representation of Bengalis and professionals on the municipal board disappeared in the early 1890s, Ward IV consistently returned a 'Malavi' and a 'Khattri', or rather, a Malaviya supporter and a member of the Tandon connection, in alternate years.[111] Once on the Board, Malaviya, his family and his associates, were close supporters of the Tandon family and their allies against the conservative party which was led by another Khattri banker, Lala Jagat Narayan. These disputes were important for the major trading communities in that after the mid-1890s they centred around control of the local octroi taxation, which could affect the through-trade in grain and cloth, and building materials with which the Tandons, with their growing commercial interests, were particularly concerned.[112] But symbolic religious issues were also crucial. The influence that Malaviya came to wield among the Hindus of the city in social matters was both a political advantage and a religious validation for Lalas Ram Charan Das, Someshwar Das and Bisheshwar Das, and Malaviya was found widely canvassing for them in the municipal elections of the early 1900s. At the election of March 1901, for instance, he was allegedly responsible for a rumour that the Jagat Narayan faction was about to raise the octroi rate on wedding clothes and other articles of religious importance.[113] The Tandons' part of the bargain was to see that Malaviya retained influence in municipal education policy when they were 'in power', and that local Hindu libraries[114] and other institutions were succoured with occasional grants.[115]

[110] *Leader*, 20 October and 25 December 1924, evidence of Brij Mohan Vyasa (executive officer of the Malavi Sabha) in a caste libel case.

[111] Source: returns to Allahabad Municipal Board in *UP* (*NWP & O*) *Gazette*, annually, part III.

[112] See, for instance, notes on octroi taxation, NWP Municipalities A December 1885, 1, IOL; and 'Report of Select Committee on Octroi', *UP Gazette*, 14 August 1909, part VIII. [113] *Prayag Samachar*, 15 March 1901, UPNNR 1901.

[114] The 'Prem Bhawan' library for instance. Malaviya and Someshwar Das also co-operated to found a Hindu orphanage. *Prayag Samachar*, 19 November 1896, UPNNR 1896.

[115] Note the importance for educated Hindus in keeping control of the board's

Another local organization which represented a development of existing relationships between Khattri commercial magnates and Brahmin professional men and publicists was the Allahabad People's Association, which also became an electorate for delegates to the early Congress meetings. Formed about 1883, it acted as a municipal pressure group, but its most strenuous activities were confined to matters with communal or religious undertones. It had a regular elective system based on the wards of the city,[116] and was found making representations for the wider circulation of municipal debates.[117] The People's Association was a strongly Hindu body and in 1886 it was temporarily successful in passing a by-law forbidding Muslim kine-slaughter within the municipal limits,[118] a tactic that proved successful because the relatives of the officers of the association were the dominant faction on the board. The large Ward IV branch of this body provided the machinery whereby most of the commercial wealth of the old city could be represented at the 1888 Congress, and its delegates were as one would expect, predominantly Khattri. The chairman of the association was Lala Bihari Lal Tandon, Head Accountant of the Allahabad Bank, while among commercial people represented was Lala Chunni Lal of the banking firm of that name. The Malavi Brahmin merchant community was also represented in Pt. Balmokund Bhatta, a kinsman of Balkrishna of the *Hindi Pradip*.[119]

Finally, it may also be possible to perceive in this relationship the symbolic beginnings of what later became a very well-defined 'interest' bringing merchants into Congress politics. Sugar and cloth were staples in the down-Ganges trade dominated by Khattris, Agarwalas and Marwaris, and these, in the NWP, were the articles most usually identified with the politicians' demand for 'swadeshi'. In 1881 a Deshi Tijrat (Home Industry) Company was opened in the chauk to sell country-made produce, and Malaviya, who was lecturing on the virtue of native industry as early as 1885,[120] quickly became associated with it.[121]

charitable donations. This was emphasized in 1916 when a temporary Muslim majority terminated grants to some Hindi libraries, etc., and devoted funds to an Islamia School. *Abhyudaya* (Allahabad), 27 April 1917.

[116] See miscellaneous circulars, notes of meetings etc. in Sunder Lal correspondence, 1884 bundle (in the possession of Mr R. Dave, Allahabad).

[117] Proceedings of the Working Committee, Allahabad Municipal Board, 25 May 1885. The association was also allowed to maintain observers during municipal elections. Proceedings Working Committee, 17 March 1886.

[118] 'Cow-slaughter', basta 269, file 123 GAD of 1887, CA.

[119] *INC 1888*, p. 126, delegate no. 627.

[120] Circular for meeting, 29 March, 1885, Dave Collection, 1885 bundle.

[121] *Leader*, 23 December 1909.

The manager of this firm was one Govind Prasad (Khattri) who attended the 1888 Congress as a delegate. Similarly, the Bengali swadeshi agitation of the 1900s called forth a response from the Malaviya group in the form of a project for the establishment of a Prayag Sugar Company with a capital of three lakhs of rupees. In this and in another swadeshi venture of the same sort, Ram Charan Das and Misri Lal were both major shareholders.[122]

The relationship between Ram Charan Das and Malaviya, or the Bhalla family and Balkrishna Bhatt, or more generally between high-status commercial people and predominantly Brahmin publicists, illustrates a wider feature of Indian political behaviour at this time. The educated client or publicist would use his influence in the developing mass media to support the interest of the *rais* who was his patron. As government devolved political resources to local bodies in which the *rais* and his clients were represented, and as the commercial families themselves developed wider and more exposed patterns of political and economic activity, such relationships were more and more expressed through electoral canvassing and directed to material goals. But their origin may often have been in concerns of religion and status, and such concerns remained omnipresent in the conduct of the business of local government even when taxation, licences and schedules of octroi were available to Indians as political tools.

(B) JAGAT NARAYAN—AN 'OUT' CONNECTION

To write of the association of 'Khattris' with nationalist politics in Allahabad, would be a false generalization. The Manohar Das family was merely the most powerful connection within the Khattri community; a dominant one perhaps, but other Khattri magnates displayed different allegiances. The group of families connected with the banking and insurance firm 'Kesri Narayan Mahabir Narayan' had a recent history similar to that of the Tandons of the Chauk and had also prospered by Mutiny service, though their appearance at Allahabad was prior to that of the Tandons, and they had received an honorary title from Shuja-ud-Daula, ruler of Oudh. The owner of the parent firm during this period, Rai Kesri Narayan, a loyal and subservient zamindar, was among those who found landed estates more profitable than banking interests.[123] But another branch grouped around the firm 'Jagat Narayan Bhagwati Narayan', known as the Chaddha amily, was the most active supporter of the collectorate throughout

[122] *Ibid.*, 23 December 1909.   [123] *DG Allahabad*, p. 61.

this period, and the long-standing rival of their caste fellow, Ram Charan Das. Jagat Narayan (1844–1909?) seems to have become above all a landed *rais* like his relative Kesri Narayan. He had been one of the largest purchasers in the district in the 1860s and '70s.[124] In the early 1880s he sat on the district and local boards for Arail pargana, across the Jumna from Allahabad, and was associated with the major land-owner of the area, in the government-sponsored 'Porter Agricultural Association'.[125] This landowner was the most bitter local opponent of the 1888 Congress, and Jagat Narayan was nominated to the municipal board in that year, which was significant also for hotly contested elec-tions in Allahabad.[126]

It was perhaps the predominance of Jagat Narayan's landowning concerns, his lack of large 'interest' in the city and the apparent small-ness of his urban income of Rs 5,000 p.a., compared with Ram Charan Das' Rs 60–90,000,[127] which accounts partly for his political stance. Whereas government reckoned him, in his role as landowner, 'a man of wealth and local status', the *Prayag Samachar*, referring to his connec-tion's lack of success at local elections, remarked that he was not 'supported by any powerful men (ready to fight), and his friends are not therefore generally successful at elections'.[128] On the other hand, Jagat Narayan was reported to have had considerable influence among the poorer classes of the community, *halwais* (confectioners), *pragwals* and the like, especially in the rural areas.[129] Jagat Narayan and his sons also held considerable property in the *mohullas* of the old city.[130] For instance, in 1911 one son, Bageshwari Narayan, was continually canvassed by a representative of the opposite party, but he 'had already promised Abdul Haq', an orthodox Muslim lawyer, the votes of his fifty or sixty tenants.[131] The connection's publicist in the protracted party struggle was an obscure Brahmin, Ram Gopal, editor of the *Prayag Samachar*[132] who was himself controlled by Jaggan Nath Vaid

---

[124] F. W. Porter, *Final Settlement Report of the Allahabad District* (Allahabad, 1878), p. 54; and Darbar list, 1892.

[125] Allahabad District revenue administration report, 1889 (original), basta 132, file 252 of 1889, CA.

[126] *Report on the Administration of Allahabad Municipality for the year 1887–88* (Allahabad, 1888), p. 2.

[127] Darbar List, 1892.   [128] *Prayag Samachar*, 15 March 1901, UPNNR 1901.

[129] Collector to Commissioner, 19 September 1890, report on district board, Allahabad, 1889–90 (original), basta 128, file 239 Judicial of 1890, CA.

[130] Proceedings of Working Committee, Allahabad Municipal Board, 1911–13, house assessment lists.

[131] *Leader*, 29 May 1911, election petition case.

[132] Ram Charan Das was supported by the *Natya Patra*, UPNNR 1898–1902.

doctor and moneylender.[133] The table below[134] suggests that at least
in so far as it was represented in municipal politics, Jagat Narayan's
party was no more a simple caste faction than his rivals'.

In ritual terms, the Tandon and the Jagat Narayan family do seem
to have belonged to different groups. Though both families had appeared in Allahabad at about the same time, the Tandons belonged to the
Eastern group which had migrated into the Ganges valley at a rather
earlier date, while the Chaddhas were Western or 'Punjabi' Khattris.[135]
In Allahabad, there were no marriage connections or commensality
between the two groups until well after 1900. In fact, the ritual distinctions as such were probably less important than the different historical antecedents of the two groups. Western Khattris were generally
connected with the Moghul courts and had to some extent acquired
'Nawabi' life styles. Certainly, Jagat Narayan and his sons were more
active landowners[136] and less active bankers than the Tandons.
However, there were also more ephemeral, factional elements among
Jagat Narayan's municipal supporters, and here the most important
factor seems to have been the connection's attraction for individuals
who had little to gain from the dominant Tandons and their allies.
Sheo Charan Lal, for instance, a Jain *vakil*, landowner and banker,
emerged as an associate of Jagat Narayan about 1901.[137] Always an

[133] Note on *Prayag Mittra*, memorandum on vernacular press of Upper India for
1885, Home Public B March 1886, 122–4, NAI.

[134]   *Caste of participants in Allahabad Municipal
                          disputes, 1896–1902.*

	Ram Charan Das	Jagat Narayan
Brahmin	2	2
Khattri	7	3
other ⎫ Vaish ⎭	1	—
Kayasth	2	2
Muslim	2	1
Bengali	1	1

Sources: References in *Natya Patra* and *Prayag
Samachar*, UPNNR 1896–1902; *Leader*, 29 May
and 29 July, 1911.

[135] Interview with Sri Hari Mohan Das Tandon, May 1972.
[136] Jagat Narayan was said to have introduced several new kinds of rice seed,
obtained at his own expense from Bareilly, into his estates. Collector's remarks appended to revenue administration report, 1888–89, basta 132, 252 Revenue of 1889, CA.
Jageshwari Narayan Chaddha (this was probably Jagat Narayan's eldest son) stood
in the landlord interest for the legislative council in 1920.
[137] *Natya Patra*, 15 March 1901, UPNNR 1901.

isolated figure, it is significant that he was only able to gain the office of municipal chairman in 1916 when the Hindus had temporarily boycotted the board to leave it in the hands of his Muslim allies.[138] Equally, there is evidence that the virtually unrepresented Sunni Muslims gravitated at times towards the 'out' Hindu connection;[139] and it is certainly true that after the death of Jagat Narayan, his sons used their bloc vote to support the local Muslim League against a party representing the rump of the old Ram Charan Das connection strengthened by the adherence of the Nehrus and Malaviyas.[140] It was in this way the fractured elements of the old *rais* connections were incorporated into the fabric of caste and party politics after 1910.

Another result of this connection's subordinate position in local politics was Jagat Narayan's close dependence on the collectorate. Since he was a nominated member and not directly responsible to the dominantly commercial electorate of the old mohullas, officials were able to use Jagat Narayan to initiate a reign of terror against those who violated the octroi regulations.[141] His period as member in charge of octroi saw a leap in income from that department along with a thorough overhaul of customs procedure and the prosecution and fining of a large number of powerful merchants including Ram Charan Das himself.[142] His unrepentant collaboration earned Jagat Narayan the enduring hatred of the mercantile community and of their 'progressive' allies, but he basked in the favour of the municipal chairman.

These events point to the extreme complexity of the forces underlying 'faction' in Indian urban politics at this time. The political aims of the local administration played an important part, as did the struggle for political spoils both within and without the municipal arena. On the other hand, ritual differences which in turn reflected different historical backgrounds were significant. What seems most clear is that the common denominator of local politics at this time was the patron and his connection. Even the caste associations of the mercantile communities with their predictable annual resolutions give an illusion of coherent

[138] *Abhyudaya*, 9 December 1916; *Leader*, 30 July 1916; and board debates 1916–17.
[139] E.g. *Natya Patra* for July 1898; UPNNR 1898. Muslims were frequently coupled with Jagat Narayan for abuse. On the board nominated Muslims and Europeans tended to vote with him.
[140] *Abhyudaya*, 14 March 1912; *Leader*, 29 May 1911.
[141] *Report on the Administration of the Allahabad Municipal Board, 1900–01* (Allahabad, 1901), p. 35.
[142] *Report on the Administration of the Allahabad Municipal Board, 1901–02* (Allahabad, 1902), p. 8. Jagat Narayan 'was bent on creating a record in octroi receipts if by any additional work and supervision that result could be obtained . . . '; Proceedings of the Working Committee, no. 3 of 1900–01, dated nil, petition dated 1 April 1900.

action that never existed in urban communities where the panchayat
had all but ceased to exist.[143] The 'Allahabad Khattri Association' which
maintained the Khattri Pathshala[144] was merely an alliance between
the relatives of Ram Charan Das and Bisheshwar Das, on the one hand,
and Jagat Narayan's sons on the other.[145] Equally, the 'Khattri
Sabha' which flourished in another quarter seems to have represented
a collusion between the connections of Ganesh Prasad Seth, cloth
merchant, and Bhowani Prasad Bhalla, banker. Professionals associated
with the major connections such as Kampta Prasad Kackar and Purshottam Das Tandon, High Court pleaders, became involved in the
management of these associations when the significance of the *rais*
connections diminished after the turn of the century; but at first they
filled a subordinate role in the politics of charity.

(c) 'NEW' GROUPS AND NEW ALIGNMENTS—THE CASE OF THE KALWARS OF MUTHIGANJ

Ritual considerations were not entirely irrelevant in local politics, for
the standing and pretensions of a community might form the background against which the connections and political attitudes of its
raises developed. Several groups of merchants from the lower rungs
of the mercantile castes had acquired wealth and status in Allahabad
by 1900, and while the Malaviya family and their associates continued
to draw support from Tandons, Bhallas and some Bengali merchants,
they became increasingly associated with the chief men of the Kalwar
community and especially a rich family of 'Jaiswal' Kalwar bankers
and traders which resided in the suburban area of Muthiganj, a little
to the south and east of the old city and within Ward V of the municipality. Ganga Prasad, a landowner and banker, figured little beyond
Kalwar social organizations,[146] but his sons Mewa Lal and Lakshmi
Narayan were typical urban *raises*; the former had an annual income
from house letting and trading of Rs 9,000 p.a. in 1911 and was also a
substantial zamindar,[147] while the latter held lands to the value of
Rs 20,000 land revenue in Allahabad, Benares and Ghazipur and a

[143] A feature of the upper mercantile communities was the absence of regular
panchayats. Caste discipline was enforced by what Blunt calls 'public opinion',
often working through caste sabhas or samajes. E. A. H. Blunt, *The Caste System of
Northern India* (reprinted Delhi, 1969), Chapter VI.
[144] *Leader*, 15 October 1917.
[145] *Abhyudaya*, 28 February 1914, fourth annual conference of the Allahabad
Khattri Sabha.
[146] He attended the Congress of 1892.   [147] *DG Allahabad*, p. 61.

retail trade and moneylending business in Kydganj.[148] Lakshmi Narayan was also an honorary magistrate and was regularly returned from Ward V of the municipality, which the family dominated. His claim to be a *rais* in his own right depended on the fact that he needed the 'nomination' of neither Ram Charan Das nor Jagat Narayan, to secure his seat—'in my ward no help is required . . .'.[149] Lakshmi Narayan was clearly influential enough to vary his support between the two rival factions, but 'generally, Sheamber Lal, Lakshmi Narayan of Daraganj, and I voted with Lala Ram Charan Das, sometimes we voted against him'. As far as elections themselves were concerned, though, the Jaiswals were always associated with the Tandon-Malaviya connection. Radha Kant Malaviya was returned from Ward V on a number of occasions, while Mewa Lal stood for Ward V with Madan Mohan Malaviya himself in 1898, which probably points to some electoral understanding between them. Mewa Lal was also active beyond the confines of municipal politics. He was a delegate to the second Allahabad Congress of 1892, a regular attender of the annual sessions after 1906, and an active protagonist at the public meetings organized by the Allahabad moderates during the 'swadeshi' period.[150] In fact, apart from Ram Charan Das himself, he was the only 'rais and banker' to be consistently associated with the public life of the city.

Whereas it was the high local status of the Khattris which facilitated their involvement with the high-caste publicists, in the case of the Kalwars it was a low ritual position which formed the background to their political motivation. In 1871, despite the wealth of some men, Kalwars were still stigmatized as 'liquor distillers' and regarded as hardly superior to Telis and similar castes.[151] The comparatively low origin of the community was shown by the absence of a well-developed gotra or clan system which distinguished the upper commercial castes.[152] But Kalwar opium and liquor contracts for government had given the community a number of extremely rich men, some of whom, like Babu Lal of Allahabad, had also become major bankers and landholders.[153]

[148] *Leader*, 26 August 1910, election petition case.

[149] *Ibid.*, 29 July, 1911, election petition case.

[150] E.g. the meeting against the imposition of Regulation 9 of 1818, *Indian People*, 2 June 1907; proposal of motion on Executive Council for UP (*Indian People*, 28 March 1909).

[151] Crooke, *op. cit.*, III, 113.

[152] *Ibid.*, III, 107: also J. Nesfield, *A Brief View of the Caste System of the North-Western Provinces and Oudh* (Allahabad, 1885), p. 54.

[153] *SR Allahabad, 1878*, p. 54.

Such men were wealthy enough to survive the progressive erosion of
their distilling monopoly by government imposition of an outstill and
official distillery system,[154] especially in Allahabad and Benares. It
was here that prominent Kalwars, who usually claimed to be of the
superior Jaiswal group, reached local importance at the beginning of
the twentieth century. More widely, Kalwars were forsaking their
traditional occupation, as a result of government action, and because
a number were taking to western education.[155] At the 1921 Allahabad
Kalwar Conference it was claimed (undoubtedly an exaggeration)
that out of 4,000 Kalwars in the city, only fifty were still actually
concerned with the liquor trade, while most had become bankers,
contractors, and even government servants.[156] Inevitably, richer men
within the community attempted to make their ritual status more
equivalent to their economic importance. In the 1890s the Kalwars
of the eastern part of the province were already claiming higher,
Kshatriya status, while their priests had begun to ascribe the richer
men to a clan, since they too derived respectability from the position
of their patrons.[157] Another method of raising status was to reduce the
force of the subcaste ranking system by joining the extreme wing
of the Arya Samaj, and indeed, many Aryas were drawn from this rank
of society.[158] Lakshmi Narayan was an Arya,[159] and was also associated
with the activities of the UP Temperance Council. This was founded
in 1909,[160] and was an alliance of Arya Samaj popular lecturers, like
Pt. Devi Dutt, and more orthodox revivalists, like the Malaviya family,
who were office bearers in the organization. Following the usual
pattern, Mewa Lal was also concerned with social work and reform in
his particular subsection, the Jaiswals, and he was later president of an

[154] Government progressively whittled away the old system of farming out contracts
to Kalwars and Pasis as it became less profitable. In 1870, for instance, the Government of India directed that each retail shop should pay a fee equal to its profitability,
and sparked off a Kalwar agitation. *Report on the Excise Administration of the NWP
for 1870-71* (Allahabad, 1871), p.8. By 1892 the outstill system, enforced in backward
areas, was the only form of excise administration directly to Kalwars' advantage.
The dwindling prosperity of their hereditary occupation may well have been a
stimulus to richer Kalwars moving into banking and commerce. Cf., Nesfield,
op. cit., pp. 54-5.
[155] Allahabad University entrants for 1905-07 from Allahabad Schools included
at least three (Jaiswal) Kalwars, *UP Gazetteers* 1905-07, pt. IV (May) Entrance Lists.
[156] Speech of Gauri Shanker Misra at the Allahabad Kalwar Conference, February
1921, *Kalwar Kshatriya Mitra* (Hindi, Allahabad), February 1921, p. nil.
[157] Crooke, *op. cit.*, III, 107.
[158] *Census of India 1901*, UP XVI, 248.
[159] UP Intelligence Report, 26 January 1909, Home Poll D June 1909, 100-7, NAI.
[160] *UP Excise Administration Report for year 1916-17* (Allahabad, 1917), p. 12.

'All-India Jaiswal Hitkarini Sabha' (Reform Association) held at Calcutta in March 1918.[161] Regarding the status of the community as a whole, he was in the forefront of the increasingly literate demand that Kalwars should be regarded as members of the Kshatriya Varna, and was prominent in the so-called 'Kshatriya Dal' which was strong enough in 1924 to demand an enquiry from the 'Second Kalwar Conference' into whether Kalwars considered themselves Vaishyas or Kshatriyas,[162] the extent to which their customs approximated to the practice of the two Varnas, and what professions they could follow and what not.[163]

As an Arya, Lakshmi Narayan had been approached by 'political suspects' in Allahabad as early as 1910, but it was after 1916 that the populist politicians became seriously interested in the Kalwar community. Malaviya's relationship with Mewa Lal was an entrée into the affairs of the urban Kalwars. Their associations with village Kalwars became relevant to an increasingly political temperance movement, and to the incipient local peasant association.

The community in Allahabad seems to have had a particularly flourishing social life centred around the activities of Jaiswal connections. In the 1890s the only organization had been a loose association of panchayats (seven in number) based upon the major subdivisions of the community.[164] But in 1902 the banker Hanuman Prasad Jaiswal formed the first Allahabad Kalwar Association whose purpose was to collect funds for the Kalwar Kshatriya Pathshala, an elementary school which was opened in 1905, and which taught English up to the sixth standard. The Sabha's energetic beginnings were reflected in two journals, the *Sansar Mitra* and the *Globe*, which were devoted to topics of reform and caste hagiography.[165] They joined to become the *Kalwar Kshatriya Mitra* about 1909. Hanuman Prasad was also a moving force in the first session of the Kalwar Kshatriya Mahasabha held in Allahabad in 1910 to coincide with the beginning of the surveys for the Census of 1911, a powerful stimulus to organization in many communi-

---

[161] *Kalwar Kshatriya Mitra*, March 1918.

[162] Blunt, *op. cit.*, p. 227, makes no mention of the Kshatriya claim, merely of that to the status of 'Batham Vaisya'.

[163] *Kalwar Kshatriya Mitra*, February 1924.

[164] Crooke, *op. cit.*, III, 108. 'Each subcaste holds a meeting of the adult males to decide caste matters, and the penalty is a feast (*bhoj*) to the brethren'; Nesfield, *op. cit.*, p. 54; *Kalwar Kshatriya Mitra*, February 1919, pp. 22–3, enumerated the following sub-divisions: Jaiswal, Sivhari, Rai Chauska, Malvi, Kharida and Jain.

[165] *Kalwar Kshatriya Mitra*, February 1921, pp. 24 ff., speech of Babu Masuriuddin at the 'Nineteenth' annual Kalwar Conference. The foundation of the sabha was probably connected with the Census operations, 1901.

ties.[166] These organizations flourished until 1913 when they ceased abruptly owing to the deaths of Lala Hanuman Prasad himself, the president of the conference, Mata Badal, and the editor of the *Mitra*. As a result, the *Mitra* became irregular, the money for the pathshala dried up and the Mahasabha ceased to exist—a good example of the extent to which so-called 'caste' bodies were largely dependent on the activities of a few *raises*. The local charity institutions continued to function under the patronage of Babu Radha Shyam, the Allahabad landowner,[167] and Lalas Banke Lal and Madhav Badal, bankers and commission agents. But these individuals represented the older generation of Kalwars, the major subcastes, and the older residential areas of the town and trading areas, like Kydganj and Bahadurganj. A new and more active body was founded in 1915: this was the Kalwar Kumar Sabha, and it was led by Ganguli Ram and Sarju Ram Bhat, but was centred in the newer residential areas of Katra and Muthiganj around the University. Finally, a third group was founded as an adjunct to this in 1917, and was called the Kalwar Youth Association. It was organized by Babu Lal, Ganguli Ram's nephew and Mewa Lal was its secretary. But the important fact about this last society, apart from the youth of its members, was that it undertook active work in the villages, and both the associations were found working in villages as far away as Cawnpore, Delhi and Fatehpur.[168]

Since rural Kalwars were both village moneylenders and distributors of liquor,[169] they were often at the root of both peasant indebtedness and peasant prodigality, so the leaders of the Allahabad Peasants' Association quickly made contact with them. On 25 January 1919 Krishna Kant Malaviya presided over a meeting of 8,000 members of the Kalwar Youth Sabha. National and caste issues were skilfully interwoven; Pandit Dev Narayan Pande (a Sanatan Dharmist) spoke on 'Duty', Pt. Devi Dutt (an Arya) on 'Dharma' and 'Temperance' and Krishna Kant Malaviya (editor of the *Abhyudaya* and *Kisan* newspapers at this time) encouraged the foundation of Kalwar reform associations in cities and big villages, and emphasized the necessity of sacrifice (viz. of wealth accumulated by distilling). From this point onwards, the *Kalwar Kshatriya Mitra* contained several articles on peasants and the various activities of Krishna Kant Malaviya.[170]

[166] In the 1901 Census the Commissioner had placed Kalwars in Group VI, 'Sudras claiming a higher status or Vaishyas depressed'. *Census of India 1901*, Vol. XVI, 221.
    [167] *Kalwar Kshatriya Mitra*, February 1921.   [168] *Ibid.*, February 1919.
    [169] *UP Banking Committee*, II, 51; and report on village 'Pandilla', Soraon, Allahabad District, *ibid*, 317–25.
    [170] *Kalwar Kshatriya Mitra*, December 1918, and following issues.

Kalwars like Mahabir Prasad and Salig Ram played an active part in all stages of the non-cooperation movement in Allahabad.[171] But as far as their general involvement was concerned, the climax came in February 1921 at the 19th annual Kalwar Conference of Allahabad. Gauri Shankar Misra,[172] Purshottam Das Tandon and Shyam Lal Nehru put in a pointed appearance. The usual temperance motion this year was larded with references to the 'orders of Mahatmaji', and the second resolution urged the community to boycott the annual auctions of liquor shops which the local authorities were about to hold.[173] Gauri Shankar Misra, President of the Peasants' Association said that their workers 'had seen in all districts how harmful liquor was to the villagers' and, shrewdly assessing the ritual pretensions of his audience, he added that some days previously in Allahabad, dhobies, cobblers and swineherds had given up the use of alcohol in panchayat; how then could the Kalwars not follow suit? In fact, social boycott was only a contributing factor to the failure of the liquor auctions. Government added the further explanation:

the combined introduction of the contract system, with prohibition of the watering of spirit in shops and the raising of the duty from Rs 6.4 to Rs 9 per proof gallon caused vendors to apprehend that the profits of the trade would vanish, and in several districts, they refused to bid for shops.

Some 'agitators' also told the Kalwars that if they boycotted the auction for a while, government would be obliged to bring the duty down.[174] In the case of the Kalwars, then, both ritual status and economic considerations, as well as longer standing connections between *raises* and the populist politicians had again contrived to give the appearance of a community involvement in Gandhian politics. The boycott of the liquor auctions was made possible, as government sources show, by the dissidence of distillers reacting against administrative change. The social boycott was effected, and the appearance of community decision was facilitated, by the longer term social and ritual aims of Kalwar magnates who had long before diversified into banking and retail trading.

[171] Mahabir Prasad styled himself 'non-cooperator' under 'profession' in a Kalwar Conference Report of 1924; Salig Ram Jaiswal and other Kalwars became active in early Allahabad socialist parties.
[172] Gauri Shankar Misra, Advocate, Allahabad; ex-editor of *Abhyudaya*, vice-president of Malaviya's Allahabad Kisan Sabha (Peasants' Association); later, secretary of the Congress.
[173] *Independent*, 16 February 1921.
[174] *Report on the Excise Administration of UP for 1921–2* (Allahabad, 1922), pp. 14–15.

F

5. Conclusion

The problem upon which this essay has focused is the relationship between monied groups in north Indian towns and a new range of political forms which emerged in the second half of the nineteenth century. The monied interests in question were the wealthy commercial families which provided many of the north Indian city notables; the new political forms were the ascriptive organizations and pressure groups which formed within the arenas of municipal and provincial politics, among which the Congress was pre-eminent. Local notables were never, of course, a dominant element in the provincial, still less in the all-India, nationalist organizations. But their association with them was important for a number of reasons. At the broadest level, it pointed to a continuity between the various levels of political activity. Local notables used Congress publicists to propagate their interests in local society, just as the publicists employed the backing of the notables to forward their careers in provincial and later in electoral politics. Again, some nationalist leaders, beginning their careers as clients or relatives of local magnates, remained indebted to them for the finance of quasi-political, educational and religious movements. This provides one important explanation of the fundamental conservatism of the Hindustani political leadership until Independence. Despite his misgivings about 'capitalists', the career of Madan Mohan Malaviya, for instance, began, from the logistical point of view, with the Allahabad Tandons and ended with the Birlas. The character of its local supporters also prescribed to a large extent both the limits within which the early nationalist movement could gain more popular support, and also the normative themes which its lecturers could use. This was politically most significant, because the rhetoric of the early Congress in Hindustan contributed to the alienation of local and provincial Muslim leadership even where compromises could have been effected in regard to the material spoils of politics. For the ears of some of the most potentially formidable figures in local politics, particularly of the *mahajan* families, were attuned to the Hindu idiom, and the organizations which they could vitalize in support of Congress were generally institutional expressions of conspicuous piety.

To demonstrate connections between various levels of politics is not, however, to describe the motives which drove some wealthy and conservative men into forms of activity which were in many ways quite alien to them. It is tempting to argue in the case of the 'political' *mahajan* what is argued more convincingly in the case of the Muslim or Kayasth government servant: that institutional change and new sources of patronage provided the incentive for these political initiatives. But there are two difficulties here. Firstly, the material interests of the commercial élites were not obviously under any great or continuing pressure from government, its taxation or even its municipalities, until after the new organizations and relationships had been forged. Secondly, if we stress the simple availability of new material resources in politics as an incentive to political development, and produce at random a number of examples where notables did move in to engross it, we are in danger of establishing a too mechanical model of social action. There is an assumption that a universal 'political man' exists who will always move in to fill a political vacuum created by administrative (or economic) change, who will always respond promiscuously to the possible access of new wealth, and who will always seize every opportunity to increase crude political control over other individuals. Government itself often pointed to the difficulty of persuading local notables, fortified with elevated ideas of their own status, to participate in public bodies and public activities, even where the pickings were by no means negligible. But the history, life-style and conceptions of status of the mid-nineteenth-century *mahajan* families give even less support to any mechanical account of political motivation. On the contrary, many of these families seem deliberately to have adopted a posture of minimum social and political investment in a locality, in the same way that they severely limited their economic initiatives by a constricting emphasis on the need for continuity and security in *mahajani* practice. In fact, the difficulties arising from the postulation of general acquisitive drives to account for social action are not new in this field. For some commentators, the upper Indian *mahajan* has long stood out as an exception to the rule that supposes the existence of a universal 'economic man' who will inevitably respond positively to any new economic incentives. The habits of 'hoarding', ideas of credit, and the patterns of investment of *mahajans*, suggest minds working on very different principles of business activity and within wholly different perceptions of the social uses of wealth from those current in more modern societies, or in more modern segments of Indian society. This essay has suggested that it was primarily in the field of religious patronage (and also ritual advancement) that the commercial notables expended the social energy derived from their wealth and abandoned the 'low profile' they otherwise maintained until well into the second half of the nineteenth century. It was initially through the active propagation of these religious and status concerns that they came to contribute to the developing public politics of upper India.

However, the background within which the urban notables set their conception of religious and community status was not static. Though often random, localized, and open to manipulation by political adventurers, the Hindu revivalism to which they contributed produced a wide range of organization which was at once new, sophisticated and capable of generalization beyond a locality. As the cow-protection movement demonstrated, its direction could also be autonomous of specific government policies. Expressed in the idiom of Hinduism, because Hinduism was the vehicle of social status, this organization derived partly from the impact of wide forces of westernization on old patterns of religious charity. It was also connected with changes in the lay of wealth within Hindustani cities, whose origins in the erosion of the power of the Muslim service gentry predated British rule. Later, during the 1880s and after, the policies of government on matters such as employment and education led to the incorporation of some of these patterns of organization into a more permanent political system, increasingly structured around the distribution of government patronage. From this point of view, early nationalism in upper India can be seen as a tenuous fusion of vested interests in government service, moving in opposition to bureaucratic change, with independently generated organizations expressing a wider cultural change. But if these wider changes are to be defined, it will still be in terms of the specific social attitudes of important local groups, rather than the generalities of cultural history.

Municipal Government and Muslim Separatism in the United Provinces, 1883 to 1916

FRANCIS ROBINSON

BRITISH rule cut down Muslim power in the United Provinces. Between 1868 and 1916, municipalities and councils acts tempered the rule of officials, many of whom were Muslims, with the rule of the people, few of whom were Muslims. Up to 1916, Muslims felt this loss of power most severely in the towns. But, because the municipalities were electorates for the provincial councils, this decline of Muslim power in the towns was reflected in the province as a whole. UP Muslims directed their politics towards compensating for this loss. They aimed for a protected share of power. This essay analyses the local origins of this Muslim demand.

In the late nineteenth century, government began to bring increasing numbers of non-official Indians into the administration of the towns. It had to do so in order to finance improvements or even to remain solvent. Between 1868 and 1883, elected municipal boards were given powers to tax, to spend, and to make bye-laws. Since government had a real impact upon the towns, non-official Indians were winning a real influence over local life.

1. The worth of a municipal seat, 1883–1908

The power of non-officials on municipal boards has been questioned, and it is true that their powers were limited.[1] Government took care to curb the freedom of municipal boards. 'The principle of self-government', it declared, 'is to be kept steadily in view, so far as may be compatible with public safety and happiness.'[2] So non-official influence over policy

---

[1] Indian politicians, thirsting for more power, were keen to give the impression that there was little worth having in the towns. See, for instance, the evidence of Madan Mohan Malaviya and Sunder Lal before the Decentralization Commission, *Royal Commission upon Decentralization in India, Parliamentary Papers* 1908, XLV, pp. 749 and 754.

[2] *Report on the Administration of the NW Provinces for the year 1869–70* [*NWP Administration Report*] (Allahabad, 1871), p. 70.

was kept in check. The elected majority of non-officials could only block official suggestions:[3] if they wished to put into operation their own proposals, they had to win official approval. The chairman was the main restricting factor. In six important municipalities he was appointed by the local government.[4] Other boards had the right to elect a non-official, but in practice they tended to choose an ex-officio member, usually the district magistrate, either because they knew that government preferred it or because they felt that an official chairman was a guarantee of impartiality or because it was difficult, particularly in small towns, to find suitable non-officials to take on a time-consuming task. Thus official chairmen became the rule, and, pressed for time, they tried to use boards as rubber stamps. Nevertheless, non-officials did have some indirect influence. In theory, the municipal board, meeting in ordinary or special session, made policy. As municipal work grew and meetings became impossibly numerous, however, some of the business came to be left to subcommittees or individuals, which was technically unconstitutional but tolerated out of expediency.[5]

Admittedly the municipal commissioner's influence over policy was slight, but it was compensated for by the control he could exercise over the administration. This depended largely on the patronage he commanded in the municipal establishment. 'The social status conferred by a seat on the board' was, according to the district magistrate of Ghazipur, 'as nothing to the power of patronage',[6] and the best job in the influential commissioner's gift was the secretaryship. The secretary himself had many jobs under his control, and he was the board's agent in everyday administration. His importance is well illustrated by events in Fyzabad. As soon as the Kayasth, Balak Ram, leader of one faction, captured the chairmanship of the board from another faction, he replaced the secretary, Jehangir Shaw, with his

[3] The UP municipal boards had the highest percentage of elected members in India. Hugh Tinker, *The Foundations of Local Self-Government in India, Pakistan and Burma* (London, 1968), p. 48, Table 3. In 1904–05, out of 1,249 municipal commissioners, 155 were nominated by Government and 155 were members ex-officio, usually the local district magistrate or joint magistrate, a deputy collector and a tahsildar. The rest were elected.

[4] The municipalities of Lucknow, Benares, Allahabad, Agra, Bareilly and Moradabad.

[5] Note on the 'Agency for the exercise of the executive powers of a municipal board', n.d., Municipal 1910, 1 E, Uttar Pradesh Secretariat Records, Lucknow [UPS].

[6] H. R. Nevil, District Magistrate, Ghazipur, to Commissioner, Benares Division, 20 June 1911 and see also J. C. Fergusson, District Magistrate, Saharanpur, to Commissioner, Meerut Division, 29/30 August 1911, Home Educ Municipal A April 1914, 22–31, National Archives of India, New Delhi [NAI].

own nominee, a Kayasth, Dwarka Prasad, and used the municipal servants as his private force.[7] At election time, his opponents were harassed by delays in the preparation of ward rolls[8] and had to contend with 'the whole host of the municipal army', deployed against them by Balak Ram.[9] In Agra the secretary was said to ensure that 'old contractors enjoy as it were a hereditary right';[10] in Moradabad, administration was brought to a halt by clashes between old municipal employees and the placemen of a new secretary.[11] It was worth getting control of the municipal establishment with its opportunities for manipulation which the municipalities' acts of 1900 and 1916 tried, without complete success, to eliminate.[12]

Towards the end of the nineteenth century, the scope of urban administration grew by leaps and bounds. The few municipal amenities which had once been donated by rich patricians[13] were now, with many new ones, provided by the municipality. Since municipal employees could be influenced, commissioners were able to affect many aspects of this expanding urban government. One of these was taxation. The amount of taxation levied in the towns was not small:

[7] Soon after Balak Ram gained the upper hand in Fyzabad, the municipal servants spent over a week decorating the city in honour of the maktab ceremony of his grandson for which they were rewarded with a holiday on the great day. *Leader* (Allahabad), 5 April 1911.

[8] *Ibid.*, 20 June 1913.

[9] *Ibid.*, 1 April 1915. 'The subordinates', a *Leader* mofussil correspondent wrote of the Fyzabad municipal employees who had gone canvassing with Balak Ram, 'generally think their loyalty consists only in their proving useful in elections and upon this their future prospects entirely depend.' *Ibid.*, 6 April 1912.

[10] *Nasim-i-Agra*, 7 December 1887, North-western Provinces and Oudh Native Newspaper Reports 1887. [Hereafter references to this source, which after 1902 were continued as United Provinces Native Newspaper Reports, will be abbreviated UPNNR.]

[11] *Jam-i-Jamshed* (Moradabad), 3 January 1892 and 27 March 1892, UPNNR 1892.

[12] *Report of Municipal Administration and Finances in the North-Western Provinces and Oudh 1900–01* [hereafter for reports up to 1900/01 NWPMAR and for reports from 1901/02 UPMAR] (Allahabad, 1902), p. 1; the report for 1914–15 declared that one of the aims of the imminent municipalities bill was to ensure that the municipal staff were 'secure in the tenure of their posts under varying party majorities'. *UPMAR*, 1914–15, p. 8.

[13] For instance, many of the glories of Muttra were supplied by its great family of Seths: the temple of Dwarakadhis, the Jamuna Bagh Chattris and the good repair of the property in the civil lines. F. S. Growse, *Mathura: A District Memoir* (North-Western Provinces' Government Press, 1874), Part I, pp. 91, 99, 103. The role of the large landowner in creating a market centre and adorning it is well illustrated in Fox's description of the activities of Rai Udai Baks Singh, Raja of Bilampur, in building up the Sahibganj area of 'Tezi Bazar'. Richard G. Fox, *From Zamindar to Ballot Box* (Ithaca, N.Y., 1969), pp. 75–77.

already by 1895 it was as much as one-eighth of the provincial budget.[14] Until 1912, this revenue was mainly raised by indirect taxation, in particular, by the octroi,[15] and as a committee of enquiry realized in 1909, the schedule of taxes could easily be arranged so as to benefit particular interests.[16] The octroi could, for instance, be used by one group of traders to attack another, or it could be used by other interests to bring pressure on traders during elections.[17] In large municipalities, the management of octroi encouraged a 'tendency to the development of hostility between the municipal bureau and the traders generally'.[18]

Influence on the municipal board could mean patronage in contracts. The large number of ambitious public works undertaken by the municipal board meant that it was usually the largest source of business in the town. In principle, members were not allowed to contract for works within their municipality, but this did not mean that their friends could not benefit: 'it is no uncommon thing', revealed one district officer, 'for members of the Finance and Works' Committees to apply for contracts under fictitious names, sanction these applications, obtain the contracts, sub-let them at a higher rate, and sit as a board of inspection on the skimped work of the sub-contractors, and pass them as satisfactory!'[19] Worse could happen. In 1911, a local correspondent reported that, in Fyzabad, where municipal affairs verged habitually on the picaresque:

Party spirit is active, of late certain municipal contracts of Porass, markets, sites etc. . . . were given by public auction by responsible members of the board to particular persons, their bid being the highest. In other instances the contracts were re-sold without any rhyme or reason in a very unbusiness-like manner.[20]

In 1907, at least sixty contractors thought it worth their while to get onto the municipal boards of the province.

[14] In 1895–96, the provincial income was Rs 324,87,000 and the total municipal income Rs 52,92,780. *NWP Administration Report, 1895–96*, pp. 67 and 148.

[15] The octroi was the traditional trading impost of Hindustan. In 1884–85, it was levied in seventy-seven towns and raised 16⅓ lakh rupees out of a total municipal taxation of 19½ lakh rupees. In 1914–15, octroi, although levied in only thirty-seven towns still provided 27½ lakhs out of a total 88⅔ lakh rupees. *NWPMAR, 1884–85*, Form 1; and *UPMAR, 1914–15*, Abstract of Statement No. II.

[16] *Enquiry into the subject of municipal taxation with special reference to the limitation of the octroi tax* (Allahabad, 1909), p. 16, Municipal 1908, 700 D, UPS.

[17] 'Octroi officials brought undue pressure to bear on the traders.' the *Hindustani* complained when Babu Sri Ram beat Bishen Narain Dar in the Lucknow municipal elections of 1892. *Hindustani* (Lucknow), 9 March 1892, UPNNR 1892.

[18] *Municipal taxation enquiry*, p. 16.

[19] Major-General Fendall Currie, *Below the Surface* (London, 1900), p. 100.

[20] *Leader*, 5 April 1911.

Naturally, municipal government affected most aspects of local life. Religion was particularly affected. The new-found influence of municipal commissioners over an increasing number of regulations, particularly concerning sanitation, bore increasingly on religious susceptibilities in the towns. Before the institution of the municipal board, control over such regulations had been in the hands of the kotwal,[21] an autocrat whose word was law. Now they were in the hands of the chairman of the municipal board whose task, in principle, was to give effect to the wishes of the majority party. Under the guise of the hygienic management of slaughter houses and kebab shops, therefore, Hindus could defend the cow and impose their standards on Muslims, while, for Muslims, the maintenance of their right to slaughter cows and eat them could become a symbol of their ability to protect their religion and culture.

Apart from power within the towns, a municipal commissionership could also be a route to added prestige, the honours list of the raj, and what were potentially even greater powers beyond the municipality. It could help to make the unknown vakil known, get a man an honorary magistracy or higher honours such as a Rai or Khan Bahadurship, while from 1892 it was the first step to a seat on the provincial council.[22] Naturally, the power, the status and the training it offered in executive government were highly valued.[23] The position was powerful because it combined deliberative and executive functions. This combination, together with the right to make and administer regulations, created wide openings for patronage, peculation and prejudice, which meant that a seat on a municipal board brought both status and power. For the commercial and professional men brought forward by British rule, as well as for some of the more adaptable established notables of urban society, in the late nineteenth century a municipal

[21] Very often the kotwal was a Muslim. Under the Mughals he was firmly abjured to avoid all points of religious tension. Abul Fazl Allami, *Ain i Akbari* trans. Colonel H. S. Jarrett, Vol. II (Calcutta, 1891), Ain IV 'The Kotwal', pp. 41-3.

[22] Under the 1892 Councils Act, the possession of a municipal commissionership was one of the qualifications for prospective candidates. The more important municipalities of the UP were divided into two constituencies which each recommended a representative from their commissioners to the provincial council.

[23] When government set about circumscribing the executive functions of the municipal commissioner in preparing for the 1915/16 municipalities legislation, local politicians protested vigorously. Under the bill, commissioners deliberated and municipal servants, with great security of tenure and under the control of a civil servant, administered. A committee on which they were represented warned that 'boards would strongly resent total exclusion from executive functions and control. . . .' Typed draft of the Lucknow committee recommendations, 8 April 1914, Municipal 1915, 230 E, UPS.

commissionership was an important means by which they could con-
solidate their local influence.

2. Patterns in competition for local power, 1883–1908

Over eleven per cent of the province's population lived in the towns.
Muslims, only fifteen per cent of the provincial population, were
thirty-eight per cent of the urban population. They were unevenly
distributed with more of them in towns in the west than in the east
of the province. In Rohilkhand, they constituted more than half the
urban population. A few, such as the Iraqis of Ballia[24] and the Pathans
of Shahjahanpur,[25] lived in the towns to trade and lend money, a
few because they were contractors, but most lived in the towns because
many towns were Muslim foundations, because their traditional occupations, whether in skilled industries or service, brought them there
and because they preferred town life. Some Muslims were absentee
landlords, owning estates which usually were situated close to the towns
in which they lived.

Among the Hindu urban population, three important groups were
traditionally occupied in service: Kashmiri Brahmins, the itinerant
administrators of two empires and the rulers of a third; Kayasths, the
traditional clerisy of northern India; and Brahmins, the family priests
and teachers. The Kashmiri Brahmins were restricted to a few large
towns such as Agra, Allahabad and Lucknow. The Kayasths were more
numerous and widespread, although more lived in east and central UP
than in the west. Brahmins were found everywhere. Large numbers of
the Hindu trading and money-lending castes, Banias, Khattris,
Kalwars, Bohras and Jains, lived in the towns because this was where
they worked. Some of them owned land, usually near the towns, and,
following much the same pattern as the Muslims, they tended to be
absentee landlords.

Municipal commissioners were recruited from these religious and
caste groups. One obvious category was the wealthy, the 'inevitable
municipal board men', big commercial raises, mainly Hindus, such
as Ram Charan Das of Allahabad, Damodar Das of Bareilly or Lala

[24] *District Gazetteer [DG] Ballia*, XXX, 81–2. The Iraqis were thought to be converts
from the Hindu Kalwars (distillers), their name being derived from *araq* or arrack.
They were generally shopkeepers or money-lenders and several owned land.

[25] For the money-lending activities of this Pathan community see E. I. Brodkin,
'Rohilkhand: A study in the Great Indian Rebellion, 1857–58', unpublished paper
delivered in Cambridge, November 1967.

Sukhbir Sinha of Muzaffarnagar and those from great landed or service families, often Muslims, such as Nawab Asadullah Khan of Meerut, Mufti Haidar Husain of Jaunpur and Raja Salamat Khan of Azamgarh. 'Inevitable municipal board men' often held the same seat for ten to twenty years and frequently sat on district boards. Their relationship with government was one of mutual interest. Many seats were taken by representatives of lesser businessmen, eager to have a say about the octroi and market rates or to win contracts. They were not always businessmen themselves. Some traders had neither the status nor the skills to operate effectively on municipal boards and so were compelled to employ a vakil to voice their interests. Lawyers, however, were not merely other men's voices; for them a seat on a board was a step closer to the legislative councils, a way of protecting their private interests and improving their standing. But no commissioner was just a trader or a lawyer. He had other interests, the most important being those of his caste or community, and as competition for local power became more intense, these interests could clash.

In the competition for places on the municipal board, wealth had the advantage. The 1883 Municipalities Act gave the vote to men of substance with incomes ranging from Rs 120 to Rs 500 or houses rated from Rs 12 to Rs 60.[26] The qualifications for candidates were three times as high. In 1889, Auckland Colvin, as lieutenant-governor, complained that the result of these regulations was that:

The class which was formerly regarded, if not as being altogether without value, at least as beneath contempt, has assumed a position corresponding to the policy of the present masters of the country, who give to education and commerce increasing consideration, and to mere social position or military skill less attention.[27]

[26]   *Guidelines laid down for individual towns under the Municipalities Act of 1883 for drawing up electoral qualifications.*

Municipalities	Municipalities with income p.a. over	Those could vote who had . . .		
		Income p.a. of	House rating p.a. of	Municipal tax p.a. of
Class I	Rs 1,00,000	500	60	5
Class II	Rs 50,000	300	36	3
Class III	Rs 12,000	200	24	2
Class IV	under Rs 12,000	120	12	1 8 annas

Source: *NWPMAR, 1884–85*, p. xvii.

[27] Note by Auckland Colvin, 11 June 1889, Home Public A August 1892, 237–52, NAI.

To bear a noble name, to have great prestige was no longer enough if the rupees were not there. There could be no better proof, Colvin continued, of the 'formidable weapon which the elective system in Municipalities has put into the hands of new men, than the hatred and fear with which the system is almost universally regarded by Muhammadans, and by the majority of Hindus of the conservative class. . . . At present it serves only as another illustration of the levelling, and what seems to them revolutionary element, introduced into their society by British rule. . . .'[28]

Colvin's assessment, though basically sound, was rather too simple. First, there were 'new men', and men to various degrees established, to be found in most sections of society. There were 'new men' among the landlords; Muslims and Hindus who had, through success at the law or government service in the early nineteenth century, been able to buy themselves landed estates.[29] On the other hand, there were some commercial men who had been landowners and men of influence in their localities for centuries,[30] and others whose local dominance had been marked before the Mutiny, had been reinforced by their loyalty at that time, and had been only strengthened further by the development of municipal self-government.[31] Nevertheless, by and large, those connected with the land were the Muslims and the Hindus of the 'conservative classes' and the 'new men' were mainly Hindu moneylenders and traders to whom the franchise gave a marked advantage. Second, the levelling effect which Colvin lamented was not the same

[28] *Ibid.*

[29] An examination of the Benares region in 1885 has revealed that of the 134 revenue payers classified as paying over one thousand rupees per year in land revenue, thirty-nine (paying thirty-one per cent of the revenue) were 'new men' most of whom owed their wealth and position to the conditions established by British rule. B. S. Cohn, 'Structural Change in Indian Rural Society 1596–1885; in R. E. Frykenberg (ed.), *Land Control and Social Structure in Indian History* (Madison, 1969), pp. 78-9.

[30] Members of the great Qanungo family of Meerut had 'from time immemorial . . . been bankers and zamindars.' The family was founded by one Jograj in the reign of Aurangzeb. At the turn of the twentieth century, three Qanungoyan, Lala Murari Lal, Lala Banarsi Das and Lala Jainti Parshad sat on the Meerut Municipal Board. *DG Meerut*, IV, 93.

[31] The fortunes of Lala Nihal Chand's family are a good example. The joint estates of his father and uncle were increased by lending British officers money during the Mutiny. By the beginning of the twentieth century they contained 41 villages. Under Nihal Chand and his son, Lala Sukhbir Sinha, the family dominated the Muzaffarnagar municipal board, where it provided vice-chairmen (up to 1910 the highest position that a non-official could usually expect to reach), and the district, where it ran the Muzaffarnagar Zamindars' Association. *DG Muzaffarnagar*, III, 113.

in all parts of the UP. The traditional influence of the commercial and landed groups varied from area to area of the province and so did the impact of economic change. To discover, therefore, where pressure on the influence of Muslims and Hindus of the 'conservative classes' was most severe it is necessary to examine more closely who commanded wealth in the different municipalities of the province. Two indicators will be used. First the distribution of trade; this will show where traders were doing well. Second, the direction in which land was being transferred; this will provide an idea of the relative strength of landed and commercial wealth. After applying these criteria, two areas of the UP with certain distinctive characteristics emerge. The first, east UP and Oudh, contains the divisions of Benares, Gorakhpur, Lucknow and Fyzabad, the second, west UP and Doab, contains the divisions of Meerut, Agra, Rohilkhand and Allaha-bad.[32]

In east UP and Oudh, the coming of the railway[33] destroyed the wealth of the riverine trade marts. The massive commerce of Benares, once the entrepôt of upper India, became largely local[34] and the merchants of the city switched their capital from trade to banking.[35] Money-lending firms deserted Mirzapur,[36] commercial capital of Bundelkhand, and Fyzabad, Ghazipur and Jaunpur were all in dec-line.[37] The railways, however, did develop two new trade centres, Gorakhpur, serving the area north of the Goghra river,[38] and Luck-now, at the hub of a road and rail network serving Oudh.[39] Elsewhere in east UP and Oudh, trade was not a major source of wealth.

[32] The division is made along administrative boundaries; see map. At first, this might appear an unsophisticated method of delineating economic regions in the vast Gangetic plain where one area shades imperceptibly into the next. But land policy had an important role in determining concentrations of wealth. The dividing line is drawn between the areas under Agra rent law and those under Oudh rent law and permanent settlement. All of Benares division is included in the division of east UP and Oudh although some of it was under Agra rent law. The reason for this is that those parts of Benares division not permanently settled nevertheless had more in common with east UP and Oudh than with west UP and Doab. This is also true of Gorakhpur.

[33] The broad-gauge reached Cawnpore in 1859, Saharanpur in 1869. During the 1870s and 1880s the broad and medium gauge traversed every district and, by 1900, even the most remote areas of the province were connected with Calcutta, Delhi, the Punjab, Bombay and western India.

[34] DG Benares, XXVI, 58.

[35] Ibid., pp. 53–5, 120–2.

[36] DG Mirzapur, XXVII, 100.

[37] DG Ghazipur, XXIX, 65–9; DG Jaunpur, XXVIII, 67; DG Fyzabad, XLIII, 44.

[38] DG Gorakhpur, XXXI, 75–8.

[39] DG Lucknow, XXXVII, 51–2.

The Table[40] shows that this area had more than half the province's population but a quarter of the trade. Only twenty-four towns were big enough to earn municipal status and only nine per cent of the population lived in them. In some, population was declining,[41] in others, there was not enough trade to justify the levying of octroi.[42]

In west UP and Doab, the picture was very different. The railway brought wealth to towns from Cawnpore to Saharanpur, from Chandpur to Shahjahanpur. Between 1873 and 1907, the rail-borne traffic in wheat, sugar and cotton of Chandausi, one of the great Rohilkhand wheat marts, grew eight times.[43] Between 1881 and 1901, Agra's rail-borne traffic rose by over forty-four per cent[44] and, between 1847 and 1907, Cawnpore's imports grew twenty times.[45] The Table,

[40]   *The distribution of Railway-borne trade by division in 1000s of maunds for the quinquennium, 1911–16, and the percentage increase since the quinquennium, 1884–89.*

	Meerut	Agra	Rohilk-hand	Allaha-bad	Benares	Oudh	Gorak-hpur	UP
Total trade 1911–16	31,221	21,152	19,732	40,348	15,767	27,445	7,601	163,270
Percentage divisional share of total provincial trade	19.12	12.95	12.09	24.71	9.66	16.81	4.66	100
Percentage increase in provincial trade since 1884–89	192.12	110.36	270.83	184.29	111.52	299.24	—	199.11
Percentage of provincial population living in divisions	12.31	10.61	11.98	11.64	10.64	26.62	13.83	100

Calculated from: *Report on the Railway-borne Traffic of North-Western Provinces and Oudh for the year ending March 31st, 1885* (Allahabad, 1886) Appendix III. *Trade Report of the North-Western Provinces and Oudh for the year ending March 31st, 1886* (Allahabad, 1887), Appendix III. *Railway Trade Report of the North-Western Provinces and Oudh for the year ending March 31st, 1887* (Allahabad, 1888), Appendix III. *Railway Trade Report of the North-Western Provinces and Oudh for the year ending March 31st, 1888* (Allahabad, 1889), Appendix III. *Annual Report on the Rail-borne Traffic of the North-Western Provinces and Oudh for the year ending March 31st, 1889* (Allahabad, 1890), Appendix III. *Annual Report on the Inland Trade of the United Provinces of Agra and Oudh for the year ending March 31st, 1912* (Allahabad, 1913), Appendix III and the same series continued to 1916.

[41] For instance, Khairabad, *DG Sitapur*, XL, 240; or Hardoi, *DG Hardoi*, XLI, 267.

[42] *DG Sitapur*, p. 121; *DG Unao*, XXXVIII, 108.

[43] *DG Moradabad*, XVI, 55–6.   [44] *DG Agra*, VIII, 52.

[45] Cawnpore's imports grew from 648,580 maunds in 1847 to 13,733,725 maunds in 1907. *DG Cawnpore*, XIX, 75.

The United Provinces: districts and divisions, 1911

The United Provinces: municipalities, 1911

footnote 40, shows that west UP and Doab had less than half the province's population but nearly threequarters of its trade. Fifty-eight towns were municipalities and nearly fourteen per cent of the area's population lived in them. Cawnpore became the great entrepôt of northern India and the largest manufacturing centre in India outside the Presidency capitals. Hathras was the commercial centre of west UP, Agra and Khurja became important manufacturing centres and most of the large towns developed native and joint-stock banking concerns.

There was, however, a connection between changes in the distribution of trade and the transfer of land. Some traders were also money-lenders, and some money-lenders engaged in trade. After the Mutiny, money-lenders pursued property with vigour. The reduction in the revenue demand, the growth of irrigation, the development of communications, the expansion of trade, the rise in prices[46] and the more efficient enforcement of law, all helped to make land worth having.[47] 'The money-lenders . . . are anxious to buy land, simply because they cannot find a better investment for their capital'[48] wrote one commentator. But the money-lender whose capital came from trade was not the only man in the land market. He competed with the large landlords, and with the richer coparceners who bought up the pattis of their poorer fellows. Some landowners were also money-lenders, such as Raja Rampal Singh of Kurri Sidhauli, head of the Baihasta Bais Rajputs, who had an income of nearly five lakhs from this source and managed several Bais Rajput estates.[49]

In east UP and Oudh, money-lenders added little to their holdings

[46] Taking 1873 as 100, the index of retail prices of food-grains in India rose from 102 for the quinquennium 1870/75 to 188 for the quinquennium 1910/15. Calculated from *Index Numbers of Indian Prices 1861–1931* (Delhi, 1933), Summary Table III.

[47] The author of the Mainpuri district gazetteer described the process. 'After the Mutiny, however, a totally new condition of things came into being. Hitherto the speculating classes had only looked upon land as a form of security and had not ambition to become landed proprietors themselves. The money-lender who intruded into a Thakur or Ahir village to oust the original owners of the land would have needed more than a common degree of courage, and the adventure was not generally considered to be worth the risk. But the reign of law and order which has prevailed since 1859, together with the great security of landed property and the high profits to be derived from it, have brought about a new era. The banking classes who before the Mutiny lent out their capital grudgingly and showed no desire to drive landlords to extremity, now compete with one another to accommodate the zamindar and encourage his extravagant habits, and by foreclosures and auctions in execution of decrees are steadily and persistently increasing their hold upon the land.' *DG Mainpuri*, p. 111.

[48] *Hindustani*, 8 June 1892, UPNNR 1892.

[49] Booklet on Lucknow Division, Revenue and Agriculture 1918, 578, UPS.

except in the vicinity of the large cities. Around Lucknow and Benares traders were prominent in the land market. They did best in Unao which was between Lucknow and Cawnpore.[50] Outside these places, they were, if anything, being dispossessed by landed magnates. In Oudh, talukdars, well protected by the law of primogeniture and by the Court of Wards, were successful in retaining their property and in buying zamindari and pattidari estates coming under the hammer.[51] In the permanently settled districts of Benares division, the landed communities were now holding their own.[52] In 1909, an observer in Ghazipur remarked: 'Of late years the old families have managed to retain their ground with more success than in the first half of the nineteenth century, and the recent acquisitions on the part of the money-lenders have been relatively unimportant.' He stressed that 'Probably the only class that has failed to improve has been that of the traders.'[53] In some parts of the remainder of Benares division and Gorakhpur, wealthy landowners such as Nawab Abdul Majid of Jaunpur did better than the money-lenders;[54] in others, the pattidari communities fought them off.[55] Therefore, land tended to circulate within the landed community rather than to be transferred from Rajputs and Muslims to Banias and Khattris. In the land market of east UP and Oudh the money-lender was no match for the landlord.

In west UP and Doab, the contrast is marked. Table I shows that money-lenders were doing well in land. Their holdings ranged from three per cent in Jalaun, to twenty-five per cent in Saharanpur, and forty-one per cent in Cawnpore. In Agra division, where there were several large landed estates—for instance, those of the Sherwanis and the Rajas of Awa and Tirwa—their holdings ranged from four per cent in Farrukhabad to nearly fourteen per cent in Agra. The purchasers were mainly Banias, Khattris, Kalwars and Brahmins. 'Among castes

---

[50] Cawnpore, although in the Doab, had considerable influence over the trans-Ganges district of Unao. Many Cawnporis owned land there and it was an area favoured by political agitators from the city.

[51] *DG Kheri*, XLII, 72; *DG Bahraich*, XLV, 71; *DG Lucknow*, p. 88; *DG Unao*, p. 83; *DG Rae Bareli*, XXXIX, 68; and *Settlement Report* [SR] *Sultanpur, 1898*, p. 10.

[52] In the first half of the nineteenth century, the landed communities had had a hard time, large quantities of their property entering the hands of civil servants, merchants and bankers. B. S. Cohn, 'The Initial British Impact on India: A Case Study of the Benares Region', *Journal of Asian Studies*, XIX, No. 4, August 1960, pp. 418–31.

[53] *DG Ghazipur*, pp. 118–19.

[54] *DG Jaunpur*, p. 91; and for purchases made by Nawab Abdul Majid see the booklet on Benares division in Revenue and Agriculture 1918, 578, UPS.

[55] *DG Basti*, XXXII, 88; *DG Azamgarh*, XXXIII, 106; and in Gorakhpur and Mirzapur, the money-lending groups had not done well enough to be regarded as proprietors, *DG Gorakhpur* p. 109; *DG Mirzapur*, P. 129.

TABLE I

Landholding and gains in land of castes associated with trading and money-lending in the UP by district at the beginning of the twentieth century

Division	Money-lending and trading castes	Land per cent held in district	Remarks
Meerut			
Dehra Dun	Bania, Khattri	11.5	Since 1886 Bania holdings increased by 57%
Saharanpur	Bania, Khattri	25.1	Since 1870 Bania holdings increased by 31%
Muzaffarnagar	Bania, Bohra	26.9	Since 1890 Bania holdings increased by 46%
Meerut	Bania	9.8	Since 1874 Bania holdings increased by 40%
Bulandshahr	Bania, Khattri, Bohra	11.1	Since 1889 Bania holdings increased by 33%
Aligarh	Bania, Brahmin	27.5	Since 1882 Bania holdings increased by 32%
Agra			
Muttra	Bania	9.3	Since 1879 Bania holdings increased by 6.9%
Agra	Bania, Khattri	13.7	Since 1870 Bania holdings increased by 96%
Farrukhabad	Bania, Sadh, Khattri	9.0	Since 1875 Bania holdings increased by 79%
Mainpuri	Bania, Bohra, Khattri	8.2	Since 1875 Bania holdings increased by 82%
Etawah	Bania, Khattri, Bohra	11.0	Since 1875 Bania holdings increased by 32%
Etah	Bania	10.0	Since 1874 Bania holdings increased by 100%
Rohilkhand			
Bareilly	Bania, Brahmin, Khattri	27.2	
Bijnor	Bania, Khattri	12.6	Since 1874 Bania holdings increased by 22%
Budaun	Bania, Khattri	15.5	Since 1873 Bania holdings increased by 78%
Moradabad	Bania, Khattri	19.3	Since 1881 Bania holdings increased by 65%
Shahjahanpur	Bania, Khattri, Kalwar	14.1	Since 1874 Bania holdings increased by 233%
Pilibhit	Bania, Khattri, Kalwar	16.0	
Allahabad			
Cawnpore	Brahmin, Bania, Khattri, Baqqal	41.3	Since 1802 Bania holdings increased by 111%
Fatehpur	Bania, Khattri, Kalwar	11.6	Since 1878 Bania holdings increased by 100%
Banda	Bania	6.1	Since 1881 Bania holdings declined by 10%
Hamirpur	Bania, Bohra	15.1	Since 1881 Bania holdings increased by 5%
Allahabad	Bania, Khattri, Kalwar	18.2	Since 1840 Bania holdings increased by 92%
Jhansi	Bania, Bohra	6.0	Bohra figure not available
Jalaun	Bania, Khattri, Bohra	3.0	Khattri & Bohra figure not available

TABLE 1—*contd*

Division	Money-lending and trading castes	Land per cent held in district	Remarks
Benares			
Benares	Bania, Khattri, Kalwar	11.7	
Mirzapur	NA		
Jaunpur	Bania, Khattri	5.3	
Ghazipur	Bania, Kalwar, Khattri	6.0	
Ballia	Bania	2.6	
Gorakhpur			
Gorakhpur	Bania, Naik	6.8	
Basti	Bania	3.4	Since 1891 Bania holdings increased by 15%
Azamgarh	Bania, Khattri	5.6	Since 1877 Bania holdings increased by 72%
Lucknow			
Lucknow	Bania, Khattri	7.3	Since 1870 Bania holdings increased by 309%
Unao	Bania, Brahmin, Khattri	28.5	Brahmins hold 18.9%
Rae Bareli	Bania, Khattri	2.6	
Sitapur	NA		
Hardoi	Bania	0.6	
Kheri	Bania, Khattri	1.7	
Fyzabad			
Bara Banki	Bania, Khattri	1.0	
Partabgarh	Bania	0.2	Since 1877 Bania holdings increased by 31%
Sultanpur	Bania	0.8	
Bahraich	Bania		"not included in the landowning class"
Gonda	Bania	0.1	
Fyzabad	Bania, Khattri.	2.4	

N.B. 1. Bania is used to describe those who are returned as Bania, Vaish or Mahajan.

2. The figures for Aligarh, Bareilly and Unao are somewhat exaggerated, because of the addition to the total of the figures for Brahmin landholding. In these districts, some members of the caste were said to be prominent in trade and money-lending.

Calculated from: *SR Dehra Dun, 1907*, p. 4; *SR Saharanpur, 1891*, p. 53; *SR Saharanpur, 1921*, p. 47; *SR Muzaffarnagar, 1921*, p. 25; *SR Meerut, 1940*, p. 10; *SR Bulandshahr, 1891*, p.2; *SR Bulandshahr, 1919*, p. 33; *SR Aligarh, 1903*, p. 7; *DG Muttra*, p. 121; *DG Agra*, p. 86; *SR Farrukhabad, 1903*, p. 13; *DG Mainpuri*, p. 104; *SR Etawah, 1915*, p. 36; *DG Etah*, p. 80; *DG Bareilly* pp. 100–01; *SR Bijnor, 1899*, p. 13; *DG Bijnor*, p. 108; *SR Budaun, 1901*, p. vii; *DG Budaun*, p. 84; *DG Moradabad*, p. 88; *DG Shahjahanpur*, p. 87; *DG Pilibhit*, pp. 101–02; *DG Cawnpore*, pp. 129–30; *DG Fatehpur*, p. 101; *SR Banda, 1909*, p. 23; *SR Hamirpur, 1908*, p. 29; *DG Hamirpur*, pp. 83–4; *DG Allahabad*, p. 104; *DG Jhansi*, pp. 105–06; *DG Jalaun*, pp. 69–70; *DG Benares*, p. 114; *DG Jaunpur*, pp. 94–5; *DG Ghazipur*, p. 96; *SR Ballia, 1886*, p. 23; *SR Gorakhpur, 1891*, p. 40; *SR Basti, 1919*, p. 33; *SR Azamgarh, 1908*, p. 11; *DG Azamgarh*, p. 106; *SR Lucknow, 1898*, pp. 23–7; *SR Lucknow, 1930*, p. 46; *SR Unao, 1931*, p. 39; *SR Rae Bareli, 1898*, pp. 28A–29A; *DG Hardoi*, p. 75; *SR Kheri, 1902*, p. 8; *SR Bara Banki, 1931*, p. 33; *SR Partabgarh, 1896*, p. 22; *SR Sultanpur, 1898*, p. 9; *DG Bahraich*, p. 70; *SR Gonda, 1903*, p. 8; and *SR Gonda, 1944*, p. 17; *SR Fyzabad, 1942*, p. 25.

Vaishyas now occupy the first place holding nearly a quarter of the district', wrote the settlement officer of Muzaffarnagar, 'The avidity with which these shrewd men of business have seized every opportunity of extending their possessions, is speaking testimony of the value of land as an investment.'[56] The dispossessed were mainly Muslims and Rajputs.[57] In 1909, a commentator on Cawnpore noticed that: '. . . nothing is more striking in the general history of the district than the disappearance of the old estates, especially those of the Rajputs. . . .'[58] In 1919, the settlement officer of Bulandshahr remarked that 'The money-lending class (Vaishyas, Khattris | and Bohras) hold a large area, about 11 per cent of the whole district, and have gained distinctly since the last settlement. The principal losers, however, seem to have been Pathans, Saiyids and Kayasths, who have lost no doubt through debt and extravagance.'[59] In west UP and Doab, money-lenders appear to have monopolized the property market.

In east UP and Oudh, just as the landed interest sustained its economic position against the trading and money-lending castes, so it succeeded in holding its political position. In 1907, landlords and zamindars held over thirty-nine per cent of municipal seats, men in the professions, landlord and government service held nearly forty-two per cent, and commercial men no more than seventeen per cent.[60] The landed interest was stronger than its percentage would suggest. Landlords had influence over those who worked on their estates as revenue agents or managers, while legal business concerning land

[56] *SR Muzaffarnagar, 1921*, p. 6. The landlord who was gaining land through money-lending was rare enough for the settlement officer of Muzaffarnagar to suggest that 'A notable exception is the influential family of Jansath town [an important Muslim family, the Jansath Saiyids] of which the members are steadily increasing their wealth by money-lending.' *Ibid.*, p. 7.

[57] Kayasths too lost land in many districts and also groups restricted to particular areas such as Gujars, but, in nearly every district, Rajputs and Muslims lost land. *DG Saharanpur*, p. 116 (Rajputs only); *DG Muzaffarnagar*, p. 117; *DG Meerut*, pp. 83-4; *DG Bulandshahr*, pp. 92, 106; *DG Aligarh*, pp. 90-2; *DG Muttra*, p.121 (Muslims only); *DG Etawah*, pp. 77-86 (Rajputs only); *DG Mainpuri*, p. 104; *DG Agra*, p. 87 (Rajputs only); *DG Farrukhabad*, p. 80 (Rajputs only); *DG Bijnor*, p. 108; *DG Budaun*, p. 84; *DG Moradabad*, p. 88; *DG Pilibhit*, p. 101; *DG Cawnpore*, pp. 129-30; *DG Allahabad*, p. 102; *DG Fatehpur*, p. 101 (here Muslims lost and Rajputs gained); *DG Hamirpur*, p. 84 (Rajputs only); *DG Jalaun*, p. 70 (Rajputs only); *DG Jhansi*, p. 116 (Rajputs only). Muslim holdings appear to remain stationary in Agra and Shahjahanpur, *DG Agra*, p. 87; *DG Shahjahanpur*, p. 87; and Muslims actually made slight increases in Saharanpur, Farrukhabad and Mainpuri, *DG Saharanpur*, p. 116; *DG Farrukhabad*, p. 80; and *DG Mainpuri*, p. 104.

[58] *DG Cawnpore*, p. 130.   [59] *SR Bulandshahr, 1919*, p. 4.

[60] Calculated from statements showing the occupation of members of municipal boards, Municipal 1908, 594 D, UPS.

supplied lawyers with the bulk of their work. The hidden strength
of the landlords is well illustrated by the way in which the Kayasth
pleader, Balak Ram, was hoisted into the chairmanship of the Fyzabad
municipal board by the Rajas of Jehangirabad and Partabgarh.[61]
Landlords also tended to be united to their service and professional
allies by links of common culture. These appear to have been particularly strong between the Kayasths who occupied one quarter and
the Muslims who held nearly two fifths of municipal board seats.[62]
They had a common past in the service of the Mughals from which
they inherited a common culture centred on the Urdu language,
both groups were highly literate, both owned land, both looked for
jobs in government service and the legal profession; indeed, no two
sections of the educated classes had more in common. Of course,
similar interests could mean competition. And, since both Kayasths
and Muslims were internally divided and seldom worked as a solid
bloc, their alliances were fragile. But in practice they often worked
together in municipal politics. Balak Ram's climb to power in Fyzabad
is an example of a Muslim-Kayasth alliance at work. So also are the
operations of the Kayasth, Ram Garib, manager of the Gorakhpur
Kayasth Trading and Banking Corporation, who employed a leading
Muslim, Qazi Ferasat Husain, and, even when relations between
Hindus and Muslims were deteriorating, backed him for the municipal
board against the leader of the Agarwal community, Jugal Kishore.[63]
In east UP and Oudh, links of caste, community, culture, and common
interest tended to unite men around a landed interest in such a way
that old notables and their allies managed to hold their own in the
new conditions.

In west UP and Doab, they did not. Traders and money-lenders
were doing better than the landed classes, both economically and
politically. Prima facie it might not seem so. Landlords held thirty-
eight per cent of the seats, men in service and the professions twenty-
eight per cent, and men connected with commerce only thirty-two
per cent.[64] But, as in the case of the landlords in east UP and Oudh,

[61] For a description of this affair, see below.

[62] Kayasths had 24.5 per cent and Muslims 38.4 per cent of seats on east UP and
Oudh municipal boards. Calculated from 'Statement showing caste of members
of Municipal Boards', Municipal 1908, 594 D, UPS.

[63] *Leader*, 25 March 1910. Qazi Ferasat Husain won and his victory was celebrated
by Muslims and Kayasths with a party given by Ram Garib at which the Muslims'
praises were sung by a Kayasth pleader in a Qasida.

[64] Calculated from statements showing the occupation of members of municipal
boards, Municipal 1908, 594 D, UPS.

the percentage disguised the extent of their influence. Ten per cent of those described as landlords or zamindars were banias, many of whom had acquired their property recently with the proceeds of commerce and retained their connection with it. In addition, trading interests were often represented by the professions. In Allahabad there was a close connection in municipal politics between the Khattri banker, Ram Charan Das, and the Brahmin lawyer, Madan Mohan Malaviya, and this was just the most important example of a general connection between Allahabad's Khattris and Malavi Brahmins.[65] Sometimes lawyers acted for caste organizations whose members would have been unwelcome on boards. In 1911, the district magistrate of Meerut observed that:

In nearly all big towns there are large and often powerful trade castes or communities which though they have strong caste organisations and frequently take concerted action over caste matters have no direct say in municipal affairs as a section or caste. They may, and often do, control elections in certain wards, but are hardly ever represented by members of their own community and their social status would in some cases make them unwelcome on the board.[66]

In east UP and Oudh, Kayasth and Brahmin professional men usually owed their living to landowners, a good proportion of whom were Muslims; in west UP and Doab, where the dominant political alignment was based not on land but on commerce, which the Hindus largely monopolized, these professional men tended to be in the pay of Hindu traders and money-lenders. Sixty per cent of Hindu municipal commissioners but only seven per cent of Muslim commissioners were commercial men.[67] So in west UP and Doab the connections of interest which often occurred between Hindus and Muslims in east UP and Oudh, were less common.

But Muslims were not simply in a minority. Their interests tended to clash with those of the Hindus. On some municipal boards in west UP and Doab, particularly in Meerut and Rohilkhand, Muslims of long pedigree and in 'reduced circumstances' sat opposite Hindu commercial men to whom they were either indebted or sold up.[68]

[65] C. A. Bayly, 'Patrons and politics in Northern India', above.

[66] J. R. Pearson, District Magistrate, Meerut, to Commissioner, Meerut Division, 16 August 1911, Home Educ Municipal A April 1914, 22–31, NAI.

[67] Calculated from statements showing the occupation of members of municipal boards, Municipal 1908, 594 D, UPS.

[68] For example, in 1907–08, four Keshgi Pathans, landowners and leading Muslims of the town, and five Vaishyas sat on the municipal board in the booming Buland-shahr cotton town and grain mart of Khurja. Some of these Vaishyas were Churuwal

Where traders were active, dispossessed Muslims found it difficult to get any representation at all.[69] Such direct opposition of economic interests sometimes determined political alignments. In Amroha, where the Syeds had lost heavily to the trading castes,[70] the Muslims usually banded together against the Hindus.[71] In Muzaffarnagar, in 1917, the district magistrate reported that 'The trouble . . . has been due [not to Home Rule protest but] to the strained relations between the old Saiyid proprietors who are now very much in debt, and the banias who have grown at the expense of the Saiyids.'[72] The conflict could be exacerbated by class factors; many of the traders were petty shopkeepers whom the Muslims detested.[73] Moreover, divisions were hardened by religious differences: the Muslims were strongest in Meerut, the old home counties of the Mughal Empire, and Rohilkhand, the former seat of the Rohilla kingdom, and here the traders and money-lenders were most vigorous in the assertion of Hindu religion and values. Traders and money-lenders provided much of the strength

Banias, the leading Hindu residents of Khurja, who owned property in many parts of India, were large bankers as well as traders and had a big interest in the cotton trade. One, Lala Nathi Mal had recently purchased the house and property of Azam Ali Khan, the last important member of a once notable, but now declining, Bhale Sultan family (Muslim Rajput). *DG Bulandshahr*, p. 259; and 'Statement of the members of Bulandshahr municipal board', Municipal 1908, 594 D, UPS.

[69] In 1907–08, Muslims were under-represented in the trading centres of Muttra, Hathras, Firozabad and Chandausi, in the major political centres of Moradabad, Allahabad, Meerut and Bareilly and in other areas where they had lost a particularly large amount of property, such as Muzaffarnagar and Sambhal.

[70] In Amroha town, 'During the past century several families have acquired wealth by trade and in many cases have bought up the revenue-free holdings of the Saiyids.' *DG Moradabad*, p. 177.

[71] *Ibid.*, p. 176.

[72] Note by Kunwar Jagdish Prasad, District Magistrate, Muzaffarnagar, 29 October 1917, General Administration Department [GAD] 1918, 603, UPS.

[73] See, for example, the comments of the following Muslim newspapers: *Amir-ul-Akhbar* (Cawnpore, Urdu), 7 April 1891, UPNNR 1891, and *Cawnpore Gazette*, 1 June 1892, UPNNR 1892. Some commercial men, particularly those from families of long standing, had much in common with the Muslims, such as, for instance, Lala Sita Ram, the leading Agarwal banker of Meerut, who corresponded in Urdu and had many Muslim friends. Sita Ram Papers, NAI. In addition, Hindu professional men such as Motilal Nehru felt much the same as the landed Muslims about commercial men. When the wife of Mohanlal Nehru attempted to launch the political career of Nehru womanhood by taking the quite unprecedented step, as a woman, of standing for the Allahabad municipal board, he wrote to his son: ' . . . imagine Mohan Rani sitting in the company of a number of pragwals, banias of sorts, and the so-called Raises whose greatness depends on the number of mistresses they keep.' He was going to have nothing to do with it. 'I am myself one of the voters . . . I hope to be better occupied elsewhere.' Motilal Nehru to Jawaharlal Nehru, 29 February 1912, Nehru Papers, Nehru Memorial Museum, New Delhi [NMM].

of the Arya Samaj. 'The Banias have always been the caste from which new sects such as the Arya Samaj have been chiefly recruited. . . .'[74] wrote the commissioner of Meerut in 1907. They were the strongest supporters of the All-India Hindu Sabha and the provincial Hindu Sabha. In both organizations, Lala Sukhbir Sinha, head of the leading Bania family of Muzaffarnagar, took a prominent role. Thus it appears that on many boards in west UP and Doab there were Hindus whose economic interests and religious beliefs tended to be hostile to a large sector of the town population—the Muslims. Competition for power tended to coincide with communal lines.[75]

3. Muslims in municipal politics and the demand for separate representation 1883–1908

Politics need not have split along communal lines. The prescriptions of religion did not prevent Hindu and Muslim from working and living together. In the 1880s, common interest in land and trade united people as much as religious solidarity. By 1900, however, politics in some towns was coming to be dominated increasingly by religion. This tendency varied markedly between the two regions of the UP.

In east UP and Oudh, the dominant factor was the connection based on the landed interests which was supra-communal and discouraged appeals to religion. In the towns religious quarrels were rare. Religious feeling was of so little importance in Lucknow politics that, in the 1893 and 1895 legislative council elections, local Hindu Congressmen felt it quite safe to put forward a Muslim barrister, Hamid Ali Khan,[76]

[74] Extract from fortnightly Demi-Official [D-O] report from H. C. A. Conybeare, Commissioner, Meerut, 20 May 1907, Home Poll D August 1907, 4, NAI.

[75] Fox's local study of Tezibazar, Jaunpur district, illustrates well some of the background and some of the characteristics of the communal antagonism that existed between Hindus and Muslims: for example, the selling up of Muslim estates to banias at the beginning of the twentieth century, the rise of the banias at the same time to challenge and to take political power from the zamindars, and the antipathy between trader and Muslim, 'The most anti-Muslim of status categories', Fox states, 'are the Baniyas and the Brahmins. . . . Local people say that Baniyas and Brahmins are especially anti-Muslim because these castes most retain the spirit of Hinduism in social habits and ideals and are therefore most inimical to Islam.' Fox, *From Zamindar to Ballot Box*, pp. 69–81 and 113.

[76] The political career of Hamid Ali Khan reflects the changing style of politics. He began as a Congressman, but by 1901 he had joined Viqar ul-Mulk and Munshi Ehtisham Ali in appealing for Muslim political organization to combat the government's Hindi resolution. In 1906 he was a member of the provincial committee of

as their candidate for the northern municipal board seat against the Kayasth talukdar and representative of the landed interest, Babu Sri Ram.[77] There were, it is true, severe communal riots in east UP and Oudh,[78] but the towns, on the whole, remained unaffected, and this was in striking contrast to west UP and Doab where towns were usually their focus.

In some towns of west UP and Doab, a narrow communalism characterized municipal self-government from the start. In the 1870s and 1880s, communal tension increased in Allahabad when Hindu traders and professional men launched a campaign to transfer the control of the Magh Mela,[79] a great source of patronage, from the Muslim Kotwal to the Hindu subcommittee of the municipal board; they succeeded in 1886.[80] This episode, which lasted over a decade, influenced the way Allahabad politics divided along communal lines. In 1888 the Muslim Anjuman-i-Rifah-i-Islam demanded that the existing municipal board be abolished and the number of Hindu and Muslim seats fixed to ensure Muslim representation.[81] Parties organized primarily around religion were found in other west UP and Doab towns. In 1891 the Muslims of Pilibhit complained that they were under-represented and that the district magistrate refused to help.[82] Communal attitudes were not new in Pilibhit. In 1871 it had seen serious

the All-India Muslim League appointed at Dacca, and by 1914 he was regarded both by the landed interest and by the government as a 'safe man'.

[77] In fact, the Lucknow Congressmen misjudged the situation. In 1892, the northern municipal board seat had five electors representing the municipalities of Agra, Bareilly, Meerut, Lucknow and Fyzabad. Meerut (a Muslim) and Fyzabad voted for Hamid Ali Khan, Agra, Bareilly and Lucknow (the local district magistrate) voted for Sri Ram. In 1895, with a broader electorate, Hamid Ali Khan lost 9–5. J. L. Hill, 'Congress and Representative Institutions in the United Provinces, 1886–1901' (Duke University, Ph.D. thesis), pp. 220–3, 239.

[78] In 1893, east UP and Oudh saw the most severe communal outbreaks of the century. But the disturbances in Gorakhpur and Azamgarh districts, as in the case of those of 1913 and 1914 in Fyzabad, were rural, not urban, affairs. J. M. Rizvi, 'Muslim Politics and Government Policy: Studies in the development of organisation and its social background in North India and Bengal, 1885–1917' (Cambridge University, Ph.D. thesis, 1969), pp. 102–03.

[79] An annual fair at the sangam at Allahabad which is thought to be the point of confluence of the mythical holy river, Saraswati, with the Ganges and Jumna. It ranks with Hardwar and Benares among the most important of Hindu bathing festivals. The management of such a festival provided considerable patronage in the grant of monopolies to pan, incense and flower sellers.

[80] C. A. Bayly, 'The Development of Political Organisation in the Allahabad Locality, 1880–1925' (Oxford University, D.Phil. thesis, 1970), pp. 231–5.

[81] Municipal B March 1888, 40, UPS, cited in J. L. Hill, 'Congress and Representative Institutions', pp. 128–9.

[82] Municipal B October 1891, 31, UPS, ibid., p. 129.

Hindu-Muslim rioting. In the following year, Moradabad had even more serious riots. Moradabad was seldom free from communal trouble, and its politicians were notorious for their bitter communalism.[83] Under the rules laid down in 1884, more Hindus than Muslims in Moradabad had the vote. But the secretary of the municipality was a Muslim. He drew the ward boundaries so that most Hindu voters, who lived in the centre of the town, were jammed into one ward, leaving Muslims with the advantage in the remaining five wards.[84] As a result, the Muslims always had a majority. In 1898, Babu Brijnandan Prasad, vice-chairman of the board, complained to the local government that:

ever since the introduction of the principle of local self-government, the Hindus in Moradabad have had no share in Municipal administration, and are really worse off than they would have been if local self-government had never been granted to Moradabad.[85]

Communal politics developed in many west UP and Doab towns. The reasons for this varied. Historical enmity based on old grievances such as at Pilibhit or Moradabad, or the changing nature of municipal government leading to a weakening of the Muslim position, seem to have played a part. These factors were also present in some towns of east UP and Oudh, but what would appear to have been crucial in west UP and Doab was that political alliances based on common interests were made within communities, and not between them.[86]

Of eighty-two municipalities in 1908,[87] the Muslims had a majority of the population in twenty-one but had a majority of Muslim elected members in only thirteen. They were handicapped by their relative poverty which gave them fewer voters than their numbers merited, and it was only in east UP and Oudh towns such as Gorakhpur that the Muslim proportion of voters was larger than their proportion of the population. The Table shows that between 1884 and 1908, the

[83] An illustration of the city's reputation lies in the Hindu saying that 'In Moradabad there are nothing but mukkhiam, macchar aur musalman,' (flies, mosquitoes and Muslims).

[84] *NWP Administration Report, 1871–72*, pp. 4, 10–12.

[85] Minute, Babu Brijnandan Prasad, vice-chairman, Moradabad municipal board, 28 February 1898, Municipal A October 1898, 92 f. UPS, cited in J. L. Hill, 'Congress and Representative Institutions', pp. 130–31.

[86] Hill stresses the prevalence of communal politics in west UP, *ibid.*, p. 130.

[87] The only figures available for UP municipal electorates are for 1911 when Muslims had a majority of voters in only ten municipalities. Home Educ Municipal A April 1914, 22–31, NAI.

proportion of Muslim seats on municipal boards fluctuated.[88] In the two regions, however, Muslim fortunes varied. In the twenty-four municipalities of east UP and Oudh, the Muslims held their position, but in the fifty-eight municipalities of west UP and Doab, they did not. They lost seats steadily in important cities such as Meerut, Agra and Cawnpore and, in the first decade of the twentieth century, the same trend was apparent in Rohilkhand towns such as Moradabad, Budaun and Chandpur.

The reasons for this decline were many. Muslim voters and candidates tended to be men dependent for their living on service, the professions or income from property. They suffered more severely than the Hindus, of whom many were traders and money-lenders, from the sharp price rise that occurred between 1880 and 1910.[89] Government action also played a part. In the Municipalities Act of 1900, government pruned the membership of many boards. The redrawing of ward boundaries which followed gave opportunities for the settling of old scores and gerrymandering. In Moradabad, the Muslim majority was now at

[88]   *Hindu and Muslim performance in municipal board elections, 1884/5–1907/8*

Towns in the region of:	Community	1884/5	1887/8	1897/8	1907/8
West UP and Doab	Hindu	60.7	62.2	56.5	65.6
	Muslim	34.1	33.5	33.5	30.1
	Other	5.2	4.3	10.0	4.3
Hindu majority over Muslim		26.6	28.7	23.0	35.5
East UP and Oudh	Hindu	62.2	64.2	60.8	64.3
	Muslim	30.1	30.1	32.0	33.5
	Other	7.7	5.7	7.2	2.2
Hindu majority over Muslim		32.1	34.1	28.8	30.8
Total UP	Hindu	61.3	62.9	58.6	64.8
	Muslim	32.7	32.3	32.5	31.1
	Other	6.0	4.8	8.9	4.1
Hindu majority over Muslim		28.6	30.6	25.9	33.7

Calculated from Returns of elections to municipal boards, *NWP and Oudh Gazette*, Part III, for the years 1884, 1885, 1886, 1887, 1895, 1896, 1897; and *UP Gazette*, Part III, for the years 1905, 1906 and 1907.

1884/5 has been taken as the base-line because this was the first year of elections under the 1883 act. Only those municipalities which existed both in 1884 and in 1908 have been analysed in order to make the figures comparable. The figures in 1897/8 go against the trend, and this is in part explained by the large increase in other members. The Municipalities Act of 1900 cut back the number of seats on municipal boards and this partly accounts for the Muslim figures for 1907/8. The evidence from this table is suggestive but not conclusive.

[89] This price rise reached peaks in the years 1897 and 1908. *Index Numbers of Indian Prices 1861–1931*, Summary Table III.

last destroyed.[90] Sheer electoral incompetence was another cause. In Bareilly, Muslims numbered fifty per cent of the population and Hindus forty-nine per cent. In 1901 each community had nine seats. But one electioneering slip by a Muslim followed by the manipulation of the electoral rolls by a Hindu changed the position to eleven to seven in favour of the Hindus.[91] The very fact that Muslims were usually in a minority did not help them: the majority and stronger community in a municipality were better placed to capture Tammany Hall. In the Allahabad elections of 1891, hired ruffians saw that only supporters of Badri Prasad reached the polling booth.[92]

In 1893, government observed that the:

general tendency towards assertion of religious privileges on both sides since the country passed under the British Government has naturally been greatest in those localities where during the previous administrations one party possessed an ascendancy which has now ceased.[93]

The process was most evident in west UP and Doab towns where communities took advantage of electoral victories to settle religious scores. Soon after the Hindus gained the upper hand in Moradabad, they compelled Muslim butchers to dry their hides outside the city.[94] In Chandpur, they ended cow slaughter.[95] In Bijnor, where Hindus dominated the board, the Hindu kotwal thrashed Muslim butchers for offering beef for sale in the market-place.[96] When Muslims had a chance, they replied in kind. Cows were openly killed in Najibabad after the Muslims gained power.[97] There was nothing to choose between Hindus and Muslims, but Muslims, as a minority, were more frequently the losers, and they came to see the need to control local government to safeguard their religion.[98] In many towns of the region, Muslims gained a taste of what it might mean to be in a perpetual political minority. As at Pilibhit, they found that nominated members and

[90] In 1897, the Muslims had a nine to eight majority on the board, but by 1907 they were in a four to eight minority. The Muslim press claimed that the Hindus had influenced the redrawing of the ward boundaries. *Naiyar-i-Azam* (Moradabad, Urdu), 26 April 1910, UPNNR 1910.

[91] Note for the Collector of Bareilly by Munshi Asghar Ali Khan, 1911, Home Educ Municipal A April 1914, 22–31, NAI.

[92] *Prayag Samachar* (Allahabad, Hindi), 19 March 1891, UPNNR 1891.

[93] Home Public A December 1893, 210–13, NAI.

[94] *Rohilkhand Gazette* (Bareilly, Urdu), 24 February 1903, UPNNR 1903.

[95] *Sahifa* (Bijnor, Urdu), 12 June, 1904, UPNNR 1904.

[96] *Ibid*, 5 August 1903, UPNNR 1903.

[97] *Gohar-i-Hind* (Najibabad, Urdu), 5 February 1902, UPNNR 1902.

[98] Note by Shaikh Zahur Ahmad, Barrister-at-Law, Allahabad, 2 February 1911, Home Educ Municipal A April 1914, 22–31, NAI.

government officials could do little to help them.[99] They were beginning to be exposed to the force of democratic politics. Uneasy about their position, Muslims began to search for protection through statutory safeguards and communal organization.

West UP and Doab was the centre of the demand for separate representation and from there came the initiative for Muslim political organization. At Muzaffarnagar, fifty-eight per cent of the population was Hindu and forty-one per cent Muslim, but, out of the four nominated and twelve elected members, there were only three Muslims, two nominated and one elected. As a solution, the editor of *Kashshaf* demanded separate representation.[100] In Allahabad, where Muslims with thirty per cent of the population found difficulty in electing a single representative, as early as 1889, the Anjuman-i-Rifah-i-Islam insisted that Muslim interests could be properly safeguarded only by giving equal representation on the municipal board to the two communities.[101] Failure in council elections produced a similar reaction. Before the grant of separate representation in the 1909 reforms, no UP Muslim succeeded in elections to the provincial council and so Muslims began to demand separate representation for the councils as well.

Admittedly, the demand for separate representation had been made by other Muslims and in earlier times.[102] But it was in west UP and Doab that this demand achieved all-India importance and was backed by an organization which claimed to speak for all Indian Muslims. It was at Aligarh that Syed Ahmed Khan built the Mahomedan Anglo-Oriental College. It was in the west UP and Doab that Aligarh leaders found most support for their political initiatives; for the United Patriotic Association, Syed Ahmed's retort to the Congress incursion into upper India; for the Mahommadan Defence Association, Aligarh's reaction against the 1892 Councils Act and the cow-protection movement; and

[99] Commenting generally upon this problem before the Decentralization Commission, Kazi Azizuddin Ahmad, Deputy Collector of Moradabad, stressed that district officers had lost a great deal of power since the introduction of the elective system in local government.

[100] *Kashshaf* (Muzaffarnagar, Urdu), 24 January 1896, UPNNR 1896.

[101] Municipal B January 1890, 36, UPS, cited in J. L. Hill, 'Congress and Representative Institutions', p. 129.

[102] In 1883, Yusuf Ali, the Muslims' spokesman on the Bengal Legislative Council, demanded separate representation as protection in local and council government and, in 1884, this was included among the demands of the National Mahommedan Association. A. Seal, *The Emergence of Indian Nationalism* (Cambridge, 1968), p. 311. In the late 1880s, separate representation in various forms was adopted in several Punjab municipalities, for instance, Wazirabad, Lahore and Amritsar. Aligarh, the only UP municipality to get separate representation before the 1916 Municipalities Act, was given communal electorates in 1890.

for the 1900 Urdu Defence Association, the Muslim response to Mac-
Donnell's Hindi resolution. Viqar ul-Mulk, who was one of the first to
attempt to organize a Muslim political association and to demand
separate representation, was a member of the west UP municipal
board of Amroha. His sphere of influence lay in the towns of Meerut
and Rohilkhand where he successfully established several local Muslim
political associations.[103] The two men who drew up the 1906 Muslim
memorial to Minto came from Syed families long connected with the
west UP and Doab.[104] To support this memorial, the Muslim League
was founded, and between 1906 and 1909 many of its leaders came
from the west UP and Doab and its policies were shaped by the needs
of that region.

4. The stakes are raised: the growth of competition and communalism, 1909–1915

Between 1909 and 1915, government's impact on the towns grew
stronger and its character changed. This development, set off by the
recommendations of the Decentralization Commission and by the 1909
Councils Act, affected municipal taxation, the extent of official control
and the relationship between municipal boards and provincial councils.
In the towns of the UP it created new sources of competition, stimulated
new political consciousness, and vastly increased the value of a municipal
seat.

Changes in municipal taxation and the extent of official control
stirred up municipal politics. In order to prepare the towns for the
greater freedom from government interference, which the Decentralization Commission recommended, the taxation system was overhauled.
The octroi was now discovered to be 'essentially dangerous, and
tolerable only where central control is exceedingly close . . .;'[105] so it
was scrapped and replaced by a terminal tax and various direct imposts.

[103] Meetings were definitely held at Moradabad and Bijnor, see reports in *Nizam-
ul-Mulk* (Moradabad, Urdu), 28 February 1903, UPNNR 1903; and *Uruj* (Bijnor,
Urdu), 14 July 1903, UPNNR 1903; there was much talk of a district political
association in Budaun, *Zul Qarnain* (Budaun, Urdu), 14 July 1903; and such associ-
ations were formed in at least two places, Saharanpur and Shahjahanpur, *Pioneer*
(Lucknow), 31 July 1903, cited in S. R. Wasti, *Lord Minto and the Indian Nationalist
Movement, 1905–1910* (Oxford, 1964), p. 60; and *Edward Gazette* (Shahjahanpur,
Urdu), 26 June 1903, UPNNR 1903.
[104] These two men were Nawab Medhi Ali, Mohsin ul-Mulk and Syed Hosein
Bilgrami, Imad ul-Mulk. While the draft memorial was being drawn up at Bombay,
Viqar ul-Mulk was one of Mohsin ul-Mulk's most frequent correspondents.
[105] *Municipal Taxation Enquiry*, p. 16.

Part of the burden of taxation now shifted from the shoulders of the traders to a much wider range of town-dwellers. This gave more people a real interest in town government which was increased by a severe price rise[106] that compelled municipalities to raise taxes. A tax on professions and trades was especially resented and it led to protest meetings in many towns, notably in the west UP and Doab. No less disturbing was the gradual introduction, after 1910, of elected non-official chairmen.[107] Now there was even greater reason for gaining control of municipal boards. Officials had less power to interfere and to protect injured minorities. The change brought home the dangers of the impending British withdrawal from municipal government.

Municipal politics were set alight, however, by the 1909 councils act. Under this act, municipal and district boards continued to work as council electorates. In eight divisions, these boards became general electorates, returning one member at each election.[108] Another four members were elected by eight major municipal boards half of which voted in alternate election years.[109] In these twelve general electorates, where both Hindus and Muslims voted, the municipalities gave the ambitious politician his best chance to climb to provincial power. But, beyond this, the Muslims were given four special electorates.[110] Government accepted their demand for separate representation and recognized the claim about their 'political importance'.[111] Consequently, the Muslims not only had the right to vote in the general electorates but also in their own special electorates which alone guaranteed them a percentage of representation greater than their proportion of the population.

The Hindus bitterly resented these Muslim privileges. In his first

[106] Index numbers of Indian prices, based on retail prices of food grains, show the following increases during this period: 1901–05, 137.6; 1906–10, 190.6; 1911–15, 197.8. 1873 equals 100. Calculated from *Index Numbers of Indian Prices 1861–1931*, Summary Table III.

[107] 17 municipalities received the privilege in 1910, a further 16 in 1912 and the remainder in the Municipalities Act of 1916.

[108] The municipal and district boards of each division elected representatives who formed a divisional electoral college by which the candidate was selected.

[109] The municipal boards were: Allahabad, Agra, Meerut, Lucknow, Fyzabad, Benares, Bareilly and Cawnpore. The first four elected members in 1909, the second four in 1912 and so on.

[110] The four Muslim constituencies were Agra/Meerut; Rohilkhand/Kumaon; Lucknow/Fyzabad and Allahabad/Benares/Gorakhpur. In these constituencies, Muslim voters had the right of direct election. This was another source of grievance for the Hindus who were compelled to operate through electoral colleges.

[111] In the 1906 Muslim memorial to Minto, Muslims had claimed a proportion of separate representation greater than their proportion of the population on the grounds of their 'political importance'.

leading article, the editor of the *Leader*, an Indian-owned English daily founded to fight the Congress cause, dilated in almost Wordsworthian terms on the 'growing feeling that new activities are coming into existence and a large life is rapidly dawning before us', but then, with a touch of bathos, pointed to the flaw in this vision of heaven, 'Lord Morley's reform scheme mingled with a message of hope is now surcharged with an element of anxiety.'[112] Muslim political gains had taken much of the goodness out of the new dose of political power. Congress Hindus planned to put the goodness back. They waged a relentless campaign against Muslim representation. Their attitude to council elections went thus: if the Muslims were not prepared to act with the Hindus, all they were entitled to was representation in proportion to their numbers. Their special electorates had given them this proportion and more; they should keep to these electorates. Any Hindu who dared to back a Muslim in the general electorate risked a bastinado from the *Leader*. Any Muslim who dared to stand in the general electorate was likely to receive a public warning of this kind:

We have heard that the Hon Khan Bahadur Ali Nabi, who represents the Agra city municipality in the Council, means to contest the division seat as the city will have no member this time. We shall have nothing to say about his offering his valuable services to the Muslim electors of the Agra and Meerut divisions, though it is nearly certain that he will not be the equal of the sitting member, the Hon Mr Aftab Ahmed Khan, who is a really able man; *but he need not thrust himself upon the mixed electorate whose 'duty' it is to elect a 'Congressman' and 'Hindu'.*[113]

The message was: position reserved for Hindus, no Muslim need apply.[114]

The obvious points where the Hindus could strengthen their position in the general electorates were the municipal boards—the district boards were still too much under government's thumb. To be sure of electing their men to the provincial councils, their best plan was to reduce Muslim influence on municipal boards. From 1909, their attempts to do so became much more determined. In 1910, the editor of Etawah's *Al Bashir* complained that in local elections Hindu bankers were exerting influence over their Muslim debtors, Hindu house-

[112] *Leader*, 24 October 1909.
[113] Cutting from the *Leader* of 12 May 1912, enclosed in Hasan Ali Khan, member, Agra District Board, to Mahomed Ali, 14 May 1912. (The words in italics were underlined in the original by Hasan Ali Khan, and he also added the quotation marks.) Mahomed Ali Papers, Jamia Millia Islamia, New Delhi.
[114] Summary of the argument of a typical leading article on the question. This one commented on Sachchidananda Sinha's address to the Provincial Conference of 1912. *Leader*, 6 April 1912.

H

owners played the same game with their tenants, and Hindu landlords threatened Muslim cultivators with ejectment.[115] Manipulation of electoral rolls became so blatant that it was officially investigated in Meerut, Saharanpur, Etawah, Aligarh and Fyzabad.[116] The life of a Hindu who failed to obey the communal whip became grim. 'It is an open secret here that the Hindu members who had promised to vote for me were put to great inconvenience.' Munshi Asghar Ali Khan of Bareilly noted in 1911. 'It was made a religious question by the friends of the other candidates and every sort of religious pressure was brought to bear upon them. They were given Muhammadan nicknames and one of them was much harassed even in private affairs. His term of office as a municipal commissioner having expired in March last, other candidates were set up and after a hard contest he had to go. . . .'[117]

Under such electoral pressures communal feeling developed rapidly. 'Never in my experience', wrote Harcourt Butler, 'has Hindu-Mahommedan antagonism been so intense as it now is in Northern India. People there are beginning to ask for separate courts of justice, separate schools etc. . . ., for the two communities. Most municipal elections turn on this question. The Mahommedans have got too much say the Hindus; we must get back a bit.'[118] Throughout the province the two communities attacked each other where they could. Hindu talukdars dismissed Muslims from their service.[119] Hindu merchants considered stopping credit.[120] Muslim pleaders and physicians were boycotted[121] and, in the full flight of communal feeling, the Hindus of Agra even went so far as to renounce the charms of their Muslim courtesans.[122] Muslims retaliated where they could, refusing to greet Hindus[123] and agitating for a separate classification of the depressed classes in the census.[124] Each community blackballed representatives of the other who applied for membership of the Gorakhpur Union Club.[125] Thus

[115] *Al Bashir* (Etawah, Urdu), 15 March 1910, UPNNR 1910.
[116] Home Municipal A August 1909, 2, November 1909, 17 and D February 1910, 3, NAI.
[117] Note by Munshi Asghar Ali Khan, 9 August 1911, Home Educ Municipal A April 1914, 22–31, NAI.
[118] Harcourt Butler to Sir James Duboulay, Private Secretary to the Viceroy, 25 November 1910, Hardinge Papers, Cambridge University Library, 81.
[119] D-O Letter from the Commissioner of Lucknow, 18 May 1909, Home Poll A October 1913, 100–18, NAI.
[120] D-O letter from the Commissioner of Agra, 21 February 1911, *ibid.*
[121] *Ibid.*   [122] GAD 1910, 442, UPS.
[123] D-O letter from the Commissioner of Lucknow, 31 August 1909, Home Poll A October 1913, 100–18, NAI.
[124] D-O letter from the Commissioner of Allahabad, 5 April 1910, *ibid.*
[125] D-O letter from the Commissioner of Gorakhpur, June 1911, *ibid.*

the communal attitudes previously confined to some west UP and Doab towns, now, by means of the electoral machinery of the reformed councils, percolated throughout the province. 'The fact is', Government commented, 'that elections to local bodies were before the introduction of the reform scheme as often as not contested on personal grounds and not on the basis of any political or religious cleavage. . . . It has been quite clear since 1909 that elections to local bodies turn, to a far larger extent than previously, on the question of religion.'[126] Increasingly the parties of local politics were becoming religious factions.

5. Muslim performance in local politics, 1909–15

As politics increasingly divided along communal lines, the Muslim electoral position might have been expected to get worse. Certainly, the UP government assumed that the Muslims were doing badly. In 1912, it called upon the Government of India to give Muslims separate representation, and to back its case it reported that, in 1909, of the members elected to municipal boards, 33.3 per cent had been Muslims, in 1910, 31.3 per cent, and in 1911, 29.1 per cent.[127] But the local government neglected to point out that only one-third of the boards were returned each year and that, in 1911, the overall position of Muslims was much the same as before 1909. This is shown by the Table.[128]

---

[126] R. Burn, Chief Secretary, Government of UP, to Secretary, Government of India Education Department, 4 September 1912, Home Educ Municipal A April 1914, 22–31, NAI.   [127] *Ibid.*

[128]   *Proportions of Hindus and Muslims elected to Municipal Boards 1907/08–1915/16*

	1907/08	1911/12	1915/16
Hindu	65.8	65.8	65.6
Muslim	30.3	30.3	30.4
Other	3.9	3.9	4.0

Calculated from: Returns of elections to municipal boards, *UP Gazette*, Part III, for the years 1905, 1906, 1907, 1913, 1914, 1915, and table showing proportions of Hindus and Muslims elected to municipal boards as on 1 April 1911, enclosed in Burn to Secretary, Government of India Education Department, 4 September 1912, Home Educ Municipal A April 1914, 22–31, NAI.

These figures and the case which they supported were prepared by Burn, the Chief Secretary, who was thought to be the real governor of the province during Meston's lieutenant-governorship, and was suspected of pro-Muslim sympathies.

But Muslim fortunes did vary in the two regions of the province. In the towns of west UP and Doab, the fact that Muslims were poor and seats more valuable might have been expected to lead to a further decline in their representation. But the Table[129] shows that between 1907 and 1915, the number of Muslim seats remained much the same, although, in Rohilkhand, as seats were won first by one community and then another, Muslims succeeded in winning three boards previously controlled by Hindus—including Moradabad, the focal point of communal rivalry in west UP.

How did the Muslims do so well? The reform of the legislative councils and their electorates had the effect of involving the landlords more directly in municipal politics. If landowners were to get their men on to the legislative councils, they had to have them elected by the divisional constituencies. This meant taking a hand in the politics of the towns. In Etawah, for example, Muslims and Hindu raises banded together to keep out candidates who were lawyers and Arya Samajists.[130] The

[129]   *Hindu and Muslim performance in municipal board elections in west UP and Doab, 1907/08–1915/16*

Towns in the division of:		1907/08	1911/12	1915/16
Meerut	Hindu	61.2	57.9	60.7
	Muslim	29.5	31.9	29.8
	Other	9.3	10.2	9.5
Agra	Hindu	78.3	83.4	84.9
	Muslim	21.7	16.6	15.1
	Other	—	—	—
Rohilkhand	Hindu	55.8	56.1	55.1
	Muslim	44.2	43.9	44.9
	Other	—	—	—
Allahabad	Hindu	77.6	78.4	80.0
	Muslim	15.3	14.4	13.7
	Other	7.1	7.2	6.3
Total west UP and Doab	Hindu	65.8	66.0	66.7
	Muslim	29.6	29.4	29.0
	Other	4.6	4.6	4.3

Calculated from: Returns of elections to municipal boards, *UP Gazette*, Part III, for the years 1905, 1906, 1907, 1913, 1914, 1915, and table showing proportions of Hindus and Muslims elected to municipal boards as on 1 April 1911, enclosed in Burn to Secretary, Government of India Education Department, 4 September 1912, Home Educ Municipal A April 1914, 22–31, NAI.

[130] *Leader*, 18 March 1911 and 28 March 1911.

pattern was this: in small district towns where landlords were influential,[131] Muslims gained seats; in large towns where merchants were strong, as the Table shows, Muslims tended to lose.[132] Thus in Meerut the Muslims lost three seats and in Allahabad they won none at all. But in the district capital of Banda they won eight seats, and in the small market town of Chandpur, for the first time in fifteen years, they won an elected majority.

In west UP and Doab, however, the landed interest was not the only factor helping the Muslims in municipal elections. Communal rivalry was growing all the time. In 1911, the commissioner of Rohilkhand reported that 'There had been fiercely contested elections and much

[131] How Muslims could benefit in a landlord-dominated electorate is illustrated by the large proportion of seats which they held, in excess of the proportion of the population, on district boards.

	Meerut	Agra	Rohilk-hand	Alla-habad	Ben-ares	Gorak-hpur	Luck-now	Fyza-bad	UP Average
Muslim Divisional population per cent	22.12	9.22	24.98	9.26	8.23	12.48	12.75	14.24	14.35
Muslim District Board seats per cent	26.19	19.76	44.05	23.81	28.57	35.29	36.86	43.06	31.65

Calculated from: Table showing proportion of Hindus and Muslims elected to district boards in the UP as on 1 April 1911, enclosed in Burn to Secretary, Government of India Education Department, 4 September 1912, Home Educ Municipal A April 1914, 22–31, NAI.

[132]

Hindu and Muslim performance in elections to west UP and Doab municipal boards with the right of direct election to the provincial council, 1907/08–1915/16

	1907/08	1911/12	1915/16
Hindu	65.9	67.8	74.7
Muslim	27.5	26.6	20.0
Other	6.9	5.6	5.3

These boards were: Allahabad, Agra, Meerut, Bareilly and Cawnpore.

Calculated from: Returns of elections to municipal boards, *UP Gazette*, Part III, for the years 1905, 1906, 1907, 1913, 1914, 1915, and table showing proportions of Hindus and Muslims elected to municipal boards as on 1 April 1911, enclosed in Burn to Secretary, Government of India Education Department, 4 September 1912, Home Educ Municipal A April 1914, 22–31, NAI.

undesirable display of racial feeling in Bareilly, Nagina and elsewhere.'[133] Nevertheless, this kind of communalism indirectly helped the Muslims in local politics. Increased competition for local power united the Muslims,[134] but at the same time it stimulated the divisions in Hindu society. In Allahabad, Ganeshi Lal, headmaster of the Kayastha Pathshala, asked 'all Kayasthas . . . to strain every nerve to bring about' the success of Girdhari Lal, general manager of the People's Industrial Bank, 'as he was a Kayastha'.[135] In Saharanpur, when a young Agarwal stood against his elderly caste-fellows, the Agarwal voters split.[136] In Cawnpore, when the Sanatan Dharma supporter, Rai Debi Prasad, launched a religious campaign against a leading Arya Samajist, Lala Anand Swarup, the Hindus divided.[137] In Mainpuri, the Muslims allied with Sanatan Dharma men against Arya Samaj candidates.[138] From the new participation of the landed interest in the towns and the new divisions among Hindus, the Muslims gained enough help to be able to hold their own.

In east UP and Oudh, they did better than that. The Table shows that between 1907 and 1915, the Muslims lost slightly in Lucknow and Benares divisions but gained steadily in Fyzabad and dramatically in Gorakhpur.[139] In Benares and Gorakhpur divisions, they not only

[133] Report by the Commissioner of Rohilkhand, cited in *UPMAR, 1911-12*, p. 2.
[134] Increased competition united the Muslims except in areas of Shia-Sunni conflict such as Amroha and Lucknow.
[135] *Leader*, 13 November 1912.
[136] Report by the District Magistrate of Saharanpur, 1 August 1909, enclosed in Hose, Chief Secretary, Government of UP Municipal Department, to Secretary, Government of India Home Department, Home Municipal A November 1909, 18, NAI; and *Leader*, 4 April 1910.
[137] *Leader*, 11 May 1912.   [138] *Ibid.*, 27 March 1912.
[139]   *Hindu and Muslim performance in municipal board elections in east UP and Oudh, 1907/08-1915/16*

Towns in the division of:		1907/08	1911/12	1915/16
Benares	Hindu	52.9	60.6	56.3
	Muslim	45.7	37.9	40.6
	Other	1.4	1.5	3.1
Gorakhpur	Hindu	78.3	62.5	48.0
	Muslim	21.7	37.5	52.0
	Other	—	—	—
Lucknow	Hindu	62.9	65.3	67.5
	Muslim	31.6	31.6	28.4
	Other	5.2	3.1	3.1
Fyzabad	Hindu	71.4	67.1	65.0
	Muslim	28.6	32.9	35.0
	Other	—	—	—

held a percentage of municipal seats beyond their proportion of the urban population, but they also either gained seats or maintained their position in every municipality except Benares itself and Mirzapur. In Gorakhpur town, they gained a majority for the first time. The type of politics which enabled the Muslims to do better in east UP and Oudh than in west UP and Doab is illustrated by the politics of Fyzabad.

In the Fyzabad municipal elections of 1886, two young pleaders, Balak Ram, a Kayasth, and Manohar Lal, a Khattri, had been returned to the board. Both retained their seats for most of their lifetime and both, during their long tenure, built factions based on members of their respective castes. Balak Ram was the brother of Babu Sri Ram, talukdar of Rasulpur in the Fyzabad district, and a 'safe' man in the government's view. His immediate followers were mainly his relatives, who were in service or law. Kayasths were the fourth largest landowners in the district, and Balak Ram's party may be regarded as one of Kayasths with landed, particularly talukdari, connections. Manohar Lal's family were rich merchants, who owned some land and were increasing their holdings. His faction was composed mainly of vakils and traders, Khattris and Vaishyas. Some were staunch Arya Samajists and were later to become Hindu Sabha men. Their politics had a nationalist tinge. Manohar Lal himself was a Congressman and a follower of Madan Mohan Malaviya. Their actions suggested that they were anti-talukdari, anti-Kayasth and pro-Congress.

As the municipal board usually elected a non-official chairman, rivalry between these factions was intense. Until 1909, Manohar Lal's faction seems to have had the advantage and from time to time he had been elected chairman. Fyzabad, a large town and divisional headquarters, was one of the few places in the region where traders were strong. But the 1909 reforms increased landlord participation in local politics and gave Balak Ram the opportunity to swing the balance in his favour. In the first election in the divisional constituency, Manohar

Total east UP and Oudh	Hindu	64.3	64.8	62.8
	Muslim	33.5	33.7	35.3
	Other	2.2	1.5	1.9

Calculated from: Returns of elections to municipal boards, *UP Gazette*, Part III, for the years 1905, 1906, 1907, 1913, 1914, 1915, and table showing proportions of Hindus and Muslims elected to municipal boards as on 1 April 1911, enclosed in Burn to Secretary, Government of India Education Department, 4 September 1912, Home Educ Municipal A April 1914, 22–31, NAI.

Lal stood against the Raja of Jehangirabad. Balak Ram naturally threw his weight behind the Raja who scraped home in the electoral college by one vote.[140] The Khattri leader reacted by launching a strong attack against Balak Ram and his nephew, Sitapat Ram, a vakil, who in 1910 were standing for re-election in both the municipal and the district board elections. In the district board elections, Balak Ram successfully opposed Triloki Nath Kapur, a Khattri, influential banker and zamindar.[141] The contest aroused so much feeling that the district authorities prohibited the carrying of lathis on election days.[142] In the municipal board elections, Balak Ram received strong Muslim support, and the affair had strong communal overtones. The *Leader* correspondent, obviously a Manohar Lal man, reported from the spot:

One most objectionable feature was that our Mahomedan friends canvassed by appealing to the religious sentiments of their co-religionists so that the Pesh-Imam went from house to house carrying with him the banner of Islam in order to induce people of his faith to flock round it, and he succeeded to such a great extent that almost all the Mahomedans went in a body for the Mahomedan candidate. Our Kayestha friends followed the footsteps of their Islamic brethren and preached Kayestha fraternity so that the entire Kayestha community with only a few honourable exceptions went in a body. . . . The election of B. Balak Ram was celebrated by cheers, loud exclamations of joy and by a band which played at the polling station when the result was declared, and his canvassers went round the city, with the band in front in a carriage just like tamashawallas who go round distributing notices of their performances. There was also a big nautch party in the People's Industrial Bank Ltd., to commemmorate his election.[143]

Having regained his municipal seat and brought the Muslims into his party on the municipal board, Balak Ram now challenged his rival for the chairmanship. In the preliminary lobbying, Jehangirabad rewarded Balak Ram for his support by putting pressure on three members of the Manohar Lal faction. Jehangir Shaw, a Parsi trader, honorary magistrate, nominated member and secretary of the board, was ordered to Lucknow. Here Jehangirabad interviewed him. He voted for Balak Ram. Two other members of the faction were also singled out for encouragement; both were Vaishyas, Ram Raghubir and his brother. The former was treasurer of the Bahampur estate. Partabgarh, a Hindu raja, and Jehangirabad urged the Raja of Bahampur to order his two clients to vote for Balak Ram, hinting that

[140] The electoral college consisted of thirty-nine delegates, eight from the municipal boards and thirty-one from the district boards—a reflection of the way in which the council regulations had been drawn up in favour of the landed interest. *Leader*, 12 December 1909.

[141] *Ibid.*, 14 January 1910.   [142] *Ibid.*, 13 March 1910.   [143] *Ibid.*, 24 March 1910.

government did not want Manohar Lal as chairman. Bahampur asked government what he should do and was told to do nothing. He obeyed. In the election the voting came out at eight apiece, and Thakur Lal Bihari Singh, the vice-chairman, and member of the Manohar Lal party, gave his casting vote for his leader. Balak Ram immediately petitioned on the grounds that first, a member of his party had missed his train and had not been able to vote, and second, that the Thakur's election as vice-chairman in the previous year had been invalid. The commissioner, to the annoyance of his superiors, vetoed the election and Balak Ram was returned in the re-run.[144]

In the municipal elections of the following year, Balak Ram proceeded to entrench his position further. Now more was at stake, since in the council elections of 1912, it would be the turn of the municipal board to elect a representative, over and above the divisional seat. Four out of five of his party succeeded. Two were Kayasths, one being Balak Ram's nephew. Two were Muslims, who ousted two Manohar Lal men, Babu Sunder Lal, a Khattri, and Ram Raghubir, by the narrow margins of four and nineteen votes. 'Were it not for their Hindu canvassers and voters' the Leader mofussil correspondent wrote of the Muslim victories, 'they would not have succeeded.'[145] In the fifth contest, P. N. Sapru, a Kashmiri Brahmin and staunch Congressman, beat the Kayasth candidate, Babu Raghunath Sahai, by four votes. In the autumn of 1912, in spite of the odds against him, Manohar Lal gamely tried for the council, but Balak Ram's Kayasth-Muslim-talukdari alliance was too strong.[146] Indeed, it was to dominate Fyzabad until the 1916 Municipalities Act, when the introduction of separate representation brought a sizeable Muslim contingent on to the board and turned factional alliances topsy-turvy.[147]

These political games in Fyzabad were not inspired by Hindu-Muslim antagonism. Jehangirabad and Partabgarh, when they put their weight behind the Kayasth faction, were supporting the landed interest.[148]

[144] Based on a note by Hose, Chief Secretary, Government of the UP, 26 May 1910, Municipal 1910, 291/98, UPS; and Leader, 10 June 1910.
[145] Leader, 18 March 1911.   [146] Ibid., 27 November 1912.
[147] H. A. Gould, 'A Working Paper on Religion, Ethnicity and Coalition Formation in Local Level Indian Politics' (unpublished paper presented at the conference on religion and political modernization, Honolulu, 22–25 March 1971).
[148] Until the 1930s, the landlords usually put their own interests before those of their communities. Thus, in 1906, Jehangirabad refused to attend the Lucknow meeting at which the Muslims drew up their memorial to Minto for fear of offending his fellow talukdars and, in 1909, Partabgarh, later a vice-President of the UP Hindu Sabha, was prepared to help a Muslim landlord into the council in preference to a Hindu Congressman. But even the landlord interest did not remain for ever

By installing a man of Balak Ram's impeccable connections as chairman of the board, they forwarded this interest in the divisional and
in the municipal constituency in the 1912 council elections. In Fyzabad,
Kayasths, Muslims and talukdars—groups associated earlier with
Muslim rule and now with service and land—banded together to keep
out Khattris and Vaishyas, Congressmen, vakils and traders. The basis
for similar alliances existed in nearly every municipality of east UP
and Oudh.[149]

6. The Muslim demand develops from separate to equal representation, 1909–1915

By 1915 the Muslims held more elected majorities in the towns of the
UP than they had done before 1909 and generally they held a better
position in municipal government than they had ever done before.
Against all expectations the growing importance of municipal boards
had worked to the community's advantage. Nevertheless Muslims
looked for more protection. The spread of communal politics in the
wake of the 1909 reforms kept them powerless both on the legislative
council and on most important municipal boards. At the same time,
the growth of Muslim political organization and a Muslim political
Press gave an edge to their agitation. A few gains were no substitute
for municipal majorities. In 1909 and 1910, the demand for separate
representation gained momentum in Press and on platform.[150] The

impervious to communalism. Reeves has shown how, in the elections of February
1937, the landlords were eventually broken by communal and factional pressures.
This he calls a 'turning point in the political development of the United Provinces.'
P. D. Reeves, 'Landlords and Party Politics in the United Provinces, 1934–7', D. A.
Low (ed.), *Soundings in Modern South Asian History* (London, 1968), pp. 261–82.

[149] In 1907, out of 20 east UP and Oudh municipal boards (information is not
available for the remaining four; Balrampur, Gonda, Nanpara and Sultanpur),
there were more Muslims and Kayasths than any other group on 12 (Benares, Mirzapur, Jaunpur, Ghazipur, Gorakhpur, Kheri, Sandila, Rae Bareli, Sitapur,
Khairabad, Nawabganj and Bahraich). By 1915, Muslims and Kayasths sat in
greater numbers on a further 5 boards (Ballia, Shahabad, Azamgarh, Fyzabad and
Tanda).

[150] For instance, *Al Bashir*, 15 March 1910; *Zul Qarnain*, 19 March 1910; *Naiyar-i-
Azam*, 26 March 1910; *Muslim Review* (Allahabad, Urdu), March 1910; *Al-Fasih*
(Bareilly, Urdu), 3 May 1910, UPNNR 1910. One of the many demands came from
the UP Muslim League, an organization that only sprang into existence for electoral
purposes. Ibni Ahmad, Secretary, UP Muslim League, to Chief Secretary, Government of UP, 2 November 1910, Mahomed Ali Papers, Jamia Millia Islamia.

lieutenant-governor was impressed. In 1908, he had advised the Government of India to stand firmly against separate representation;[151] but, by 1912, he argued that 'it would not now be right to deny to the Muhammadans the only means of securing for their adequate representation by election to local bodies on the ground that this act of bare justice would be offensive to the Hindus'.[152] Consequently, the UP Government asked every municipal and district board in the province for its views on the question of separate electorates for Muslims and the proportion of seats they should receive.[153] Their replies made the situation clear. Most Hindus were opposed to separate representation on principle; most Muslims demanded it on principle. Even that great nationalist, the Raja of Mahmudabad, called for 'the proper weapon of defence to enable them to protect their rights in all matters. . . .' with the warning, so ironically prophetic in his case, that 'the Mohammedans are aware of their lot if unsupported by the British Government and they fully know their existence here would be impossible but for the protection afforded by their Rulers.'[154] A few Muslims from east UP paid lip service to the principle of separate representation but denied that it suited their local situation.[155] If it was implemented, they stood to lose the benefit of their recent electoral successes in the localities. But, outside east UP, most Muslims felt that if the official element was to be squeezed out of local government, then, as Shaikh Zahur Ahmad of Allahabad argued:

[151] J. M. Holms, Secretary, UP Municipal Department, to Secretary, Government of India Education Department, 16 March 1908, Home Public A October 1908, 116–46, NAI.

[152] Opinion of Sir John Hewett, quoted in R. Burn, Chief Secretary, Government of UP, to Secretary, Government of India Education Department, 4 September 1912, Home Educ Municipal A April 1914, 22–31, NAI.

[153] Burn to Commissioners of Divisions, 22 April 1911, *ibid*.

[154] 'Note by the Hon'ble Raja Sir Muhammad Ali Muhammad, Khan Bahadur, of Mahmudabad on Separate Representation of District and Municipal Boards', 18 October 1911, Home Municipal B April 1914, 28, NAI.

[155] This point was made strongly by the Muslim members of the Jaunpur municipal board, Home Educ Municipal A April 1914, 22–31, NAI. Local conditions were also reflected in the comments of the district officers. Those from east UP divisions wrote of communal harmony and argued that separate representation was not necessary. See, for example, the report on Gorakhpur. J. Hope Simpson, District Magistrate, Gorakhpur, to Commissioner, Gorakhpur Division, 14 August 1911, *ibid*. Most officers from west UP, Doab and even Oudh reluctantly conceded that the communities were divided, and, ignoring the recommendations of the Decentralization Commission, wanted government to continue to hold the ring. See, for example, H. C. Ferard, Offg. Commissioner, Agra Division, to Secretary, Government of UP, 21 November 1911; and C. A. Mumford, Chairman, Allahabad Municipal Board, to Commissioner, Allahabad Division, 21 July 1911, *ibid*.

In these circumstances to give preponderant influence to one community would mean grave injustice to the other; and it would be an evil day for India if the mass of any community comes to think that its interests have been left at the mercy of the other and the British Government has in any way deviated from its well established principle of holding the balance even in India. In these circumstances, since it is the majority of votes that decides all questions in municipal and district boards, a community whose members are less than 50 per cent will naturally be at the mercy of the predominating community and this in the absence of the personal *dabao* and influence of the official president means the sacrificing of the interests of the minority to those of the majority. The only solution of such a difficult problem lies in giving equal representation to both the communities or distributing the number of representatives in such a way that if the non-partisan members oted with the Muhammadan members the issue may be decided accordngly.[156]

From this standpoint, separate and equal representation was the only guarantee of the community's security; and throughout 1910 the provincial Muslim League clamoured for it. As the prospect of independence in local government became real, the Muslim demand moved from separate to equal representation.

7. Government and the Hindus concede separate representation to the Muslims, 1915–1916

The government enquiry into separate representation was part of a larger effort to increase non-official participation in local government and make it more efficient. The draft legislation that emerged in 1915 was the product of eight years' work by the civil service compiled in eighty-four fat files; a tribute to bureaucratic activity so mountainous that, when piled up, it reached from floor to ceiling in the UP secretariat record room. The bill was the outstanding achievement of Meston's rule as lieutenant-governor. In July 1915, it was introduced into the provincial council. The bill aimed at removing official influence from the boards, and at separating executive and deliberative functions, but it made no provision for separate representation. Meston discarded Hewett's recommendation that Muslims be given separate representation and a large weighting,[157] because it would 'arouse a storm of

[156] Note by Shaikh Zahur Ahmad, Barrister-at-law, Allahabad, 2 September 1911, *ibid.*

[157] Hewett, basing his policy on the 'Burn Circular', recommended that where Muslims numbered less than one-third of the population they should be given a proportion of elected seats on municipal boards equivalent to half as much again as their proportion of the population; where they accounted for between a third and a

indignation among the Hindus which will do us more harm with them, than good it will do us with the Muhammadans'.[158] As a result, the bill merely contained the provisions of the 1900 Act which had empowered government in particular cases to make rules regarding representation by notification. When the first World War broke out, the UP government was ready to postpone the bill. But it soon realized that the war was raising the level of political aspiration. Fearing that delay might destroy the bill they wanted, the UP government asked Delhi for permission to introduce the legislation as soon as possible.[159] What governed UP politics, and, to a large extent, all-India politics from this moment, was the unbending determination of the UP government to rush its legislation through. This brought Hindu and Muslim attitudes towards the devolution of power to a head.

If government was prepared to set aside the question of separate representation, the communities of the province were not. Most Muslim politicians in the UP were agreed about what they wanted. Their parties had to do less with policy than with factional struggles for power. To their own rough divisions they gave the titles of the 'Young Party' and the 'Old Party'. The 'Young Party' was Aligarh-bred, English-educated and largely professionally employed or unemployed. When Mahomed Ali was interned, Wazir Hasan, a young Lucknow lawyer, became its leader and the Raja of Mahmudabad its main financial support. The 'Old Party', a grouping of aristocratic landlords, successful lawyers and retired government servants, men such as Muzamilullah Khan of Bhikampur, Nawab Abdul Majid, Aftab Ahmad Khan and Viqar ul-Mulk, had no acknowledged leadership. 'Young Party' politicians had hoped for power from the 1909 Councils Act, but had gained nothing. 'Old Party' men monopolized

half of the population, Muslims should have half of the total number of seats; where Muslims were more than half of the population of a town, they should have a percentage of seats equal to their percentages of the population. If implemented, the result would have raised the number of Muslim elected members of boards from 30.3 per cent, the proportion on 1 April 1911, to 46 per cent.

[158] Private note by Sir James Meston, 6 September 1913, Meston Papers, Mss Eur F 136 6, India Office Library, London.

[159] In urging the change of plan, the UP government wrote: 'As you will understand, it is likely to make a great difference to the prospects of passing a workable Bill if we are able to introduce it into Council shortly and to get it through by, say July next. In any case there is likely to be considerable opposition to some of the most necessary provisions; but that opposition will probably be much greater if the consideration of the Bill is postponed long enough for the present vague expectations of radical changes to crystallise.' A. W. Pim, Secretary, Government of UP Financial Department, to L. Porter, Secretary, Government of India Education Department, 24 December 1914, Home Legislative A July 1915, 1–5, NAI.

almost all Muslim seats in the legislative council[160] and dominated all other channels of Muslim representation from the Muslim University movement to the All-India Muslim League. However, in 1912, the 'Young Party' had succeeded in capturing the All-India Muslim League organization at Lucknow, and had set about agitating for further council reforms which, they hoped, would give them control of Muslim politics in the province. They changed the creed of the Muslim League, made overtures to the UP Congress Committee, joined in a Congress agitation over elementary education and took a leading part in pressing for a provincial Executive Council. In November 1915, they threatened to hold the annual Muslim League session at the same time and in the same place as the Congress. 'Old Party' politicians were too disunited to oppose them effectively. But, in spite of their differences, Muslims, 'Young' and 'Old', all agreed on the need for separate representation in municipal government and many of them wanted equal representation.

Hindu politicians with narrow local interests were wary about overtures from the 'Young Party' Muslims. They did not like the provincial concessions which were the price of the Muslim alliance. Stiffened by the warnings of the Arya Samaj and the Hindu Sabha, they prepared to oppose separate representation and those Hindus ready to grant it.[161]

Hindu politicians with provincial and all-India interests saw matters rather differently. The war brought council reforms closer, and the chance of making a common demand with the Muslims brought them nearer still. In the House of Lords, MacDonnell and Curzon had used communal differences to argue against the further devolution of power. The leaders of Indian Muslims lived in the UP, and so the arguments against further reform that were used in the UP might easily be used against reform in India as a whole. If the Muslim condition for supporting municipal reform was separate representation, the Congress

---

[160] Between 1909 and 1912, the following 'Old Party' men sat in the provincial council: Nawab of Rampur, Nawab of Pahasu, Nawab Abdul Majid, Nawab Asadullah Khan, Raja of Jehangirabad, Shaikh Shahid Husain, Munshi Asghar Ali Khan, Aftab Ahmad Khan and Syed Ali Nabi. The last named, at this time, was regarded as an 'Old Party' man although later he veered towards the 'Young Party'.

[161] In 1915, all-India and provincial Hindu Sabhas were formed in the UP in reaction to the possibility of further council reforms and the success of Muslim demands. In April, while the provincial political conference at Gorakhpur demanded self-government after the war but refrained from passing the usual resolution against separate representation, an All-India Hindu Sabha was formed at Hardwar by men from the west UP, many of them Vaishyas and Khattris. In December, while Wazir Hasan in Bombay was turning the joint Hindu-Muslim front into a reality, a provincial Hindu Sabha was formed at Allahabad.

Hindus had to concede it. This was the primary consideration on which negotiations over the municipalities bill were based.

In the legislative council, the Muslim reaction was predictable. They wanted nothing to do with an increase of power in municipal government, unless their share was guaranteed. Outside the council, they stepped up their agitation. On 19 October 1915, Syed Ali Nabi, president of the provincial Muslim League, declared:

that in recent years there has never been such a consensus of opinion among all the Musalmans on any political question as there exists today among them on the question of separate representation on local bodies.[162]

The Hindus, in the beginning, took a larger view of the bill. Members of municipal boards attacked the separation of functions because it reduced their personal powers in local government. They feared that government was using the executive officer, the instrument of separation, to increase rather than diminish its power. This fear lay behind the bulk of the resolutions passed at a conference of non-officials on the bill in September 1915. However, the all-India politicians could not ignore the growth of Muslim agitation. A select committee of the September conference of non-officials headed by Sapru, was prepared to make a concession to the Muslims. It recommended that the Muslims should have a fixed proportion of seats according to the proportion of their population in each town, for which both Hindus and Muslims would vote. Moreover, if this did not satisfy the Muslims, the committee would concede the Muslim demand for weighting; it suggested that the fixed proportion of Muslim seats could be larger than the Muslim proportion of the population in those towns where Muslims formed less than one quarter of the total population.[163]

But this initiative did not spring solely from a desire to compromise. The government had made it clear that it would set up separate electorates by regulation if necessary. Thus, if the bill became law, government might at any time propose such regulations without taking Hindu opinion into account. The Cawnpore Mosque affair had given Hindus some idea of how their rulers reacted to determined Muslim agitation. Since Muslims were so implacable in their demand for electoral privileges and some concessions were inevitable, Hindu politicians felt that they could protect their positions most effectively by conceding

[162] Syed Ali Nabi, President of the UP Muslim League, to Secretary, Government of UP, 19 October 1915, Municipal 1915, 230 E No. 58, UPS.

[163] Representation of the Sapru Committee on the Municipalities Bill, to Secretary, Government of UP Municipal Department, *Leader*, 29 October 1915.

the principle of separate representation in order to have a say in its detailed application.

Meanwhile, a select committee of the legislative council was examining the bill. Among its members were four non-officials; two Kashmiri Brahmins, Motilal Nehru of Allahabad and Jagat Narain Mulla of Lucknow, one Vaishya, Lala Sukhbir Sinha of Muzaffarnagar and one Muslim, Munshi Asghar Ali Khan of Bareilly. The non-officials on this committee were quite happy chipping away at the executive powers of the government, but were chary of having to come to a decision on separate representation. After consulting all-India politicians at an imperial legislative council meeting in Simla,[164] they decided to try to wreck the bill. Led by Motilal Nehru, they asked the government to postpone the bill, arguing that it was impolitic to push through controversial legislation during the war.[165]

The non-official members on the legislative council's select committee reckoned without the government's determination to legislate. Meston had no time for such tricks. 'It is a performance of sheer "funk";' he noted on 22 October, 'and if they refuse to serve on the Select Committee we must hold a meeting of Council and appoint another which will work. It is all nonsense about the measure being controversial.'[166] The lieutenant-governor successfully called their bluff. Having failed to sabotage the bill, the Hindus had to accept the need to compromise. On October 26, the council's committee again went into session. When separate electorates were considered, the Muslim member immediately demanded that the principle be recognized. Motilal Nehru was against separate representation. But he saw that it would have to be conceded if Muslim opinion demanded it. However, Muslims should not be allowed to vote in the general electorates. Nehru did not want the Muslims in the municipalities to have the double advantage they had in the council electorates. Jagat Narain Mulla and Lala Sukhbir Sinha agreed with him. The Sapru committee of the Hindu conference had been prepared only to give Muslims a fixed number of seats in which Hindus as well as Muslims would vote for Muslim representatives; but now the select committee of the legislative council offered a separate electorate excluding Hindus. This was a further concession to the Muslims. But, while the committee members agreed that Nehru's concession should form a substantive part of the bill,

---

[164] Note by Meston 22 October 1915, Municipal 1915, 230 E No. 57, UPS.
[165] Letter from Simla signed by all the non-official members of the Select Committee, to the Secretary, UP Legislative Council, 11 October 1915, *ibid*.
[166] Note by Meston, 22 October 1915, *ibid*.

they could not agree what proportion of representation Muslims should have. Despite Meston's efforts to get agreement, government had to settle for a bill which included separate electorates but left the proportion of Muslim representation unresolved.[167]

Thus the bill came out of the select committee acknowledging the principle of separate representation, although Nehru, Narain and Sinha appended minutes of dissent stating that they still preferred joint electorates with a fixed number of Muslim seats. Since non-officials did not want to leave the division of power and the power to divide in the hands of the government, they were all agreed that a definite numerical formula about Muslim reserved seats would have to be inserted in the bill. But Hindus and Muslims could not agree on what this formula should be. So the bill included no formula. In this unsatisfactory state it was sent to the Government of India.[168]

Delhi reacted slowly and it was not until the second week of March 1916 that Meston had the Government of India's opinion. They approved all the clauses except clause eleven which dealt with separate representation. However, Delhi was prepared to sanction the legislation if the non-official members of the council could arrive at an agreement which was acceptable to government. If no compromise was possible, clause eleven was to be removed and it was promised that the matter would be re-considered after the war.[169] When non-official members of the legislative council met to discuss the situation,[170] Hindus and Muslims took as common ground their acceptance of the principle

[167] Three formulas to settle the proportion of Muslim representation were discussed. Nehru recommended that minorities should have thirty per cent weighting (as it was technically called) in excess of numerical proportion, provided that this in no case resulted in giving them more than one-third of the total number of seats. The Muslim League asked for fifty per cent of the seats, irrespective of the proportion of population. Asghar Ali Khan stood by the suggestion of the Hewett administration that Muslims should have fifty per cent weighting provided it did not result in giving more than fifty per cent of the seats. Compromise proved impossible, although it was generally agreed that moderate Muslim opinion would accept forty per cent weighting with a proviso that this should not result in giving more than forty per cent of the seats. Meston was left frustrated, and reiterated the official position that the matter would be taken up after the war. Based on a note by A. W. Pim, 27 October 1915, Municipal 1915, 230 E No. 62, UPS.
[168] 'Report of the Select Committee on the United Provinces Municipalities Bill', 25 December 1915, *UP Gazette Extraordinary*, 1915.
[169] A. Muddiman, Secretary, Government of India Legislative Department, to Secretary, Government of UP Municipal Department, 10 March 1916, Municipal 1916, 230 E No. 74, UPS.
[170] It was extremely fortunate that the Government of India's reply coincided with a meeting of the legislative council, enabling Meston to call together the non-official members on 13 March 1916 to explain the situation.

I

of separate representation and of separate electoral rolls; but they were not sanguine about the chances of agreeing on the ratio of seats to be reserved for Muslims. But, at the same time, they did not want to go ahead with the bill unless that ratio was prescribed in it. The Hindus were perhaps less insistent on this point; but they felt that since Muslims demanded preferential treatment, the limits of these concessions should be clearly defined. Muslims, on the other hand, were most emphatic; they were against any devolution of power unless their share was guaranteed by law. Government's promise of future legislation on separate representation satisfied neither party.

It was soon evident that no separate representation meant no bill. Government could have forced the bill through the council only in the face of fierce opposition from both communities. It was clear that only a compromise on the number of Muslim seats would save the situation. After much prevarication, the leading men of each community agreed to meet to discuss a formula. On 13 March, Syed Riza Ali suggested that minorities above forty per cent should get no additional seats, that those between twenty-five and forty per cent should have forty per cent of the seats and that those under twenty-five per cent should have a ratio of seats equal to their proportion of the population plus one-third.[171] On the following day, the Hindus agreed to a formula drawn up by Motilal Nehru that was substantially the same as that of Syed Riza Ali, and the Muslims assured Meston that it had their support.[172]

Time was now very short as there was only one more session before

[171] Note by Meston 14 March 1916, Municipal 1915, 230 E Confidential, UPS.

[172] The following was the compromise formula drawn up by Motilal Nehru on 14 March 1916 and included in the final reading of the bill:

1. That the figures representing the proportion of the Mohammedan population within municipal areas be derived from the total population within those areas according to the last census as compared with the whole population within the same areas.

2. That in Municipalities where the Mohammedan population is less than 25 p.c. they may be allowed a weighting of 30 p.c. on their actual number.

3. That in Municipalities where the Mohammedan population is not under 25 p.c. of the total population but under the average arrived at under (1) above they may be allowed such weighting as will raise their number to the said average.

4. That where the proportion of the Mohammedan population is over the said average the number of seats to be given to them shall be in accordance with their ratios to the total population.

5. That where the percentage arrived at under (1), (2), (3) & (4) results in a whole number and a fraction over ½ the number of elected seats attached to the boards be increased by 1— the seat so created to be given to the minority.

6. That the same principles be applied *mutatis mutandis* to non Moslem minorities.

From 'Original note by P. Moti Lal Nehru regarding the terms agreed to at the meeting of Hindus on March 14th. A. Pim 16.5.1916'. In pencil, Municipal 1915, 230 E Confidential, UPS.

the council dissolved. But the lieutenant-governor, having come so far, was not going to lose over the last furlong. On 21 March, Meston wrote to the Government of India stressing that it was of the 'highest importance' that he should know their views before the council met on 29 March, because in April the council went out of office, 'and if the Bill is not passed before then, we should have to begin all our difficulties again with a large number of new members'.[173] Delhi gave its assent in time. On the 29th, the bill was given its final reading. An amendment containing the Nehru formula was moved by the Raja of Jehangirabad and seconded by Sapru. The amendment was passed. Neither the UP government nor the all-India politicians of the province wanted separate representation. Both had agreed to accept it, the former to avoid radical reform in the province, the latter to win it in the country.

8. Separate representation in the UP Municipalities Bill, 1916

By December 1915, separate representation had been conceded to the Muslims in the Municipalities Bill. Its details were set out in the Jehangirabad amendment of March 1916. This was the result of a compromise between the Hindu and Muslim members of the legislative council. The reasons why these politicians supported or opposed the Jehangirabad amendment are significant. They reveal that government always had some men in its pocket; they underline the differences in political attitude between east UP and Oudh and west UP and Doab; they illustrate that politicians in their provincial roles could not ignore municipal or national considerations.

The way men voted on the Jehangirabad amendment shows where members stood on the issue of separate representation; the division on whether the bill should be introduced provides collateral evidence. Tables 2 and 3 set out the vote on both those divisions. On the basis of this and other evidence, Table 4 attempts to list those who were for and those who were against separate representation as it emerged in the bill.

Some council members always supported the government. Three of the nominated Hindus had too much at stake to risk government disfavour: the Maharaja of Benares was keen that government should

---

[173] It was most unusual for a lieutenant-governor to write a letter of this nature; it is an indication of his eagerness to get his legislation through. D-O letter Meston to Muddiman, 21 March 1916, Home Public B September 1916, 70–2, NAI.

Tables 2 and 3—Voting on the introduction of the Municipalities Bill and the Jehangirabad Amendment in the UP Legislative Council, 29 March 1916.

44 men were present: 22 officials, 1 Anglo-Indian non-official and 21 Indian non-officials.[174]

TABLE 2
Voting on the introduction of the Municipalities Bill

For	Against	Present but did not vote
Muslims 6	*Muslims* 1	*Hindus* 7
Syed Abdur Rauf	Syed Karamat Husain	Tej Bahadur Sapru
Syed Riza Ali	*Hindus* 6	Jagat Narain Mulla
Shaikh Shahid Husain	Motilal Nehru	Mahadeo Prasad
Raja of Jehangirabad	Brijnandan Prasad	Balak Ram
Syed Ali Nabi	Gokul Prasad	Narsingh Prasad
Asghar Ali Khan	Bishambhar Nath	Prag Narain Bhargava
Hindus 1	Sukhbir Sinha	Maharaja of Benares
Tara Dat Gairola	Raja Rampal Singh	
Anglo-Indian 1		
Officials 22		
Total 30	7	7

TABLE 3
Voting on the Jehangirabad Amendment[175]

For	Against	Present but did not vote
Muslims 7	*Hindus* 3	*Hindus* 5
Syed Abdur Rauf	Brijnandan Prasad	Mahadeo Prasad
Syed Riza Ali	Sukhbir Sinha	Balak Ram
Shaikh Shahid Husain	Gokul Prasad	Narsingh Prasad
Raja of Jehangirabad		Bishambhar Nath
Syed Ali Nabi		Raja Rampal Singh
Asghar Ali Khan		
Syed Karamat Husain		
Hindus 6		
Tara Dat Gairola		
Prag Narain Bhargava		
Tej Bahadur Sapru		
Jagat Narain Mulla		
Maharaja of Benares		
Motilal Nehru		
Anglo-Indian 1		
Officials 22	3	5
Total 36		

[174] Eight non-official members of the Council did not attend on 29 March 1916: Maharaja of Balrampur, Rana Sheoraj Singh, Rai Shanker Sahai, Raja Kushalpal Singh, Babu Moti Chand, Nawab of Pahasu, Nawab of Rampur and Pandit Sunder Lal.

[175] The Council proceedings do not give a breakdown of the voting on the amendment. The list is based on evidence from the Council debates and newspapers. It is

TABLE 4
Indian Non-officials for and against separate representation in the UP, 1916.

Hindus		Muslims	
For	Against	For	Against
Motilal Nehru (Kashmiri Brahmin)	Brijnandan Prasad (Vaishya)	Syed Karamat Husain	None
Tej Bahadur Sapru (Kashmiri Brahmin)	Sukhbir Sinha (Vaishya)	Syed Abdur Rauf	
Jagat Mulla (Kashmiri Brahmin)	Gokul Prasad (Kayasth)	Syed Riza Ali	
Maharaja of Benares (Bhumihar Brahmin)	Bishambhar Nath† (Vaishya)	Shaikh Shahid Husain	
Tara Dat Gairola (Brahmin)	Raja Rampal Singh† (Rajput)	Raja of Jehangirabad	
Mahadeo Prasad* (Kayasth)		Syed Ali Nabi	
Balak Ram (Kayasth)*		Ashgar Ali Khan	
Narsingh Prasad (Kayasth)*			
Prag Narain Bhargava (Bhargava)			
Total 9	5	7	0

* These three men abstained from voting on both occasions. They have been included as supporters of separate representation because they did not join the agitation against the Jehangirabad amendment. Mahadeo Prasad spoke forcefully for the amendment in Council; Narsingh Prasad knew that it would destroy the Muslim position in Gorakhpur and so enable him to get back into power; Balak Ram had every reason to believe that more Muslims on the Fyzabad board would strengthen his position, although in fact they did not.
† These two abstained from voting on the Jehangirabad amendment. Both voted against the introduction of the bill. They have been included among the opponents of separate representation because both were strong Hindu Sabha men, both agitated against the bill and Rampal Singh presided over the Benares Hindu Conference which was convened specifically to consider how the Jehangirabad amendment might be opposed.

tentative. The Council proceedings record that the voting was thirty-six to three. Twenty-two officials and the Anglo-Indian were certain to vote with the government. The *Leader* states that the Hindus who supported the amendment were five nominated members and Nehru which leaves seven remaining votes, the same as the number of Muslims. We can assume that all seven Muslims voted for the amendment. Three men voted against the amendment. It is again reasonable to assume that these were the three Hindus who spoke against it. This leaves five Hindus in the last column, present but not voting. There is one small problem in this division. Mahadeo Prasad spoke forcefully for the amendment but yet, according to the *Leader*, he abstained from voting for it. *Proceedings of the Council of His Honour the Lieutenant-Governor, United Provinces of Agra and Oudh, assembled for the purpose of making laws and regulations, 1916* [hereafter *UPLC*] (Allahabad, 1917), pp. 178–9 and *Leader*, 14 April 1916.

raise his status, Tara Dat Gairola had been nominated for Kumaon as a favour and Prag Narain Bhargava who owned the Newal Kishore Press had large government contracts. Even officials called poor old Prag Narain a 'dummy'.[176]

The way more independent Hindu members divided over separate representation illustrates the difference in political attitude between east UP and Oudh and west UP and Doab. Six out of nine of those for separate representation came from east UP and Oudh.[177] All were members of service and landed families. Mulla was one of the Kashmiri triumvirate,[178] who were accused of being 'little better than Muhammadans'.[179] He was a typical east UP and Oudh man. He practised at the Lucknow Bar with Muslim League leaders. He was given civil and criminal work by the Muslim rajas of Mahmudabad and Jehangirabad.[180] He joined, with his Golaganj neighbour, the Nawab of Shish Mahal, in being the patron of Lucknow's most celebrated annual mushaira. Interest and conviction led him to adopt a supra-communal attitude.

Four out of five of those who opposed separate representation came from west UP and Doab.[181] All were strictly provincial politicians, and leading members of the Hindu Sabha. Three were connected with trade or money-lending. Their spokesman, Brijnandan Prasad of Moradabad, did all he could, as Meston complained, to 'wreck' the bill and 'after each of his attacks on the various principles of the Bill had also failed, one after the other, he followed up with amendments of paragraphs and sub clauses. . . .'[182] He poured scorn on the naivety of 'My nationalist friends [who] are willing to make every concession in the pious hope of having a glimpse, distant and hazy though it be, of the millennium when separation will lead to compact union.'[183] Separate representation, 'if allowed to grow will make local self-government impossible . . . will make majorities and minorities

---

[176] H. V. Lovett to Pim, 20 June 1914, Municipal 1915, 230 E, UPS.

[177] These six were: Jagat Narain Mulla, Prag Narain Bhargava, Maharaja of Benares, Mahadeo Prasad, Balak Ram and Narsingh Prasad.

[178] Sapru and Nehru were its other two members.

[179] Extract from the diary of the Superintendent of Police, Cawnpore, 8 April 1916, Municipal 1915, 230 E No. 80, UPS.

[180] So friendly was Mulla with the Mahmudabad family that he witnessed the will of Raja Mahomed Ali Mahomed.

[181] These were Brijnandan Prasad, Sukhbir Sinha, Bishambhar Nath and Gokul Prasad. Gokul Prasad represented Benares division but practised in the High Court and lived at Allahabad which was the site of his consuming interest, the Kayasth Pathshala.

[182] *Pioneer* (Allahabad), 3 April 1916.   [183] *UPLC 1916*, p. 167.

permanent and will lead to bigots and extremists being returned on both sides. The party in power will continue in power, and being imbued with communal fanaticism will be tempted to tyrannize over the other.'[184] Separate representation had 'sprung up like a noxious weed in the fair garden of national unity and mutual goodwill, marring and stunting the growth of beautiful and refreshing flowers of national advancement.'[185] Brijnandan Prasad ignored the fact that Hindus themselves, only seventeen years earlier, had wanted to plant the 'noxious weed' in Moradabad.[186] His attitude was strictly communal.

Local considerations dictated reactions to separate representation just as they had driven Muslims to demand it. Their importance was increased because elections for a new council were about to be held. In west UP and Doab, the Jehangirabad amendment reduced Hindu representation in municipalities; in Sukhbir Sinha's Muzaffarnagar, Bishambhar Nath's Cawnpore, and Gokul Prasad's Allahabad, Hindus lost seats. In Moradabad the Muslims gained an unshakable majority; the bitterest exchanges in council were between the two members from this city, Brijnandan Prasad and Riza Ali. In east UP and Oudh, the effect of the amendment was not uniform. In Fyzabad, Balak Ram no doubt thought that more Muslims on the municipal board would bring him security. In Gorakhpur, the Muslim majority was destroyed; fewer Muslims meant more power for Narsingh Prasad, who depended on a straight Kayasth vote.[187] In Rampal Singh's case the desire to play a provincial role tempered the force of local considerations. This Oudh talukdar, who was a leading member of the provincial Hindu Sabha, opposed separate representation. But generally the needs of local politics were paramount throughout the provinces.

Those who tried to ignore these needs found themselves in trouble. Sapru and Nehru were politicians with all-India aspirations. Meston's determination to force through the municipalities legislation threatened Hindu-Muslim unity in the UP and put the growing Congress-League alliance in jeopardy. To preserve this all-India alliance, they were willing to make concessions to Muslims in the UP. But by so doing, Sapru and Nehru risked their political existence in the province.

[184] UPLC, 1916, p. 231.   [185] Ibid., p. 229.
[186] Minute by Babu Brijnandan Prasad, vice-chairman of Moradabad municipal board, 28 February 1898, Municipal A October 1898, 92 f, UPS; J. L. Hill, 'Congress and Representative Institutions', p. 131.
[187] Gorakhpur Kayasths were divided by faction. One group led by Ram Garib operated with Muslims in municipal politics, the other of which Narsingh Prasad was an adherent consisted only of Kayasths.

Sapru had no interest in municipal politics. His political base was
the province and his concern was for all India. Supporting the Jehangirabad amendment in the Council, he stressed the importance of all-
India considerations. '. . . the evolution of India to higher and freer
political institutions, depends . . . wholly, upon a satisfactory re-
adjustment of inter-communal relations'. He continued, 'were it not
that I believed in and hoped for higher things to come; were it not
that I hoped that we are not going to rest content with merely local
self-government, I should not be so willing to accept an amendment
which I know is not approved by my friend . . . Brijnandan Prasad.'[188]
Sapru's willingness to sacrifice Hindu municipal seats on the altar
of all-India political progress did not go down well. He was burned
in effigy[189] and it seemed so certain that the Hindu Council members would take revenge by refusing to elect him to the imperial
legislative council that the lieutenant-governor offered to nominate
him.[190]

Nehru, however, was closely tied to a municipal base. Only by extraordinary contortions could he match principle with survival. Nehru
and many members of his family sat on the Allahabad municipal board
and he hoped to be elected to the new legislative council from it. But in
Allahabad communal relations were always strained. So Motilal
Nehru had to tread warily. In the select committee of the legislative
council, he seemed willing to accept the Muslim claim to have more
municipal seats than their population warranted. Two months later,
he changed his stand. He tabled an amendment that either the separate
representation clause should be omitted or that the proportion of
elected seats for Muslims should be no larger than the proportion of
their population.[191] A month later, at the 14 March meeting, he again
reversed his position. He came out in support of compromise by now
offering the Muslims a larger proportion of municipal seats than they
had ever been offered before. In council, he continued his double game.
He was the only Hindu who both voted against the moving of the bill
and yet supported the Jehangirabad amendment. He betrayed his

[188] *UPLC, 1916,* pp. 217–18.
[189] Sapru and Mulla were burned in effigy in Lucknow. CID Memo No. 3304
Allahabad 17 April 1916, Municipal 1915, 230 E No. 80, UPS.
[190] Meston to Sapru, 8 April 1916, GAD 1916, 222, UPS. In making this offer,
Meston was rewarding Sapru for the stand he had taken. It is clear from the correspondence that passed between them in the days from the March 14 agreement to the
Council debate that Meston was relying on Sapru to bring recalcitrant Hindus
into line.
[191] Note for Meston by A. W. Pim, 15 February 1916, Municipal 1915, 230 E
Confidential, UPS.

uneasiness in correspondence with his son.[192] The ambivalence of his position was summarized in a letter to the *Indian Daily Telegraph*. In it, he wrote about the need for political union with advanced Muslims and stood by the principles of his formula, but he protested against the details of its application in Allahabad.[193]

The Muslims accepted the terms of the Jehangirabad amendment. But not all Muslims were equally keen to do so. The great drive for separate representation came from the Muslims of the west UP and Doab, Asghar Ali Khan, Riza Ali and Ali Nabi. They supported the amendment; it greatly improved the Muslim position in their municipalities. Local advantages, however, were not the only considerations. By early 1916, further devolution to the provinces had become a distinct possibility. Both the Congress and the All-India Muslim League were known to be preparing reform schemes. The crucial point of negotiation between the two organizations was likely to be separate representation. With this in mind, no doubt, those hostile to the League's move towards Congress, such as Abdur Rauf and Karamat Husain, called for equal representation; 'this is a great concession they [his Muslim colleagues on the council] have made', Rauf declared. The Jehangirabad amendment 'certainly falls much below my expectation, . . .'[194] 'Young Party' men such as Riza Ali and Ali Nabi, on the other hand, were keen that the Congress and League should agree. For them the Jehangirabad compromise on Muslim representation was of immense importance for the negotiations that were to take place later in the year at Lucknow. It showed that Congress leaders were prepared to make generous concessions in order to gain Muslim support for devolution. It enabled UP Muslims, the creators of the League's rapprochement with the Congress, to support a united demand for Indian political reform.

[192] Motilal to Jawaharlal Nehru, 20 July 1915, 29 March 1916 and 30 March 1916, Nehru Papers, NMM.

[193] Motilal Nehru to Editor, *Indian Daily Telegraph* (Lucknow), published 30 August 1916. The *Leader* refused to publish this statement of Nehru's position, so, with the help of 'Young Party' leader Wazir Hasan, it was published in the Lucknow paper. Municipal 1915, 230 E No. 83, UPS.

[194] *UPLC, 1916*, p. 229.

Non-cooperation and Council Entry, 1919 to 1920

RICHARD GORDON

GANDHI's passive resistance campaigns in South Africa and his satyagraha agitation against the Rowlatt Bills in 1919 were conceived in wholly different circumstances; and the non-cooperation programme of 1920 was designed to meet conditions which were different again. To regard the non-cooperation movement simply as the logical consequence of the 1919 satyagraha and as the political application of Gandhi's ideology is to fail to appreciate just how experimental and uncertain Gandhi's politics were during this period. His ideas could and did change rapidly; he maintained a flexible approach. Consequently he was able to take advantage of an uncertain and confused political situation. During 1919 most politicians, both established men and ambitious parvenus, were driven by the tides of discontent into uncharted waters as they strove to retain or to improve their position. This was the context within which Gandhi tried to find a following and a policy by which he could unite political India under his leadership.

In 1919 Gandhi still lacked a firm and well-organized base outside his native Gujarat. He had some support in the Bombay branch of Mrs Besant's All-India Home Rule League which he used for his satyagraha. But Gandhi did not control any organization with truly all-India connections. During 1919 Gandhi tried to build an organized following outside and independent of the established associations, such as the Home Rule Leagues and the Congress. But when satyagraha failed and the Satyagraha Sabhas swiftly collapsed after their inconclusive foray into Punjab, Gandhi found his standing as a political leader with a rational policy much reduced. Between August 1919 and the middle of 1920 Gandhi gradually altered his strategy to recoup his losses and to regain his prestige. To do this he had to place less emphasis on building up his own political organization and more on working inside established political bodies: in particular the Home Rule League and the Central Khilafat Committee. In September 1920 at Calcutta Gandhi captured the Congress. He succeeded in doing this by a deliberately organized campaign inside the framework of conventional politics and not as the apostle of a new and revolutionary order.

The Satyagraha Sabhas had been first formed in the early months of 1919. They began as offshoots of the Bombay city branch of the All-India Home Rule League. Their strength came from Home Rule League members in Bombay city and Gujarat; outside these places, the Sabhas received little support.[1] The Deccan Nationalists of Tilak's camp wanted to have nothing to do with the 1919 satyagraha. In upper India and Bengal, few leaders were prepared to endorse it fully. In Allahabad, Motilal Nehru refused to associate himself with the local Satyagraha Sabha, and in March he was pointedly absent from a public meeting to welcome Gandhi to the city.[2] At the Bengal Provincial Conference in April, C. R. Das tried and failed to rush through a resolution committing the conference to full support of satyagraha, including passive resistance and civil disobedience.[3] Some influential Nationalist leaders in Madras were prepared to endorse both stages of the satyagraha pledge in principle, but they showed little inclination to do so in practice.[4] Nationalist leaders in the major provinces were cautious, taking at most a nominal part in the general hartal of 6 April.[5] The hartal was a time-honoured technique in Indian politics; participating in it did not require any great commitment to the more stringent provisions of Gandhi's satyagraha programme or support for the larger issues which Gandhi was trying to raise. Once disturbances broke out in Delhi and Punjab in April 1919, the Nationalists hastily withdrew their conditional support for a limited satyagraha.

The reason why the Nationalists were so lukewarm about the satyagraha movement had little to do with their opinions about Gandhi's aims and objectives. Rather it had to do with their uncertainty about the fate of the reforms scheme. The Government of India Act of 1919 was a long time in the making. It did not take its final shape until June 1920. In 1918, the Montagu-Chelmsford Report had laid down the broad principles which were to form the basis of the Act, but the Southborough Committee was left to work out its details. The committee's recommendations were incorporated in a bill which a Joint Committee of the Houses of Parliament considered before it became

---

[1] In March 1919, of 600 signatories to the satyagraha pledge, 369 were members of the Bombay city Home Rule League and 120 were from Kaira district of Gujarat. Together these accounted for 81.5 per cent of the total. The rest of India was represented by only 111 signatures. Home Poll D April 1919, 48, National Archives of India, New Delhi [NAI].

[2] *Leader*, 13 March 1919.

[3] Das could not even carry his own supporters. They threatened to revolt and he was forced to amend his resolution. Home Poll B June 1919, 494–97, NAI.

[4] Home Poll D July 1919, 46–47, NAI.   [5] *Leader*, 8 April 1919.

law. At every stage of this process a variety of groups and interests, ranging from the simple to the sophisticated, lobbied government for favourable concessions under the new order. The visit of the Secretary of State and the sittings of the Southborough Committee in India, and the meeting of the Joint Parliamentary Committee in Westminster were all attended by carefully arranged delegations of Indian opinion and interest. However, the Government of India retained a good deal of latitude in the framing of the Rules and Regulations under the Act, in regard both to questions not settled by the Joint Committee (such as the representation of non-Brahmins in Madras and Maharashtra), and to the final settlement of the constitution of the legislative councils and the drawing up of the electoral rolls.

In 1919, the Indian National Congress was divided over the reforms, making it easier for Gandhi to intervene. The factions could not agree on what measure of responsible government would make the reforms acceptable. What was at issue was not advance at the centre but autonomy in the provinces. Politics at this time were governed by the particular circumstances in each of the provinces. Congress politicians were influenced by the probabilities of their coming to power under the reforms. Three broad all-India alliances emerged. The largest faction was led by B. G. Tilak of Poona and C. R. Das of Calcutta. It was loosely named Nationalist and was associated with Tilak's Home Rule League. The second faction was led by Mrs Besant. It was organized through the Theosophical Society, and by mid-1919 most of its supporters were theosophists.[6] The third faction consisted of the Moderates who had lost control of the Congress in 1917 and 1918 to the Nationalists and who had then seceded from it to form the various Liberal Associations. The Nationalists were strongest in Maharashtra and Bengal, but after the Besant Home Rule League split, they gained some support in the UP from Motilal Nehru's party and from that of S. Kasturi Ranga Iyengar in Madras. Nehru and Iyengar had parted with Besant over the demand for provincial autonomy and the extension of agitation among peasants and workers.[7] Unlike Mrs Besant or the Liberals, the Nationalists were ready to agitate and to form trade unions and peasant organizations to demand full provincial autonomy. The Nationalists in Madras formed a Madras Nationalist party and declared for satyagraha immediately after breaking with Mrs Besant.[8]

[6] See H. Owen, 'Towards Nation-wide Organisation and Agitation: The Home Rule Leagues, 1915-18', in D. A. Low (ed.) *Soundings in Modern South Asian History* (London, 1968), pp. 172-3.

[7] Home Poll D August 1918, 28, NAI.

[8] Home Poll D March 1919, 16-17; April 1919, 48, NAI.

The satyagraha against the Rowlatt Bills was launched when it seemed that Conservative opinion in England, and special interests such as the non-Brahmins in India, would succeed in whittling down the reforms.[9] By giving conditional support to passive resistance, the Nationalists hoped to discourage Government from succumbing to diehard pressures.

The Satyagraha Sabha, the main organization behind the Rowlatt agitation was dominated, in effect, by a small clique of Bombay merchants who were the backbone of the city's branch of the All-India Home Rule League.[10] Umer Sobhani, a member of an influential Memon family in Bombay, Jamnadas Dwarkadas, and L. R. Tairsee were among the members of the Sabha active in the speculative commercial boom which preoccupied Bombay throughout 1919. Sobhani was trying to corner the Bombay cotton market by the technique of taking over established companies and forming new ones. Sobhani, with Jamnadas Dwarkadas and Shankerlal Banker, had galvanised Bombay city politics in the aftermath of the industrial boom of the war years. As L. R. Tairsee witnessed, Sobhani was the 'motive power and the cheque book of the Home Rule movement.'[11] It was this group who first approached Gandhi to lead the agitation against the Rowlatt Bills. The campaign was conceived without consulting any of the major political leaders in other provinces, and without much thought about how the campaign was to be run. The central meetings of the Satyagraha Sabha in Bombay were attended mainly by men from the city and Gujarat. Outside Bombay, the only significant support came from the small group of advanced politicians in Allahabad such as Sunderlal Srivastava, a Kayastha journalist and a leader of the young party in 1907, and Jawaharlal Nehru, both inexperienced and relatively unimportant politicians.[12] With the exception of C. Rajagopalachari of Madras, none of the major Nationalist leaders took part in the proceedings of the Central Satyagraha Sabha.

It is difficult to resist the conclusion that in 1919 Gandhi had no definite political intentions. He was indecisive and hesitant, and reluctant to push his chosen methods to their conclusion. In any case, there was so little agreement about these even among his supporters that Gandhi was content to make it appear as though he had been

[9] *Leader*, 13 April 1919.
[10] The committee included Gandhi, Horniman, Dr Sathaye, Shankerlal Banker, Umer Sobhani, Mrs Naidu, Jamnadas Dwarkadas, Manu Subhedar, a Parsi merchant, Hansraj Thackersey and Mrs A. Gokhale. *Ibid.*, 5 March 1919.
[11] *Bombay Chronicle*, 7 July 1926.   [12] Home Poll D August 1919, 50, NAI.

overwhelmed by events. When Gandhi called off the satyagraha after violence broke out in Punjab he made use of a technique which he was to deploy effectively time and again in later years. This was the device of cloaking essentially practical decisions in a parade of moral scruples. Interestingly enough, Gandhi made no attempt to involve the Congress in the satyagraha movement. Unofficially it was organized by the Home Rule Leagues, and by the Bombay city branch at that. However, between May and August of 1919, Gandhi was faced by a split in the Bombay city Home Rule League, and confusion in his own ranks. He was presented with the alternatives of losing control over the Bombay Home Rule League or of abandoning the satyagraha. When Gandhi announced his intention to go ahead with the campaign in May by courting arrest through civil disobedience in Punjab, several of his influential followers began to dissociate themselves from the campaign. In the final week of May, at least twelve members of the executive committee of the Satyagraha Sabha, including Jamnadas Dwarkadas and some of his fellow theosophists, and over a hundred ordinary members had resigned.[13] Every day another two or three members resigned, and after 26 July the Satyagraha Sabha did not meet again. A similar pattern was repeated in upper India, and in Punjab the situation was characterized by utter disarray and Gandhi's loss of his erstwhile supporters. Late in May 1919, Swami Shradhananda, who had been organizing a vigorous campaign to involve the Arya Samaj in the agitation,[14] publicly dismissed Gandhi's scheme as unpractical and incapable of being implemented without provoking a mass upheaval.[15]

Meanwhile, throughout India the divisions between the more advanced party and the followers of Mrs Besant were growing more acute. The split finally occurred in May 1919 when Besant's All-India Home Rule League broke up, and Besant herself was forced out of the League and prevented from going to England as its representative before the Joint Committee of Parliament.[16] With the consequent departure of the theosophists the All-India Home Rule League passed into the hands of the anti-Besant factions led by M. A. Jinnah in Bombay, S. Kasturi Ranga Iyengar in Madras and Motilal Nehru in the UP.[17]

By June 1919 Gandhi was a somewhat isolated figure on the national scene. In many quarters he was regarded as a harmless crank. His

[13] Home Poll D August 1919, 50, NAI.
[14] CID Report, 23 June 1919. Home Poll D June 1919, 701–704, NAI.
[15] *Leader*, 30 May 1919.   [16] *Ibid.*, 6 May 1919.   [17] *Ibid.*, 8 May 1919.

campaign had made no impact on Bengal and Maharashtra (including Berar and the Marathi districts of the Central Provinces). It had not won the support of the leaders of the advanced Nationalist party in the Congress organization in those regions which were thought to be the most prepared for full provincial autonomy. In fact, the satyagraha agitation had followed closely the organizational connections built up by the All-India Home Rule League with its branches in the towns of Gujarat and Sind, Bombay, Madras city, in Allahabad and Patna—all urban centres in regions which had less political and cultural homogeneity than Bengal or Maharashtra. As a Gujarati, based in Bombay city, Gandhi fell naturally into the pattern of politics which the All-India Home Rule League had established. As Hugh Owen has observed, Gandhi used the League's membership as the basis of his agitation.[18]

When satyagraha collapsed Gandhi found himself in an embarrassing position. Between May and June 1919 he was anxiously searching for new causes to extricate him from it. On 25 June he launched a Swadeshi Sabha in Bombay urging its adherents to take a swadeshi vow to boycott all foreign goods, especially cloth.[19] With more lasting consequences, however, Gandhi now began to consider the possibility of an alliance with the Khilafat movement. On 18 August 1919, at a conference sponsored by the Bombay Khilafat Committee, Gandhi, the only prominent Hindu to attend the gathering, associated himself directly with the Muslim demands about the Khalifa. He used the occasion to chastise the Khilafat Committee for its lack of direction and precise aims. With the moral support of tens of thousands of Hindus, he urged, the Muslims could dictate their own terms to Government. Gandhi followed up his rallying cry to the conference with an article in *Young India* calling on the Khilafat Committee to make their demands clear and unambiguous.[20] Having failed to carry the Home Rule Leagues with him in his Rowlatt Bills agitation, Gandhi turned his full attention to the Khilafat question and offered to construct a coherent political organization out of the loose and conflicting strands of Muslim opinion that were gathering around the Khilafat.

The reaction to the Lucknow Pact in 1916 had shown how large the differences were between Muslims in the different provinces. Under the pact, the Muslim minorities in the UP, Bombay and Madras did

[18] Owen, 'The Home Rule Leagues', in Low (ed.), *Soundings*, p. 184.
[19] *Leader*, 25 June 1919.
[20] Home Poll D November 1919, 15, NAI.

well, but the Muslim majorities in Punjab and Bengal did badly.[21] The Muslim League in Punjab and Bengal consequently refused to ratify the Pact, and protested against the sacrifice of their interests to those of Muslims in Bombay and the UP.[22] But concerns further from home were also agitating Indian Muslims.[23] Between 1916 and 1920 the twin streams of religious revivalism and the new enthusiasm for politics coalesced in an agitation for the preservation of the secular and religious status of the Khalifa, overwhelming the Muslim League. In September 1919 the Central Khilafat Committee was formed at Lucknow. With the Congress this Committee dominated Indian politics between 1919 and 1923.

Though in retrospect the Khilafat movement appears as an emotional and religious upheaval, the political origins of the campaign were fitful, and rent with the differences and jealousies that riddled the Muslim community. In 1919 the first formal Khilafat Committee was set up in Bombay by a group of rich merchants anxious to protect the Holy Places, for which the Khalifa had become a potent symbol.[24] This Committee had little connection with the neo-political religious bodies in north India, such as the Khuddam-i-Kaaba of Abdul Bari of Lucknow. From the beginning, the Khilafat issue was connected with factional squabbles in the Muslim League, particularly in Punjab, UP and Delhi. In December 1918 the 11th Annual Session of the League was held at Delhi. At this meeting the extremist party in the League allied with those ulama who, under the lead of Abdul Bari, were to form the Jamiat-ul Ulama-i-Hind to press the claims of the Khalifa in the League, in an effort to wrest control of the League from the Raja of Mahmudabad's faction.[25] The radicals held a special meeting of welcome for the ulama in an effort to show that they had the backing of the Muslim theologians, but it was estimated that only 10 were present at the League session.[26] When the extremist party

[21] Under the terms agreed at Lucknow, Bengali Muslims, with 52.6 per cent of the population of the province, were allowed 40 per cent of the seats on the Bengal Council, while Bombay Muslims, with 20.4 per cent of the population (Sind included) were to get 33.3 per cent of the seats and UP Muslims, accounting for 14 per cent of the provinces' population, were to have 30 per cent of UP Council places.

[22] Nawab Syed Ali Chaudhury, zamindar and President, Central National Muhammedan Association, Bengal, to S. P. O'Donnell, Reforms Commissioner, 28 January 1920. Home Reforms Office Franchise B January 1920, 244–45, NAI.

[23] For a personal, colourful, account of the effect of Turkey's entry into the war see Chaudhury Khaliquzzaman, *Pathway to Pakistan* (Lahore, 1961), pp. 20–35.

[24] Home Poll D August 1919, 51, NAI.

[25] CID Weekly Report, 18 January 1919. Home Poll D January 1919, 160–3, NAI.

[26] *Ibid.*

K

failed to win the League, which in any event was ill-suited for popular agitation about the Khalifa, the Central Khilafat Committee was formed at Lucknow in September 1919.

Gandhi's public support had a dramatic effect on the Khilafat cause.[27] Hitherto it had been an amorphous campaign within the Muslim League, but now it emerged to all-India significance. The timing of Gandhi's decision to take up the Muslim cause is significant. When he appeared in Bombay in August 1919 championing the Khilafat cause, satyagraha had just collapsed and the Khilafat issue showed distinct signs of developing into an India-wide agitation. The Bombay Khilafat Committee had taken great pains to get support from upper India, and from Abdul Bari in particular. Later in September the Bombay meeting was followed by a larger conference at Lucknow, when the Central Khilafat Committee was formally launched.[28] However, the Committee was torn by rivalries between Bombay and north India for control of the movement. Gandhi was mainly responsible for seeing that the agitation got off the ground and was not dissipated in ineffectual protest and intrigue.

As soon as the Central Khilafat Committee decided to call for a hartal on 1 November, Khilafat day, Gandhi struck swiftly. He artfully suggested that Muslims should abstain from the peace celebrations.[29] The Central Committee did not want to go so far, but pressure from the ulama in north India forced a Khilafat Conference to endorse Gandhi's proposals for the boycott. The conference, held in Delhi late in November, was dominated by delegates from the UP. They pressed for total boycott and authorized the ulama to draw up a fatwa prohibiting Muslims from participating in the peace celebrations.[30] The ulama and the north had come to play an increasingly important role in the Central Khilafat Committee. An attempt was made to transfer the headquarters of the Committee from Bombay to Delhi or Lucknow. But if north India was the power-house of the movement, Bombay was still the treasury. It was Bombay's superior financial resources and the important merchant influence in the Central Khilafat

[27] This was not the first time that Gandhi had associated with Muslims. Soon after his return from South Africa he had made contact with Muslim leaders in north India. In 1918 he had won the warm approval of Abdul Bari by writing to the Viceroy in support of Muslim claims about the Khalifa. He maintained contact with the Ali brothers, even during their internment. Home Poll D July 1918, 9; CID Report, 16 June 1919. Home Poll D June 1919, 701–04, NAI.

[28] Fortnightly Report [FR] Bombay and UP, September 11 1919. Home Poll D November 1919, 15, NAI.

[29] FR Bombay, 1 November 1919. Home Poll D January 1920, 5, NAI.

[30] FR Delhi, 11 November 1919. *Ibid.*

Committee that helped Gandhi to keep the headquarters of the movement in Bombay and to tone down the boycott resolutions.[31] The President of the Khilafat Committee, Chhotani, a rich Memon merchant who had made a fortune in war contracts, not only paid for the Khilafat Deputation to England but also financed much of the agitation in upper India.[32] Bombay city retained effective control of the Executive Committee and benefited under the new constitution adopted in February 1920: Bombay city was given fifty-four places on the Committee compared with twenty for Sind, twenty-five for Bengal, fifteen for Madras, and eighty-six for the rest of India. Moreover, with the exception of the secretary, Shaukat Ali, the Executive Committee was drawn entirely from Bombay city.[33]

Between November 1919 and March 1920, Gandhi restrained the more forward elements which threatened to pull the movement apart and to lead to violence, introduced stronger central control from Bombay, and evolved a uniform policy for the Khilafat Committee. He did this by avoiding any hasty action or commitments. As in the satyagraha campaign he organized all-India hartals and demonstrations, designed to unify the movement and to keep a tight control over it. This allowed him to play for time, since it was still uncertain where the agitation would lead. His counsels of moderation to the Khilafat leaders were also designed to attract Hindu support. Although they sympathized in public, most Hindu leaders were reluctant to associate themselves with what they considered to be a factitious agitation, bearing little relation to their immediate concern with the reforms. The evolution of Gandhi's final programme of non-cooperation was intimately associated with his attempt to link his Muslim support with a new following in the Home Rule League and, more particularly, the Congress.

The first major step in this campaign was the publication of Gandhi's manifesto on the Khilafat on 7 March 1920. For the first time he urged the adoption of non-cooperation if the minimum Muslim demands were not met.[34] Although appealing for Hindu support, he said little about the precise programme of non-cooperation he envisaged.

[31] FR Bombay 11 November 1919. *Ibid.*
[32] FR Bombay, 1 February 1920. Home Poll D July 1920, 88, NAI.
[33] The membership of the Committee was also predominantly Sunni. Of 70 members of the Subjects' Committee at the February conference only 1 was a Shia, 3 Borahs and 2 Khojas, while the remainder were Sunnis, save for 2 Hindus. FR Bombay, 11 February 1920. Home Poll D July 1920, 89, NAI.
[34] *Collected Works of Mahatma Gandhi* [*CWG*], XVII (Ahmadabad, 1965), pp. 73–6.

The timing of the manifesto was important. It came immediately
after the Calcutta Conference of the Khilafat Committee which had
passed resolutions on total boycott of which Gandhi disapproved.[35]
Again Gandhi appeared to be taking the initiative boldly when in
fact he was forced to move in order to contain the violence threatened
by the Calcutta resolutions. Later in March 1920, at a joint Hindu-
Muslim leaders' conference in Delhi, he was faced with Abdul Bari's
wild demand for immediate jehad and hijrat. But Gandhi succeeded
in getting the matter shelved. A subcommittee of five was appointed
to draw up a plan of action in case the Khilafat demands were not
met by the Government.[36] Gandhi's appeals were essentially practical.
He stressed that he opposed violence because of its inherent impracticability in Indian conditions. 'They had no weapons', he warned,
'and were weak. If they killed one white man, 2000 Indians will be
killed in return.'[37] Thus, the conference was inconclusive. Most of the
Hindu leaders present followed Madan Mohan Malaviya's lead.[38]
He spoke for an hour, an unusually short speech for him, opposing the
movement. Lajpat Rai alone was sympathetic. He urged the delegates
to fall back on the tried methods of the swadeshi period. His 'views
were very much liked as he was more practical than others', and he
was made a member of the subcommittee.[39]

An important part of Gandhi's strategy was to win the support of
that loosely allied group of politicians in upper India who formed the
political core of the Hindu Mahasabha. Just as he had flirted with north
India Muslim leaders upon his return from South Africa, so Gandhi
had been anxious to make himself acceptable to the Hindu religious
leadership of the UP and Punjab. In 1915 he had attended the Kumbh
Parva in Hardwar and he was prominent at the meeting at which the
Mahasabha was formed.[40] By 1916 he had won a reputation as a supporter of the various associations pressing for Hindi to be recognized as
the *lingua franca* of India. At the Lucknow Congress in December 1916 he
presided over the first 'All India One Script and One Language
Conference'.[41] In 1919 he became President of a subcommittee of the
Hindi Sahitya Sammelan. This association was liberally financed by

[35] FR Bombay 1 March 1920. Home Poll D July 1920, 90, NAI.
[36] Home Poll D April 1920, 4, NAI.   [37] *Ibid.*
[38] Gandhi, M. M. Malaviya, Tilak, Khaparde, Lajpat Rai, V. J. Patel, C. P.
Ramaswami Iyer, Lala Harkishenlal and the Hon'ble Mr Chanda. *Ibid.*
[39] The members were: Gandhi, Lala Lajpat Rai, Hakim Ajmal Khan, Shaukat
Ali and Maulana Abul Kalam Azad. *Ibid.*
[40] Home Poll File 40 of 1925, NAI.
[41] *Leader*, 6 January 1917.

the Marwari communities of Bombay and Calcutta,[42] and worked to popularize Hindi in the Bombay and Madras Presidencies.[43] With characteristic judiciousness, Gandhi had allied himself with movements which were becoming increasingly important in Indian politics.

At the Amritsar Congress in December 1919, Gandhi's alliance with Malaviya, the grand old man of Hindustani revivalism, enabled north Indian interests to challenge the old dominance of Bengal and Maharashtra, represented by Das and Tilak. Indeed, the *Leader* went so far as to describe the Amritsar Congress as a joint meeting of the Hindi Sahitya Sammelan and the Urdu Conference.[44] This showed how significant Gandhi's bid for support from both the Hindus and Muslims of upper India had become.

Gandhi deliberately ignored the Nationalist leaders who had come to power in the Congress with the rise of the Home Rule movement and the secession of the Liberals. Ever since they had been opposing counsel in the Dumraon case in Bihar, Motilal Nehru and C. R. Das had resented Gandhi's independent line. In February 1920, Motilal wrote to his son:

That Gandhiji is going to take up an attitude not in complete accord with Congress resolutions is fairly clear. Our only grievance is that while he has evidently taken Shastri and Malaviya into his confidence he has left us severely alone. It will then be for us to consider whether we shall take it for our guide or not.[45]

In an earlier letter, Nehru had warned that the general drift of Gandhi's policy statements meant trouble, and he told Das that 'we must be prepared for a big tussle'.[46] But at this stage, Gandhi's aims were so uncertain that Nehru was contemplating a compromise with the Government.[47] This was a view shared generally by the Nationalists, and by Tilak in particular who barely concealed his contempt for Gandhi's crankiness and the impracticability of his programme. As late as June 1920, Tilak complained to V. J. Patel that the Punjab troubles had been neglected as a possible 'lever to work up the British people for the reforms', the blame for which he attributed to Gandhi and Malaviya. 'As for myself,' he continued,

I do not think we can do much here unless Malaviya and Gandhi are prepared to help us. They are the men on the Punjab Committee who should have taken the work in right earnest. Not only would they not do it but they

[42] *Ibid.*, 16 June 1920.   [43] *Ibid.*, 24 April 1919.   [44] *Ibid.*, 8 January 1920.
[45] Motilal to Jawaharlal, 29 February 1920. Nehru Papers, Nehru Memorial Museum, New Delhi [NMM].
[46] Motilal to Jawaharlal, 27 February 1920. Nehru Papers, NMM.   [47] *Ibid.*

do not much value foreign agitation as you know. Moderates are what you know. . . .[48]

Yet the Nationalists misjudged Gandhi. This was to be a crucially important factor at Calcutta in September 1920 when he took most of them completely by surprise.

On 28 April 1920, Gandhi announced that he had joined the All-India Home Rule League which had ejected Mrs Besant so unceremoniously in July 1919. Gandhi told the Press that he was attempting to broaden the basis of his support and to provide himself with an additional organization to the Khilafat Committee. To free himself from his dependence upon the latter, Gandhi tried to gain control of the Home Rule League, and announced a programme calculated to win him wider support. In his programme, Gandhi referred specifically to swadeshi, Hindu-Muslim unity over the Khilafat, the adoption of Hindustani as the *lingua franca* of India, the reorganization of the provinces on the basis of language, and the abolition of untouchability.[49] The manifesto was a daring move to capitalize on underground political movements in the Congress. For the growing importance of north India coincided with the growth of separatist movements. They were particularly strong in the old Presidencies. In Gujarat and Sind in Bombay Presidency, in Kerala and Andhra in Madras Presidency, and in the Karnatak, submerged linguistic groups challenged the dominance of Marathi and Tamil speakers. Separate Congress provinces had been constituted in Andhra and Sind in 1918, while Gujarat and the Karnatak[50] had been pressing for a separate Congress province. Through his contacts with the Servants of India Society, Gandhi took up the case of Orissa and gave his blessing to the agitation for the amalgamation of the Oriya tracts under one administration.[51] But, except for Gujarat, Gandhi's programme for linguistic provinces was more a bid for new support than evidence of backing from these regions.

Gandhi's tactics contrasted strikingly with those of his Nationalist

---

[48] Tilak to V. J. Patel, 26 June 1920. File 94 of 1920, All-India Congress Committee [AICC] Papers, NMM.

[49] *CWG* XVII, pp. 347–8. Gandhi had not, previously, been a member of the League.

[50] See, for example, B. V. Joshi to C. P. Ramaswami Iyer, 28 November 1917, urging the formation of provinces along linguistic lines. 'We have seriously realised that we have fallen behind in the race for political progress by reason of unequal competition with more advanced peoples. We are of opinion that the creation of a Kannada Provincial Congress circle will ensure our progress . . .' File 1 of 1917, AICC Papers, NMM.

[51] *CWG*, XVII, pp. 396–8, 403–05.

opponents. While he was attempting to create an all-India following by espousing all sorts of grievances, the Nationalists were content to cultivate their own provincial gardens. For the Nationalists, all-India politics took second place to provincial interests, and their alliance at the all-India level was geared towards serving them. The demand for full autonomy in the provinces under the reforms, preferably unhampered by the more politically backward provinces, had come from the Nationalists. In 1917 the Bengal Provincial Conference had demanded autonomy for Bengal only.[52] At Delhi in 1918, the Congress moved a resolution that the advanced provinces should receive self-government; but the representatives of the supposedly backward regions created such a furore that the resolution had to be withdrawn.[53] What distinguished the advanced and the backward regions was the varying ability of their representatives in Congress to dominate the reformed councils. The advanced provinces had sophisticated electoral organization; the backward provinces had no organization at all. The Presidencies were well prepared for the elections to the reformed councils, to be held in November 1920. Under the auspices of the Bangla Jana Sabha in Bengal, Tilak's Democratic Party in Maharashtra and the Nationalist Party in Madras, the Nationalists collected funds, nominated candidates and got their slogans ready.[54] At the Amritsar Congress it was a good tactic for the Nationalists to appear to reject the Reforms as inadequate and disappointing. But they soon showed that their real interest was to contest the elections and, if possible, to win office. In other provinces electoral arrangements were far behind those in the Presidencies. In the UP, for example, as late as June, just four months before the elections, no arrangements had been made.[55]

The Nationalist preparations for the elections were not co-ordinated on an all-India basis. In June, at the annual conference of the Indian Home Rule League, Tilak claimed that his Congress Democratic Party Manifesto had been prepared in consultation with Nationalist leaders in other provinces. This was denied by some of the Nationalist

---

[52] The motion moved by Bepin Chandra Pal at the Conference, which marked the entry of C.R. Das into the forefront of Bengali politics, called for 'complete provincial autonomy and responsible Government in Bengal.' *Leader*, 7 December 1917.
[53] CID Weekly Report, January 1919. Home Poll D January 1919, 160–63, NAI.
[54] Maharashtra was the most advanced of all. On his return from England Tilak launched the National Democratic Company with a capital of Rs 10 lakhs. FR Bombay, 1 January 1920. Home Poll D January 1920, 78, NAI.
[55] Motilal to Jawaharlal, 16 June 1920. Nehru Papers, NMM.

leaders he claimed to have consulted.[56] Until the All-India Congress Committee met at Benares in May 1920, it was not clear what role the Congress would play in the elections, despite the activity of some of the Provincial Congress Committees. At the AICC meeting the Nationalists and Besant's Home Rulers struggled for control of the Congress organization. Besant's party wanted to stop the Congress from participating officially in the elections but the Nationalists successfully secured Congress support for their electoral campaigns. The AICC decided not to set up a central body but to allow the various Congress Committees to run the elections within their own provinces.[57]

It is significant that, before July 1920, boycott of the reforms was not part of Gandhi's programme of non-cooperation. In his March manifesto Gandhi had stressed that the Khilafat issue should take precedence over the reforms and made no mention whatsoever about the possibility of a boycott.[58] At Amritsar in 1919, Gandhi had joined with Malaviya to support a resolution in favour of working the reforms although he professed to be reluctant to take part in the elections. It is clear that until July 1920 it was quite possible for politicians to give a guarded support for Gandhi's proposed non-cooperation and to plan to fight the election campaigns. Gandhi had not publicly suggested a boycott of the reforms. Although he was a member of the Congress Punjab Disorders Enquiry, Gandhi had as yet made no effort to link the 'Punjab wrong' with the Khilafat question. Indeed, even members of the Khilafat Committee were engaged in electioneering and espoused the Khilafat issue as part of his campaign.[59] Until the end of June 1920, the non-cooperation programme was that ratified at a meeting of the Central Khilafat Committee in Bombay on 12 May. It was envisaged that non-cooperation would be in four stages: first, the giving up of titles and the resignation of honorary posts; second, resignation of public servants from Government employment; third, the resignation of the police and the army; and fourth, the suspension of the payment of taxes. Speaking of the third stage Gandhi said that this was 'a distant goal' while the fourth stage was 'still more remote'.[60] This was the programme, with some modifications, which Gandhi put before the joint meeting of Hindus and Muslims at Allahabad in June. Few Hindu leaders attended. Neither Tilak nor Das was present, and although Gandhi later tried to claim that the vote for non-cooperation was a joint decision of Hindus and Muslims, all the Hindus withdrew before the vote was

[56] *Leader*, 26 June 1920.   [57] *Bombay Chronicle*, 7 June 1920.
[58] *CWG*, XVII, pp. 73–6.   [59] *Leader*, 10 June 1920.
[60] *CWG*, XVII, pp. 389–90.

taken. Nehru, Sapru, Malaviya and Lajpat Rai all spoke against non-cooperation and voiced fears that it might precipitate an Afghan invasion.[61] Until June, therefore, Gandhi could claim little support for non-cooperation even from the Hindu leaders of upper India with whom he had been conducting an elaborate flirtation since his return from South Africa in 1915. Even this programme of non-cooperation was revised by the Muslims, and a subcommittee was appointed to prepare the final scheme.[62]

What marked the politicians' attitude to the non-cooperation proposals, however, was their diplomatic silence. The north Indian Hindu leaders did not commit themselves to non-cooperation, and Congress leaders in other provinces decided to wait and see. Masterly inactivity was the order of the day. Gandhi's non-cooperation proposals were considered at the Benares meeting of the AICC in June 1920, but no decision was taken. The matter was postponed to a special meeting of the Congress to be held at Calcutta in September. Tilak and Lajpat Rai were against adopting non-cooperation immediately and emphasized the practical difficulties in the way of its success.[63] The Bengal leaders were silent. The Council of the Muslim League, and its president, M. A. Jinnah, took no part in the public discussion. However, the Benares meeting of the AICC did make it clear that the programme of non-cooperation before them did not involve a boycott of the reforms. The discussion of non-cooperation at Benares was brief and inconclusive; the AICC instead concerned itself with settling the role that the Congress was to play in the forthcoming elections.[64] In an interview after the meeting, Tilak expressed the general opinion that the Congress should do nothing about non-cooperation until the Muslims had decided upon some definite course of action.[65] Not surprisingly, most of Tilak's interview was concerned with his party's preparations for the elections.

The Khilafat, ulama and joint Hindu-Muslim meetings at Allahabad from 1 to 3 June and the AICC meeting at Benares suggested that, apart from a vague general support for the principle of non-cooperation which was never in doubt, Gandhi's non-cooperation programme would gain very little support even from among the Muslims. During the meetings of the Khilafat Committee it became clear that only Sind, the Punjab, Madras and the Northwest Frontier Province were pre-

[61] CID Report. Home Poll B July 1920, 109, NAI.
[62] 'The Mohammedan Decision', *Young India*, 9 June 1920 quoted in *CWG*, XVII, pp. 484-85; Home Poll B July 1920, 109, NAI.
[63] Letter from Jamnadas Dwarkadas, *Bombay Chronicle*, 7 June 1920.
[64] *Bombay Chronicle*, 7 June 1920; *Leader*, 8 June 1920.
[65] Interview with Tilak, *Bombay Chronicle*, 8 June 1920.

pared to support the movement in its entirety. Some delegates from the UP and the CP tried to limit the movement to the first two stages only, while the Bengal Muslim leader A. K. Fazl-ul Haq urged that Bengal 'where sentiment was still backward should be left out of the scheme for the present'.[66] An amendment, which was moved by the Muslim politicians from the UP and which was supported by the Delhi leaders, Dr Ansari and Hakim Ajmal Khan, and most of the Bombay city members of the Committee who resigned subsequently, called for the adoption of the first stage only. Support for Gandhi in the UP came from the ulama party in which Abdul Bari and Hasrat Mohani were prominent. The breach between the politicians and the ulama was already a pronounced feature of the Khilafat campaign and the squabbles between the political and the religious wings were to become more acute as the campaign developed. On the second day of the meeting, the Khilafat Committee adopted all four stages of the non-cooperation programme. But only forty persons were present when this was done, compared with an attendance of 125 on the first day. Indeed, the fate of the movement was so uncertain that Gandhi asked for and was given dictatorial powers, subject only to the requirement that he take advice from the Non-cooperation Committee appointed to draw up the final programme.[67]

Under Gandhi's dictatorship, this subcommittee was to be free from the restraints of the Khilafat Committee. Its headquarters, however, were to be in Bombay and its members were mainly from Bombay city, so there was close liaison with the central body. On the first day of the joint meetings, Gandhi announced his intention of adding several new items to the non-cooperation programme. The boycott of schools and colleges and the law courts would now form part of the first stage, and this, Gandhi argued 'would cripple the Government'.[68] He also announced, again for the first time, that he would 'get through all the stages in four or five months one by one'. According to a police report, not one of the handful of twenty-five politicians who were present was

[66] A CID Report estimated provincial attendance as: Bombay Presidency and Sind 20, Madras 6, Punjab 6, UP 50, Delhi 5, Bihar 10, Calcutta 5 and the CP 5. Home Poll B July 1920, 109, NAI.
[67] The committee members were Gandhi, Shaukat Ali, A. S. Khatri (Bombay), Hakim A. Y. Ispahani (Bombay), Md. Ali Dharavi (Bombay), A. K. Azad (Bihar), Hasrat Mohani (UP), and Dr Kitchlew (Amritsar). *Ibid.* The president of the Central Khilafat Committee, Chhotani, refused to be nominated to the Non-cooperation Committee.
[68] Stage one was to be put in operation for one month; stage two for a further month; the third and fourth stages were to be taken up simultaneously for one month, when all four would be kept in force. *Ibid.*

prepared to support the movement beyond the first two stages; most of them showed little enthusiasm for the scheme as a whole. The first joint meeting broke up in confusion when Hasrat Mohani suggested that Muslims should liberate India with the help of the Afghans. The Hindu reaction, especially from the leaders from upper India, showed their real attitude to the whole movement. 'The matter was only *politically interesting* to the Hindus' Lala Lajpat Rai told the meeting,

while to the Muslims it was of importance religiously. That made a lot of difference. Hindus could only side with Mussalmans till such a stage as the political betterment of India was not damaged. If they smelt the least danger, the Hindus would not only withdraw co-operation with the Mussalmans but they would take steps to counteract the danger.[69]

So the position in early June was this: neither of the two joint Hindu-Muslim meetings had come to a decision and the meeting of the Khilafat Committee, which adopted the non-cooperation resolution, was extremely poorly attended.

Until June 1920, therefore, paying lip-service to non-cooperation did not cost the Congress politicians much. They remained sceptical about it and instead busied themselves with the immediate problem of getting ready for the elections in November. In the second week of June, further Rules and Regulations under the Government of India Act were published. They introduced a wholly new element into the political situation. By determining the final shape of the reforms and by settling the representation in the councils and the exact nature of the franchise, these Rules and Regulations for the first time made the boycott of the councils an issue in practical politics. In facing this issue, the initiative came not from Gandhi but from that political chameleon, Lajpat Rai. At the Benares session of the AICC Lajpat Rai had opposed non-cooperation as unpractical. Once the Rules for the Punjab were published, it was clear that the last-ditch attempt of the Punjab PCC to gain more seats in the Provincial Council for the urban areas had failed,[70] and that urban Hindus in Punjab would have little chance of power under the new reforms. At this point, Lajpat Rai, apparently without consulting other Punjab leaders, called for the boycott of the

[69] Hindu leaders who were at the meeting included Sapru, Chintamani, Motilal Nehru, Malaviya, Jawaharlal and Shamlal Nehru (UP), B. C. Pal (Bengal), Satyamurthi and A. Rangaswamy Iyengar (Madras), Jamnadas Dwarkadas (Bombay city), Jairamdas Doulatram (Sind), Lala Goverdhan Das, and Lala Lajpat Rai (Punjab), and Mrs Besant, representing the three major factions in the Congress, the Liberals, the Nationalists and the Theosophists. *Ibid.*

[70] See, Punjab PCC Memorandum on the Reforms Scheme, 16 April 1920. Home Reforms Office Franchise B May 1920, 129-34, NAI.

council. Writing in his Urdu journal *Bande Mataram* on 25 June he outlined his reasons for advocating a boycott:

Sir Michael O'Dwyer looked down on the educated community of the Punjab and with approval on those *reises* and representatives of the agricultural classes who, to secure his goodwill, considered the educated people of the Punjab as nothing more than empty noise makers. The Rules which the Reforms Commission in the Punjab has framed with the approval of the Lt. Governor of the Punjab under the Reform Act, partake of the same character which means, that although by his courtesy Sir Edward Maclagen has changed, to some extent, the external guise of the official policy, the original policy stands unchanged on principle and has undergone no modification.[71]

Issued without the sanction of the Punjab PCC, Lajpat Rai's letter entirely changed the character of the discussion over non-cooperation.

Gandhi's reaction to the letter was immediate. He acted swiftly. On 30 June, five days after Lajpat Rai had called for boycott of the councils, Gandhi endorsed the suggestion in a cleverly worded letter to the Press and drew the conclusion that council boycott was 'but one step in the campaign of non-co-operation'. 'Needless to say', he wrote,

I am in entire accord with Lala Lajpat Rai on the question of the boycott of the reformed Councils. For me it is but one step in the campaign of non-co-operation and as I feel equally keenly on the Punjab question as on the Khilafat, Lala Lajpat Rai's suggestion is doubly welcome. . . .[72]

Before this announcement, Gandhi's attitude to the reforms had been consistently ambiguous, and he had made no specific stand about the elections. At Amritsar he had supported the resolution to work the reforms, but he had, nevertheless, kept his options open. His Home Rule Manifesto in March had stated that the Khilafat should take precedence over the reforms. But, only a month before the publication of Lajpat Rai's letter, he had suggested in an article in *Young India* and *Navajivan* that men should vote at the elections for candidates of principle and proven public merit, irrespective of party affiliations.[73] By adopting Lajpat Rai's suggestion, and making it his own, Gandhi had much to gain. Of course his move struck at the core of the Nationalists'

---

[71] Translation in *Bombay Chronicle*, 28 June 1920. The agricultural classes included the Hindu, predominantly, Jat, peasantry of the Ambala Division. Commenting on the Punjab PCC Memo on the Reforms, Chhotu Ram, President of the Rohtak DCC, wrote: 'The whole of this (precious) document breathes a spirit of ungenerous hostility towards rural representation and indulges, to a nauseating extent, in special pleading on behalf of the commercial and urban classes.' Chhotu Ram, High Court vakil, Rohtak, to Secretary, Home Department, Government of India. Home Reforms Office Franchise B May 1920, 129–34, NAI.

[72] *CWG*, XVII, p. 521–2.   [73] *CWG*, XVII, pp. 416–18.

political campaigns for the past four years, and indeed at the whole
Congress strategy since its foundation in 1885. But its advantages from
Gandhi's standpoint were obvious. It enabled him to join together the
Punjab and the Khilafat issues. As he pointed out, this was an opport-
unity that India, and indeed he himself, could not 'afford to miss'.[74]
Such a chance might not come again for a hundred years.

With equal alacrity Gandhi persuaded the Non-cooperation Committee to adopt the boycott of the reformed councils as a central plank
in its programme. In a manifesto published on 4 July the committee
outlined a programme which was radically different in detail from the
plans it had first made in February and March. It made council
boycott the rule not only for Punjab but for the whole of India. Although
the details for the first stage only were set out, Gandhi now decided to
begin this stage of non-cooperation on 1 August, a month before the
Special Congress was due to meet at Calcutta.[75] His intention was to
try to win popular support for the entire programme, especially the
boycott of the councils, and to put the Nationalists in a position where
they would have either to accept the council boycott or to come out
against non-cooperation as a whole. The decision to launch the campaign before September was also a deliberate move by Gandhi to
drum up support for himself at the Calcutta Congress, where he knew
he had to expect serious opposition.

Before July, council boycott had not been included in Gandhi's
programme. Between July and September it assumed the most important place in his propaganda. In an article in *Navajivan* on 18 July,
Gandhi wrote that the 'most important programme now facing the
country is the boycott of councils',[76] adding the boycott of the visit
of the Prince of Wales as an afterthought. Gandhi planned to capture
the Congress by a three-pronged attack: through the All-India Home
Rule League, the Khilafat Committees and through such support as
he could muster in the Congress Committees themselves. The regions
which Gandhi now visited tell us from where he expected this support.
In July his full non-cooperation programme was endorsed by the
Gujarat Provincial Conference and the Swarajya Sabha in Bombay city.
But Gandhi's greatest effort was devoted to a personal tour of the
principal Muslim areas in Madras, Punjab and Sind, the three provinces which had supported the full programme of non-cooperation
at the Allahabad meeting early in June. During this tour Gandhi

[74] *Bombay Chronicle*, 30 June 1920.
[75] *CWG*, XVIII, pp. 13–14.
[76] *Navajivan*, 18 July 1920, in *CWG*, XVIII, pp. 55–56.

142 RICHARD GORDON

spoke mainly to Muslims and not to Hindus. In Madras city, at a meeting organized by the ulama of a local mosque, Gandhi called on all the Muslims 'to go to the Congress and make it impossible for the Congress to give any other verdict'.[77]

As the Special Session of the Congress approached, and Gandhi was busy persuading delegates to go to it, the Provincial Congress Committees began to consider what their policy towards non-co-operation should be. It was a foregone conclusion that they would adopt non-cooperation in principle. The important question was whether they would support the boycott of the councils or not. Only the Sind PCC declared full support for Gandhi's full programme of non-cooperation which he had spelt out on 4 July and in his letters to the Viceroy on 14 and 16 July.[78] The UP PCC accepted the broad outlines of Gandhi's proposals but suggested some important modifications; lawyers were not to be asked to leave the courts and the local government was not to be boycotted.[79] None of the leading UP politicians— Motilal Nehru, Malaviya, and the President and the Secretary of the AICC, Iswar Saran and Gokaran Nath Misra—were present at the meeting of the PCC when the vote was taken. All of them were known to be against adopting the non-cooperation resolution.[80] The PCCs of Bengal and the Central Provinces were the only ones which specifically opposed the boycott of the councils. Bengal stated that it was against a uniform policy for the whole of India. It wanted the details of non-cooperation to be left to each province 'to shape its course with due respect to its own circumstances.'[81] Bihar also wanted a programme tailored to provincial circumstances, and appointed a committee to assess Bihar's special needs.[82] Madras's position was more equivocal, but no less unfavourable to Gandhi's programme. As the local Congress secretary put it, the Madras PCC favoured 'a policy of NCO and has voted against Mr Gandhi's programme'.[83] When Gandhi visited Madras, he failed to win round the PCC, and even Yakub Hasan, who had once led the Khilafat Committee, came out against council boycott.[84]

[77] *Bombay Chronicle*, 14 August 1920.　　　　　　　[78] *CWG*, XVIII, pp. 104–05.
[79] Resolution of the UP PCC, 22 August 1920. File 13 of 1920, AICC Papers, NMM.
[80] The resolution was carried by a very narrow majority. *Leader*, 25 August 1920.
[81] Resolutions of the Bengal PCC, 15 August 1920. File 13 of 1920, AICC Papers, NMM. Secretary, CP PCC, to General Secretary, AICC, 28 August 1920. *Ibid.*
[82] Secretary, Bihar PCC, to General Secretary, AICC, 9 August 1920. *Ibid.*
[83] Secretary, Madras PCC, to General Secretary, AICC, 26 August 1920 [italics in original]. *Ibid.*
[84] *Bombay Chronicle*, 14 August 1920.

Lajpat Rai, realising that few provinces were prepared to join Punjab in boycotting the councils,[85] changed his position. Moreover, Lajpat Rai's call for boycott had met with a poor response from the urban classes in Punjab and in particular from the leaders of the Punjab Hindu Sabha.[86] On 4 July the Punjab PCC met but failed to come to a decision since its president, Lala Harkishenlal, opposed the boycott of the reforms. On 8 August, the PCC merely endorsed the principle of non-cooperation but postponed consideration of a detailed programme until after the meeting of the Special Congress.[87] Meanwhile, in a signed article in *Bande Mataram*, Lajpat Rai had modified his earlier position. Sensing that opinion in Punjab was drifting against Gandhi and boycott, he was unwilling to commit his province to a policy which might cut it off from the mainstream of political activity in the country.[88] The Bombay and Andhra PCCs adopted much the same line as Punjab; they accepted non-cooperation in principle but left the details to be settled by a subcommittee to be appointed by the Special Congress.[89] The Bombay position reflected the delicate balance between the strong Gandhi party in Bombay city and Gujarat and the Tilak party in Maharashtra. If the resolutions of the PCCs are any guide, the dice were loaded against Gandhi. It seemed probable that non-cooperation in principle would be accepted by the Special Congress but that the detailed programme would be trimmed to suit the interests of the Nationalists. This meant that non-cooperation would be left sufficiently flexible to permit entry into the councils along the lines outlined by Das and Tilak at Amritsar in 1919.

At the Special Congress at Calcutta the vote in the open session recorded a clear victory for Gandhi's full programme. Historians have been misled by this fact. Gandhi had a large following among the delegates, but he won in the Subjects Committee, the only body that really mattered, by a very narrow margin. Once he had carried the Subjects Committee, victory in the open Congress was a matter of course. So the situation in the Subjects Committee, not the vote in the open session, needs to be examined. It is, of course, difficult to analyse the composition of the Subjects Committee, but certain points emerge.

---

[85] For example, the influential Calcutta Daily, *Amrita Bazar Patrika*, told its readers that the atrocities in Punjab were a local grievance to be remedied by a local boycott of the councils in Punjab alone. See Punjab letter in *Bombay Chronicle*, 6 August 1920.
[86] Home Poll D July 1920, 106, NAI.   [87] *Bombay Chronicle*, 10 August 1920.
[88] *Leader*, 16 July 1920 and 20 July 1920.
[89] Joint Honorary Secretary, Bombay PCC, to General Secretary, AICC, 16 August 1920, File 13 of 1920, AICC. The Andhra PCC resolution is not in the file but see M. R. Jayakar, *The Story of My Life*, I (Bombay, 1958), p. 397.

Gandhi's tours in the preceding two months, encouraging delegates to come to the Congress, paid high dividends. Khilafat special trains brought to Calcutta delegates, mainly Muslim, from Bombay, and Madras.[90] The high proportion of Muslim delegates at Calcutta was clearly reflected in the Subjects Committee. The Madras delegation, for example, had the right to elect fifteen delegates to the Subjects Committee; it returned at least seven Muslims. The pro-council-entry partly led by S. Kasturi Ranga Iyengar failed to get one man elected to the Subjects Committee.[91] By careful canvassing, two Muslims were elected to the Committee from Bombay city and, more surprisingly, one from the Southern division.[92] There are few details about other delegations. But Bengal, for example, had thirty seats on the Subjects Committee, and in addition ten seats as the hosts of the Congress; Muslims, it can be assumed, took their share of these forty seats. Indeed Jayakar believed that one reason why the Congress was invited to Calcutta rather than to Bezwada or Berhampore was Muslim strength in Calcutta.[93] It seems that on most delegations Muslims held the balance between those for and those against Gandhi, and were sufficiently numerous on the Subjects Committee to tip the balance in Gandhi's favour.

The second important factor in the voting in the Subjects Committee was the defection of certain politicians who had until this moment opposed the non-cooperation movement, in particular Motilal Nehru of the UP and Gangadhar Rao Deshpande, Tilak's chief lieutenant in the Karnatak. Nehru's conversion was crucial, as Das, who was deeply angered by it, realised. Nehru was important to Gandhi. This can be gauged by Gandhi's readiness to water down the non-cooperation resolution by inserting the word 'gradual' in relation to the boycott of schools, colleges and courts.[94] Nehru's volte-face came at a stage when it looked as if Gandhi would be forced to compromise with the Nationalists. By appearing to oppose non-cooperation the Nationalists found themselves in reluctant alliance with Mrs Besant and her theosophists. To disassociate themselves from the theosophists, who came in for a good deal of abuse, Das and his Nationalist allies proposed a compromise. His plan contained four parts: the first, that the Congress should enter the councils to work for the immediate attainment of

[90] The Madras 'Khilafat Special', for example, carried some 200 delegates to Calcutta, most of them Muslims from Bangalore, Trichinopoly and North Arcot. FR Madras, 1 September 1920. Home Poll D September 1920, 70, NAI.
[91] Leader, 9 September 1920.   [92] Bombay Chronicle, 6 September 1920.
[93] Jayakar, The Story of My Life, I, p. 393.
[94] Bombay Chronicle, 9 September 1920.

swaraj by forcing government to amend the constitution; the second, that only Congressmen who pledged to refuse office should be elected; the third, that where it achieved a majority, the Congress party should work to make government impossible; and finally, that where it won a minority of the seats, it should resign and seek re-election, and repeat this tactic with the same objective, namely to bring government to a standstill.[95]

It seemed that Das's compromise might succeed, since some supporters of non-cooperation began to reassess their position. Lajpat Rai now suggested that Nationalists should be allowed to stand for election if they agreed to resign from the councils whenever Congress by committee decided they should do so. Although he was unwilling to stand for election himself, Lajpat Rai stated that he was not prepared to bind other provinces to the boycott of the councils.[96] Gandhi himself was by no means certain that he would win. As Kapil Deva Malaviya later recorded, Gandhi held a meeting of the Swarajya Sabha (the old Alls India Home Rule League) during the sittings of the Subjects Committee, at which he discussed alternatives in case he lost.[97] When the vote in the Subjects Committee was finally taken, Gandhi's motion was carried by a small majority of only fifteen votes, 148 voting for and 133 against.[98]

Nehru's defection may well have swung the UP delegation in favour of Gandhi. In 1918 Nehru had been the only leader of any standing in the province to follow the advanced Home Rule party and he had been able to capture the Provincial Congress by working through the branches of the Muslim League and the Home Rule Leagues. To a large extent, Nehru depended upon Muslim political support, and was widely known for his pro-Muslim sympathies. As an Urdu-speaking Kashmiri Brahmin, he had voted with the Muslims for the UP Municipalities Bill in 1916 and he had kept clear of the agitation against it which the Hindu Sabha and the Provincial Congress launched. When Nehru saw how strongly Muslims supported non-cooperation in 1920, he may have been persuaded to tolerate the movement against his better judgement. But his decision rested, ultimately, upon more rational considerations than his wish to curry Muslim favour. It was based upon his calculations about the chances of the UP Congress of winning a majority at the 1920 elections, and of being able to

[95] Ibid.
[96] From the *Times of India* correspondent, *Leader*, 11 September 1920.
[97] Letter in *Leader*, 2 March 1923.
[98] *Bombay Chronicle*, 8 September 1920. Bepin Chandra Pal's motion was lost by a similar margin of 133 for and 151 against.

L

dominate the new council. Electoral preparations in the UP had not gone far. Nehru calculated that Congress had little chance of winning the elections. So for the time being council boycott made sound political sense. At Calcutta in November 1922, Nehru told the AICC that he had seconded the non-cooperation resolution at Calcutta in 1920. 'I recently had the opportunity', he went on,

of seeing that speech of mine and I am glad to tell you that the reasons which held good then hold good today. That reason was related to the actual entry into the Councils and not to standing for election, and it was the main and real reason that it was *absolutely certain then* that it [the Congress] *would not possibly get a majority*.[99]

The crucial issue at Calcutta was the boycott of the reforms. The vote was taken on this issue and this alone. With the exception of the Muslims, the provincial leaders voted according to calculations of expediency. In other words, they decided according to their estimate of the Congress's chances of winning a majority at the elections in their provinces. So not surprisingly the Nationalists in Maharashtra, the Central Provinces and Bengal, who had made the most elaborate preparations for the elections and who had the best chances for success at the polls were the most strongly opposed to the boycott. The split in the Madras PCC between the parties of S. Kasturi Ranga Iyengar and of C. Rajagopalachari, the latter in alliance with the Provincial Khilafat Committee,[100] reflected their different reactions to the success of the non-Brahmin Justice Party at the elections to the Madras Legislative Council in 1919.[101] Kasturi Ranga Iyengar and the Madras Nationalists, many of them Brahmins, were confident that Brahmins would hold their own at the elections in 1920, notwithstanding the Justice Party and the reservation of eighteen seats for non-Brahmins under the Meston award.[102] Rajagopalachari, however, assumed that the Brahmins were unlikely to win many seats, and voted accordingly. Similarly, the Congress in Bihar had relatively little chance of winning the elections against the landowning interest, and so it is understandable why some of its delegates voted for boycott on the Subjects Committee.

At Calcutta, Gandhi did not sweep to power on a wave of enthus-

---

[99] File 8 of 1922. AICC Papers, NMM [my italics].
[100] CID Notes, Annexure G, Madras Letter, 20 November 1920. Home Poll D December 1920, 48, NAI.
[101] Madras letter, *Leader*, 6 August 1919.
[102] Home Reforms Office General Franchise A May 1920, 31–43, NAI.

iasm for his programme.[103] The dominating fact of the Congress was the large Muslim contingent. This was the first time Muslims came in significant numbers to the Congress. In his closing speech as President, Lajpat Rai referred pointedly to these Muslims, adding that he was 'a little sorry that Mr Gandhi in his wisdom should have considered it necessary and proper in a way to tack the Indian National Congress to the Central Khilafat Committee.'[104] Granted the determined opposition of the Nationalists, Gandhi could not have captured the Congress without the support of the Central Khilafat Committee. The largest difference between the Congresses of 1918 and 1919 and the Special Congress of 1920 was the presence of the Khilafatists at the latter. The Central Khilafat Committee, both inspired and led by Gandhi, was calling the tune in Indian politics in September 1920, and took the Nationalists by surprise. Few could have thought that Gandhi would carry the day and no one tried to counter Gandhi's elaborate preparations throughout July and August.

But Gandhi's victory at Calcutta did not mean that he had captured the Congress organization. The Nationalists still controlled most of the PCCs and their influence within the AICC was strong. Gandhi was in no position to dictate to the Congress. Gandhi depended upon the Central Khilafat Committee and the Swarajya Sabha for the prosecution of his programme between September and the Nagpur Congress in December.[105] When the AICC met in October to discuss the report of the Non-cooperation Subcommittee, Gandhi's relative weakness was exposed. This Subcommittee had been appointed at Calcutta to prepare draft instructions for the detailed application of the programme, and consisted of Gandhi, Motilal Nehru, and V. J. Patel.[106] Gandhi had tried to interpret the Congress resolution as support for all four stages of non-cooperation, including the non-payment of taxes and withdrawal from the civil and the military services. This interpretation was rejected by the AICC and deleted from the report. Similarly, Gandhi's specious interpretation of the word 'gradual' was rejected when the AICC authorized the 'gradual' withdrawal from schools, colleges and law courts. The AICC also rejected the statement in the report that the Congress resolution on the boycott of British goods was

---

[103] *Bombay Chronicle*, 9 September 1920.

[104] *Times of India*, 11 September 1920. One delegate interpreted Lajpat's speech as a warning: "In fact, as the Lalaji remarked, what the Central Khilafat Committee had done today the Hindu Sabha might do tomorrow." *Leader*, 17 September 1920.

[105] Circular Letter to Home Rule branches, before 25 September 1920, *CWG*, XVIII, pp. 285–86.

[106] *CWG*, XVIII, pp. 279–84; Patel's minority report, *ibid.*, pp. 489–92.

'an unfortunate interpolation due to a misapprehension.'[107] The report was passed with these three substantial amendments.

The report pointed to the major tasks before the non-cooperation party: above all, hard and sustained work and the urgent need to collect funds. Since there were large differences, even among those who had voted for Gandhi at Calcutta, over such items in the programme as the boycott of educational institutions and the suspension of practice by lawyers, this meant that Gandhi and his men had to take the line of least resistance. He managed to secure a consensus which favoured placing the boycott of the reforms at the forefront of the programme. This was an astute move by Gandhi. It offered the best and most immediate chance to produce some tangible results, but paradoxically it also provided the means for keeping the Nationalists within the Congress. Their defeat at Calcutta raised an uncomfortable dilemma for the Nationalists. They had to decide whether to stay in Congress or get out. Since their political future outside Congress seemed dismal, they quickly decided to withdraw from the elections. In the two key provinces of Bengal and Maharashtra the Nationalists issued manifestos withdrawing from the elections; but they also reaffirmed that they opposed the boycott of the councils and reserved to themselves the right to seek to alter the Congress programme at some future date.[108]

It is generally held that the Nationalists, outmanoeuvred by Gandhi at Calcutta, decided to rally their forces for the Nagpur Congress in December to reverse the decision on the boycott of the councils.[109] Calcutta is thus seen as a dress rehearsal for the greater Gandhian triumph at Nagpur. This view is entirely misleading. It distorts what happened at Nagpur and misjudges the strategy pursued by the Nationalists. It has already been noted that the major task of the Congress after Calcutta was the boycott of the elections, a duty which the Nationalists, once they had decided to stay in Congress, were only too eager to fulfill. They were more active than most in preaching the boycott. By setting up dummy candidates, they hoped to keep seats warm for their eventual return to the councils, and to make the election of their moderate opponents as difficult as possible.

The obvious point most historians have ignored is this. By December the elections were over, and consequently there was no point in the

[107] *Leader*, 4 and 7 October 1920; FR Bombay, 11 September 1920. Home Poll D December 1920, 84, NAI.

[108] *Amrita Bazar Patrika*, 15 September 1920; *Bombay Chronicle*, 21 September 1920. 23 Nationalists withdrew in Bengal and 17 in Bombay.

[109] See, for example, J. H. Broomfield, 'The Non-cooperation Decision of 1920: A Crisis in Bengal Politics', in Low (ed.), *Soundings*, pp. 225–54.

Nationalists attempting to reverse the Calcutta decision at Nagpur. When they reserved their right to alter the Congress decision at some future date, they did not plan to do this at Nagpur. As the November elections had come and gone, entry into the councils, for the time being, ceased to be an immediate issue. The actions of C. R. Das who, after Tilak's death, emerged as the leader of Gandhi's opponents at Calcutta, illustrate the tactics of the Nationalists. After withdrawing from the elections, he made a move to come to some kind of compromise with Gandhi. This was certainly Motilal Nehru's impression when he wrote to his son:

You must have seen the paragraphs which have appeared in the Calcutta papers about the case under the head of 'NCO'. My own impression is that they are inspired by Das who ought to have no doubt in his mind that he is going to lose. These paragraphs suggest an immediate compromise.[110]

Das's subsequent actions prove the point. He was building up support in an attempt to force Gandhi's hand and gain as much control as possible over the non-cooperation movement. Although he had lost at Calcutta, Das was not prepared to allow Gandhi to run the Congress as he chose. As the meeting of the AICC late in September had shown, there was considerable dissatisfaction with the way in which Gandhi was running the campaign. Lajpat Rai had publicly supported Patel's dissenting note to the Report of the Non-cooperation Subcommittee and voiced doubts about the practicality of Gandhi's methods.[111] Gandhi's unsuccessful sallies against the Benares Hindu University and the Aligarh College, and his failure to provide alternative educational facilities for the students whom he urged to leave the schools, attracted a good deal of hostile comment.[112] Das's view seems to have been that unless the programme was radically altered non-cooperation would before long prove an egregious failure.

Calcutta had taught the Nationalists that they would have to work together if they were to bargain successfully with Gandhi. Calcutta had also shown that the natural alliance between Maharashtra and Bengal no longer dominated the AICC or the Subjects Committee. So Das called a conference of Nationalists at Benares in the last week of October and prepared a draft statement for publication which was circulated secretly to all leading Nationalists. He hoped to publish it with the approval of leading Congressmen in Maharashtra, Bengal,

110 Motilal to Jawaharlal, 19 September 1920. Nehru Papers, NMM.
111 Letter in *Leader*, 4 October 1920.
112 CID, Note by DCI, 11 October 1920. Home Poll D October 1920, 51, NAI.

Madras and northern India.[113] In his statement Das made a bold move to hoist Gandhi with his own petard. He pressed for the adoption of all stages of non-cooperation simultaneously. The Calcutta resolution, he argued, 'emphasized inessentials to the neglect of essentials' and by placing a purely negative emphasis upon boycott offered no work of a practical nature for the 'masses'. Significantly, he said nothing about council boycott as 'it is no longer a matter of immediate practical importance.' Das' plan was more comprehensive than Gandhi's, and it placed as much emphasis on economic as on political boycott. Politically, non-cooperation should mean a complete boycott of all governmental machinery; economically, it should entail the boycott of foreign goods and British agency houses. Men and money should be withdrawn from all British enterprises in India. In the last resort the country should refuse to pay taxes.[114] At the same time, Das called for the reorganization of the Congress, the creation of a special fund, and a membership drive. When Congress extended its organization and recruited a wider following, 'particular efforts should be made to enrol at least a majority of those who are entitled to vote under the new Reform Act.'[115]

Though Das's statement was never published, he repeated the burden of his argument in an interview in Calcutta early in December. He declined to comment upon what had been discussed or settled upon at the conference in Benares, but he again stated that he supported the adoption of all four stages of non-cooperation simultaneously.[116] It is reasonable to assume that Das hoped to strengthen the negotiating position of the Nationalists at Nagpur, with an eye to compromise. He attempted to do this by splitting the ranks of the non-cooperators, some of whom could be expected to opt for the larger programme he was propagating, while others would prefer to stick to the more limited Calcutta resolution.

In the event, the Nagpur Congress was something of an anti-climax. Much play was made of Das's supposedly miraculous conversion at the last moment. It was Das who proposed the non-cooperation resolution in the open Congress, which was passed by acclamation. But, far from being a personal triumph for Gandhi, the Nagpur Congress witnessed Gandhi's capitulation to Das. For it was Das's programme of non-cooperation that was adopted at Nagpur and not Gandhi's. Gandhi's

[113] B. R. Moonje to V. J. Patel, 5 December 1920. File 2 of 1920, AICC Papers, NMM.

[114] *Ibid*. Das's letter was enclosed by Moonje in his letter to Patel.

[115] *Ibid*.   [116] *Leader*, 4 December 1920.

draft resolution[117] contained only a few minor amendments to the Calcutta resolution. They included the deletion of the word 'gradual' when referring to the boycotts, and putting in a reference to the foundation of national schools and arbitration courts. But Gandhi's resolution said nothing about adopting all four stages of non-cooperation at once. The final resolution[118] proposed and passed in open Congress was different, both in principle and in spirit, from Gandhi's draft. It resolved to endorse all four stages of the programme at once, to form a body of workers to be known as the National Service, to collect a Tilak Swaraj Fund, to undertake a full economic boycott and to establish Congress Committees in every village. These additions were grafted upon Gandhi's draft. They were, in substance, drawn from Das's proposals. Further, two other resolutions, on the boycott of contracts and the organization of trade unions, were passed at Nagpur. Both were drawn from Das's programme.[119] The Nagpur resolutions put a new emphasis upon economic boycott. This was something which Gandhi had opposed consistently since 1919. It shows how far Das succeeded in putting his imprint on the Nagpur Congress and in forcing Gandhi to compromise.

As Subhas Bose pointed out, Das did not give in to Gandhi at Nagpur. Rather he entered into an agreement with him.[120] There is no way of knowing precisely what the terms of this agreement were. But there are some clues. In the resolution passed at Nagpur Gandhi's promise of *'swaraj established within one year'* was heavily stressed.[121] This and subsequent statements by other Nationalists suggest that Gandhi and the Nationalists concluded an informal pact to work the non-cooperation programme for one year only. At Ahmadabad in May 1923, V. J. Patel publicly stated that 'He and his colleagues supported the boycott of Councils at Nagpur simply *because it was a programme of one year.*'[122] At the AICC meeting at Calcutta in November 1922 the Jagat Guru Shri Shankaracharya said that when the Maharashtrian party had accepted non-cooperation at Nagpur 'it was merely in deference to the Congress mandate and it was only for the swaraj year 1921.[123] Das himself was quite explicit. Speaking at Tanjore in June 1923, he defended himself against the charge of being inconsistent:

[117] *CWG*, XIX (Ahmadabad, 1966), pp. 182–3.
[118] *Ibid.*, pp. 576–8.
[119] *Indian Annual Register*, 1921, Part III, p. 184.
[120] S. C. Bose, *The Indian Struggle, 1920–1942* (Calcutta, 1964), p. 44.
[121] *CWG*, XIX, p. 578.
[122] *Hindu*, 24 May 1923 [my italics].
[123] File 8 of 1922. AICC Papers, NMM.

There is a belief that at Nagpur I changed my position. That is absolutely untrue. I ask you to read the Nagpur resolution and you will find nothing in it inconsistent with my position here. It was at my instance and upon my insistence that the clause with regard to the boycott of Councils was moved. Mahatma Gandhi removed the clause because at the time of the Nagpur session the elections were over practically. I insisted on the removal of the clause because, otherwise said I, I could not support the resolution. And lower down in the same resolution you will find a clause put in, again at my instance and upon my insistence.[124]

At Nagpur, Gandhi also was anxious for some kind of settlement. At Calcutta he had been prepared to modify the non-cooperation resolution to win over Motilal Nehru, and at Nagpur he was eager to draw Das into the net. At Calcutta Gandhi had won in the Congress by relying on the Muslims, and his plea for a national coalition hardly masked his desire to free himself from his dependence upon the Central Khilafat Committee. If Gandhi wanted to lead an all-India agitation, he could hardly ignore the two most populous provinces, the UP and Bengal. By winning over Motilal Nehru, Gandhi gained a much needed counterweight to the more extreme party of the ulama in the UP led by Abdul Bari and Hasrat Mohani. Since the beginning of 1920 Gandhi had experienced the greatest difficulty in restraining the ulama from a more violent course of action. So Gandhi needed Nehru and Das, and his dependence upon them was to become even more pronounced during 1921 when the movement Gandhi led threatened to fall apart.

To some extent Madras and Maharashtra remained outside this centre party that emerged at Nagpur. The results of the Madras elections and the spectacular victories of the non-Brahmins and the Justice Party[125] pushed many of the Brahmin politicians who had been undecided, into non-cooperation. Better the Congress on any terms, than the Justice Party. The sudden shift of opinion in Madras political circles was evident in the selection of C. Vijayaraghavachariar, who at the Calcutta session had been an outspoken opponent of Gandhi, to be the president of the Nagpur Congress, and in the 'conversion' of S. Kasturi Ranga Iyengar.[126] Of all the old Nationalist groups, the

[124] *Hindu*, 14 June 1923.

[125] Of 74 seats open to Hindus, of which 28 were reserved for non-Brahmins, non-Brahmins secured 54 and Brahmins 20 seats. 'Return Showing the Results of Elections in India, 1920', *Parliamentary Papers Cmd.* 1261, 1921, p. lv.

[126] The Report of the Madras PCC for 1920–21 stated clearly the difficulties of the decision. 'The activities of the non Brahman party in this Presidency rendered the boycott of the Councils a very difficult sacrifice to make. It meant in other provinces the suffering involved in allowing an unrepresentative body of Moderates to take

Tilak party in Maharashtra was the least reconciled to non-cooperation. They continued to criticise Gandhi's programme, and they at once expressed their determination to revise the Congress programme so as to be in a position to contest the next general elections in 1923.[127]

This analysis of the calculations behind the non-cooperation decision of 1920, suggests that to argue that non-cooperation was adopted because the Reforms of 1919 were inadequate is historical fiction. The boycott of the councils was an afterthought, tacked on to Gandhi's original programme when political rivalries and prospects in Punjab brought forth the suggestion. The politicians who supported council entry and those who supported the boycott both realized that the reforms of 1919 devolved substantial powers to Indians. They did not disagree that the patronage and office which the constitution offered were desirable; they only differed in their calculations about the ability of the Congress in the various provinces to elect a majority capable of winning power. Council boycott appealed to those who felt they could not win the elections in 1920. The centre party that emerged at Nagpur in December was, by its nature, a temporary one. The Nationalists retained a distinct factional identity within the supposed Gandhian Congress. Moreover they accepted non-cooperation for a limited period only. N. C. Kelkar was not far wrong when he wrote that it was 'Mr Gandhi himself who is on trial. We do not say this in a spirit victimizing Mr Gandhi but only for pointing out the quarter in which the centre of gravity of the responsibility lies.'[128] The role of the Swarajya party in the nineteen-twenties suggests that Gandhi's victory in September and December 1920 was by no means complete; and that the politics of council entry and provincial calculation remained to be fought another day.

charge of immediate administration of several departments of Government and have the ear of bureaucracy generally. But in this province it meant the voluntary surrender of a considerable degree of power for mischief to a party which placed the interests of particular communities above the call of the country as a whole and openly opposed the most bitter sentiments against a minority which had hitherto played the most prominent part in public affairs.' *Hindu*, 23 June 1921.

[127] N. C. Kelkar, 'The N.C.O. Resolution', *Mahratta*, 19 September 1920.
[128] *Ibid.*

Country Politics: Madras 1880 to 1930

DAVID WASHBROOK

Introduction

THE period from the 1880s to the 1930s was one of major change in the political organization of India. Indians joined the British in the highest offices of state; government greatly increased its activity through legislation and through the trebling of taxation; elective institutions and legislatures steadily replaced the discretionary rule of bureaucrats; a nationalist movement of great size and force appeared; the means of communication—through road, rail and press—improved beyond recognition to bring together for the first time the diverse peoples of India. This was the critical epoch in the formation of the modern Indian state and many aspects of it have been the subject of historical study. Yet, paradoxically, the political history of rural India at this time has been much neglected. While we can turn to several works on national government and the Congress and to investigations of provincial political activity, we find considerably fewer on the organization of local politics and virtually none at all that deal with matters outside the principal towns. Until the rural locality has been examined, our knowledge of the political development of India must remain small, for it takes no great insight to see that most of India's wealth and population were to be found in the countryside. Whether the success of an Indian government be judged by the mid-Victorian standard of revenue or the mid-twentieth century standard of votes, it could be achieved only through rural control and support. This essay is meant as a tentative contribution to our understanding of political change in the country-side.

Its primary concern is, therefore, the peasant. Although the peasant was not the only element in rural society, his position as the main producer of wealth makes him central to any discussion. To a consider-

I should like to thank Dr C. J. Baker of Queens' College, Cambridge, for his help in putting together much of the political material in this essay; Dr Carolyn M. Elliott of the University of California, for first interesting me in rural politics; and the other contributors to this volume for their patience and their criticisms which helped to make the arguments put forward here less like the wandering cart tracks which they once were.

156   DAVID WASHBROOK

able extent, the structure of power in rural India was determined by the structure of power among the peasantry.[1] However, the almost infinite variety of conditions in different parts of India threw up different types of peasant political organization. And there are almost as many different ways of attempting an analysis of them. This essay concentrates on two important aspects of peasant life—the ways in which agrarian production was organized and the ways in which peasants were related to governmental authority.

Section 1 examines a region of the Madras presidency organized for 'dry' cultivation. The area includes the Ceded districts (Kurnool, Bellary, Anantapur and Cuddapah) and most of hinterland Tamilnad (the districts of Salem, Coimbatore, Madura, Trichinopoly, Tinnevelly, and North and South Arcot).[2] It tries to show how changes in economic and administrative conditions produced a distinctive 'style' of peasant participation in politics. Section 2 analyses a region of 'wet' cultivation in Madras—the Kistna and Godaveri deltas. It attempts to demonstrate how a different set of relationships between agrarian production and the administration led to a different style of politics. Section 3 assesses the influence of these two regional polities on the supra-regional political organizations—the Congress and the provincial legislatures—of which they were part.

I

Between the great famine of 1876–78 and the depression of 1929–30, the Ceded districts and hinterland Tamilnad experienced slow but definite economic growth. Certainly there were regular rain-failures and shortages, but their effect in contracting the economy seldom lasted more than a year or two. The great famine, by contrast, had driven back cultivation in the Ceded districts to such an extent that it was twenty years before the cropped area reached its 1876 level. Between the mid-1880s and the mid-1920s, the acreage under cultivation kept pace with the growth of the population. According to the census the population of

[1] The arguments presented below are pitched at a high level of generality. Consequently, I have isolated 'the peasant' as the most useful general social category with which to investigate rural society.

[2] As the 'dry' region is categorized by a type of cultivation, it is not meant to include those parts of 'dry' districts in which 'wet' rice cultivation was to be found. In the districts of hinterland Tamilnad it thus excludes about 20 per cent of Tinnevelly, Trichinopoly and Madura where rice cultivation took place along the banks of rivers and large tanks.

these districts increased by about 30 per cent[3] while the area under ryotwari tenure—the only form of tenure for which we have information—went up by a third.[4] Admittedly, some of this new land was poor, but the area under irrigation—mostly from wells and tanks—also increased by about 25 per cent.[5] Moreover, changes in the use of land helped to raise the profitability of agriculture. Most of the land was under dry grain crops—cholum, ragi and combu—which were of little value. But as transport facilities developed, and as opportunities in world markets grew, the area under cash crops, particularly cotton and oilseeds, expanded.[6]

Together with the rewards of cash cropping, a steady rise in the price of grain helped to promote prosperity in the area. Grain prices, of course, were subject to wild fluctuations according to both the locality and the time of the year, but improved communications helped to control these fluctuations and to stabilize prices at higher levels.[7] As more was earned from the land, the share which the state took in land revenue became smaller. Although in theory the ryotwari revenue system, which covered three-quarters of Madras and nearly all of the dry districts, allowed the government to raise assessments to keep pace with prices, in practice this was never possible. Districts were resettled and prices reviewed only every thirty years and even then, as we shall see, government was not the master of its own administration. During the period under study the government at Fort St George was able to raise its assessment on dry land from an average of Rs 1.10 per acre to Rs 1.18, and on wet land from Rs 5.2 to Rs 5.8—increases of only

[3] Calculated from Dharma Kumar's estimate of population in 1886, D. Kumar, *Land and Caste in South India* (Cambridge, 1965), p. 116 and *Census of India 1921 Madras. Volume XIII. Part II* (Madras, 1922), p. 4.

[4] *Reports on the Settlement of the Land Revenue in the Districts of the Madras Presidency for Fasli 1294 (1884–85)* (Madras, 1886), pp. 40–44; *Reports on the Settlement of the Land Revenue in the Districts of the Madras Presidency for Fasli 1330 (1920–21)* (Madras, 1922), pp. 17–20. (Hereafter this series of reports is abbreviated as *Land Revenue Reports for Fasli . . .*)

[5] *Ibid.*

[6] Allowing for changes in the area covered by the statistics, between 1884–85 and 1920–21 the area under cotton grew by 40 per cent and that under ground-nut by 100 per cent. By the mid-1920s, these two crops occupied about 15 per cent of the acreage of most dry districts. *Agricultural Statistics of British India. Quinquennial series* (Calcutta, 1884–85 to 1920–21), Vol. I, 'Area under Crops'.

[7] The fluctuations remained sufficient to make it difficult to give an accurate idea of the scale of the price rise. But, roughly, dry grains were selling between 50 and 70 per cent more in the years 1910–17 than in 1880–87. During the shortages of 1918–20, prices went even higher. Calculated from 'Statements showing the prices of food grains' in *Land Revenue Reports for Fasli 1290 (1880–81)* to *Land Revenue Reports for Fasli 1335 (1925–26)*.

between 7 and 12 per cent.[8] Its increased income from land revenue depended on the fact that more acres were assessed and more land became irrigated.

There is much to suggest a modest buoyancy in the agrarian economy at this time. Government censuses of cattle, ploughs and carts, however inaccurate they may have been, all indicate a steady growth in capital investment on the land.[9] Although there was no such thing as a free market in land, the evidence suggests a slow growth in land prices.[10] By the time of the First World War, the Madras government found itself under constant political pressure from rural areas to expand road and railway communications along potential trade routes.[11] Trade in agrarian produce was developing, albeit gradually and fragmentarily. Of course, this prosperity did not necessarily mean that everybody was getting richer. Indeed, many may have been getting poorer. A variety of economic, social and political factors stood between the cultivator and the fruits of his labour. Hence it is necessary to look closely at the nature of agrarian organization to see how crops were produced, who produced them and, perhaps most important of all, how they were sold.

The land in these districts was marked by the small size of the holdings and the extreme poverty of the holders. In 1900, for example, rather more than 70 per cent of all the ryotwari pattas issued by the government were for the payment of less than Rs 10 per annum in land revenue. In Coimbatore, the richest district, about 67 per cent of the holdings paid less than Rs 10; in Cuddapah, the poorest district, 77 per cent of the holdings were so rated.[12]

The amount of land represented by a Rs 10 patta was barely enough to support a family in good years, and in many years the rains failed. Even among these minute pattas, many were meant to support more than one family. In the early 1890s, Sir Frederick Nicholson, one of Madras' few agrarian experts, attempted to give an idea of how many so-called landowners held smallholdings of this type: 'their immense numbers may be judged from the fact that about 86 per cent of the

[8] Calculated from 'Statements of the Ryots' Holdings', *Land Revenue Reports for Fasli 1290 (1880–1881)* to *Land Revenue Reports for Fasli 1335 (1925–26)*.

[9] See *Agricultural Statistics of British India*. Quinquennial Series, 1884–85 to 1920–21, 'Live-Stock'.

[10] See comments on land prices in *Reports of the Provincial Banking Enquiry Committee, 1929–30* (Calcutta, 1931) 'Madras' [*RPBC*], p. 79.

[11] For example, see the district board campaigns in Ramnad, Madura and Coimbatore to get a railway to the West Coast, *Hindu*, 1 February and 17 May 1915.

[12] *Land Revenue Reports for Fasli 1310 (1900–01)*, pp. 71–7.

Madras ryots pay less than Rs 10 and on average Rs 4 in assessment'.[13] However, in every district—almost in every village—there were a few large pattadars whose holdings made a mockery of Sir Thomas Munro's claims that the ryotwari system created a society of equal peasant farmers. In Coimbatore and Tinnevelly there were several hundred, and in the Ceded districts several dozen, men paying more than Rs 250 per annum on a single patta. In 1900, the 7.5 per cent of pattas at the top of the revenue table paid more than 43 per cent of the land revenue.[14]

The growth of cash cropping in the dry areas produced a diversification rather than a specialization of crop patterns. Peasants seldom devoted the whole of their holdings to cotton or oilseeds but continued to sow dry grains alongside the more valuable crops. This was because they could not rely either upon the weather or upon prices. The Banking Inquiry noted how, in some 'dry' localities, ryots would grow as many as five different crops on the same land in the hope that, should some fail, the others at least might survive.[15] Equally, the prices of cotton and groundnut were fixed by international market conditions which varied from year to year but which were barely related to local conditions.[16] When the grain harvest was poor and prices were high, the peasant who had turned all his land over to cash crops could find himself in difficulties, as his income did not meet the cost of his food. Cultivators, even near markets, did not usually put more than a quarter of their land under a single cash crop;[17] and in villages more remote from the auction block, the proportion was less.

These crop patterns, together with the general poverty of the region, tended to limit marketing areas. In the poorest parts of the Ceded districts most ryots did not trade outside their village;[18] farther south,

[13] F. A. Nicholson, *Report regarding the possibilities of introducing Agricultural Banks into the Madras Presidency* (Madras, 1895) [*RAB*], Vol. I, p. 232.

[14] *Land Revenue Reports for Fasli 1310 (1900–01)*, pp. 71–7. The problem of the zemindari ryot, who appears occasionally in the dry and more often in the wet region, is more difficult. However, on the basis of landholding size and rent payment, there is evidence of little real distinction between him and the government ryot. Most commentators thought that the structure of landholdings under zemindars was roughly the same as that under government and that, although zemindari rents were higher, they were collected less regularly. S. Srinivasa Raghavaiyangar, *Memorandum on the Progress of the Madras Presidency during the Last Forty Years of British Administration* (Madras, 1892), p. 76; *RPBC*, pp. 7–8.

[15] *RPBC*, p. 14.

[16] *RPBC*, p. 108.

[17] See *Madras Provincial Banking Enquiry Committee* (Madras, 1930) [*MPBC*], Vol. V. 'Reports by Investigators' for examination of 'dry' villages in Madura, Coimbatore and Bellary districts.

[18] F. A. Nicholson, *RAB*, Vol. I, p. 230.

men bought and sold in shandies which served small circles of villages.[19] There was little scope for a fast-moving grain trade which, in other parts of India, often formed the backbone of commerce. As most villages grew most of their wants, 'the food-grain needed for local consumption is seldom shifted very far'.[20] Of course, most of the rice eaten had to come from outside, but in these areas, rice was a luxury available only to a few. All villages had some wells, usually on the land of the richer ryots, which provided sufficient irrigation to grow vegetables. Cloth was often locally produced and hand-loom weaving was an important village industry.[21] Household utensils and agricultural implements were made by village artisans. Most villagers had little use for imports.[22]

Of course, everything that was grown in the village or village circle was not consumed there: cotton and groundnut were exported from India and grain was needed in the towns. But the ordinary cultivator had nothing to do with these transactions. The government's revenue demand had to be met immediately after the harvest, and most peasants had to sell as quickly as they could to pay on time; and the usual conventions of credit required debts also to be repaid at the harvest, forcing the peasant to sell at once.[23] Further, capital was needed to transport grain by cart to the towns, and capital was in short supply. Most peasants therefore disposed of their grain immediately in the village or village shandie.

Cotton and groundnut cash crops also presented marketing difficulties. Both were sold, ultimately, to European and Indian companies which were based in the major towns. These companies usually operated through commission agents (dallals) who could combine to "dominate the market" at the expense of small, disorganized sellers.[24] In addition, cotton and groundnut fetched high prices only after they had been processed: most ryots were in no position to do this. They sold their raw produce relatively cheaply in the local shandie or even in the field.[25]

[19] *RPBC*, p. 119; *Royal Commission on Agriculture in India, Appendix*, Vol. XIV (London, 1928), p. 269.

[20] *RPBC*, p. 121.

[21] *Royal Commission on Agriculure in India, Appendix*, Vol. XIV, p. 270.

[22] Except for cattle; and the cattle trade was highly decentralized, being carried on and financed by itinerant pedlars.

[23] Both these factors applied also to zemindari ryots. *RPBC*, p. 106; 'Report on Kurnool' pp. 4–5 in *Land Revenue Reports for Fasli 1312 (1902–3)*; *MPBC*, Vols. II–V, *in passim*.

[24] *RPBC*, p. 110.

[25] *Royal Commission on Agriculture in India, Appendix*, Vol. XIV, p. 269. *MPBC*, Vols. II–V, *in passim*.

The Cotton Commission (1925–28) found that, in the area of the Ceded districts which it investigated, 87 per cent of the cotton crop had been sold initially in the village where it had been grown.[26] As the Royal Commission on Agriculture (1928) discovered, 'the keynote of the marketing system . . . is the predominant part played by the middle-man'.[27]

The middle-man was the main beneficiary of the marketing system. In the grain trade, he could make profits either by transporting part of the crop to the towns or simply by keeping some of it where it was. As most ryots had to sell at the harvest, they glutted the grain market and drove down prices. The merchant who bought and stored made money as prices rose again during the next agricultural year.[28] In cotton and groundnut, he gained even more. Not only could he greatly enhance the value of the produce by processing it, but, if he operated on a sufficiently large scale, he could crack the hegemony of the urban dallal. The seller who guaranteed the delivery of many tons of decorticated groundnut or cotton kapas was in a strong bargaining position. Indeed, it was usual for a big rural trader to employ his own dallal to negotiate directly with the various purchasing companies.[29] If he kept the produce he had collected in a warehouse in the town, he could raise a loan on it without difficulty from urban sources, and wait for the best offer before selling it.

The middle-man played a key role in the economy of the dry areas, but it is difficult to discover who he was. In some parts of the region there were distinctly commercial groups: Komatis in the north, Devangas, Nadars, Vannigas and Tamil Muslims in the south. In localities which had been particularly stimulated by cash cropping, Marwaris and Multanis had moved in. But the absence of a thriving grain trade, and the problem of obtaining impersonal security for loans, tended to restrict their activities to the towns.[30] In the countryside,

26 *Indian Central Cotton Commission. General Report on Eight Investigations into the Finance and Marketing of Cultivators' Cotton. 1925–28* (Bombay, n.d.), p. 21.

27 *Royal Commission on Agriculture in India, Appendix*, Vol. XIV, p. 268.

28 *RPBC*, p. 106; *MPBC*, Vol. III, pp. 658, 946; 'Report on Kurnool', pp. 4–5 in *Land Revenue Reports for Fasli 1312 (1902–3)*.

29 *RPBC*, p. 112, 123; *Royal Commission on Agriculture in India, Appendix*, Vol. XIV, p. 268.

30 None of the evidence, not even the individual village surveys, attempts to distinguish exactly who was involved in rural trade. In most of the dry region this would have been difficult anyway because at every harvest urban merchants or their agents set out from the towns with empty carts and picked up what they could from whichever villages they passed through. There was little routine in this aspect of marketing. However, in some localities it is clear that these trading groups had established some-

M

trading connections followed closely those of debt: to most cultivators, trade and debt were two sides of the same coin. As Nicholson observed:

Probably it would, at least for an immense number of villages and for the majority of small ryots and cultivators, be safe to say that the rural credit of this presidency is chiefly grain credit, all the poorer ryots habitually and annually borrowing from the richer ryots at the sowing season, and repaying advances at the harvest. It may also be said that the rural creditors of this presidency are, for the vast bulk of the loans ryots, not men of the Marwari class. In Tinnevelly, South Arcot, Coimbatore and other districts where the short mortgage is in vogue, from 85 p.c. to 73 p.c. even of such loans are granted by ryots; similar figures are found in loans upon simple bonds. In the Ceded Districts, such as Anantapur where mortgages are rare, there will be a few simple bonds due to men—often well-to-do landholders— outside of the village, but the bulk is due to the richer ryots within the village and nearly every seer of borrowed grain, the commonest form of loan in these districts, is due to co-ryots of the same village.[31]

Nearly forty years later, the Banking Inquiry found that this analysis still applied.[32] Since the commercial groups found it so difficult to enter the trading and moneylending business in the villages, the rural economy rested firmly in the hands of those few peasants with a surplus from their own lands.

The tiny élite of rich peasants in the dry districts were perfectly placed to dominate the village economy and to grasp a profit from any new opportunities. Their relatively large holdings and substantial crops meant that they did not need to sell grain as soon as it was harvested. They were able to invest in carts and to process their crops. From this secure base, the large landholder could launch himself across the market. His surplus enabled him to buy up cheap grain at the harvest and to advance loans to his poorer brothers. The interest on grain loans was extremely high and left very little with the debtor who had to borrow again next year.[33] It was also usual for creditors to demand the right to buy the debtor's crop at a fixed and low price as a condition of loan.[34]

thing of a more permanent relationship with the economy. Yet almost all the evidence indicates that rich ryots were heavily involved in trade and controlled most—varying in different reports between 60 and 90 per cent—of the rural credit. Allowing for the fact that, here and there, non-landowning trading groups were important, I have chosen to concentrate on the ryot-rural capitalist who was much the most typical commercial agent in the region as a whole.

[31] F. A. Nicholson, *RAB*, Vol. I, p. 230. See also, *Statement exhibiting the Moral and Material Progress and Condition of India during the year 1901–02 and the nine preceding years*. *PP* 1903, Vol. XLIV, p. 354.
[32] *RPBC*, p. 79.
[33] F. A. Nicholson, *RAB*, Vol. I, p. 232; *RPBC*, pp. 79, 106.
[34] *Ibid.*

The position of the rich ryot was greatly enhanced by the lack of alternative sources of credit in the area. Faced with the government's demand for revenue, regular rain-failure and social pressures to spend lavishly on family ceremonies, petty cultivators had to find patrons: 'they could not begin to cultivate without borrowing seed, cattle, grain for maintenance, etc.'[35] But few of their fellow villagers were likely to be able to meet their needs. A Bellary witness told the Banking Inquiry that ryots needed a minimum of twenty acres of land to begin to market their own crops.[36] This was presumably good dry land which would pay about Rs 30 per annum in revenue. In Coimbatore this qualification would have excluded about 93 per cent of the landholding population from trading and lending on their own account. In poorer districts like Cuddapah or Bellary it would have excluded 97 per cent of ryots. Not surprisingly, the most usual form of credit relationship was that between a petty cultivator and a single creditor who regularly supplied most of his wants: 'Under each rich ryot there will be a set of ordinary ryots who depend on him for money. When once a ryot goes to a particular rich ryot for money then a convention is established that the poor ryot is the client of the rich ryot.'[37]

The large landholder's local dominance was further assured by his ability to provide employment. In the 1890s, S. Srinivasa Raghavaiyangar estimated that 8 dry acres were needed to keep a family and that 75 per cent of the cultivators held less than 5 acres.[38] Obviously most ryots required extra work in order to survive. The rich ryot, who possessed more land than he could cultivate, paid labourers to till it, or leased it out on annual, unprotected, tenancies. Many nominally independent revenue payers were thus already tied to a patron as his employees and tenants.[39] Naturally, they looked to him as their principal sowcar and were in no position to refuse his overtures or deny him their crop. Borrowing, labouring and tenancy were often different aspects of the same relationship:

The Sahukar charges his own rates of interest as the ryot can no longer bargain with him: what is worse the ryot has next to plough the lender's field

[35] F. A. Nicholson, *RAB*, Vol. I, p. 232.   [36] *MPBC*, Vol. II, p. 298.
[37] *MPBC*, Vol. III, p. 664. See also *Report on the Famine in the Madras Presidency during 1896 and 1897* (Madras, 1898), Vol. I, p. 50.
[38] S. Srinivasa Raghavaiyangar, *Memorandum on the Progress of the Madras Presidency*, p. 75.
[39] In the villages investigated by the Cotton Commission in Bellary district, about 35 per cent of the ryots worked the land of other ryots as well as their own. *Indian Central Cotton Commission. General Report on Eight Investigations into the Finance and Marketing of Cultivators' Cotton. 1925–28*, p. 50.

gratis and to do any other work at his bidding. The younger members of the family, the sons and brothers, are sometimes engaged as the private servants of the Sahukar without payment and in partial payment on the interest of the amount borrowed.[40]

The rich peasant ran an estate which stretched far beyond the boundaries of his own land into that nominally owned by his dependents who 'are thus in the worst cases little more than tenants of the lender who can prescribe what crops they shall grow and demand what terms he pleases'.[41]

In the Ceded districts, the bulk of the grain trade was in the hands of the richer Reddis who built their houses on top of enormous grain pits.[42] Much village trade consisted of borrowing from and returning to these pits.[43] Near Adoni, in Bellary district, the Cotton Commission found that although the scale of advances on the cotton crop was second only to that in Sind, the amount owed directly to urban creditors was only 27.3 per cent of the total.[44] Ryots and landlords were responsible for 56 per cent of the loans—far more than in any other part of India.[45] But even if the loans were not from urban merchants, they still bound the debtor and his crop to the lender.[46] In the marginally more prosperous south, members of the principal peasant castes—Gounder and other Vellalas, Reddi migrants from Andhra, and agricultural Maravars—were responsible for moving much of the grain, cotton and groundnut crop from the fields and smaller shandies to the markets. They often kept warehouses in their villages and in the towns, paid for the decortication of their groundnut, and hired dallals to act as brokers for their cotton.[47] From their positions at the centres of commerce, some of the more successful among them built up broad economic connexions. In the north, the growth of mica mining was financed by

[40] *MPBC*, Vol. III, p. 699.

[41] F. A. Nicholson, *RAB*, Vol. I, p. 232.

[42] *Appendix to the Report of the Indian Famine Commission, 1898, being Minutes of Evidence, etc. Volume II. Madras Presidency*, p. 101, *PP*, 1899, Vol. XXXII; *Report on the Famine in the Madras Presidency during 1896 and 1897* (Madras, 1898), Vol. I, p. 48; Vol. II, p. 139.

[43] F. A. Nicholson, *RAB*, Vol. I, p. 230.

[44] *Indian Central Cotton Committee. General Report on Eight Investigations into the Finance and Marketing of Cultivators' Cotton. 1925–28*, p. 14.

[45] *Ibid.*, p. 16.

[46] *RPBC*, p. 109; *Royal Commission on Agriculture in India. Volume III. Evidence taken in the Madras Presidency* (London, 1927), p. 55.

[47] *RPBC*, pp. 112, 123, 108; *Royal Commission on Agriculture in India, Appendix*, Vol. XIV, p. 233, 268; *MPBC*, Vol. III, pp. 319, 750, 946, 972; *Indian Central Cotton Committee. General Report on Eight Investigations into the Finance and Marketing of Cultivators' Cotton 1925–28*, p. 64.

landowning Reddis;[48] where British military or railway enterprises touched the local economy, it was often wealthy peasant families who picked up the construction and supply contracts;[49] where petty industry began to appear, both in the towns and in the villages, it was often the investment of local peasants—in decortication machines, cotton presses and, by the 1930s, cotton mills—which supported it;[50] in district capitals such as Madura and Coimbatore, Gounders moved between trade and banking, and played an important part in urban and regional economic development.[51]

The wealthy and commercially mobile peasant used his profits to extend and tighten his control in the locality. He was helped by the peculiar nature of the money-market. In Madras, the usual securities for loans were moveable properties and personal knowledge of the borrower. Land might have seemed the most obvious collateral; but titles to it were complicated by the interests of the joint-family and by a revenue system in which a man seldom owned the fields he cultivated. The petty cultivator, who had little property save his miserable crop, and who was unknown outside his village circle, could raise money only in his neighbourhood. The rich ryot, however, who had crops stored both in his village and in the town, and who was known to be credit-worthy among urban financiers, had much less difficulty in obtaining credit.[52] Money borrowed in the town, where it was quite plentiful, could be lent out at a considerable profit in the village, where it was scarce. As the market opportunities in the dry areas increased, the more important and the more dominant the rich ryots became in the working of the rural economy.

[48] See biography of K. Audinarayana Reddi in Reforms (Franchise) B, March 1921, 34–99, National Archives of India, New Delhi [NAI].

[49] In North Arcot district, where there was a great deal of military and railway contracting available, the leading contractors were drawn from the locally dominant Palli caste. One of the most famous, A. Dhanakoti Mudaliar, who came from a rich landowning family, extended his contracting empire to Madras city where he was a member of the Corporation in the 1880s. Also, see biography of M. Venkatarajaghaoulu Reddiar in Hindu, 19 May 1919.

[50] For example, the Vellakina Gounder family, of which V. C. Vellingiri Gounder was a member, built a cotton mill in Coimbatore district in the 1930s. For examples of Land-owning families involved in urban commerce see biographical notes on K.S. Ramaswami Gounder in Directory of the Madras Legislature (Madras, 1938), p. 231; on M. Vydyalinga Reddy in V. L. Sastri (ed.), Encyclopaedia of the Madras Presidency and the Adjacent States (Cocanada, 1920), p. 767.

[51] For examples, see biographical notes on G. Eswara Reddi, ibid., p. 751; C. S. Ratnasabhapati Mudaliar, ibid., p. 609; and for involvement with urban co-operative banks, P. S. Kumaraswami Raja in Directory of the Madras Legislature, p. 144; V. K. Palamsami Gounder, ibid., p. 196; K. A. Nachiappa Gounder, ibid., p. 176.

[52] RPBC, pp. 87–9.

One of the main problems the historian confronts in trying to trace
the increasing power of the richer peasants is that the sources upon
which he has to rely were not concerned with this question. The
revenue statistics reveal something about movements in landholding
but the economic power of the rich peasant did not necessarily depend
upon formal ownership. Most land was worth no more than the crops
and the cultivators on it. Through his manipulation of credit and trade,
the rich peasant already possessed effective control over the land and he
could find better ways of spending his money than idly pursuing title-
deeds. Moreover, the assumption of legal possession brought with it
great hazards. Titles to land in ryotwari Madras were documents of
dubious value, but even to get hold of them, the money-lender had to
follow a course which was fraught with danger. Court cases were
expensive and lengthy; under the Usurious Loans Act, they could
end in disaster for the money-lender who foreclosed. Judges could cut
agreed interest rates almost at will. Most loans were unsecured by any
formal document and so most money-lenders seldom went to court.[53]
The actual amount of land transferred in Madras each year by legal
possession, gift or will, was remarkably small.[54] Essentially, the rich
peasant operated his informal economic empire through personal
connexion with his debtors: the amount of land which he formally
acquired in no way represented his influence.

Nonetheless, the little movement of land that we can trace, indicates
an increasing stratification of landholding as larger proprietors accumulated more land and as the number of small ryots grew. Between
1886–87 and 1925–26, the proportion of total revenue paid by pattas of
more than Rs 250 per annum increased from 4.2 per cent to 6.7 per cent
and by pattas of less than Rs 10 from 24.3 per cent to 31.2 per cent.[55]

[53] F. A. Nicholson, *RAB*, Vol. I, p. 230; *RPBC*, pp. 87, 173–5, 181–2.

[54] On average, about 1–1½ per cent of the cropped area per annum. Unfortunately,
from 1913–14, the Madras Government ceased to keep central records of the
acreage transferred but there is little reason to think that the pattern of transfers
established in the 1884–1914 period altered radically before the depression. See
Agricultural Statistics of British India. Quinquennial Series. 1884–85 to 1912–13, 'Land
Transfers'.

[55] These figures cover both joint and single pattas. Although there were administrative differences between the two, it would in practice have been difficult to find
any real distinctions. Most single pattas were regarded as joint-family property
although legally registered only in the name of one member. The growth in the
number of joint patta holders in the twentieth century was due more 'to the growing
desire on the part of the people to secure documentary evidence in support of their
joint interest in land' than to any change in the character of landholding itself.
Hence I have put single and joint pattas together as units of possession. *Land Revenue
Reports for Fasli 1310 (1900–01)*, p. 26. Table 1 calculated from 'Statement of the

This growth at the top and bottom ends of the patta scale was, of course, at the expense of holdings in the middle. Table 1 expresses the development in terms of the growth of revenue paid by particular classes of patta.

TABLE 1

Growth in Revenue paid by pattas 1886/87–1925/26[56]

Less than Rs 10	72.4%
10–30	24.1
30–50	19.3
50–100	4.7
100–250	7.5
250–500	137.6
500–1,000	41.5
More than Rs 1,000	138.6

If anything, the land revenue figures minimize, rather than maximize, the movement of land towards the larger proprietors. They are statistics of pattas, not pattadars, and there was nothing to stop one man from holding more than one patta. However, pattas included all the land held by a man in one revenue village, so that the multi-patta holder had his lands quite widely spread. In view of this fact, the rich ryot was infinitely more likely than the poor one to own several pattas, and the land revenue figures would not show the true position of his accumulating wealth.

The growing economic importance of the rich peasant found its reflection in social and political life. The ties of debt operated by the wealthy ryot in the village were, of course, political as well as economic:

His power and prestige must at any cost be secured by having a large number of village people at his disposal. Consideration of his importance influence the advance of money rather than profit from usurious rates of interest.[57]

Rent-Roll' in *Land Revenue Reports for Fasli 1296 (1886–87)* and *Land Revenue Reports for Fasli 1335 (1925–26)*.

[56] Calculated from *ibid*.

[57] The quotation continues '... Nevertheless, the lifelong dependence of the borrower upon the landlord and a variety of free services to be rendered to the latter during agricultural seasons are features closely associated with this system. It is not unusual that the smaller agriculturist borrowers are obliged to sell their produce to the apparently obliging landlord'. *MPBC*, Vol. III, p. 1034; see also *ibid.*, p. 770.

As he often stood between starvation and his clients, he seldom had difficulty in obtaining their allegiance:

Experience shows that this unfortunate class of ryot have not only to work in the ryot's fields for bare subsistence but what is worse they have to help in all village politics and factious quarrels and in all kinds of litigation.[58]

Increasing wealth enabled him to deepen and extend his village empire. He could also spend more lavishly on religion and ritual. Not only did this bring him more influence over priest and service groups in his village, but it heightened his social status and distinguished him more clearly from his fellows.

As the rich peasant became involved in higher forms of economic organization, he was also drawn into larger forms of social and political organization. The principal market towns drew together village élite families from the surrounding countryside and gave them the means to further their ambitions. Marriage connexions affected economic and political, as well as social, life. The towns became focal points for marriage brokerage among wealthy landowners.[59] They were members of peasant sub-castes which sprawled across an area larger than that from which they normally took their spouses. But when dominant families came to live in the same town, they began to create much wider geographical connexions.[60] This also opened the way for marriages between wealthy families in different sub-castes. Such growth of literacy as there was in this region took place among the superior peasantry. Able to read and to write, the rich peasant had a better chance of taking the opportunities afforded him in the market towns.

This examination of the dry areas of Madras emphasizes two features. In the first place, growing market opportunities helped to increase the wealth of groups already landed and rich. Through the extension of ties of debt and trade, this élite was able to extend its own economic control over its neighbourhood without any serious challenge from outside. Secondly, as rich peasants were attracted from their villages into marketing centres, they could work in larger economic and social structures. By borrowing cheap money in the towns, pursuing different kinds of economic openings in the districts, and establishing

---

[58] *Ibid.*, p. 699.

[59] *Royal Commission on Agriculture in India. Appendix*, Vol. XIV, p. 233.

[60] For interesting discussions on the importance of expanding marriage ties among South Indian peasants see Carolyn M. Elliot, 'Caste and Faction Among the Dominant Caste: the Reddis and Kammas of Andhra' in R. Kothari (ed.), *Caste in Indian Politics* (New Delhi, 1970), pp. 129–71. Also, J. Maner, 'The Evolution of Political Arenas and Units of Social Organizations: the Lingayats and Vokkaligas of Princely Mysore' (forthcoming).

distant marriage and political alliances, they were able to build a series of socially horizontal connexions which reinforced their position. Naturally, such connexions were denied to their clients in the villages. For most poorer peasants, economic connexions with the outside world took place only through the rich peasant who diverted most of the rewards to himself.

There is much to suggest that the social patterns produced by administrative development were similar. Professors Frykenberg and Mukherjee have shown that the British, in their early settlements, failed to interfere directly in the village political structures which they found.[61] None the less, the conquerors certainly exercised a considerable indirect influence over village political society. The village—as an administrative or political unit[62]—was intimately related to the institutions of government above it, and the British greatly changed the nature of those institutions. For much of the eighteenth century, Madras had been torn apart under the rule of small princes or wandering bands of warriors who had pressed heavily on the village in search of surplus wealth. By establishing peace, the British removed this threat and replaced the many authorities which had ruled Madras with one uniform but more distant authority. They relaxed the pressure which had built up on the village.[63]

However, the British, like the previous native régimes, also had to govern rural Madras, and this meant that they had to connect their administration to the village. To effect this, they relied less on naked force—such as had characterized the administration of Hyder Ali and Tipu Sultan—than on establishing contacts inside village society with collaborators who would do their work for them. In the later nineteenth century, as the British administration became the most powerful Madras had ever seen, the position of these collaborators inevitably became strengthened. Those who directed village administration added to their local power through their links with extra-village authority.

The principal office on which the British built their administration

[61] R. E. Frykenberg and N. Mukherjee, 'The Ryotwari System and Social Organization in the Madras Presidency' and R. E. Frykenberg, 'Village Strength in South India' in R. E. Frykenberg (ed.), Land Control and Social Structure in Indian History (Madison, 1969), pp. 217–26; 227–47.

[62] The administrative village, of course, was not necessarily the same as the economic village or village circle we have discussed above. Nor were either necessarily the same as the 'physical' village of habitation. Village, as used in this article, is shorthand for the unit of face-to-face relations in rural society. Later, we shall be discussing the actual size and shape of this unit.

[63] See B. Stein, 'Integration of the Agrarian System of South India' in R. E. Frykenberg (ed.), Land Control and Social Structure in Indian History, pp. 207–12.

was that of the village headman. Certainly, the kurnam (accountant) who kept the revenue records was also, and sometimes independently, powerful. As he was usually the member of a literate family, the kurnam might also have relatives in government offices beyond the village. But in a system in which 'all influence is sought to be exercised through the Village Magistrate or headman'[64] whose post 'becomes daily of greater influence',[65] the headman was usually at the centre of village politics. Dependent on the support of established leaders, the British recruited their headmen from the principal peasant landowning castes and from families which had, or pretended to have, been recognized as headmen by previous régimes. In 1802, Fort St George confirmed them in office and guaranteed their hereditary rights.[66] This meant that it threw away its best lever on the village establishment. For three-quarters of a century, it was folk-lore at Fort St George that hereditary village officers could be dismissed if they failed to perform their duties. But in 1884 J. H. Garstin, of the Board of Revenue, studied the practical difficulties of enforcing this rule, and reported that the only offence for which a village officer could be dismissed (short of a criminal conviction) was that of being a woman.[67]

Land revenue systems have always been the most important aspects of Indian government. The system favoured by the British in most of Madras was ryotwari. Under this, the government took responsibility for measuring and assessing for revenue every field in the presidency. It spawned a vast bureaucracy, the senior officers in which were 'little more than post-boxes' passing huge quantities of paper which came to them from subordinates on to superiors.[68] The lowest officials in the pyramid were those appointed in the village—the kurnam and the headman who were responsible for collections, and for issuing notices of demand and restraint of defaulters' property. Dr R. E. Frykenberg has shown how the British locked themselves out of their own administrative system by giving too much unchecked authority to those serving low down in it.[69] Although reforms, particularly from the 1870s, checked the worst abuses at higher levels, the independence of local

[64] *Administration Report of the Madras Police for the year 1885* (Madras, 1886), [*Madras Police* . . .], p. 4.
[65] F. A. Nicholson, *RAB*, Vol. I, p. 312.
[66] B. B. Misra, *The Administrative History of India 1834–1947* (Oxford, 1970), p. 461.
[67] J. H. Garstin to Secretary, Revenue Department, 3 April 1884 in G.O. 787 (Revenue) dated 24 June 1884, Tamil Nad Archives [TNA].
[68] For a critique of the weaknesses of the revenue department written by senior officials inside it, see G.O. 173 (Revenue) dated 20 February 1902, TNA.
[69] R. E. Frykenberg, *Guntur District 1788–1848. A History of Local Influence and Central Authority in South India* (Oxford, 1965).

COUNTRY POLITICS: MADRAS 1880 TO 1930

administrations remained intact in Madras Presidency until at least
1900. In 1885, for example, a Board of Revenue investigation in
Tanjore, generally considered one of the better governed districts,
uncovered a network of intrigue and private connexion which stretched
from the Huzur Sheristidar to hundreds of village officers. The dominant
office clique had used a flood in the winter of 1884 as an excuse to claim
Rs 8 lakhs of remissions from Fort St George; the Board of Revenue
found Rs 4 lakhs of these to be fraudulent. The investigator, H. S.
Thomas, who had nearly thirty years' experience of Madras, doubted
whether his findings were the result of peculiar conditions in Tanjore.
He thought that the same kind of hidden organizations existed everywhere; they had been uncovered in Tanjore only because their private
demands on the revenue had overstepped the bounds of common
sense.[70]

Such a loosely organized revenue administration gave great power
to those who connected the village to the taxation system. In 1902,
Lord Ampthill, the Governor, described to his Secretary of State the
operations of the annual jamabundi:

What happens is this: All the lands on which the crops have failed have to be
inspected by subordinate agency which, as you know, is very amenable to
bribery in this country. The consequence is that the well-to-do ryot who can
afford to bribe the village officers or revenue inspectors gets them to report
that his crops are withered or totally lost, so as to entitle him to remission. . . .
Again it is by no means infrequent that the remissions never reach the ryots
for whom they were intended as the village officers deceive the ryots by
telling them that no remissions were granted, collect the full assessment and
pocket the money themselves.[71]

Within the limits of a known and relatively fixed 'tribute' to the
superior government, the village revenue establishment dictated
village payments. When they came to resettle the land, the British
discovered that the area cultivated often bore no relation to what was
in the records. Wet land was listed as dry; good quality soil as bad;
and many fields were not listed at all.[72] Village officers also controlled
the sale of revenue defaulters' land and saw that it went to their clients

---

[70] H. S. Thomas, *Report on Tanjore Remissions in Fasli 1294 (A.D. 1884–85)* (Madras, 1885).

[71] Ampthill to Hamilton, 6 August 1902, Ampthill Papers, Eur. MSS. 233/7. India Office Library [IOL].

[72] See, *Madras District Gazetteers*: W. Francis, *The Niligiris* (Madras, 1908), Vol. I, p. 281; J. F. Hall, *South Kanara* (Madras, 1938), Vol. II, p. 28; F. J. Richards, *Salem* (Madras, 1918), Vol. I, Part II, pp. 35–6; W. Francis, *Madura* (Madras, 1906), Vol. I, pp. 203–4; *Selections from the Madras Records Vol. XXII* (Madras, 1870), p. 18; 'Report on Coimbatore', pp. 2–3 in *Land Revenue Reports for Fasli 1280 (1870–71)*.

at give-away prices.[73] As late as 1929 the Banking Inquiry was told that in many places no outsider could acquire land without the permission of the village revenue establishment.[74]

Police administration also was built onto the authorities within the the village. At no time in the nineteenth century was Fort St George able to employ more than one centrally appointed policeman to every 1,500 inhabitants.[75] Keeping the peace, such as it was, rested firmly in the hands of the village headman who, by Sir William Robinson's reforms of 1863, acquired greater formal powers than ever before. He was given money to hire more kavalgars, and usually he could keep all other law-officers out of his village.[76] He was well placed to operate a rule of terror, which doubtless had always been part of his prerogative. The grim situation in Salem, described by its Superintendent of Police in 1896, was typical of the area:

all the violent crime in the district is committed by Koravars, who act in very many cases as private Kavalgars in the villages. He considers that in very many cases these men are in the hands of the Village Magistrates, who use them as their servants and in consequence protect them, taking care when crimes occur not to mention any of their dependents in their first reports, on which the Sessions Court sets such value. The Village Magistrates, of course, obtain a considerable share of the proceeds of these looting expeditions.[77]

Headmen used the gangs under their protection to force the obeisance of subjects in their little kingdoms and to harass and plunder their enemies.[78] When the police and courts outside the village took a hand, they proved usually to be the unwitting allies of the village powers. The district police only came into the village when the headman called them, and his word was taken by the courts as that of authority.[79]

[73] *Report of the Indian Famine Commission. Appendix. Volume III. Condition of the Country nd People*, PP 1881, Vol. LXXI, Part 2, p. 416.

[74] *MPBC*, Vol. III, p. 679.

[75] See *Madras Police 1878–1900*. And their 'provincial' policemen were ineffective: 'Dishonesty in investigation is, we are told, prevalent everywhere. . . .', *Statement of the Police Committee on the Administration of the District Police in the Madras Presidency* (Madras, 1902), p. 50.

[76] For an assessment of the workings of the reforms, see *Madras Police 1885*, pp. 1–5.

[77] *Madras Police 1896*, p. 35. For similar reports on headmen in Coimbatore, Cuddapah, Tinnevelly, Madura, Chingleput and North Arcot, see *Madras Police 1888*, App. C, pp. xxi–xxii; *ibid., 1895*, pp. 33, 185; *ibid., 1912*, p. 10.

[78] 'But many Reddis or Village Magistrates keep gangs of retainers—generally Yerikalas—who, when not committing depredations, act as bravos in paying off old scores against rivals'. Report on Cuddapah in *Land Revenue Reports for Fasli 1314 (1904–05)*, p. 72.

[79] *Madras Police 1897*, p. 12.

In the early twentieth century, false reports and charges brought by headmen against their enemies—often headmen in neighbouring villages—became so numerous that the Madras Government began to keep two registers of crime—one 'false' and one 'true'.[80]

Headmen also possessed some powers as criminal and civil magistrates in their own right. Although these powers were little used in the later nineteenth century this does not mean that the headman's influence was on the wane.[81] His formal powers in criminal matters were extremely limited. Fifteen days in prison or a spell in the stocks were hardly awesome threats in a society where life was so cheap. Most people who appeared before the headman did so voluntarily to answer petty charges of social misdemeanour. His informal influence was far greater than the limits of his judicial power suggest. In civil matters, it was generally recognized that headmen arbitrated many more, and far more important, disputes than ever got into their ledgers.[82] Indeed, in the Ceded districts, where the Reddi was pre-eminent, the headmen did not bother to send in returns of the cases they tried.[83] In the early twentieth century, when government began to insist on records, litigation in village courts increased prodigiously.[84]

In spite of the recommendation of the Madras Torture Commission (1855) that police, magisterial and revenue functions should not lie in the same hands, the village headman possessed all three. Not only was it extremely difficult for the British to intervene in his affairs, but normal administrative procedures guaranteed that, whenever they were called in, it was to support his authority. In the later nineteenth century, as the government began to do more and more, the headman's role in government grew larger. The administration of the income tax, introduced in 1886, was attached to his revenue office;[85] the Famine

---

[80] For example in 1918, the police were called out in answer to 5,290 false complaints and found themselves involved in 4,160 false prosecutions. *Madras Police 1918*, pp. 18–21.

[81] In the later nineteenth century although relatively few village headmen tried civil cases, they nonetheless covered about two-thirds of the litigation in their competence. F. A. Nicholson, *RAB*, Vol. I, p. 312.

[82] *Ibid.*

[83] See *Report on the Administration of Civil Justice in the Presidency of Madras* 1881–1925 (annual series); *Report on the Administration of Criminal Justice in the Presidency of Madras* 1881–1925 (annual series).

[84] In 1881, village munsiffs heard 47,656 civil cases; in 1910, they heard 96,597; and between 1913 and 1918, with the help of panchayats, they heard an annual average of 126,959. *Report on the Administration of Civil Justice in the Presidency of Madras in 1881* (Madras, 1882), p. 31; *ibid.*, *1910*, p. 4; *ibid.*, *1920*, p. 3.

[85] For comments on the arbitrary nature of assessment see Proceedings of the Board of Revenue, No. 46 (Ordinary) dated 15 January 1892, TNA. Also *Report on the*

Code provided him with cheap government loans and grain to distribute, almost without supervision, in his village;[86] the development of Takavi loans permitted him to hand out—or withhold—government-backed credit for long-term loans;[87] the District Boards Act of 1884 put him on village unions with powers of local taxation and considerable administrative interference.[88] The British elaborated a vast administrative system which sought to govern entirely through him. In the last decades of the nineteenth century the village headman, in some parts of Madras, was more powerful than he had ever been before.

As the Madras government became more concerned with district administration, it demanded greater efficiency from the headman whose powers it had increased. While security and the regular payment of revenue were its main concern, the government did not enquire too closely into the affairs of the village; but when it wanted to do more, the headman's independence could prove a problem. The revenue resettlements, which began in the 1860s, showed how irrelevant policy made in the capital was to the practice of the village. On investigation the revenue system was found actually to prevent the centre from meddling too much in the localities.[89] To exercise control the British realized that they would have to change the entire system, and that they would have to put the police on a quite different footing.[90] From the 1880s the new revenue settlements cut down some of the worst abuses in the village. Village officers had now to demonstrate some competence in their work—they had to be able to read—before their sanads were recognized. Their right to issue notices of demand and restraint at will was curbed and many of the minor posts of village watchmen and servants, which had provided the headman with useful patronage, were discontinued. Between the 1860s and 1906, headmen were paid increasingly by centrally administered stipends. Districts and

Administration of the Income Tax under Act II of 1886 in the Madras Presidency for the year 1888–89 (Madras, 1890), p. 39.

[86] *Appendix to the Report of the Indian Famine Commission, 1898, being Minutes of Evidence, etc. Volume II. Madras Presidency.* PP, 1899, Vol. XXXII, pp. 33, 165, 169; *Report on the Famine in the Madras Presidency during 1896 and 1897* (Madras, 1898), Vol. II, p. 203.

[87] Takavi loans were administered through the regular revenue machinery.

[88] Village officers were *ex-officio* members of village unions—collections of villages brought together for administrative purposes. By 1920, there were nearly 600 of these, with an average annual income of Rs 3,000. G.O. 1337 (Local and Municipal, Local) dated 13 July 1921, TNA.

[89] See J. H. Garstin, *Report on the Revision of Revenue Establishments in the Madras Presidency* (Madras, 1883).

[90] Radical police reform was recommended after an inquiry ordered by Lord Curzon. See *Statement of the Police Committee on the Administration of the District Police in the Madras Presidency* (Madras, 1902).

taluks were reduced in size, and more supervisory officials were appointed.

However, it must be doubted whether any of these reforms seriously curtailed the independence of the village officer, at least before the mid-1920s. For the Government of India cheap government and good government were synonymous. Reforms cost money, and Calcutta would not give Madras the funds necessary to launch an effective attack on the village administration.[91] In 1883 a modest request for Rs 4.6 lakhs to improve the revenue department was turned down.[92] In 1896, when approached for money to reform the police force, the Government of India only permitted an increase in expenditure sufficient to issue the existing policemen with badges and night-sticks.[93] Faced with parsimony on this scale, all the efforts of Fort St George were mere tinkerings. They could not undermine the village officer because they could not afford to replace him.

Moreover, village officers themselves exercised influence which went far beyond the bounds of their office. Exact figures of their landholding, apart from their inams, do not exist; but everybody in Madras knew that they were the richest of the rich peasants.[94] In 1921 the Government announced that it would not raise their stipends to meet inflation because their stipends formed only a very small part of their income. Few members of the Legislative Council bothered to challenge this; some carried it further and argued that senior village officers did not need to be paid at all.[95] The vital offices of government in the locality had been settled on the principal landowning families of village Madras, who, by inter-marriage, formed distinguishable élites within small territories. They were precisely the same families who were tightening their control over the local economies. The government's attempts at reform chipped at only one of their many pillars of authority. These local bosses made dangerous enemies and, during the Home Rule League-Congress agitations of 1916–22, when the nationalists tried to

[91] During our period, the Government of India took, under various headings, between 68 and 78 per cent of Madras revenues.

[92] G.O. 369 (Revenue) dated 25 March 1885, TNA; India Office, Public and Judicial Department, File 251 of 1888, IOL.

[93] *Madras Police 1897*, p. 5.

[94] Some fragments of evidence on their landholdings, however, are available. For example, according to a report of 1865, the village officers of Bellary held 650,000 acres of land in the district. W. Francis, *Bellary* (Madras, 1904), Vol. 1, p. 175; or again 168 Cuddapah village officers mentioned in a resettlement operation, admitted to paying Rs 22,507 a year in land revenue between them. 'Report on Cuddapah' p. 10 in *Land Revenue Reports for Fasli 1285 (1875–76)*.

[95] Government of India, Home Judicial Files 1–2 of 1922, NAI.

link up their agitation with protests from the village élites, the British had cause for alarm.[96]

The government had many reasons for not launching a full-blooded assault on their village officers. When a government order of 1894 forced village officers to prove their literacy and to attend classes on their work, it contained a clause which permitted all those village officers and their immediate heirs who registered within two years to avoid the penalties for failure.[97] It was a generation before the order began to have any impact, and then all the government found it could do with men who failed the tests was to ask them to come back the next year.[98] The attempts to enfranchise service inams were expensive and still incomplete by the time they were stopped by the Government of India in 1906. In any case, village officers took advantage of their possession of the records to surrender as little land as possible. Their new stipends were worth far more than the fields they lost.[99] Since the government could not easily dismiss them, the control-through-payment which the British had hoped to achieve remained purely notional.[100] Some of the most glaring abuses of the revenue system were ended, but the resettlement operations did not prevent the village officers from continuing to manipulate the administration. More land was assessed for revenue, but the Madras government still knew remarkably little about who paid what. In the end, the British did little more than irritate the headman by clipping some of his perquisites and patronage; they never solved the central problems of his existence and the nature of his rule.

The headman's success in fending off attack was made clear by

[96] In 1916, Home Rule League agitators picked up the cause of indentured labourers and demanded that the Government restrict emigration to Burma and Ceylon because of the appalling conditions of service there. In fact, as the British recognized, this move was intended less to aid the labourers than to connect with the protests of landlords in several parts of Madras who feared that emigration was taking away their cheap labour supply. The government acted quickly and imposed restrictions in order to prevent the development of a serious threat to order. Home Political Deposit, March 1917, 32 and 33; April 1917, 61, NAI.

[97] G.O. 361 (Education) dated 24 May 1894, TNA.

[98] See *Hindu*, 1 August 1919.

[99] For example, in 1870, the village officers of Trichinopoly surrendered 16,304,37 acres of inam land and had to pay about Rs 10,000 p.a. assessment on it. In return, the cesses collected by government and distributed to them increased from Rs 642 p.a. to Rs 1,72,340 in 1875. 'Report on Trichinopoly', p. 10 in *Land Revenue Reports for Fasli 1280 (1870–71)*; and *ibid., for Fasli 1285 (1875–76)*, p. 68.

[100] 'The irregularities committed by these servants (which are very frequent) cannot, however, be well punished by suspension or dismissal as it has been found by experience that such a course causes great inconvenience to the public service...', 'Report on Cuddapah', p. 21 in *Land Revenue Reports for Fasli 1285 (1875–76)*.

the failure of two particular reforms. In 1918, thirty-five years after it had been first suggested, the Government of Madras introduced a bill to abrogate the hereditary rights of village officers. Faced with open agitation on an unprecedented scale, Fort St George shelved the bill before its first reading.[101] The second triumph was over police reform. Between 1905 and 1907, 2,000 men were recruited as deputy-inspectors in the districts, to fill the gap between the village and the distant circle police stations.[102] Within five years, it had become apparent that this scheme was not working. The new deputy inspectors doubled the cost of the police and drove down the detection rate.[103] In many regions open war was declared between the village and the police. Once village headmen withdrew their co-operation, the problem of maintaining order became more impossible than ever.[104] By 1915, the Madras Government had to compromise, and the right to appoint the deputy inspectors was taken from the Commissioner of Police and given to committees of local notables.[105] Once again the village headmen had preserved their immunity from outside control.

The fate of the police reforms set a pattern for the future relationship between the government at Fort St George and that in the village. Instead of curbing the village administration the Madras government built upon it. Local panchayats were far more important in Madras Presidency than anywhere else in India.[106] To control the production and consumption of alcohol, the government decided in 1908 to enlist the aid of local committees.[107] When the forest conservation policy caused friction with local groups, the government made local committees responsible for carrying it out.[108] From about 1915 irrigation panchayats steadily took over the distribution of water.[109] During the 1920s village courts were encouraged to take a larger share of litigation.[110] The

---

[101] For discussion of the bill, see G.O. 1958 (Revenue) dated 14 August 1920, TNA. Also, Government of India, Home Judical Files 1–2 of 1922, NAI.

[102] *Madras Police 1919*, Appendix D, p. x.

[103] *Madras Police 1912*, p. 9; *ibid., 1915*, pp. 17–18.

[104] *Madras Police 1907*, pp. 5–6; *ibid., 1912*, p. 33; *ibid., 1914*, pp. 72–76.

[105] *Madras Police 1915*, p. 18.

[106] *Royal Commission on Agriculture in India. Appendix*, Vol. XIV, pp. 256–8.

[107] *Report on the Administration of the Abkari Revenue in the Presidency of Fort St. George for the year 1915–16* (Madras, 1916), p. 4.

[108] Forest panchayats developed out of a report by the Forest Committee in 1913. The government hoped that they 'will go far to remove or reduce the friction of forest subordinates and the public which has been such an unsatisfactory feature of past administration'. Quoted in *Hindu*, 14 April 1915.

[109] *Royal Commission on Agriculture in India. Appendix*, Vol. XIV, p. 256.

[110] *Report on the Administration of Civil Justice in the Presidency of Madras. 1920–30* (annual series).

N

Madras Government had to use village leaders in order to govern. By using them the government made these leaders more powerful.

The main theme of this economic and administrative analysis of the dry areas of Madras has been the growth of social stratification. Of course, Madras rural society was hierarchically organized long before the British arrived; and the British did not change the social order of that hierarchy. But the distance between the rich and the poor, between those with administrative power and those without it, was becoming greater. Further prosperity came to individuals and to families who were in a position to control the village economy and the local administration rather than to whole castes or communities. Communal organizations among dominant peasant castes were weakened.[111] In the countryside politics were marked by factionalism rather than by conflict between castes or classes. Peasant leaders, often of the same ritual rank, fought each other for land, loot and pre-eminence within a restricted locality. Their followers were socially heterogeneous and drawn together by their dependence on a common leader.

The restricted locality over which the peasant boss held sway was not limited to the village, although there were many faction fights inside villages. Most of the powers at the disposal of the peasant leader could be exported beyond the village boundary. Connexions of debt, kin and terror could embrace several villages. Since the Madras village was usually a collection of hamlets brought together for administrative convenience, village officers might have jurisdictions covering several square miles. Further, by waging war against his neighbours, a successful village leader could influence an even larger territory. A typical example of local politics in this area was the long-standing feud between Chinnarappa Reddi and Thimma Reddi in the Gooty taluk of Anantapur district. Both men were large landholders connected with village office families. They had been quarrelling for many years, but in 1904 their rivalry broke out into an open vendetta. Thimma was arrested for the murder of a young Reddi lawyer who was Chinnarappa's man. Thimma was acquitted, and extended the fight by acquiring land inside Chinnarappa's territory. Chinnarappa countered by hiring P. Kesava Pillai, a lawyer and well-known provincial politician, who had considerable influence with the local administration. Over the next few years Thimma was arraigned before the local magistracy on various charges of violence no fewer than thirty-three times and several

[111] For example, by 1907, of all the Vellala sub-castes in Trichinopoly district, 'only a few of the sub-divisions, namely the Kodikkals, Kongas and Aru-nadus, have caste panchayats'. F. R. Hemingway, *Trichinopoly* (Madras, 1907), Vol. I, p. 102.

of his hench-men were imprisoned. Chinnarappa also used Kesava Pillai's influence to block police action against himself. He drove Thimma's labourers off his land and attacked his dependents. Supporters of each man were murdered—sometimes at the rate of two or three a month—but Kesava Pillai intervened six times to prevent the Madras authorities from stationing punitive police in the district. In better days Thimma had bought a pleadership certificate from a local official. This was revoked by the courts when Kesava Pillai accused him of moneylending. Through violence, and by bending the law, Chinna-rappa smashed Thimma's empire and became 'the sole monarch of forty villages', exacting tribute from his subjects and settling their disputes.[112] Police reports from other districts make it clear that there was nothing unusual in this conflict.[113] Forty villages might seem a sizeable realm, but it was simply a fraction of one revenue firka. Such battles were essentially fought out face-to-face with resources gathered from a small area. They rarely intruded into the higher levels of the administration, although individual superior police and revenue officials were sometimes called in to help one or the other of the sides.

The general development of administration, however, began to create institutions in which the resources available to engage in such petty battles could be drawn from a much wider area. Just as the economic élite found that the development of the economy enabled them not only to strengthen their local position but also to participate in new forms of economic activity, so the administrative élite were pulled out of the locality and placed in a framework in which new administrative—or political—opportunities were available. The most important of these institutions, although by no means the only ones, were the rural boards.[114]

Although the Madras Government had been forced by Ripon in 1884 into following the letter of the legislation about decentralization, it did not begin to follow its spirit until about 1909. The district

---

[112] The story emerged in the course of a trial which was fully reported in the *Hindu*, 20, 22, 29 and 30 June and 16 July 1925; see also P. Kesava Pillai to S. M. V. Osman, the Collector of Anatapur, 1 July 1922, and P. Kesava Pillai to C. P. Rama-swami Iyer, 14 May 1925, P. Kesava Pillai Papers, Nehru Memorial Museum, New Delhi [NMM].

[113] The dry districts in general and Coimbatore, Salem, Cuddapah and Anantapur in particular, had much the highest murder rates in the presidency. Superior police officials invariably attributed the prevalence of the crime to faction. See *Madras Police 1910*, p. 15; *ibid., 1918*, p. 12; *ibid., 1920*, p. 14.

[114] As important, and subject to the same pattern of growth, were the temple committees. See C. J. Baker, 'Political Change in South India (1919–1937)' (Fellow-ship dissertation, Queens' College, Cambridge, 1972), pp. 65–74.

boards, which sat on top of a pyramid of taluk boards and village unions, remained extensions of various government departments, whose officers ran them as part of their general duties. A. Subbarayalu Reddiar, who took over the Cuddalore taluk board in 1912, reported to his patron Sir P. S. Sivaswami Iyer:

As matters have stood, with the exception of Dispensaries, Schools and Taluk Board Roads, almost the whole of the outdoor work was managed by the Revenue divisional agency. The Village Sanitation, the maintenance and opening of the village roads, the repair and construction of the drinking water wells, and ponds, the clearance of encroachments, the removal of prickly pear, etc., were all in the hands of the revenue department.[115]

The dispensaries were run by the Medical Department; the schools by the Education Department; and the taluk board roads by the Public Works Department. In the rural boards, as much as in the departments, rivals for favours jockeyed around the official and tried to divert his authority to their course. Village unions and taluk boards were mostly run by the lowest officials who were *ex-officio* members of them.[116] Elections to the district boards, which were made by taluk boards, were controlled by these officials.[117] The political bankruptcy of these early rural boards has been perfectly described by the Tamil novelist A. Madhaviah:

In these assemblies, I first discovered what a shameful farce local self-government was. Not a few of my fellow members were almost illiterate, and altogether innocent of the English tongue in which our deliberations were conducted. They were wealthy and so they were elected. They came more for the travelling allowance they obtained for attending meetings than for the subjects discussed at those meetings, unless they happened to hold a secret brief from a contractor to get an extravagant bill passed.[118]

From about 1909, Fort St George began to implement Ripon's policies more fully. Madras district boards had never lacked funds— they were the richest in India, and some, by the 1890s, had even begun to construct their own railways[119]—but now they became enormous pools of patronage. Between 1909 and 1919, budgets of the rural boards increased by 70 per cent to a district average of 11 lakhs a year, and

[115] A. Subbarayalu Reddiar to P. S. Sivaswami Iyer, 12 April 1912. P. S. Sivaswami Iyer Papers, NAI.

[116] See article on Tindivanum taluk board in *Hindu*, 9 August 1897.

[117] Memorandum 31-4L, dated 5 February 1915, in Confidential Proceedings of the Madras Government, 1916, Volume 23, IOL.

[118] A. Madhaviah, *Thillai Govindan* (London, 1916), p. 118.

[119] The earliest district board railway was that constructed in Tanjore in 1897–98. See *Hindu*, 10 and 17 June 1896.

between 1919 and 1929 they more than doubled again.[120] At the same time their administrative competence, which had always been considerable, was increased. They controlled a large slice of primary and some secondary education, the right to license all markets in the district, to route and maintain all important roads, to grant building permission, to levy taxes and to organize religious festivals. More significantly, from 1909 the Madras Government began to withdraw its officials from these boards and to replace them with local non-officials in the executive offices. It also increased the number of elected seats.[121] The effects of these changes are not difficult to guess:

Landlords with local influence discovered that, as presidents and members of local boards, they could wield a large amount of influence in their locality, and exercise greater power over their neighbours.[122]

It did not take local politicians long to recognize and use the potential of the district board. In 1917, for example, A. Subbarayalu Reddiar, a

[120]

Total Revenue of Rural Boards

Year	Rupees
1909–10	1, 52, 77, 794
1919–20	2, 68, 49, 522
1929–30	5, 78, 07, 952

G.O. 1702 (Local and Municipal Local) dated 12 December 1910; G.O. 1337 (Local and Municipal) dated 13 July 1922; G.O. 1568 (Local and Municipal) dated 9 April 1931, TNA.

[121]

Presidents of Rural Boards

a. District Boards

Year	Total	Nominated Official	Nominated Non-Official	Elected
1911–12	25	25	—	—
1922–23	25	1	14	9
1926–27	24	1	4	19

b. Taluk Boards

Year	Total	Nominated Official	Nominated Non-Official	Elected
1911–12	95	73	19	3
1922–23	125	1	13	111
1926–27	129	—	14	118

Source: *Annual Report on the Working of Local Boards in Madras* for 1912, 1923, 1927.

[122] M. Venkatarangaiya, *The Development of Local Boards in the Madras Presidency* (Bombay, 1939), pp. 66–7.

rich landed magnate and lawyer, moved from the president's office of the Cuddalore taluk board to the chair of the South Arcot district board, and rapidly began to build a district-wide political machine. He replaced revenue department employees with his men;[123] he demanded the right to appoint all taluk board staff, something no collector had done;[124] he stood on his rights to nominate taluk board members and presidents beneath him;[125] and he used his powers to drive out his enemies from local board seats. In particular, he was able to unseat his old rival in Cuddalore town and taluk politics, M. Razak Maracair, from the district board, on which he had sat since 1886, and fill the vacancy with his closest ally A. T. Muthukumaraswami Chetty, another rich landlord and banker.[126]

It was not only that the local self-government reforms created district arenas in which politicians could participate: the growing power of the boards and the fact that they were available to enemies meant that every man of local influence had to take part or suffer the consequences. For example, the main concern of A. K. D. Dharma Raja, a rich landlord from Rajapalayam in Ramnad district, was to run his private market. From its beginnings in 1900, he had protected it from the avaricious gaze of government by getting his brother, who was a village officer, to forget to notify his superiors of its existence. Later, however, its appearance was noticed for it was taking business away from the licensed market. Dharma Raja then contacted his tahsildar, T. S. Ramaswami Iyer, who agreed to look after its interests in the taluk board where it was licensed for a nominal sum. In 1920 the raja of Ramnad became the first non-official president of the Ramnad district board and promptly began to treat the whole district as part of his estate.[127] In particular, he tried to obtain control of all the markets in the district. Dharma Raja now found himself dragged into a district arena simply to maintain himself locally, and he sought election to the district board.[128] Dharma Raja's history was not unique: all over

[123] *Hindu*, 5 February 1918.
[124] *Ibid.*
[125] G.O. 1021 (Local and Municipal, Local) dated 8 August 1918, TNA.
[126] *Hindu*, 12 June 1918, 9 October 1920.
[127] The raja became involved with various Nattukottai Chetties, whose whole south Asian banking empire was centred on Ramnad, in a district dog-fight for control of the principal markets. G.O. 783 (Local and Municipal) dated 3 May 1922; G.O. 811 (Local and Municipal) dated 9 May 1922 TNA; *Hindu*, 31 July and 16 March 1922.
[128] G.O. 1984 (Local and Municipal) dated 7 September 1923, TNA. Dharma Raja was related to P. S. Kumaraswami Raja (see footnote 51) and their family was typical of our peasant-capitalist élite. They owned Rs 20,000 worth of land, had

Madras rural leaders were forced to take account of the new institutions. Scarcely surprisingly, the Chinnarappa Reddi vs. Thimma Reddi conflict was now drawn into a larger arena. Both became taluk board members and Chinnarappa showed who was dominant when Thimma was thrown off the board for associating with known criminals— the result, it was said, of Kesava Pillai's influence in Madras city.[129] In 1920, Chinnarappa was elected to the district board.

The district boards placed the rural élite in a broader political context. Rivals no longer fought each others' armies only with sticks: they had to shift around their districts, seeking alliances with men whose bases could be a hundred miles from their own, in order to gain control of district institutions. The need to make wider horizontal political connexions within an extending locality also fostered wider social and marriage connexions. Although the political conduct of the élite changed, there was very little alteration in the vertical structure of politics. The rural leaders, scrambling over each other to gain district office and rewards, still preserved as tight a grip as ever over their localities. Madhaviah's comment on the electoral importance of wealth applied throughout this period; and the British fully recognized the influence village officers possessed over district and provincial elections.[130] The rural board franchise was based on tax-payment, and included only a small fraction of the population.[131] Even so, many voters were dependents of the rural élite and their votes were cast long before they reached any polling booth. Most men did not have the vote, and this served not only to preserve the importance of the active élite but actually to enhance it. For if any member of this voteless majority wished to obtain anything from the district institutions, he could do so

interests in banking and a cotton ginning factory and possessed village office. See A. K. D. Venkata Raja, *A Brief Life Sketch of P. S. Kumaraswami Raja* (Rajapayaiyam, 1964).

[129] G.O. 180 (Local and Municipal, Local) dated 27 February 1920. TNA.

[130] Between 1920 and 1930, the electorates to the Legislative Council and to the taluk boards were roughly the same. When considering action against village officers, C. Todhunter, a senior British official, thought: 'the village officers are likely to have so much influence over the electorate under the Montagu–Chelmsford Reforms that it would be easy for them to secure a mandate to elected members to oppose interference with hereditary right'. Note, 11/12/19 in G.O. 1958 (Revenue) dated 14 August 1920, TNA.

[131] No exact statistics of the rural board electorates exist. On the basis of information collected for the 1920 and 1937 Legislative Council reforms, it seems probable that, between 1920 and 1930, about 2½ per cent of the rural population could vote in rural board elections and, between 1930 and 1937, about 13 per cent. See *Madras Government Evidence to the Southborough Committee on Franchise 1918–19.* (Calcutta, 1919), Appendix 1; Government of India, Home Political, File 129 of 1937, NAI.

only by approaching somebody who was capable of influencing decisions inside them. In other words, he had to become a client.

Rural board and district politics were the preserve of small groups feeling little direct pressure from below. The dependents of the rural élite were unable to come together to constitute a separate force, or even much of an organized interest. The effects of this can be judged by the absence of organized protests against government policy and by the failure of attempts to introduce popular issues into district politics. From its creation in 1878, the forest department sought to control the use made of jungles and lands unfit for cultivation. This meant that, in areas like the Ceded districts, Coimbatore and Salem, it restricted access to land from which ryots traditionally obtained grazing for their cattle, crude fertilisers, fire-wood and various food stuffs. Relations between the forest department and the ryots under its jurisdiction were always strained. Although Legislative Councillors from the dry districts—such as P. Kesava Pillai[132]—continually pressed Fort St George to reform forest administration, and although all Congress conferences in the area tried to enlist local support by raising the forest issue, there was no organized response. The local rural élite dealt with the forest department on the ground. By bribery, threats and the occasional murder, powerful ryots came to satisfactory arrangements with forest subordinates.[133] They gained access to the forests while the poorer cultivators, who lacked 'influence', were kept out. From 1915, the development of forest panchayats put the élite even more firmly in control. Since the leaders had little to gain by raising the masses, it proved impossible to get a forest agitation moving.[134]

Attempts to get a wider political response by using the propaganda of caste were also doomed. From the 1910s to the early 1930s they seldom unbalanced the existing structure of politics. Indeed, in many ways they re-inforced the power of members of the rural élite, since caste movements were often only the public manifestations of existing connexions of kin. 'The Reddi scare' in Anantapur in 1926, for example, was really the attempt of a Chinnarappa Reddi-led faction to get rid of P. Kesava Pillai and to replace him with a Reddi lawyer.[135] Equally, the activities of the Gounders around Coimbatore in 1921 stemmed

[132] While on the Legislative Council, P. Kesava Pillai was popularly known as 'the Honourable Member for Forests and Jails'.

[133] See *Report of the Forest Committee*, (Madras, 1913), 2 vols.

[134] *Appendix to the Report of the Indian Famine Commission, 1898, being Minutes of Evidence, etc. Volume II. Madras Presidency*, p. 214, *PP*, 1899, Vol. XXXII.

[135] P. Kesava Pillai to Dr Subbarayon, 5 December 1926, P. Kesava Pillai Papers, NMM.

from V. C. Vellingiri Gounder's efforts to impose some discipline on the members of his caste in his 'territory'.[136] Such movements were never intended to broaden the context of political action or even to provide a permanent series of alliances between men of importance. Both Reddi and Gounder movements rapidly dissolved as their leaders began to fight each other and to return to profitable cross-communal alliances. The caste platform which cut across these ties quickly collapsed. In South Arcot in the early 1920s, for example, several young Padayachi lawyers and literati tried to create a communal constituency for themselves in the Padayachi-dominated taluks. They did not win the support of any patron who mattered, and, in the 1926 Legislative Council election, their two candidates were severely beaten. However, another Padayachi, who had no contact with them and who stood on 'the Brahmin' Swarajya Party ticket, with the backing of several notables— whether Padayachi or not—was returned triumphantly.[137]

The decentralization of government established the rural élite in district institutions but it also started to draw them towards the centres of provincial government. The British, but much more the native politicians who increasingly shared the responsibilities of government with them at the provincial capital, made sure that considerable powers of patronage in the rural boards remained with the local self-government department controlled from Madras. Until 1926, virtually all district board presidents, and, until 1930, a large number of the seats on the boards, were filled by nomination from the capital. In the Montagu-Chelmsford Councils, the Justice Party Ministry, in the words of its Chief Whip, 'Lived on patronage.'[138] From 1921, the chief minister was always the minister for local self-government, and he kept his ministry solvent by trading his nominations on the boards for support in the Madras Council.[139] This gave all district politicians a close interest in the affairs of the Legislative Council and, until 1937, most members were also members of rural boards.

In the dry areas, the steady involvement of a powerful rural élite in district and provincial politics began to have important consequences on the social composition of the political world. While contacts

---

[136] The movement developed from incidents which had led to the murder of some Gounders in a toddy shop brawl. Its most concrete form was the drive by Vellingiri Gounder and his henchmen to close down all the toddy-shops in their area. See C. J. Baker, 'Political Change in South India', pp. 353–4.

[137] Ibid., pp. 241–2; Hindu, 25 November 1926.

[138] R. V. Krishna Ayyar, In the Legislature of Those Days (Madras, 1956), p. 45.

[139] Indian Statutory Commission. 1930. Oral Evidence taken at Madras, Vol. I, 5th meeting, p. 19.

with government above had remained personal and fragmentary, most important rural politicians had found it convenient to work through intermediaries. They lacked the education, the social background and the family connexions which would bring them into close touch with the top bureaucrats. Members of the Western-educated classes were, of course, only too willing to perform the function of go-between, which took them out of the debating chamber and gave them an income, social importance and attachment to a more real political system. The relationship of Kesava Pillai to Chinnarappa Reddi was similar to that of many provincial politicians to their backers before 1920. In Salem and Coimbatore districts, for example, the Tamil Brahmin lawyer B. V. Narasimha Iyer, a Legislative Councillor between 1912 and 1921, was close to many of the principal families among the Gounder gentry. In 1913, he toured the Coimbatore countryside organizing an agitation on their behalf against the Coimbatore district board which, under the control of a Coimbatore town clique, was swelling its treasury by raising rural taxes.[140] Equally, in Nellore, the Brahmin lawyer, A. S. Krishna Rao, sat on the Legislative Council continuously from 1910 to 1926 as the representative of the interests of various Reddi leaders. Indeed, so important were his local supporters that the Justice Party had to swallow its communal pride and twice re-nominate this Brahmin to the presidency of the Nellore district board.[141] In the Ceded districts, A. Kaleswara Rao noted that 'the Reddi Sirdars' controlled the elections to Legislative Council in 1920 but they did not bother to return many Reddis.[142]

However, the development of the boards meant that the rural élite could no longer leave its affairs to agents. The price of security was constant vigilance, and agents anxious to become principals might turn the new power in the boards against their backers. District board politics also brought members of the rural élite into close contact with senior government officials and gave them greater opportunities of influencing important decisions. These trends provided a further stimulus to education. Before 1920, the Legislative Council and provincial politics had been the domain, almost exclusively, of Western-educated lawyers. The era of the Montagu–Chelmsford Councils saw the rural élite move in. At the very first elections, a few of the more

[140] *Hindu*, 22 and 24 September and 1 and 7 October 1913.
[141] *The Cult of Incompetence, being an impartial enquiry into the record of the First Madras Ministry* (Madras, 1923), pp. 37–9.
[142] A. Kaleswara Rao, *Na Jivita Katha–Navya Andhramu* (Vijayawada, 1959), p. 333 (Telugu).

substantial rural magnates had been returned. Among those members representing Coimbatore was V. C. Vellingiri Gounder, who paid land revenue of Rs 2,000 in villages in Coimbatore taluk and had banking interests in the district capital. He was, of course, a prominent district and taluk board member. North Arcot elected A. Thangavelu Naicker, a member of the wealthiest ryotwari landlord family in the district. Beside A. S. Krishna Rao of Nellore, sat K. Audinarayana Reddi, whose income was said to be Rs 40,000 a year from land and from mica mining.[143] All three of these men's families had made alliances by marriage with other leading families in their district.[144]

During the 1920s and 1930s prominent peasant families increasingly took a hand in provincial politics. In Kurnool, Cuddapah and Anantapur, for example, which were deep in the territory dominated by rich Reddis, only two of the six Council members elected in 1920 actually were Reddis;[145] by 1930, all six seats were filled by their men.[146] In South Arcot in 1920, only A. Subbarayalu Reddiar, of the three men elected, might have been said to belong to the dominant peasant élite, and he, rather ahead of his brethren, was a Western-educated lawyer; by 1930, all three South Arcot members came from the élite.[147] Similar developments may be seen in North Arcot, Trichinopoly and Salem. The 1937 election, on the franchise extended by the 1935 Government of India Act, carried the process further. In South Arcot four of the five seats went to rural magnates; in Coimbatore six of the seven; in Anantapur two of three; in Cuddapah two of two; in South Arcot four of five; in Chittoor three of four.[148]

As the rural élite was drawn closer to the centres of government, the professional middle-man, who had no importance save the expertise with which he represented the interests of others, was progressively eliminated. In Nellore, for example, no Brahmin lawyer emerged to

[143] Biographies of Madras Legislative Councillors in Reforms (Franchise) B, March 1921, 34–99, NAI.
[144] V. C. Vellingiri Gounder possessed marriage connexions with several of the pattagar families—the religious leaders—of the Gounder community. Besides religious status, the families were among the richest in the Coimbatore–Salem area. A. Thangavelu Naicker was related to the largest landowning Palli families in the Arcot region and was the nephew of A. Dhanakoti Mudaliar, the Arcot and Madras city contractor. K. Audinarayana Reddi was credited with connexion to many of the principal Reddis of Nellore.
[145] Results in Reforms (Franchise) B, March 1921, 34–99, NAI.
[146] Results in Hindu, 10 to 21 September 1930.
[147] These were K. M. Dorasami, R. K. Venugopal Reddi and K. Ramachandra Padayachi.
[148] For brief biographies see Directory of the Madras Legislature (Madras, 1938).

take over from A. S. Krishna Rao.[149] In Salem, after Narasimha Iyer's retirement from politics, the leadership of district-level affairs passed to a European zemindar, a Devanga merchant and various Gounder landlords.[150] In 1926, Chinnarappa Reddi switched his support from P. Kesava Pillai to a Reddi lawyer and Kesava Pillai lost his Legislative Council seat.[151] The development of political institutions in the countryside allowed the rural élite to stand on its own. Through an apparently endless series of factional alliances and confrontations, rural leaders established their own district empires which gave them seats on the Legislative Council. Secure in their home-bases from disturbances and threats from below, and capable of dealing directly with each other in rural institutions, they were the heirs of the economic and administrative developments of the late nineteenth and early twentieth centuries.

II

The Kistna and Godaveri deltas were very different areas from the dry region we have been examining. Whereas major pilgrimage centres in the dry districts were few and dispersed—notably Tirupati, Madura, Kalahasti, Srirangam—both the Kistna and Godaveri rivers were considered sacred to Hindus and attracted large numbers of pilgrims. In the deltas irrigation works were centuries old and had long made it possible to cultivate rice commercially. This may have been one reason why the dominant peasant castes, particularly the Kammas, had broader marriage patterns than in the dry region.[152] The wealth generated by wet cultivation could also be seen in the many small temples which dotted the countryside. Since medieval times the deltas had been the centre of Telugu culture. Brahmins were more numerous here than in the dry regions: 5 per cent of the population compared to about 2 per cent in most of the dry districts.[153] Long before the British arrived, the inhabitants of the deltas were more mobile and wealthier

---

[149] Reddi landowners consistently took one district Legislative Council seat and the family of the Venkatagiri zemindars the other.

[150] Notably T. Foulkes of the Salem zemindari, S. Ellappa Chetty and P. Subarayon, who owned the small Kumaramangalam estate.

[151] P. Kesava Pillai to Dr Subbarayon 5 December 1926, P. Kesava Pillai Papers, NMM.

[152] In 1891, about 40 per cent of the 850,000 people returning themselves as Kammas did not specify a sub-caste and another 35 per cent claimed one particular sub-caste—that found predominantly in the Kistna area. *Census of India. 1891. Madras* (Madras, 1893), Vol. XIII, Part 1 pp. 237–38.

[153] *Census of India. 1881. Madras* (Madras, 1883), Vol. II, p. 140.

than their neighbours in the dry zones. Since British rule did not shape society anew but rather tended to develop its existing characteristics, the different bases of economic and social organization in the dry and wet districts of Madras meant that the two areas diverged further under the same rule.

Between the 1840s and 1860s British engineers under Sir Arthur Cotton restored and greatly extended the irrigation works on the Godaveri and Kistna rivers. New channels built to carry the water inland brought about one and a half million acres of land under irrigation for the first time.[154] The 'flush' irrigation produced by the scheme, which led to the inundation of the fields, was perfect for the cultivation of rice and, by the later nineteenth century, the Andhra deltas fed the upper classes in much of the Presidency. A contemporary observer saw

that the whole country looks like a single rice field, the groves around the villages, the road avenues and the white sails of the boats gliding along the main canals breaking the uniform sea of waving green crop.[155]

Statistical eccentricities, zemindaries, and the peculiarity of early settlements in the deltas make it difficult to determine the changes in landholding occasioned by the extension of irrigation. By 1900, however, it seems clear that the distribution of wealth from land in the deltas was significantly different from the pattern established in the dry regions. In Godaveri district, for example, barely 4 per cent of the ryotwari wet land was held in pattas paying less than Rs 10 per annum. The bulk of wet land—about 62 per cent—was held in the middle range of pattas paying between Rs 30 and Rs 250.[156] Holdings were still small in extent—most cultivators held less than eighteen acres—but the land was more productive. Eighteen acres in the dry districts paid between Rs 4 and Rs 30 a year in revenue; eighteen acres in the wet areas paid on average Rs 100 a year. By converting dry, or at best mixed, cultivating villages, into part of a huge complex of wet cultivation, the British irrigation works had, within a few decades, created a large class of prosperous peasant farmers.

Since the deltas specialized in rice to the exclusion of almost all other crops, they developed their own distinctive trading patterns. Most of

---

[154] A. V. Raman Rao, *Economic Development of Andhra Pradesh (1766–1957)* (Bombay, 1958), pp. 86–90.
[155] Quoted in O. H. K. Spate, *India and Pakistan. A General and Regional Geography* (London, 1954), p. 690.
[156] These figures calculated from 'Statement of the Rent-Roll' in *Land Revenue Reports for Fasli 1310 (1900–01)*.

the local crop had to be exported, and everything else had to be imported in return.[157] This greatly expanded trade was further facilitated by excellent internal communications by track, rail and water. The rail-heads and ports grew quickly in response to the rising volume of trade passing through them.[158] Marketing operations centred on a few towns which served wide areas, including their neighbouring dry taluks. In contrast to Coimbatore and Salem which in 1929 had 134 and 112 licensed markets respectively, the whole of Guntur had only six.[159]

The thriving commerce of the area meant that urban merchants were active in developing rural trade. Komati merchants expanded their family-based grain and moneylending networks deep into the countryside as they handled ever larger quantities of goods. Marwaris and Multanis flocked to the deltas. Rice was in such high demand in the rest of the presidency and elsewhere, and rice land so valuable, that they buried their scruples and risked their capital in rural moneylending and grain dealing.[160]

The delta ryot, himself, took full advantage of these developments.[161] His position as medium-sized landowner, with irrigation to free him from the vagaries of the weather, meant that he was seldom pressed by the government revenue demand into selling his crop cheaply at harvest time. He may have been in debt—probably rupee for rupee he was more in debt than the average dry cultivator—but the character of indebtedness in the deltas was very different from that in the dry region. The opening up of commerce provided the delta ryot with a multiplicity of sources of credit: the agents of urban merchants, innumerable ryots in his own village and even town banks supplied his needs. From 1904, Co-operative Credit Societies grew rapidly and with conspicuous success.[162] Security for loans was not a serious problem.

[157] *Royal Commission on Agriculture in India. Appendix*, Vol. XIV, p. 270.

[158] A. V. Raman Rao, *Economic Development of Andhra Pradesh (1766–1957)*, pp. 251–54. The market towns of the delta area were among the fastest growing in the presidency. See *Census of India. 1921.* (Madras, 1922), Vol. XIII, Part 2, pp. 8–12. *Census of India. 1931* (Madras, 1933), Vol. XIV, Part 2, pp. 10–16.   [159] *RPBC*, p. 119.

[160] *RPBC*, pp. 219–20; *MPBC*, Vol. III, pp. 740–3, 1146.

[161] Rich delta ryots were, of course, as much involved in credit and trade in their own right as wealthy ryots in the dry districts. *MPBC*, Vol. III, p. 743.

[162] In the Godaveri delta villages investigated by the Banking Commission, co-operative credit loans accounted for about one-third of all admitted loans. This was far higher than the average of dry district villages investigated. *MPBC*, Vol. V, pp. 86–255. Commercial expansion in the 1920s stimulated the development of several joint-stock banks, such as the Andhra Bank, and land banks, such as that started by the raja of Pithapuram.

The value of his crop guaranteed him a large and regular annual turnover so that he was unlikely to become bonded by the accumulation of debt to any one creditor. Most delta ryots took a hand in the market. Many carted or sailed their own produce to the towns and sold it directly to the export merchants.[163] As it was easier to export husked and boiled paddy, rice mills shot up in many of the larger villages—often built with the capital of local ryots. These mills, of course, bought locally, but they had to buy on different terms from those who bought grain in the Ceded districts. They had to compete in a relatively open market with many other buyers and they could not hope for annually glutted markets or a succession of bad seasons to drive peasants into dependence on them. If their rates were not close to those offered in the main towns, their mills would grind to a halt. The Royal Commission on Agriculture summarised the contrast between the delta and the dry areas thus:

It is the cultivator's chronic shortage of money that has allowed the intermediary in the dry areas to achieve the prominent position he now occupies. Where the cultivators are tolerably well-off, as in the Kistna and Godaveri deltas, his position is not by any means so strong. There, the ryot, once he has paid his land revenue (kist) keeps a steady eye on the prices prevailing for rice imported from Burma, and is in no haste to come to terms with the agent or buyer if the terms do not suit him. The ultimate market for his produce (Madras city and the inland districts of Coimbatore and Salem) is close at hand; he sells his husked rice to local mill-owners who hull it before passing it on and who are at least as much concerned to keep their mills working as they are to beat down prices.[164]

Rice grown for the market integrated the economy of the deltas area and brought their peasant populations into close market relations with the towns.

Since there was so much more contact between town and countryside, the effects of their interaction went further in the deltas than in the dry zone. The marriage links between various Kamma sub-castes began to leap the boundaries of sub-castes themselves.[165] Prosperous delta ryots began to imitate urban ways in their villages. Bricks replaced mud, and tiles thatch in respectable houses;[166] traditional status deferences were abandoned;[167] peasants became increasingly involved in the religious

[163] RPBC, p. 106.
[164] Royal Commission on Agriculture in India. Appendix, Vol. XIV, pp. 268–9.
[165] See Carolyn M. Elliot, 'Caste and Faction among the Dominant Caste: the Reddis and Kammas of Andhra' in R. Kothari (ed.), Caste in Indian Politics, pp. 129–71.
[166] A. V. Raman Rao, Economic Development of Andhra Pradesh (1766–1957), p. 192.
[167] MPBC, Vol. III, p. 744.

and cultural revivalism of the towns; the more adventurous village families sent their sons to the towns, and by sub-letting their holdings, they sometimes moved there themselves.[168]

Significant developments also took place in litigation and education. From the 1880s, 'litigation [was] developing with extraordinary rapidity' in the superior courts on the deltas.[169] Of course, a simple rise in litigation does not tell us much. Wherever there were zemindaris there was bound to be litigation. The courts of Ramnad and North Malabar were filled with cases, although both areas were extremely primitive. The zemindars of Kistna and Godvari also kept the courts busy, and their delta districts stood near the top of the litigation league.[170] But some of the rise was because the new courts were attractive to peasants. The Collector of Guntur complained that his courts were clogged with extraordinarily intricate village factional disputes.[171] Throughout our period, the slowest courts in completing cases in the whole province were those on the delta. In 1890, for example, the average time between filing and obtaining judgment in a suit before the Ellore district munsiff was 549 days; while his neighbour at Rajah-mundry took 435 days.[172] Both of these were twice the presidency average. The main rivals of Ellore and Rajahmundry for the title of most arduous posting in the Madras judicial service were the courts at Guntur, Bezwada and Masulipatam. It was not that these courts handled significantly more cases than others in zemindari areas, but that the cases themselves were not the block filings of a zemindar, which could be sorted out by a single judgment. A great many cases were individual litigations and were contested every inch of the way.

The last decades of the nineteenth century also saw a rise in literacy in the delta districts. In general, the Northern Circars were more backward in education than were the southern districts of the Presidency, having neither the great cities of Madras, Trichinopoly or

[168] *Land Revenue Reports for Fasli 1315 (1905–06)*, p. 72.
[169] The comment particularly referred to the district munsiffs' courts at Bezwada and Masulipatam. *Report on the Administration of Civil Justice in the Presidency of Madras in 1890* (Madras, 1891), p. 14.
[170] In 1890, for example, the zemindar of Telaprole, in Kistna, alone filed 2382 cases. *Ibid.*, p. 15. Kistna, Godaveri and, after 1905, Guntur were usually in the top half dozen districts in the presidency for the number of cases filed in ratio to population. See *Reports on the Administration of Civil Justice in the Presidency of Madras* (annual series).
[171] *Statistics of Criminal Courts in the Madras Presidency for the year 1915* (Madras, 1916), p. 2.
[172] *Report on the Administration of Civil Justice in the Presidency of Madras in the year 1900* (Madras, 1901), p. 5.

Madura, nor the great concentration of religious traditions in a few ancient temple towns. However, between 1891 and 1931, the literacy rate in Kistna and Godaveri districts rose faster than anywhere else. Much of this development was in the vernaculars and took place among the main peasant castes—the Kammas and Kapus.[173] It was not confined to the towns. In 1908, for example, the Collector of Godaveri was horrified to discover 'seditious' vernacular newspapers circulating in many delta villages. Their readers were not only Brahmins—whom he considered to be beyond the pale—but also peasant landholders.[174] By 1929 the Banking Inquiry found a male literacy rate of between 15 and 20 per cent in the villages of Ramachandrapuram taluk in Godaveri district. This village rate compares with a 1931 average of only 21 per cent for the whole Presidency, including the towns, Madras city (52 per cent), and the advanced districts of Tanjore and Malabar (more than 30 per cent).[175]

Religious and cultural revivalism in the later nineteenth century shows the extent to which the delta countryside had been integrated with the towns. One of the most famous vernacular dramatic societies, the Rajahmundry Hindu Theatrical Company, financed by local landholders, performed in all the leading Andhra towns, and it toured the larger villages.[176] Religious agitation moved from peasants to townsmen. During the muhurram of 1884, for example, a small army gathered in Gudur, a village near Masulipatam, and marched through the countryside picking up support. 'The movement was not headed by any chief and was made from village to village with a flag bearing the imprint of an idol Anjamar'. It converged on Masulipatam and caused a riot outside the main mosque.[177] In the dry areas, this sort of religious violence was virtually unknown in the countryside, although there were occasional outbreaks among weaving-communities in the towns.

In the deltas the traffic between town and country moved both ways. Vernacular newspapers, which dealt mostly with religious and cultural matters, were published in the towns but read over a wide area.[178]

[173] Census of India. 1931 (Madras, 1933), Vol. XIV, Part 1, p. 283; ibid., Part 2, pp. 276–7.
[174] M. Venkatarangaiya, The Freedom Struggle in Andhra Pradesh (Andhra) (Hyderabad, 1968), Vol. II, pp. 266–76.
[175] MPBC, Vol. V, pp. 86–255; Census of India. 1931, Vol. XIV, Part 2, p. 283.
[176] V. L. Sastri (ed.), Encyclopaedia of the Madras Presidency and the Adjacent States (Cocanada, 1920) p. 501.
[177] Madras Police 1884, p. 7.
[178] The delta towns easily led the Madras mofussil in the size and scope of their vernacular journalistic activity. By 1925, for example, Rajahmundry had at least 5 daily or weekly vernacular newspapers with a combined circulation estimated at

Another connexion was provided by urban groups such as the Komatis, who had many agents in the villages. Not only did they begin to exercise a tighter control over rural trade through Chambers of Commerce and joint-stock companies,[179] but they also spent money on temples dedicated to their caste saint, Kanyaki Parameswami, which served as focal points for the community. Komatis in the villages came back to the towns for religious festivals and to lay claim to a share of communal funds.[180] Their strong connexions can be seen in the cow-protection movement, in which many of the principal families in the delta towns and villages were involved.[181]

Most of the problems of government faced by the British in the delta districts sprang from the failure of their administrative system to take account of the social changes promoted by economic development. In the first decades of the nineteenth century, when the differences between this area and the dry region had been less remarkable, the delta ryotwari tracts had been settled on a uniform plan. Parts of the deltas had originally been settled under zemindars, but many of these had collapsed by 1850. From the 1870s the Madras government deliberately attempted to make the wet districts conform more to the general ryotwari pattern. Zemindari village officers became tied more closely to the tahsildar and the police superintendent than to their landlord, and they were paid from a government-administered cess.[182]

4,700; Masulipatam maintained at least 5 with a circulation of 8,000; and Ellore at least 3 with a circulation of about 2,000. Government of India, Home Political, File 261 of 1926, NAI.

[179] See, for example, the report on the foundation of the Guntur Cotton, Paper and Jute Mills Company, which involved the Lingamalee, Pydah and Majeti families, in *Hindu*, 13 September 1904. A Guntur Chamber of Commerce, consisting almost entirely of Komatis, was founded in about 1911 to regulate district commerce. See *Hindu*, 29 January 1913.

[180] For a description of the expansion of Komati religious and communal activity see the petitions of Komatis from various Andhra towns against the Hindu Religious Endowments Act of 1926 in G.O. 3666 (Local and Municipal) dated 8 September 1928. State Archives, Hyderabad. From 1907, a Komati caste conference developed from Guntur.

[181] Report of the Director of Criminal Intelligence, 9 April 1910, Home Political B, June 1910, 17–25, NAI; also G.O. 216 (Local and Municipal, Municipal) dated 3 February 1914, TNA.

[182] These developments, which were the result of administrative activity, received legislative ratification under the Zemindari Village Officers' Services Acts of 1894 and 1895. For discussions of the ways in which government had undermined the zemindars' authority in their estates see G.O. 351 (Revenue) dated 3 March 1925; G.O. 875 (Revenue) dated 12 June 1925, TNA. The presence of zemindars, of course, influenced the social and political life of the localities in which they lived. Zemindars both drew and spent a large income, which gave them many dependents. However, our main concern is the peasantry and there was as little difference in administrative

In the later nineteenth century, British administrative practice followed precisely the same course in the deltas as elsewhere. Village establishments were given greater powers: they managed the income tax, police, government-backed credit schemes, and village unions. Yet the whole edifice of government was being built on shifting foundations.

For an administrative system based on the village to work well, the village itself must be an important and coherent social unit. By 1900, in the deltas, this was no longer the case. So many rural people were involved in educational, marketing and legal adventures in the district towns that their society would be better characterized as an urban hinterland than as one of a collection of separate villages. Further, the great mobility of the labouring population undermined the autonomy of the village community. In the dry region, most villages had more labour than was necessary for their own needs, but in the deltas rice cultivation demanded twice in the year many more hands than were locally available. At transplantation and harvest, thousands of day labourers from the upland taluks and Ganjam and Vizagapatam districts poured into the delta and settled for a few weeks in camps on the outskirts of the villages. They were usually paid in cash and returned home as soon as their work was done.[183] Their bi-annual influx destroyed the cohesion of the delta village.

The Madras government's model of village government depended on the existence of village leaders who could rule. In the delta villages such leaders were hard to find. Certainly, there were some ryots who were much richer than others, and many of them were village officers. But they did not control the trade and moneylending of their localities to the same extent as the village Reddis of the Ceded districts and Gounder headmen of Coimbatore and Salem. Town courts undercut their powers of arbitration in local disputes. Their control over revenue payments was restricted by the ease with which others in the village could call in urban lawyers and officers. They could not overawe their highly mobile subjects who could always summon the outside world into battle against them. In the delta villages there was no entrenched, dominant, and unassailable peasant élite.

From the later nineteenth century, social and political control in the deltas was breaking down, and in the twentieth century it often collapsed. The village police could not maintain order. There was more crime in the Kistna and Godaveri districts than anywhere else in the

organization as in economic organization between ryotwari and zemindari peasants. Indeed, many zemindari village officers joined the rent-strike against government in 1921–22.   [183] *Royal Commission on Agriculture in India*, Vol. III, p. 316.

Presidency. But this crime was not the organized murder and looting thrown up by the factionalism of the dry districts, but petty theft and housebreaking which were the product of social instability.[184] Even the revenue administration—the centre of the entire British system— threatened to come to a standstill. Faced with large numbers of rich and independent peasants in his village, the village officer had to rely more on consensus than force to collect his revenue. Of course he had Leviathan behind him, but the district courts were far from the village and expropriation took time. If the British had had to use force to collect the land revenue, then their government in India would have been impossible. In the dry region, the authority of the village establishment guaranteed the smooth running of jamabundi. The decision to pay was taken and enforced by the élite. The delta village establishment, however, had to be more circumspect or it would face vigorous opposition. During the civil disobedience movement, many delta peasants refused to pay, and, in many places, the flow of revenue dried up. The village officers were not behind this: in many villages 'the rich ryots' simply ordered them to stay collections. When the government tried to punish the establishments of defaulting villages, it found that many village officers had been swept away on a tide they could not control.[185]

In the dry region, Fort St George's efforts to control its village agents had succeeded merely in irritating them. In the deltas they had more serious consequences. Here the leadership of the village official was already under pressure from the people below and the interference of government from above weakened it further. In the dry regions, government's inroads on the power and patronage of its overmighty servants only clipped a fraction of the authority of the Reddi and the Gounder; but in the deltas they knocked away the few remaining props on which the village officer leant. By the early twentieth century, many officers felt that there was little point in continuing to wear the hollow crowns of authority. Many men with long traditions of government service, finding more attractive opportunities open to them elsewhere, resigned or sold their posts. The Brahmin family of A. Kaleswara Rao, for example, auctioned its kurnamship in a village near Bezwada and moved permanently into the town.[186] At a lower

[184] See *Madras Police* for 1878–1925. G.O. 639 (Public) dated 5 June 1931, TNA.
[185] G.O. 938 (Public) dated 11 September 1931; G.O. 939 (Public) dated 11 September 1931; G.O. 980 (Public) dated 21 September 1931; G.O. 1075 (Public) dated 20 October 1931, TNA.
[186] A. Kaleswara Rao, *Na Jivita Katha–Navya Andhramu* (Vijayawada, 1959), p. 19. (Telugu).

level, the Collector of Kistna noticed many petty village servants quitting to work as labourers in the rice fields, where they could earn more money.[187] In the dry areas, by contrast, men were still willing to pay Rs 5,000 for just such petty offices which carried stipends of only Rs 4 per month.[188] Those who clung to office vigorously opposed all the government's changes. Between 1907 and 1914 Curzon's deputy police inspectors were most seriously obstructed in the delta districts.[189] By the time of the First World War, even the revenue department found itself in trouble. The Collector of Kistna reported in 1914:

My taluk officers inform me that they find constant recurring difficulties in getting their ordinary revenue duties done by the village servants. Resignations are very common, temporary absence from duty of regular monthly occurrence and wholesale strikes are by no means unusual.[190]

Paradoxically perhaps, the very linkages between town and village, which had contributed so much to the decay of village government, provided irate officials with a powerful means of making their grievances known to government. When they learnt that government intended to end their hereditary rights, village officers organized association after association; they held regular taluk and firka conferences and published newspapers to publicize their cause.[191] Home Rule Leaguers and Congressmen from the towns played a large part in these organizations, seeing a chance of winning a following. As the power of village officers waned, their protest grew more violent. Finally it spilled over into Gandhi's non-cooperation movement with an officer-led rent strike in several parts of Guntur, Kistna and Godaveri districts.[192] The government fairly easily broke the move-

[187] *Madras Police 1913*, Appendix, p. 9.
[188] See comments of raja of Ramnad in Government of India, Home Judicial Files 1–2 of 1922, NAI.
[189] G.O. 1675 (Judicial) dated 18 August 1913, TNA; *Madras Police 1913*, Appendix, p. 9; *ibid.*, *1914* Appendix D, p. 72; *ibid.*, *1919*, Appendix E, p. 68.
[190] *Madras Police 1913*, Appendix, p. 9. See also report of a Legislative Council debate on village officer resignations in *Hindu*, 3 February 1915.
[191] For reports on various village officer association meetings see *Hindu*, 12 November 1920; and *Andhrapatrika*, 4 February 1919 and 7 September 1920; *Desabhimani*, 8 January 1919; *Gramapulana*, 10 September 1921, in *Reports on the Native Press in the Madras Presidency*, IOL.
[192] The most famous of the strikes was in Pedanannipad firka of Guntur district, which was not, strictly speaking, in the deltas. However, most of the original drive for a strike had come from delta villages. As early as August 1920, for example, village officers in Northern deltaic Guntur had begun their own strike. *Andhrapatrika*, 7 September 1920 in *Reports on the Native Press in the Madras Presidency*, IOL. And in December 1921, the Andhra Desa Village Officers' Association had called for resignations at Rajahmundry and had obtained them from about half the officers in this wet

ment,[193] but the campaign showed, by the desperation of the village officials, how meaningless the village had become as the basic unit on which the administration was supposed to rest.

The pattern of public politics shown in the non-cooperation campaign was nothing new in the area. The ease of communication, the existence of obvious centres for organization, and, above all, the large number of wealthy people in the countryside, made it possible to develop, and, for the government, impossible to prevent, widespread popular participation in political movements. Whereas we saw that the challenge of the forest department in the dry areas produced little organized protest, the challenge of the Public Works Department in the deltas was met with widespread popular resistance. The Public Works Department controlled the flow of piped water to many fields, and PWD men were said to be totally corrupt and to extort money by threatening to withold water supplies. Of course, delta ryots paid the bribes and, on N. G. Ranga's testimony, exchanged threat for threat,[194] but no small all-powerful élite existed with a vested interest in the system. Anti-PWD protest became a popular pastime. Urban-based stump orators never wanted an audience when they slanged the PWD.[195] At every Legislative Council election from 1892, prospective candidates had to make village pilgrimages to demonstrate their hatred of the PWD.[196] The earliest district conferences in Madras were those of Kistna (1892) and Godaveri (1895). They drew a large support from peasants and were often held in large villages.[197] During the First World War, anti-PWD agitation spread through the deltas even faster than the village officers' campaign. Dozens of small taluk conferences were held, newspapers—such as N. G. Ranga's *Ryotpatrika*—were

taluk. The Andhra Congress, which was wary of associating itself with such an obviously dangerous movement, held back from the village officers' campaign for sixteen months. Finally, in January 1922, it was forced to join in order to keep up its political credibility. It organized the strike in Pedanandipad, which was immediately adjacent to Guntur town, the Andhra PCC headquarters, with the help of P. Virayya Choudhari, a Kamma with close village officer connexions in Pedanandipad as well as political ties with Guntur town. The Pedanandipad affair was probably the least spontaneous although the most celebrated of all the strikes. See M. Venkatarangaiya, *The Freedom Struggle in Andhra Pradesh (Andhra)*, Vol. III, pp. 43, 244, 250–308; also K. Venkatappayya, *Sviya Caritra* (Vijayawada, 1952), Vol. I, pp. 226–301 (Telugu).

[193] 'Collector's Report about the Situation in Guntur–5', in M. Venkatarangaiya, *The Freedom Struggle in Andhra Pradesh (Andhra)*, Vol. III, p. 305.

[194] N. G. Ranga, *Fight For Freedom* (New Delhi, 1968), pp. 8–9.

[195] See, for example, the meeting of ryots at Ellore in 1894, addressed by S. Bhimasankara Rao, Rajahmundry muncipal chairman. *Hindu*, 12 October 1894.

[196] *Hindu*, 4 October 1894.

[197] *Hindu*, 17 April and 5, 6, 11, 12. 15 June 1896.

founded, and permanent organizations were set up.[198] The political culture of the delta districts was markedly different to that anywhere else in Madras.

The British developed their rural administration—through district and taluk boards and village unions—in precisely the same way in the delta districts as elsewhere. And there can be little doubt that here, as elsewhere, these institutions attained a paramount significance in the determination of local political positions, and contributed to the linking of district to provincial political arenas. Clearly, there were likely to be considerable differences, between the deltas and the dry districts, in the ways in which rural boards politics operated. In the deltas, the franchise extended to a larger proportion of a population which itself was more independent and possessed many more opportunities for establishing other kinds of political associations. Of course, there were men in the deltas who had great wealth, and who held many of the strands of personal power which went into the making of rural magnates; and it would be impossible to deny that faction was the most usual political structure in the area. Yet the battlefield on which factions met was of greater size and the armies involved very numerous. No politician could afford simply to sit on his personal dependency network and make secret treaties with allies. He had to use public techniques and to raise issues and causes in order to focus on him the attention of the considerable 'floating', or at least not directly tied, vote. In 1920, for example, M. Venkataratnam Naidu, a long-term opponent of the Godaveri district board president, D. Seshagiri Rao, attempted to split the board and undercut the president's majority by introducing the non-Brahmin issue into its deliberations.[199] No dry area district board paid the slightest attention to such matters of public conscience. At about the same time, P. C. N. Ethirajulu Naidu, the Guntur district board president, found that his enemies were raising a public outcry against him on the ground that he was 'a foreigner'—he came from the neighbouring district of Nellore.[200] During periods of nationalist agitation, many district board politicians found it expedient to identify with the Congress movement, and several rural boards passed funds to Congress-inspired national education colleges.[201]

[198] For the Ryots' Central Association, Guntur, see *Hindu*, 17 September 1918; taluk conferences at Razole and Amalapuram, *Hindu*, 27 December 1918; Bezwada Ryots' Conference *Hindu*, 17 February 1919.   [199] *Hindu*, 7 May 1920.
[200] G.O. 776 (Local and Municipal, Local) dated 21 June 1919, TNA; also K. Kotilingam to P. S. Sivaswami Iyer, n.d. but probably in the spring of 1919, P. S. Sivaswami Iyer Papers, NAI.
[201] G.O. 211 (Local and Municipal, Local) dated 15 February 1919, TNA. In 1921,

Indeed, some crucially important rural district politicians, such as
Dandu Narayana Raju and Maganti Sitayya, both of whom came from
very rich west Godaveri families, openly identified with the nationalist
movement, and sought to capitalize on their association at rural board
and Legislative Council elections throughout the 1920s.[202] It is not
surprising that in 1920 the only Legislative Council candidates who
thought it necessary to issue manifestos and to campaign from public
platforms, were those who stood in the delta districts.[203]

The vigour of rural board politics can be seen in the very different
history of emotive 'caste' politics in the region. The 'Kamma scare'
which beset Guntur in the mid-1920s, unlike the Reddi scare of 1926
and the early Gounder agitation, was something of a public movement.
Of course, it did not appear spontaneously and it was part of a factional
struggle between élite politicians. But, through the use of the press and
public platform, it managed to recruit previously uncommitted support
to a caste flag and it achieved great local significance. In north-eastern
Guntur, a rich group of Kamma families, finding itself locked out of the
district board by a cross-communal clique (which included some Kammas) based on Guntur town, mobilized behind it members of its
'dominant caste'. The group won over several independently constituted Kamma taluk board factions in other parts of the district.
A venomous publicity campaign, which spawned associations and newspapers, attended its efforts, in part successful, to win Legislative Council
seats. Finally, it contrived to upset the prevailing pattern of district
alliances and to seize the district board presidency.[204] For six or seven
years, the movement demonstrated the unusual power of emotional
appeals in delta district politics. And when it broke up—shortly after
the district board presidency had been won—its members did not
desert the public platform and shut themselves away in sealed rooms,

the Guntur taluk board protested at the arrest of non-co-operators. G.O. 873 (Public)
dated 18 November 1921, TNA.

[202] C. J. Baker, 'Political Change in South India 1919–1937', pp. 214–36.

[203] This produced analyses of the programmes put forward by the various parties
and candidates. See P. Govindarow Naidu, *The Legislative Council Elections*. (Rajahmundry, 1920).

[204] The group of families was based around Nidabrolu in Bapatla taluk and was led
by P. V. Krishniah Choudhary, his relative N. G. Ranga, and J. Kuppuswami who
was one of the richest ryotwari landlords in the district, paying over Rs 8,000 a year
in land revenue. They linked up with Kamma-based factions in the Guntur and
Tenali taluk boards and overthrew P. C. N. Ethirajulu Naidu's district board
presidency in 1929. P. V. Krishniah Choudhary and J. Kuppuswami also became
Legislative Councillors. See C. J. Baker, 'Political Change in South India 1919–1937',
pp. 196–213.

as the Reddi and Gounder élites had done. Rather, they split up to follow new and potentially more profitable lines of agitational politics. The north eastern Guntur families, for example, became prominent in the anti-zemindari campaign.[205] Although this required them to reshuffle their alliances in typical élite fashion (they now had to appeal to peasants other than Kammas to work against zemindars who included Kammas), they still had to appeal for support to 'the mass' of delta district voters.[206] In spite of their great influence, their political ascendancy was never sure.

Yet if delta district board politicians had to start hares in order to attract publicity, they also had to chase the hares started by others in order to keep it. Caste, religious, class and cultural movements and protests against the administration were capable of developing an existence quite separate from the formal institutions of local politics. The men who organized them could gain popular support even though they held no major office. The loss of a district board seat was not political death in the deltas as it was so often in the dry region. Indeed, in the delta districts the leaders of these independent movements often influenced affairs in the formal institutions in which they did not sit. For example, the Bezwada lawyer, A. Kaleswara Rao, was involved in the Andhra movement, the National Education movement, various vernacular and religious associations and countless other undertakings. Between 1916 and 1922, he was active in ryot and village officer protest. He was a successful lawyer, his family had important village connexions and he worked for the Komatis of Bezwada town. In 1922 he led a campaign which put his Komati backers into power in the Bezwada municipality.[207] At the same time, he acted as broker between the many factions in Kistna district politics. In 1926, he successfully challenged the powerful zemindar of Mirzapuram at the Legislative

---

[205] This was particularly N. G. Ranga's agitation. See his *The Modern Indian Peasant* (Madras, 1936); *Economic Conditions of the Zemindari Ryots* (Madras, 1933); *Revolutionary Peasants* (New Delhi, 1949). It is of interest that, until about 1930, he and his political group in Guntur, had looked to the favour of the zemindar-based Justice Party in provincial politics.

[206] This was more of a break than it may sound. The Kamma movement had hit particularly hard at the Telaga caste, of which P. C. N. Ethirajulu Naidu was a member. Now the Kamma leaders had to try to win the allegiance of Telagas who were an important group in the agricultural community.

[207] A. Kaleswara Rao, *Na Jivita Katha–Navya Andhramu* (Vijayawada, 1959), pp. 291–360 (Telugu); G.O. 919 (Local and Municipal, Municipal) dated 24 May 1921; G.O. 945 (Local and Municipal, Municipal) dated 30 May 1921; G.O. 167 (Local and Municipal, Municipal) dated 24 January 1922;G.O. 2322 (Local and Municipal, Municipal) dated 27 November 1922, State Archives, Hyderabad; *Hindu*, 9 June and 5 December 1922.

Council elections, and later, in company with the peasant leader,
M. Pallamraju, he helped to break the zemindar's influence by dividing
the Kistna district board.[208] His local authority never depended on
office-holding, for apart from two short terms as Bezwada municipal
chairman, he never held any local positions.

Similarly, Konda Venkatappayya, a Brahmin lawyer from Guntur
town, had a considerable rural following. Like Kaleswara Rao, his
urban-backing came from rich Komatis. With several other Brahmin
lawyers, he founded schools and organized religious festivals on their
behalf. In 1917 he and the municipal chairman, N. Hanumantha
Rao,[209] both of whom were deeply involved in the Home Rule League,
helped to foment a riot between the Komatis and the local Muslims.
When the police came out onto the streets, the two of them led 'the
Hindu party' against them and won great reputations. They filled the
Home Rule coffers from the flood of donations which followed.[210]
Equally, Venkatappayya had contacts with several of the richer Kamma
families in the environs of Guntur town.[211] Although Venkatappayya's
hopes of rural board dominance were destroyed by the favours heaped
by government on his major rival (the tobacco-merchant P. C. N.
Ethirajulu Naidu, who was president of the taluk and district boards
and chairman of the municipality), Venkatappayya's rural influence
showed up in the non-cooperation campaign: the Kamma headmen of
Pedanandipad were linked to Guntur town and Venkatappayya, while
British investigators noted the presence of private armies of village
Komatis who were 'centrally directed' to prevent defections from the
rent-strike.[212]

The political élites of the delta districts were differently composed
from those of the dry region. The peasant take-over of district levels or
politics was not as complete as it was in the dry zone. Certainly, from

[208] A. Kaleswara Rao, *Na Jivita Katha–Navya Andhramu*, pp. 434–60.

[209] N. Hanumantha Rao also played a large part in the organization of the Komati-
supported cow protection movement. G.O. 216 (Local and Municipal, Municipal)
dated 3 February 1914, TNA.

[210] See letters of E. A. Davis, Collector of Guntur, and S. V. Narasimhachari,
Deputy Magistrate of Guntur, in G.O. 2461 (Home, Judicial) dated 26 November
1917, TNA. The political implications of the Komati–Brahmin publicist patronage
relationship became clear in the 1890s when Guntur municipality was allowed to
have a majority of elected members and to elect its chairmen. In 1892, the Komati
caucus Taxpayers' Association, led by the Brahmin lawyer V. Bhavarnacharlu, won
all the elected seats and put its representatives into municipal office, G.O. 1298
(Local and Municipal, Municipal) dated 5 August 1892, TNA.

[211] Particularly, P. Virayya Choudhari. M. Venkatarangaiya, *The Freedom Struggle
in Andhra Pradesh (Andhra)*, Vol. III, pp. 43, 244.

[212] *Ibid.*, pp. 264–70, 288–9.

the 1910s, increasing numbers of peasants were becoming literate and capable of conducting themselves in the larger district institutions. Indeed, there were many more of them than in the dry region. But political success did not hinge simply on the possession of small but secure vote banks and on bargaining in the district boards. The needs of publicity and organization guaranteed that there would still be a place, alongside peasant leaders, for the professional middle-man, the pure politician who had only organizational expertise. In some ways, as the political population of the deltas expanded in the 1930s, and as more voters entered the game, the middle-man became more important than ever. His ability to batten on any public issue kept him in touch with the sources of power in the deltas, and provided him with a viable political platform. A. Kaleswara Rao, who, we have seen, was no simple urban politician, did not suffer the fate of a Kesava Pillai. He was elected to the Legislative Council from Kistna in 1926, and to the Legislative Assembly from Bezwada-Masulipatam in 1937. Konda Venkatappayya was the only man to be elected to the Legislative Assembly in Madras in 1937 who had also sat in a Morley-Minto Council.

III

Two quite distinct patterns of district politics have emerged from our discussion. In the dry areas, economic and administrative development combined to produce an extremely powerful rural élite which kept localities tight under it and monopolized access to government institutions. There was little room for direct popular participation in politics, and the government's district boards came to form the major, and, for all practical purposes, the only, arena of district politics. By contrast, economic development in the wet region produced a wealthier and more mobile peasantry whose interests and influence did not stop in the locality. Many people were engaged immediately in far-reaching economic, social and political transactions. District politics developed as much as a result of movements 'from below' as of the government's imposition of district institutions 'from above'. This meant that not only were district board politics necessarily conducted with reference to a greater splay of public opinion but also political institutions emerged which were rivals of the boards, and which influenced the character of district politics.[213]

213 Of course, there were a number of other elements in the composition of district politics which we have had to neglect. Rich urban merchants or zemindars, particularly

Political development, however, did not stop at the district level. The same factors of administrative decentralization, the creation of larger political institutions and the transfer of power from British to Indian hands also worked to produce provincial and national politics. Under the Montagu–Chelmsford reforms Legislative Councils were expanded in size, and Indian ministers with considerable local powers were made responsible to the Legislature. In Madras, this period witnessed the beginnings of 'party' government. Further, of course, the nationalist movement developed in parallel to the constitution, and rapidly came to form its own political system which competed with that of the government. Yet, in many ways, these larger political organizations were built on top of firm district structures which were independent and could continue to exist without them. In Madras, between 1920 and the mid-1930s, the various labels of provincial and national politics really adhered to groups factionally determined in the district rather than to groups consciously organized along party lines from the capital. As Dr C. J. Baker has shown, the leadership of provincial parties existed quite distinctly from any district followings they might possess.[214]

District institutions were the largest political organizations in Madras which directly administered their own patronage and power. Under the Montagu–Chelmsford constitution, the ministries—in image of the British—possessed only a supervisory role over the districts and were forced to administer indirectly through channels opened for them in the districts. This meant that the ministry was dependent on the support of powers constituted by political processes within the district and it could do little of its own volition. In the rural boards, for example, the ministries were faced with a majority of members elected locally. Certainly, they could nominate presidents and a few members but they had no influence over the way most members of district boards claimed their seats. The most that ministers could do was to support the dominant faction which emerged from district board bargaining. If they set up a president who was unacceptable to the majority, he simply could not work. The raja of Panagal, the chief minister from 1921 to 1926, had to back down on several occasions from confrontations with district board powers.[215] Indeed, in order to work the district

clever lawyers, particularly insensitive goverment officials, or even small social groups which had become disproportionately wealthy by means outside the main lines of the agrarian economy, could distort some of the behavioural patterns we have tried to establish.

[214] See C. J. Baker, 'Political Change in South India 1919–1937'.

[215] In 1921, for example, Panagal tried to reward the loyal Justice Party man

boards at all he had to destroy the *raison d'être* of his so-called party. He led a nominally anti-Brahmin party, yet, when it was necessary, he supported powerful district Brahmin politicians and neglected many of the faithful of the 1917–20 non-Brahmin agitation.[216] The Montagu–Chelmsford Councils turned the ministries into the lackeys rather than the masters of district factions. The Justice Party's weakness in its relations with the district boards was reflected in the composition of the Legislative Council. If the ministries could not direct the affairs of the district boards, they certainly could not control the electorate. In fact, the Montagu–Chelmsford electorates were constituted in such a way that no 'party' or central organization could operate in them. The constituencies had several members, but each voter had only one vote. Unless there was an elaborate caucus organization to distribute votes, two members of the same party who stood in the same constituency had to take votes away from each other. The Justice Party never attempted to build such a caucus. It stayed in power by buying support from district politicians whose methods suited the electorates. It was entirely a conciliar party dependent for its majority on the jobs, district board places, nominations to temple committees, and other gifts, which it distributed to anyone who would vote for it. Its ultimate failure in 1937 came from the disappearance of most of its gifts and their replacement with a whip. From the later 1920s, further measures of decentralization meant more elections and fewer nominations in district politics. Much of the Justice Party's patronage was therefore liquidated. The ministry, still needing the support of district politicians, began to use threats instead of rewards. In 1930 the raja of Bobbili, the new chief minister, began to supersede awkward local bodies. The policy went awry, for while earlier ministries had managed to win the favour of dominant district factions, Bobbili, on nearly every occasion, contrived to madden them. In 1937 when they revolted against him, the Justice Party was beaten out of existence.

P. L. Ramaswami Naicker with a seat on the Salem district board. The board president, the European zemindar T. Foulkes, however, would not have him and insisted on the nomination of a Brahmin client of his own. Panagal was forced to give way. During the course of an angry exchange of letters with Panagal, Foulkes neatly summarized the weakness of the Council ministry: 'On general principles if Government is going to nominate members without reference to responsible local opinion, it is merely a matter of time when Government is going to land itself in difficulties'. G.O. 1295 (Local and Municipal) dated 5 July 1921, TNA.

[216] Such as T. Desikachari, Nyampalle Subba Rao, A. S. Krishna Rao, T. M. Narasimhacharlu and P. Siva Rao. *The Cult of Incompetence, being an impartial enquiry into the record of the First Madras Ministry*, pp. 37–8. Those neglected formed themselves into the 'Anti-Ministerial' Justice Party.

Even Bobbili lost his seat in his home district—to a professional Congress worker called V. V. Giri.[217]

The history of the Justice Party shows how far the district remained the most vital level of political organization. Yet the Justice Party was not the only organization attempting to win support from the districts. Although the Congress was formally opposed to constitutional politics for much of the period between 1920 and 1937, it also needed to show its district following, if it were to have any credibility in politics. Its ability to compete with the Justice Party for district affections depended very much on the nature of district politics and, as might be expected, its success differed considerably between our 'wet' and 'dry' regions. These differences came to be expressed not only in the size of the different Congress organizations but also in their character and in what they were trying to do.

In the dry districts, the formal institutions of politics had achieved such a massive importance that no party could succeed without paying heed to their connexions with the Legislative Council. The Congress offered no way of influencing political events in the district institutions. Lacking a base for popular politics it offered no alternative system of politics. Non-cooperation made little impact on the rural élite of this region, save for sporadic fighting over the forests here and there. In so far as it won any support at all, this came from the towns and from a few isolated rural groups which had been at odds with the administration for many years.[218] If the Congress were to find a role here, it would have to be as a constitutional party, involved, somehow, in obtaining Legislative Council rewards for its followers. During the 1920s, the tensions between Gandhian agitation and constitutional co-operation wrecked the Tamil Nad Provincial Congress, which represented most of the dry region, and led to the development within it of two separate parties with opposing ideologies. The first, led for most of the time by C. Rajagopalachari and supported by an extraordinary assortment of political malcontents, clung desperately to the Gandhian ideal. There was never any question that it could succeed in constitutional politics in the 1920s; it had no influence in district affairs, no secured localities under it, and little hope of winning any election. The other Congress, led by S. Srinivasa Iyengar, A. Rangaswami Iyengar and S. Satya-

[217] C. J. Baker, 'Political Change in South India 1919–1937', pp. 451–4.

[218] The one exception to this would be the area around Coimbatore where non-cooperation anti-drink propaganda fitted in with V. C. Vellingiri Gounder's caste movement. Yet Vellingiri Gounder's intrinsic lack of interest in the wider purposes of the Congress campaign was clear in his refusal to resign the Legislative Council seat he had won in 1920.

murthi, all of whom had powerful contacts in the Secretariat, the High Court and the university in Madras city, had expressed a deep revulsion from Gandhian politics in 1920, and sought to bring the Congress back to reality.[219] In 1926, in the form of the Swarajya Party, they defeated the Justice Party ministry at the polls. Their victory, of course, was not because they had a programme which could mould a new public consciousness; as Dr R. A. Gordon has seen, they achieved it largely by allying with men in the districts, many of whom had sat or stood for election in the Legislative Council when the Congress was noncooperating.[220] The Swarajya Party consisted in the main of district bosses who had been unable to reach satisfactory arrangements with the Justice Party and were looking for an alternative government. Although in the end Srinivasa Iyengar did not accept office, it was by no means clear at any time before the election that he would not, and he only refused to do so after extreme pressure was put on him by the all-India leadership of the Swarajya Party.[221] Torn by bitter fighting between the two schools of thought, between non-cooperation and civil disobedience, the Tamil Nad PCC had a small and very irregular following. Apart from the 1926 election, it took no significant part in the politics of the presidency.

By comparison, the Andhra PCC, which was run from the delta districts, was a permanent and powerful political institution at the district level. While a moderate such as Sir P. S. Sivaswami Iyer could mock the supporters of Tamil extremists as 'the rabble in the towns'[222] nobody could treat the followers of T. Prakasam, A. Kaleswara Rao or Konda Venkatappayya in such a cavalier fashion. Although they operated from the towns, their connexions with Komati networks, with vernacular newspapers read in the countryside, with religious revivalism and with local grievances enabled them to build a large and influential rural following. As early as 1894, the Rajahmundry Hindu Theatrical Company, of which T. Prakasam was a member, had used plays to convey the Congress message to rural Godaveri.[223] In the

---

[219] *Hindu*, 23 and 24 June and 16 August 1920.

[220] Of the 47 Swarajysts elected, 20 had sat in the 1923 Council, and 4 others had stood for election in 1923 but had been defeated. Only 7 of the 47 had been members of the original Swarajya Party formed by Congress politicians in 1923–24. R. A. Gordon, 'Aspects in the history of the Indian National Congress, with special reference to the Swarajya Party, 1919–1927' (D. Phil thesis, Oxford University, 1970), pp. 292–4.

[221] C. J. Baker, 'Political Change in South India 1919–1937', pp. 406–8.

[222] P. S. Sivaswami Iyer to G. A. Natesan, 13 August 1920. P. S. Sivaswami Iyer Papers, NAI.

[223] *Hindu*, 1 October 1894.

Extremist-Moderate confrontation of 1906–08, the Andhra Extremists
spread their propaganda widely. In Godaveri, British officials smelt
'sedition' in many villages, while in Kistna the influential editor of the
Kistnapatrika added to his rural fame by combining political meetings
with wrestling matches.[224] Of all the Extremist groups in Madras,
those in the Andhra deltas were alone in founding permanent institutions. They established a National School at Masulipatam which taught
practical subjects entirely in the vernacular. Between 1911 and 1917,
this leadership channelled the strong but incoherent currents of
vernacular revivalism into the Andhra movement and finally won its
own provincial Congress committee. Above all, the leaders of the
Andhra Congress were able to turn the chronic irritation against the
administration to their own advantage. At one time or another they
had all been involved in anti-PWD agitation. Between 1916 and 1922,
they were able to count on considerable support, from ryots and village
officers alike, in the nationalist movement.

During the difficult 1920s, the Andhra Congress remained the focal
point of many popular protests. This propped up its importance in the
political situation created by the development of the rural boards.
At the same time it kept its own organization and much of its membership. Local politicians fought each other to use its organizations in
their squabbles. At rural board elections, candidates paraded their
Congress affiliations.[225] It could influence district board affairs, as we
have seen from the experiences of A. Kaleswara Rao, whose greatest
asset was his high place in the Congress. In the delta districts, it was
important to be a Congressman. This was shown in the way the
Andhra Congress was prepared to obey the orders of the all-India
Congress leadership at all times, no matter how asinine those orders
might appear from a local standpoint. For example, Kaleswara Rao,
Prakasam and Venkatappayya non-cooperated in 1920; undertook
'constructive work' between 1922 and 1926; accepted the Swarajya
Party's mandate in 1926 and, in Kaleswara Rao's case, won election to
the Legislative Council; and offered civil disobedience in 1930. Although

[224] M. Venkatarangaiya, *The Freedom Struggle in Andhra Pradesh (Andhra)*, Vol. II,
pp. 177–311.
[225] In the Rajahmundry area, for example, municipal and taluk board elections
were fought on party tickets between 1921 and 1923. *Hindu*, 10 May 1921, 4 September
1922, 14, 19, 20 April 1923. The local position of the Congress became so strong that
fights for power in local institutions were conducted within it. *Hindu*, 11 September
1924. In Ellore, the struggle for power between Mothey Gangaraju and Dandu
Narayan Raju, which dominated local affairs between the mid-1920s and 1937, was
fought at the polls on Justice Party–Congress lines. C. J. Baker, 'Political Change in
South India, 1919–1937', p. 224.

there were major faction fights for control of the Andhra PCC,[226] they did not, as in Tamil Nad, lead to a split over the very purpose of the Congress, or to the exit for long of the losing faction. For many politicians, membership of the Congress was too important to be thrown away simply because they disapproved of the course Congress was taking.

From the end of civil disobedience, the Congress parties of Andhra and Tamil Nad moved closer together as it became clear that the Congress itself was to take office. The 1934 Legislative Assembly elections and, above all, the 1935–36 district board elections which put the key to Legislative Council success into the hands of the Congress, pointed the way to 1937. Yet the Congress parties which won in the dry and wet regions were of different characters, indicating the differing histories of the Congress and the differing nature of district politics in the two areas. In the dry districts, the majority of Congressmen elected to the 1937 legislature had come over to the Congress only since the end of civil disobedience and the collapse of the Justice Party's political machine. Their interest in Congress awakened only when it promised to provide them with a government in Madras city which would help them. Most of them were rural board politicians, still working within the framework of the government's institutions. Of the 50 Congressmen returned from this region, only 13 had been sufficiently active in civil disobedience to have gone to prison.[227] But among Congress members from the delta districts, there were many more old party stalwarts. Although they were also rural board politicians, many of the new members of the Council could also show membership of the Congress going back without a break to 1920. Of the 15 Congressmen elected, no fewer than 9 had been to prison in civil disobedience and two others were well-known supporters of the movement.[228] Even as the Congress stood proclaiming victory for a national ideal, the ambiguities of trying to construct provincial politics on a base of district-level institutions stood out clearly.

Conclusion

Although the area of our inquiry has been confined to two fragments of a single Indian province, it is hoped that our findings suggest approaches to many of the more general problems of rural history in our period.

[226] Between 1920 and 1937, Kaleswara Rao, Venkatappayya and Pattabhisittara-mayya (who was thoroughly unsuccessful) spent a great deal of time feuding with each other for Congress pre-eminence.
[227] *Directory of the Madras Legislature* (Madras, 1938).   [228] *Ibid.*

Clearly, a basic question which emerges from our discussion is the way in which British administrative institutions 'fitted' the political hierarchy which developed from agrarian economic relations. Control of the economic resources of the countryside put one form of power into the hands of certain men, and, in various areas, the provincial governments of British India tried to use or to destroy the bases of this power. Recent research on the United Provinces, for example, suggests that, beneath many of the estates of taluqdars and zemindars, economic conditions were fairly similar to those we have seen in our dry region.[229] Political and economic control in the village, and a monopoly of the connexions between the village and higher administrative organizations, rested firmly in the hands of a small and resilient village élite. Yet the administrative development of the United Provinces was very different from that in dry Madras. Rural boards never achieved anything like the same significance, and the village élite was never encouraged to participate in the broader structures of government. Rather, the British built on the shaky foundations provided by zemindars and taluqdars who packed the district and provincial-level institutions of government. The incongruity between lines of actual rural power and of access to the political institutions of the British might be seen to account, at least in part, for the social tensions which produced kisan disruptions and the extinction of the landlords in the 1937 election.

Another feature of our analysis which has possible implications elsewhere is the character of political society in rural areas possessing large numbers of wealthy, mobile and market-oriented peasants. The problems of finding any political system capable of maintaining stability were virtually insurmountable: controls supplied by the economy simply could not hold down enough people, while the ease of communication prevented the acceptance of any single system of formal political institutions. In the Andhra deltas, men who lost out in the district boards or in the division of spoils by the administration were able to manufacture their own rival political systems based on agitation, protest and publicity. In looking for points of comparison with other parts of India, we might notice that Midnapore in Bengal and Bardoli in Gujerat, whose rent-strikes posed similar problems to government during the days of high Gandhian politics, were also areas in which the moderately rich peasant, with a large number of direct connexions to the market, abounded.

[229] See P. J. Musgrave, 'Landlords and Lords of the Land: estate management and social control in Uttar Pradesh 1860–1920' in *Modern Asian Studies*, Vol. 6, Part 3, July 1972, pp. 257–75.

An essay of this nature must necessarily exclude a great many particularities which influenced the nature of specific events. Its purpose has been to try to paint some background against which the action in the foreground becomes more readily comprehensible. Out of the many possible factors which affected the growth of rural political society in the period, it has selected the two which seem to indicate the most obvious lines of comparison with organization in other parts of rural India. All peasants had to earn a living and all were involved in some kind of administrative structure. This essay has tried to put these two types of activity into a single context.

Partition, Agitation and Congress: Bengal
1904 to 1908

GORDON JOHNSON

1. Introduction

AT the beginning of the twentieth century the Lieutenant-Governor of Bengal administered the largest province in India. In addition to the Bengali-speaking area, it included parts of Orissa and virtually all of Bihar.[1] Nearly two-thirds of the population were Hindus, and just over one third were Muslims. However, the Hindus predominated mainly in Bihar, Orissa and west Bengal, while the Muslims lived mainly in the east. In Bengal Proper there were, by 1901, more Muslims than Hindus.[2] The province was ruled from Calcutta, the only large city in the region. Until 1912 Calcutta was also the capital of India itself. The city was a great economic, political, administrative and educational centre, and few other towns exercised such an influence over their surrounding districts as Calcutta did over Bengal.

The pre-eminence of Calcutta did not mean, however, that Bengal was effectively governed: the province was too heterogeneous and unwieldy for that. Moreover, the historical legacies of early British expansion in Bengal worked against close administration. Coming to a rich but politically confused province, the East India Company had risen to success by acting as broker between Indian interests. Once acknowledged as supreme, the Company had in turn established its rule by

The following abbreviations have been used in this article:
DR DCI: Daily report of the Director of Criminal Intelligence.
FR Bengal: Fortnightly report on the agitation in Bengal.
FR EB&A: Fortnightly report on the agitation in Eastern Bengal and Assam.
IOL: India Office Library, London.
NAI: National Archives of India, New Delhi.
WR DCI: Weekly report of the Director of Criminal Intelligence.

[1] *Census of India 1901*, Vol. I, Part II, Table 1. See also A. Seal, *The Emergence of Indian Nationalism: Competition and Collaboration in the later Nineteenth Century* (Cambridge, 1968), pp. 36–64.
[2] In Bengal there were 21,790,006 Muslims and 20,544,023 Hindus. *Census of India 1901*, Vol. VI, Part II, Table VI. At the 1881 census there were 18,432,518 Hindus and 18,212,893 Muslims in the same Bengali-speaking districts. W. W. Hunter, *The Imperial Gazetteer of India* (2nd edition, London, 1885), Vol. II, pp. 285–6.

contracting out many of the functions of government to Indians capable of mediating between it and the numerous local societies of which the Bengal territories were composed. Of course, British rule had been established in a similar fashion in other places, but perhaps nowhere else did the spirit of the original arrangements last for so long. During the course of the nineteenth century, in northern, western and southern India, the government slowly but surely began to impress itself more directly upon the notice of its subjects. It did so especially through its revenue policies (however perverted they became in practice), and by tightening its control over its administrative machinery (however much government servants managed to manipulate it for their own ends). Yet in Bengal, after the bargains struck in the Permanent Settlement, revenue policies and the administrative machinery designed to implement them were difficult to change. At the end of the nineteenth century, parts of Bengal—particularly the eastern districts where the shifting river courses made communications difficult and which had become neglected in the Company's drive westwards through the Indo-Gangetic plain—were notoriously undergoverned.

Although much government in Bengal was distant, the British found among Bengalis some of their closest associates. These were the people who not only settled their own province under the Company's rule, but who went with that rule into other parts of India, arranging contracts, staffing the administration, and later pleading in the courts and teaching in the schools. Being among the first Indians to commit themselves wholeheartedly to the new regime, they were among its earliest beneficiaries. Land in Bengal was made over to them; public money was put at their disposal for schools and colleges; government employment became their preserve; and, as the century progressed, they made the new professions their own.

Many, although not all, of these Bengalis were high-caste Hindus. While the ritual standing of powerful men in Bengal's towns and countryside was as various as that found among urban bosses and landowners in any other province,[3] and while the literate and professional callings were by their very nature open to the talents, as often as not in Bengal, Brahmins, Baidyas and Kayasthas occupied these positions. Families drawn from these castes were so numerous within the bhadralok, as the upper-crust of Bengali society was loosely named, that their dominance could be characterized fairly as a 'despotism of

---

[3] See, for example, S. N. Mukherjee, 'Class, Caste and Politics in Calcutta, 1815–38', in E. Leach and S. N. Mukherjee (eds), *Elites in South Asia* (Cambridge 1970), pp. 46–50.

caste, tempered by matriculation'.[4] Of course, impeccable ritual status
did not of itself bring social, economic or political power, and consequently by no means all high-caste Hindus scaled the ladders to success.
Moreover, caste-names simply placed men in broad ritual categories, or
indicated certain ties of kinship, which did not encompass all social
relationships. Men of equivalent ritual status might be widely separated
in wealth, learning or position, and many of their strongest connections
might be with men of other castes. But caste and communal affiliations
had also an administrative significance: they were the bricks with
which the government made policy and with which Indian leaders built
up their demands. Consequently, whatever their social reality, they
became charged with political meaning. These considerations must be
remembered when convenience, the source material, or the political
vocabulary dictate the use of caste terminologies or of such general
social descriptions as 'bhadralok'.

Bengal's high-caste Hindus were not spread thinly over the province.
Although Brahmins were to be found scattered throughout Bengal, over
half the province's Kayasths lived in the eastern districts of Mymensingh, Dacca, Faridpur, Bakarganj, Tippera, Noakhali and Chittagong;[5] and over half the Baidyas lived in six of the same seven districts,
almost one third of them in Bakarganj and Dacca alone.[6] Calcutta was
also their stronghold. At the time of the 1901 census, almost a third of
the Hindu population of that city was Brahmin, Baidya or Kayasth.[7]
The groups from which the social elite of Bengal was drawn were
settled in a few eastern districts and in the capital itself.

In east Bengal, with its predominantly Muslim peasantry, high-caste
Hindus were prominent as landlords. The 1911 census recorded that
one third of the landlords in east Bengal were Brahmins and Kayasths.[8]

[4] *Bengal District Administration Committee, 1913–1914, Report* (Calcutta, 1915), p. 176.
Quoted in J. H. Broomfield, *Elite Conflict in a Plural Society: Twentieth Century Bengal*
(Berkeley and Los Angeles, 1968), p. 15.
[5] *Census of India 1901*, Vol. VI, Part II, Table XIII, p. 228. They were most
numerous in Mymensingh where there were 110,180 Kayasths, and within the
district they were most densely settled in Netrakona and Kishorganj sub-divisions,
ibid., and F. A. Sasche, *Mymensingh District Gazetteer* (Calcutta, 1917), p. 38. For a
description of Kishorganj and life in the town at the turn of the century see N. C.
Chaudhuri, *Autobiography of an Unknown Indian* (London, 1951), pp. 4–48.
[6] *Census of India 1901*, Vol. VI, Part II, Table XII, p. 195.
[7] *Ibid.*, Part II, Table XIII, pp. 195, 204, 228. The largest single group of migrants
from the suburban districts to Calcutta were Brahmins and Kayasths. P. Sinha, 'The
Suburban Village in Bengal in the Second Half of the 19th Century—A Study in
Social History.' *Bengal Past and Present*, Vol. LXXXII, Part II, July–December
1963, p. 141.
[8] *Census of India 1911*, Vol. V, Part I, p. 553.

In Mymensingh, most of the zemindars came from these two castes,[9] and men from the same groups held many of the intermediate tenures (of which there could be up to twenty) which separated the zemindar from the peasant.[10] The government was not able to interfere effectively in agrarian relationships. Large zemindars, of whatever community, presided over a local spoils system in which each party, from the cultivator upwards, took as much as he could get away with. East Bengal districts had long histories of zemindari–tenant friction, and cases of agrarian rioting were frequent. A government report confessed:

The majority of the larger landlords are absentees and leave the management of their estates to agents. Attempts made from time to time to intercept a portion of the raiyats profits from valuable staples by enhancing current rates of rent have given rise to combinations formed for the purpose of withholding all payments. Hence a perpetual friction between landlord and tenant, culminating in outbursts of serious agrarian crime. The two largest districts, Backergunge . . . and Mymensingh . . . have attained a special notoriety in this respect. Cases of rioting have increased in a single year by forty per cent in the former and no less than sixty-two per cent in the latter district.[11]

Although the alluvial deposits of eastern Bengal were fertile, only a few zemindars made a comfortable living from their land. Sandwiched between superior zemindars and rioting villages, many intermediate tenure-holders did less well. Further, throughout the nineteenth century the amount of income they derived from their lands declined as, according to laws of inheritance, properties became subdivided. The size of the rent-receiving class in Bengal increased by 23 per cent between

---

[9] *Mymensingh District Gazetteer*, p. 38.

[10] J. C. Jack, *Bakarganj District Gazetteer* (Calcutta, 1918), p. 94. The following figures show the extent to which high-caste Hindus relied on receipts from land:

	% living on income from rent	% employed as agents or managers
Baidyas	31.7	10.3
Brahmins	19.1	8.5
Kayasths	13.7	36.7

The figures are for north and east Bengal. The figure for Kayasth employment as agents or managers includes those who were cultivators of all kinds. *Census of India 1911*, Vol. V, Part I, p. 553.

[11] *Memorandum on the Material Condition of the Lower Orders in Bengal. 1881–82 to 1891–92* (Calcutta, 1892), p. 13. For the delicate balance maintained between zemindari oppression and peasant rioting see R. Carstairs, *The Little World of an Indian District Officer* (London, 1912), *in passim*.

1901 and 1911, and by another 9 per cent between 1911 and 1921.[12] Not only were there more people dependent upon the land but the size of estates, and consequently of their incomes, was small. In 1882–83 less than one zemindar in two hundred in Bengal and Bihar held really large estates, and 88.4 per cent held estates of less than 500 acres.[13] Mymensingh was the only eastern Bengal district where most of the land-revenue was paid by large zemindars, although even here 81 per cent of the estates paid less than fifty rupees land-revenue a year.[14] The 1921 census operations revealed that the average gross rent received by tenure-holders came to fifty rupees a month (which meant a gross annual income of £41) and that of this at least 10 per cent had to be deducted to pay the land revenue and to cover the costs of its collection.[15] Thus although many respectable Hindu families had some claim on the land, few of them were rich in consequence. The great majority had to supplement their incomes with other work, and this they found in the offices and courts of Calcutta, Bengal, Bihar, Orissa, and further afield.

High-caste Hindus provided almost all the literate people in eastern India. The following table shows the proportion of Brahmin, Baidya and Kayasth men who were returned as literate at the 1901 census compared with the total population:[16]

	Total population	Baidya	Kayasth	Brahmin
Male literates	10.4%	64.8%	56%	46.7%
Male English literates	0.9%	30.39%	13.23%	7.37%

[12] *Census of India 1921*, Vol. V, Part I, p. 385. Both these increases were three times as great as the increase among the population as a whole during these decades.

[13] Size of estates in Bengal and Bihar 1882–83: Area over 20,000 acres—457 estates or 0.41 per cent total; area 500 acres to 20,000 acres—12,304 estates or 11.1 per cent total; area less than 500 acres—97,695 estates or 88.4 per cent total. B. H. Baden-Powell, *The Land Systems of British India* (Oxford, 1892), Vol. I, p. 441.

[14] Mymensingh: number of estates paying an annual revenue of:

418	less than 1 rupee
5,156	Rs 1 – Rs 10
2,881	Rs 10 – Rs 50
628	Rs 50 – Rs 100
620	Rs 100– Rs 500
92	Rs 500– Rs 1000
108	Rs 1,000 +

Out of a total annual revenue assessment of Rs 8,75,239, the 108 estates paying more than Rs 1,000 contributed Rs 5,46,872. *Mymensingh District Gazetteer*, p. 101.

[15] *Census of India 1921*, Vol. V, Part I, p. 385.

[16] *Census of India 1901*, Vol. VI, Part I, pp. 305, 309. Excluding Eurasians and

In Bengal alone the proportion of Brahmin men who knew English was 15.7 per cent, and that of Kayasths 14.7 per cent.[17] The commissioner reported 'Amongst the lower castes who form the great bulk of the population, there are practically none who are acquainted with English.'[18]

Education was the key to positions of influence and power. Twenty-two of the twenty-seven Indians who worked in the Covenanted service in the Bengal government were Brahmins, Baidyas, and Kayasths, and men from the same castes held over 80 per cent of all other high posts.[19] They also monopolized positions in the professions as well, as the following table shows:[20]

Chinese, twelve castes returned a male literacy greater than 40 per cent. They were: Mahesri (70.5 per cent), Oswal (64.9 per cent), Baidya (64.8 per cent), Vaisya (61.5 per cent), Kayasth (56.0 per cent), Agarwala (54.4 per cent), Karan (52.8 per cent), Subarnabanik (51.9 per cent), Gandhabanik (51.0 per cent), Aguri (49.8 per cent), Brahmin (46.7 per cent), and Moghal (41.7 per cent). *Ibid.*, p. 309–10. But while Brahmins, Baidyas and Kayasths totalled 4,208,741 in the entire province the other nine castes together totalled only 616,889. *Ibid.*, Part II, Table XIII, pp. 192, 193, 195, 204, 211, 226, 228, 238, 248, 259, 265, 283. Apart from the Karans who were the Orissan writer caste, and the Moghals who were aristocratic Muslims in west Bengal, the other castes listed were primarily trading and mercantile castes. Again, apart from Eurasians and Chinese, ten castes in the province were returned with a male literacy in English greater than 7 per cent. They were: Baidya (30.39 per cent), Subarnabanik (26.85 per cent), Gandhabanik (17.56 per cent), Kayasth (13.23 per cent), Moghal (12.05 per cent), Vaisya (8.35 per cent), Kansari (8.11 per cent), Brahmin (7.37 per cent), Khatri (7.36 per cent), Mayra (7.11 per cent). *Ibid.*, Part I, pp. 309–310. The seven other castes in this case totalled only 557,880. *Ibid.*, Part II, Table XIII, pp. 195, 204, 211, 225, 228, 231, 242, 259, 265, 283.

[17] *Census of India 1901*, Vol. VI, Part I, p. 302.

[18] *Ibid.*, Part I, p. 303.

[19] Of the 2,185 most senior positions in certain Government Departments in the Lower Provinces, 795 posts were held by Europeans and 11 by Native Christians. Of the remaining 1,379 posts 1,104 (80.2 per cent) were held by Brahmins, Baidyas and Kayasths; 131 (9.5 per cent) by other Hindu castes; 141 (10.3 per cent) by Muslims. The remaining three were held by Parsis. *Ibid.*, p. 506. Looked at from the opposite point of view 'the Rajputs and Khatris, though they number nearly a million and a half, hold only 5 high appointments, and the Babhans with over a million hold none. The Goalas with nearly 4 millions claim but 1 appointment—a subordinate post in the Medical Department. Numerous castes are entirely unrepresented in the higher grades of the Civil Service of the State, amongst whom it will suffice to mention the Rajbansis and Namasudras with an aggregate strength of nearly 4 millions, and the Kurmis and Bagdis, each numbering over a million.' *Ibid.*, p. 486. Of course, there was no good reason why any of these people should want to become involved in clerical work.

[20] *Census of India 1901*, Vol. VI, Part II, Appendix to Table XVI, pp. 502–6.

Profession	Total posts held by Hindus	Total held by Brahmins, Baidyas and Kayasths	Per cent held by Brahmins, Baidyas and Kayasths
Officers of Government	1,083	786	72.6
Clerks, Inspectors, etc.	23,886	17,256	81.5
Inspecting and Clerical staff of Local Bodies	1,817	1,215	67.0
Officers in Postal and Telegraph Department	1,471	848	57.5
Agents and Managers of Landed estates	10,942	7,005	64.0
Professors and Teachers	37,184	21,491	58.0
Lawyers and Law agents	9,869	7,606	77.0
Medical Practitioners	31,728	18,397	58.0

The figures in the Table are for the whole of the region governed from Calcutta. In this area these three castes amounted to 9 per cent of the Hindu population.[21]

Monopoly of white-collar employment did no more than dominance as landlords to secure prosperity for the Hindu literates. By the late 1870s when tenures were increasingly sub-divided, more youths were seeking English education only to find that the range of employment available did not meet their aspirations. The output from schools and colleges far outpaced the number of vacancies in government service and the professions. In Dacca division between 1881 and 1891 the number of schools teaching up to University entrance increased from twenty, with 5,791 pupils, to forty-two, with 10,379 pupils. This meant that

2,500 lads are yearly turned out with just enough education to render them useless for any profession but that of ministerial service. The numbers who leave the middle English schools with an education still more rudimentary, but ambitions quite as high, are not less than 3,500 annually, a total of candidates for employment of at least 6,000, while vacancies do not reach a tithe of that number. This process is at work in the central and western districts and in Western Bihar; and its outcome is a yearly swelling class of hungry malcontents.[22]

For every well-educated young man who secured a good post in the administration or built up a flourishing legal practice, there were many

[21] *Ibid.*, Table VI and Table XIII, pp. 195, 204, 228.
[22] *Memorandum on the Material Condition of the Lower Orders in Bengal during the ten years from 1881–2 to 1891–2*, p. 15.

half-educated who were forced to take low-paid jobs: in Mymensingh *naibs* were paid less than 360 rupees a year, and *muharrirs* got only eight or nine rupees a month.[23] The prospect of poverty and unemployment was further increased by the very rapid growth of education, particularly in eastern Bengal.[24] By 1900 the competition for jobs in Bengal had become very fierce.

From the end of the nineteenth century, changes in government policy also began to hit hard those groups in Bengal which had previously seemed to hold a privileged position. Those high-caste Hindu families, living in east Bengal and in Calcutta, who were dependent on white-collar employment to supplement declining shares in revenue from land, were particularly vulnerable to shifts in the government's policies about public employment and education. The lack of Biharis, Orissans and Muslims in the Subordinate Executive Service had by the late 1880s shown signs of encouraging 'feelings of race jealousy and antagonism' in the province.[25] The Lieutenant-Governor of Bengal decided in 1889 that he could no longer recruit the Subordinate Executive Service from a competitive examination, and resolved to nominate two-thirds

[23] *Mymensingh District Gazetteer*, p. 65. The cost of living was also high in the towns. In Mymensingh no house could be rented for less than ten or fifteen rupees a month, and a Government Officer earning 150 rupees a month might pay up to thirty rupees for satisfactory accommodation. *Ibid.*, p. 62.

[24] English High Schools and their pupils in eastern Bengal:

	1896–97	1901–02	1910–1911	1921–22
Dacca				
Schools	20	38	47	78
Pupils	5,164	10,212	13,323	17,455
Bakarganj				
Schools	44	46	64	81
Pupils	3,904	3,432	6,310	5,862
Faridpur				
Schools	7	23	26	49
Pupils	1,416	5,173	6,660	8,815

I owe these figures to Dr A. Basu.

[25] Memorandum by Sir S. C. Bayley. Enclosure to Govt. India to Secretary of State, 1 November 1893. *Parliamentary Papers* (1894), Vol. LX, p. 93.

[26] One-third of the vacancies in the Lower Provinces Subordinate Executive Service (of which there were about ten a year) were filled by pure competition; one-third were selected from the remaining candidates who got more than one-third of the marks in the examination 'in such a way as to distribute the appointments fairly among the various divisions, races and creeds of the Province' and one-third by nomination, usually promotions from the ministerial service—the lowest grade in the administrative hierarchy. *Ibid.*, p. 94.

of the vacancies to try to make provision for the less educationally advanced groups.[26] Since 1885 it had been government policy to encourage Muslim education so that they would gain a fairer share of government employment.[27] Money for lower-caste and Muslim schools would, however, have to be diverted from existing institutions. Curzon's proposed reform of higher education, which was intended to improve the quality of university and college graduates at the expense of their quantity, seemed further to work against the immediate needs of the traditional literate groups.[28] The notion that their main patron was sacrificing their interests became a certainty when the bhadralok learnt of the plans for the partition of Bengal.

II. The partition of Bengal

During the 1890s the Government of India considered several minor alterations to the boundaries of Bengal,[29] but it was not until 1903 that more far-reaching proposals for making Bengal a smaller and more manageable province were put forward. In that year, the incorporation of Berar into the Central Provinces provided an opportunity for

[27] In 1885 the government decided that no special exemption from the tests of suitability could be given to Muslims but that every effort should be made to improve their educational standing, and that they should be employed where consistent with considerations of administrative efficiency. By 1900 progress had been so slow that the government of Bengal issued an order that sub-inspectors of schools should be distributed between Hindus and Muslims in proportion to their respective proportions of the total population. This does not seem to have had much effect. Extract from Proceedings of the Lieutenant-Governor, Eastern Bengal and Assam, 15 February 1907. Home Establishments A, May 1907, 103, NAI. How far the policy was successful is a different question, for the evidence points towards the Hindus retaining their monopolistic position, even in the very lowest ranks of the service. Hindu dominance in posts carrying a salary of Rs 75 a month and over was very clear. In 1904 there were 4,469 such appointments in Bengal. 2,700 were held by Hindus and 302 by Muslims. Statement of Civil Appointments . . . Part A, General Tables, Government of India . . . Resolution, 24 May 1904. Home Establishments A, June 1904, 103, NAI. The Government of Eastern Bengal and Assam found that Muslims, although constituting two-thirds of the Province, only held one-sixth of ministerial appointments in divisional, sub-divisional and district offices. Govt. EB & A to Govt. India, 30 November 1906. Home Establishments Deposit, December 1906, 8, NAI.

[28] A. Basu, 'Indian Education and Politics 1898–1920' (Ph.D. thesis, Cambridge, 1967), pp. 7–92.

[29] See the map on the next page. The alterations proposed during the 1890s concerned the hilly frontier between Bengal and Assam. The South Lushai Hills were actually transferred from Bengal to Assam in 1898. This had been urged six years earlier in order to make the task of controlling the Lushai and Chin tribesmen easier. Resolution of the Foreign Department, 25 July 1892. Home Public A, October 1892, 149, NAI.

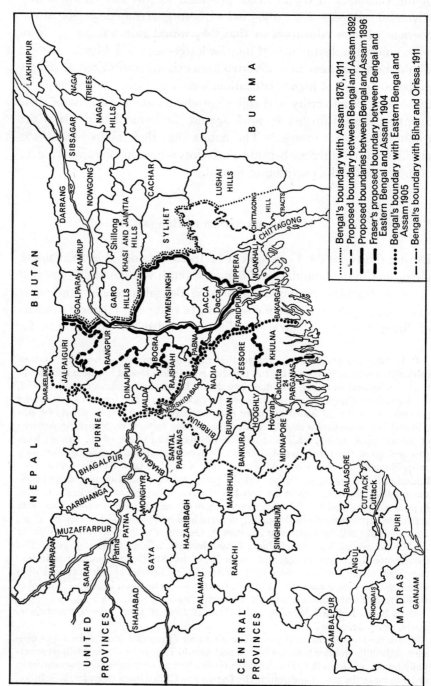

Bengal, Bihar, Orissa and Assam, showing districts under British administration

discussing major boundary changes. Submitting his decision about Berar to London, Curzon wrote:

Later will follow our proposals for adding to or subtracting from the Central Provinces, Bengal, Assam and Madras in other directions. I should like to fix the provincial boundaries (which are at present antiquated, illogical and productive of inefficiency) for the next generation.[30]

The government not only wanted to make Bengal more manageable, but it wanted to end the anomaly whereby the Uriya-speaking districts were distributed between three provinces, and it wanted to encourage the development of Assam. The problems presented by the Uriyas and the backwardness of Assam could be solved by one move: the Uriya-speakers could be added to Bengal and Bengal relieved by transferring some of the eastern districts to Assam. In the event the Madras government refused to let its part of Orissa go, and only Sambalpur, the Central Provinces' one Uriya-speaking district, was added to Bengal.[31] But by the time that this had been agreed, the governments of India and of Bengal had become more convinced of the need for a radical change in the north-east.

The transfer of several east Bengal districts to Assam would help the development of north-east India in several ways. Economically the province would benefit by having a sea-port at Chittagong. Chittagong was neglected by the Bengal government, for it was not easy 'for a Local Government dominated by the interests of a great port like Calcutta, to do much towards promoting the advancement of a humbler rival, situated so short a distance away.'[32] The Assam–Bengal railway would gain by being placed under one administration. This railway ran from the Assam Valley through Cachar, Sylhet, and Tippera to the Bay of Bengal and when complete it would link the oil wells of Digboi and Makum, the coal-mines of Margharita, and the tea plantations of the Upper Brahmaputra, with the sea at Chittagong.[33]

A further reason for expanding Assam was to enable it to recruit its own civil service instead of having to rely on Bengal. The Assam civil service was the smallest in India. In 1897 there were 489 posts carrying a salary of more than Rs 75 a month, but of these, 295 were within the Rs 75–Rs 200 range, and only 29 posts paid more than Rs 1,000 a

[30] Curzon to Godley, 17 June 1903. Curzon Papers, Mss Eur F 111/162, IOL.
[31] This was the scheme as proposed in 1903. Govt. India to Govt. Bengal, 3 December 1903, Home Public A, December 1903, 155, NAI.
[32] Govt. India to Govt. Bengal, 3 December 1903. Home Public A, December 1903, 155, NAI.
[33] Ibid.

month.[34] Inevitably a province that could only offer the prize of one
commissionership, that was remote and in a backward province, did not
attract the best civil servants. An enlarged Assam would draw and
retain men of mark, and become 'a vigorous and self-contained administration, capable of playing the same part on the North-East frontier of
India that the Central Provinces have done in the centre, and that the
Punjab formerly did on the North-West'.[35]

The arguments for adjusting the boundary between Bengal and
Assam were strong, and for almost a decade government officials debated
not whether but where it should be redrawn. The commissioner of
Chittagong had suggested in 1896 that an enlarged Assam should
include Chittagong Division and the districts of Dacca and Mymensingh.[36] This scheme was adopted again in 1903, as being most likely
to achieve the Government's ends.[37] It was only after further investigation into the state of the administration in the eastern Bengal districts
themselves, which Sir Andrew Fraser, the Lieutenant-Governor of
Bengal,[38] found deplorable (an impression which was endorsed by the

[34] The number of posts in other provinces in 1897 was as follows:

	Total Posts over Rs 75 a month	Posts over Rs 1,000 a month
Bengal	3,968	214
Bombay	3,109	177
Madras	3,012	167
United Provinces	2,390	169
Punjab	2,348	136
Central Provinces	678	48

From: Statement of Civil Appointments ... Part A, General Table,
Enclosure to Resolution of Home Department, 24 May 1904. Home
Establishments A, June 1904, 103, NAI.

[35] Govt. India to Govt. Bengal, 3 December 1903. Home Public A, December
1903, 155, NAI. These same arguments had been used to support the proposals of
1896. Govt. Bengal to Govt. India, 13 August 1896. Home Public A, May 1907, 204;
Govt. Assam to Govt. Bengal, 25 November 1896. Home Public A, May 1897, 228,
NAI.

[36] Commissioner of Chittagong to Govt. Bengal, 7 February 1896. Home Public A,
May 1897, 205, NAI.

[37] Govt. India to Govt. Bengal, 3 December 1903. Home Public A, December
1903, 155, NAI.

[38] In 1901 Fraser, as Chief Commissioner of the Central Provinces, had restored
Uriya as the court language of Sambalpur district and had requested the Government
of India to relieve the Central Provinces of so difficult a charge. A. H. L. Fraser,
Among Indian Rajahs and Ryots (London, 1911), pp. 313–16. It was Fraser again, who on
promotion to a seat on the Viceroy's executive council, had proposed the grouping
of all the Uriya-speaking districts under Calcutta. Note by A. H. L. Fraser, 28 March
1903. Notes, Home Public A, December 1903, 149–160, NAI.

Viceroy after he had toured the districts in February 1904) that the government decided to create a much larger province, with its capital at Dacca. The new province would be large enough to support its own administration and would be a province 'of much commercial importance, containing nearly the whole of the tea and jute production of N.E. India, besides silk factories in Rajshahi and Malda, and some indigo in the latter district.'[39]

The government's plan did not meet with unanimous approval. The first rumours of change, which had circulated in the 1890s, produced a crop of petitions against it. Inhabitants of Chittagong resented the loss of a seat on the Bengal Legislative Council;[40] it was argued that transferring districts from a Regulation province to a Non-Regulation province was a retrograde step;[41] land-owners were concerned lest the powers of the Bengal Board of Revenue be vested in the Chief Commissioner of Assam,[42] and those who owned land in districts which would fall under two administrations did not want to be put to the trouble of employing lawyers in Shillong and Calcutta.[43] But these objections were all met as the final scheme evolved. The new province was to have its own Legislative Council, and so would be a Regulation province; it was to have its own Board of Revenue; and Bakarganj and Faridpur were included in it to avoid splitting up big estates between two administrations.[44]

The possibility that the jurisdiction of Calcutta High Court might not extend to the new province caused wider concern. Lawyers objected to any scheme which tampered with constitutional checks on the executive and feared unemployment if the volume of work at Calcutta was decreased. Bengalis were supported in their protests by the European community.[45] This unlikely alliance was forged because the latter were

[39] Govt. Assam to Govt. India, 24 September 1904. Home Public A, February 1905, 162, NAI.

[40] Memorials from Chittagong, Govt. Bengal to Govt. India, 13 August 1896. Home Public A, May 1897, 204, NAI.

[41] Registrar, High Court of Judicature at Fort William in Bengal, Appellate Side to Govt. Bengal, 30 June 1896. Home Public A, May 1897, 210, NAI.

[42] Memorials from Chittagong, Govt. Bengal to Govt. India, 13 August 1896. Home Public A, May 1897, 204, NAI.

[43] British Indian Association to Govt. Bengal, 3 February 1896. Home Public A, May 1897, 215, NAI.

[44] Fraser's enlarged scheme of 1903 added these two districts to the new province because several major zemindars, like Sitanath Roy and his brothers, held land in them as well as in Dacca and Mymensingh. Govt. Bengal to Govt. India, 6 April 1904, Home Public A, February 1905, 157, NAI.

[45] Bengal Chamber of Commerce to Govt. India. *All About Partition* (Calcutta, 1906), pp. 103–4.

Q

against any reform which would take the districts where its economic interests lay out of the ultimate jurisdiction of Calcutta with its strong contingent of British lawyers and judges: a supreme court at Dacca might well have a preponderant Indian element. The government, in view of the strong Bengali and British opinion on the matter, decided to maintain the *status quo*, but, to the dissatisfaction of both communities, the final scheme envisaged a future date at which the new province would have an autonomous High Court at Dacca.[46]

But the main objection to the boundary changes was no minor matter, and it was one ignored by the government. As in more recent cases, the issue aroused controversy because provincial boundaries affected the distribution of government patronage and influenced its policies of public employment. As education spread and competition between regions and castes increased, there was bound to be a demand that local governments be staffed by local men. Consequently backward areas and communities might find in changed provincial boundaries new opportunities for advancement, particularly if boundaries were redrawn along racial or linguistic lines; while other social groups whose high literacy had enabled them to dominate the administration and courts far beyond their homes might find their position undermined.

The literate communities of eastern Bengal felt that they stood to lose considerably by the change. Almost one third of the Indians employed in the government offices of Bengal came from Bikrampur in the Munshiganj sub-division of Dacca district.[47] Dacca district supplied more than one tenth of the posts in the subordinate judicial and executive services in the forty-eight districts of Bengal,[48] but their position was no

[46] Govt. India to Secretary of State, 2 February 1905, Home Public A, February 1905, 166, NAI. At a protest meeting held in Calcutta Town Hall 7 August 1905, the Maharaja of Cassimbazar was concerned that the jurisdiction of Calcutta High Court would not be maintained, despite the Resolution of the Government. 'I fear that in the course of time a Chief Court will be established in the new province. And then what will become of our High Court? Thus emasculated and shorn of its jurisdiction and of its prestige and dignity it will, I fear, be reduced to the status of a Chief Court,' *All About Partition*, p. 90. Curzon did not give his audience at Mymensingh on 20 February 1904 much satisfaction on this point. He said: 'I have not here or at Dacca said anything about the jurisdiction of the High Court, because it is not proposed to remove the new province from it. To this I observe, it is replied that there is no guarantee that that may not some day be done. No more, I answer, is there now. The jurisdiction of the High Court is as likely to be affected by the congestion of its own business as it is by any administrative arrangement.' *Ibid.*, p. 45.

[47] *Imperial Gazetteer of India* (new ed., London, 1908), Vol. VIII, p. 220. Bikrampur pargana contained the ancient capital of the Hindu kings of Bengal.

[48] Memorial from the People's Association and the Landholder's Association, Dacca, 4 March 1904. Enclosure 8 in Govt. Bengal to Govt. India, 6 April 1904. Home Public A, February 1905, 157, NAI. The Subordinate Service contained the

longer unchallenged. Any change which might exacerbate the competition for employment was bound to be regarded with alarm. This was precisely what the partition of Bengal would do. In Bengal more posts would be given to Biharis and Orissans, while in the new province of Eastern Bengal and Assam, not only would there be fewer appointments available than in undivided Bengal, but the Muslims and the Assamese would be encouraged to take a large share of them.[49]

In 1896 a petition from Chittagong had put the case against making any alteration to Bengal's boundaries. The petitioners argued that a large number of posts hitherto reserved for Covenanted Civilians had recently been opened to the Uncovenanted Service and that the greater employment of natives in Bengal was a privilege granted because of the Bengalis' advance in education. The transfer of Chittagong Division would deprive both officers, and aspirants to the service, of opportunities for appointment and promotion. They regarded the proposed boundary changes as 'nothing short of a national calamity'.[50] In Dacca the fear of unemployment was greater. Many who worked in Calcutta and educated their children there, came from Dacca. If they had to leave Calcutta and return to live in Dacca, they would add to local unemployment, and, since the educational facilities in Dacca did not match up to those in Calcutta, their children would be placed at a disadvantage in the future and swell unemployment still further.[51] The

high posts not reserved for the Covenanted Service, so the proportion given here does not contradict that given in the *Imperial Gazetteer*, which includes all Government posts.

[49] There were Assamese protests against the partition also. The administration of Assam had once been almost monopolized by immigrants from Dacca and Mymensingh, but since the separation of Assam from Bengal in 1874, education had made better progress and the people of Assam were 'beginning to gather a substantial share of the loaves and fishes of office'. (Govt. Assam to Govt. India, 6 April, 1904. Home Public A, February 1905, 156, NAI.) If a new province was created including most of eastern Bengal, Assam would be 'overflooded with Dacca graduates and undergraduates, and the appointments at the disposal of the Administration will be more than insufficient to meet the demand'. (Note by Rai Dulal Chandra Deb, Chairman, Municipal Committee, Sylhet, 22 March 1904. Enclosure B, *ibid.*) One petitioner was prepared to countenance the new province provided 80 per cent of all posts were reserved for local inhabitants. (Note by Manik Chandra Barna, 27 February 1904. Enclosure 7, *ibid.*) The government of Assam really only wanted to take over Chittagong division, but the government of India considered the fear that the change would in effect be 'rather the annexation of Assam by Eastern Bengal than the transfer of Eastern Bengal to Assam' was 'if not exaggerated, at any rate not formidable'. Govt. India to Govt. Bengal, 3 December 1903. Home Public A, December 1903, 155, NAI.

[50] Memorial from the Tripora Hitasadhini Sabha to the Govt. Bengal, 16 January 1896. Home Public A, May 1897, 211, NAI. See also similar memorials from Tippera, Chittagong, Noakhali, the Indian Association and others in the same file.

[51] 'The middle class population of Dacca is composed of numerous small land-

collector at Bakarganj and the magistrate at Tippera found that the fear that partition would increase unemployment underlay the objections from their districts.[52]

The government did not think that these objections were of sufficient weight to stop the proposals; indeed, the very fact that literate Bengalis were so agitated about the change became an argument in its favour. The only people to lose by the creation of the new province were a self-interested minority who had for too long exercised an excessive influence in Bengal and who had prevented the advancement of less fortunate communities. Nowhere did this seem more true than in eastern Bengal. There the Muslims formed the bulk of the community,

and yet they find that the Hindus are the leaders in all branches of life whilst they remain the hewers of wood and the drawers of water. To the Hindus belong the land and the capital, for the majority of the landlords and landlord's agents are Hindus and so also are the great majority of the money-lenders and traders. Again, the Magistrates and Judges to whom the Muhammadans have to submit their cases are mostly Hindus, and so also are the police officers who investigate them and the lawyers to whom they have recourse to conduct them.[53]

A government which prided itself on its beneficent and impartial administration and which had a special concern for the peasant masses,

holders who have to supplement their income from land from other sources, and, consequently, from the earliest times they have had recourse to service and especially to employment under Government. The descendants of the industrial classes, whose industries have died out on account of competition with the Western nations, have also fallen to service as their vocation. In order to fit them for Government service, these people give them the best education available in the country. Thus the educated men of this district have always supplied large contingents to all Departments of Government Service, whether Judicial, Executive, or Ministerial. It has always been recognized by Government that the District of Dacca has supplied it with numbers of intelligent, able and faithful servants in all its Departments. Your Memorialists understand that the people of this district alone hold more than one tenth of the posts in the Subordinate, Judicial and Executive services in the 48 Districts in Bengal, Behar and Orissa which form the Administration of the Lieutenant-Governor of Bengal, not to speak of the innumerable Ministerial appointments they hold in all these Districts. By the intended separation the young men of this District would be deprived in future of their claims to appointments not only in the remainder of the territories under the rule of the Lieutenant-Governor of Bengal, but also in Assam.' The People's Association and the Landholder's Association, Dacca, to Govt. Bengal, 4 March 1904. Enclosure 8 in Govt. Bengal to Govt. India, 6 April 1904. Home Public A, February 1905, 157, NAI.

[52] Collector Bakarganj to Commissioner Dacca Division, 1 February 1904. Enclosure in Enclosure 19, *ibid.*; Collector Tippera to Commissioner Chittagong Division, 4 February 1904. Enclosure in Enclosure 20, *ibid.*

[53] Commissioner Dacca Division to Govt. EB & A, — July 1907. Enclosure, Govt. EB & A to Govt. India, 17 August 1907. Home Political A, December 1907, 58, NAI.

felt justified in trying to alter this inequality. The commissioner of
Chittagong had used the depressed state of the peasantry as an argument for transferring his charge to Assam in 1896,[54] but it was not until
Curzon toured the districts and found that hardly any Englishmen
served in them that the condition of eastern Bengal became one of the
most compelling reasons for the change. The Viceroy reported:

I find the case for a complete reform in the present system of administration
stronger even than I anticipated. In the whole of Mymensingh, with 4,000,000
of people, there is only one British Executive officer! Further, the Bengal
officers who are sent to these parts strike me as an inferior lot. They dislike the
part of the country, and the work suffers.[55]

The new province would be 'characterized by a prominence of Mus-
sulman interests,'[56] and consequently plans to educate Muslims and
employ them in government service, which the Government had
declared its policy in the 1880s, might at last have a chance of success.
The Muslim case although the most obvious, was not the only one which
attracted attention. High-caste Bengali Hindus had held too great a
share of Government patronage throughout eastern India. But at the
end of the nineteenth century other classes were beginning to demand
a share. Risley wrote that the 'Brahman and Kayasth monopoly has
endured for generations and the spread of education justifies the
attempt to break it up.'[57]

From the Government's point of view the time seemed particularly
ripe for appearing solicitous for the more backward peoples. The
Bengali bhadralok were the most political of Indians and were the most
incessant in their demands for reform. Curzon informed Brodrick

Calcutta is the centre from which the Congress party is manipulated throughout the whole of Bengal, and indeed the whole of India. Its best wire-pullers
and its most frothy orators all reside here. The perfection of their machinery,
and the tyranny which it enables them to exercise, are truly remarkable.
They dominate public opinion in Calcutta; they affect the High Court;
they frighten the Local Government; they are sometimes not without
serious influence upon the Government of India. The whole of their activity
is directed to creating an agency so powerful that they may one day be able
to force a weak Government to give them what they desire. Any measure in

[54] Commissioner Chittagong Division to Govt. Bengal, 7 February 1896. Home
Public A, May 1897, 205, NAI.
[55] Curzon to Brodrick, 23 February 1904. Curzon Papers. Mss Eur F 111/168,
IOL.
[56] Govt. Assam to Govt. India, 24 September 1904. Home Public A, February
1905, 162, NAI.
[57] Note by Risley, 5 December 1906. Notes, Home Establishments Deposit,
December 1906, 6-9, NAI.

consequence that would divide the Bengali-speaking population; that would permit independent centres of activity and influence to grow up; that would dethrone Calcutta from its place as the centre of successful intrigue, or that would weaken the influence of the lawyer class, who have the entire organization in their hands, is intensely and hotly resented by them.[58]

Although grossly overstated, and intended to appeal to the retired civilians on the India Council,[59] the argument of political advantage capped the partition proposals. What had begun life as a solution to administrative absurdities blossomed into an anti-babu extravaganza. Believing the change to be 'sound and statesman-like' and destined to be recognized 'as a great and indispensable administrative reform'[60] the government did not care if some Bengali interests were trodden under foot. Indeed, by affecting an Olympian disinterest as it moved the boundaries on its survey maps, the government seemed to have planned the partition to spite the bhadralok.

III. The agitation breaks

On 4 July 1905 it became known from the Secretary of State's reply to a question in the House of Commons that a boundary revision had been sanctioned by London. The agitation in Calcutta, already noisy, was even greater when it was discovered that the final scheme envisaged the transfer not of four but of fifteen eastern Bengal districts. The new province immediately became a Machiavellian device for dividing the Bengali nation, one hatched in conspiratorial secrecy by the hated Curzon. Finding that mere expression of Bengali opinion had not deflected the Government from its policy, the Bengalis decided to stiffen their protest with a call to boycott English cloth. The idea was taken up by the Calcutta leaders and yoked to a movement for the development of indigenous industries, the swadeshi movement.[61] The object of the boycott was to arouse interest in England by the most positive means possible. If English manufacturers began to lose money as a result of the

[58] Curzon to Brodrick, 2 February 1905. Curzon Papers. Mss Eur F 111/168, IOL.
[59] The partition proposals encountered a great deal of criticism from the India Council in London. The Under-Secretary of State consoled Curzon 'the opposition of the Congress Party will of course help matters considerably, so far as our Council is concerned'. Godley to Curzon, 26 January 1905, *ibid.*
[60] Curzon to Brodrick, 15 June 1905, *ibid.*
[61] Note by C. J. Stevenson-Moore, 2 December 1905, Notes, Home Public A, June 1906, 169–86, NAI. J. C. Bagal, *History of the Indian Association, 1876–1951* (Calcutta, 1953), p. 164.

partition then they would put pressure on the government, through their powerful lobbies at Westminster, to abandon the project. Further, by clearing the markets of foreign goods, the Indian leaders hoped they would assist the growth of industries in Bengal, making the economy altogether less dependent on the Imperial power. Such a method, which combined striking a more defiant blow than was possible by petitions, and a positive attempt to solve India's economic difficulties, appealed to the Calcutta politicians. It enabled them to draw attention to their grievance, it gave substance to their socio-economic theories, and it gave them an opportunity to demonstrate their political strength.

The Indian Association convened a meeting on 7 August under the Chairmanship of Raja Peary Mohun Mukherjee, at which the new methods of agitation were launched. The Indian Association determined to put itself and Calcutta firmly at the head of dissatisfaction expressed spontaneously at other district towns.[62] The mofussil leaders were invited to send delegates to the 7 August meeting, but there was not sufficient time for them to make the necessary arrangements. Babu Anath Bandhu Guha of Mymensingh wrote to Surendranath Banerjea asking that the meeting be postponed to allow the country people more time to get organized. But, as Surendranath recorded,

having regard to the strength of the feeling that had been aroused, and the eagerness to fire the first shot without delay, I wrote back . . . that time was the important element, and that the first great demonstration should be held early, so as to give the movement a lead and direction which would co-ordinate its future development and progress throughout the province.[63]

The gathering at the meeting proved to be so immense that three meetings had to be held simultaneously to satisfy the crowd who attended.

There were first the titled men—the Rajas and the Maharajas and the minor title-holders—the big Zemindars, the professional men—the Barristers, the Vakils and the pleaders from almost all the different districts of Bengal, the merchants' clerks, the school-masters and last but not the least the Marwaris of Barabazar, the shopkeepers of Chandney Chowk, Colootola, Harrison Road, College Street, Shambazar and Bagbazar.[64]

The meeting passed a resolution in which the Partition of Bengal was condemned. By 'dividing the Bengalee-speaking race' it would

---

[62] 'The leaders of the Indian Association and those of the new school sat together for days to thrash out the best means of guiding this national determination and popular upheaval into proper channels.' J. C. Bagal, *History of the Indian Association*, p. 165.

[63] S. N. Banerjea, *A Nation in Making* (2nd ed., Calcutta, 1963), p. 174–75.

[64] *All about Partition*, p. 86.

interfere with the social, intellectual, moral and industrial advancement of
the vast population concerned, while it will entail heavy expense, initial
and permanent that must add to the burdens of an overtaxed people and
indefinitely postpone all prospects of financial relief which the country so
urgently needs.[65]

The second resolution protested against the secrecy which had surrounded the final discussions of the plan,[66] and the third initiated the
idea of the boycott. The resolution was moved by Narendranath Sen,[67]
and seconded by Surendranath Banerjea. It read:

That this meeting fully sympathizes with the Resolution adopted at many
meetings held in the mofussil, to abstain from the purchase of British manufacturers so long as the Resolution on partition is not withdrawn as a protest
against the indifference of the British public in regard to Indian affairs and
the consequent disregard of Indian public opinion by the present Government.[68]

A fourth resolution pledged that the meeting would do all it could to
bring about the withdrawal of the order by constitutional means.
Indeed, the Calcutta leaders saw the boycott and swadeshi movement as
a strictly constitutional weapon. In a speech supporting the boycott
resolution Narendranath Sen said:

The proposal before you is one which affects the commercial interests of
England to some extent. I do not know whether and to what extent it will be
effective, but it is the only constitutional means which we can best adopt to
express our disapproval of the present system of Government in this country.
Our object is not retaliation but vindication of our rights; our motto is—
'Defence, not Defiance'.[69]

The Calcutta men set out to propagate the new gospel of swadeshi.
Speeches and exhortations were the order of the day. Hindu audiences
in the mofussil were encouraged to support the movement by being told
that English sugar was polluted with the bones and blood of cows in
the course of its manufacture. The argument was taken up by the
Amrita Bazar Patrika which added Liverpool salt and English cloth to
the list, and, for the benefit of its Muslim English-reading subscribers,
included the guts of pigs in the processes of manufacture.[70] Religious

[65] *Ibid.*, p. 87.
[66] *Ibid.*
[67] 'It would have been impossible to have found among the ranks of the Bengali
leaders one who by his moderation and patriotism was so well qualified for the task.'
S. N. Banerjea, *A Nation in Making*, p. 179.
[68] *All about Partition*, p. 87.
[69] *Ibid.*, p. 102.
[70] Note by C. J. Stevenson-Moore, 2 December 1905. Notes, Home Public A,
June 1960, 169–86, NAI.

authority was invoked to support the agitation. A. C. Bannerji went to Santipur[71] and Bhatpara[72] to persuade the Pundits to preach swadeshi. The doctrine was taken up at Midnapore temple, and at Kalighat in Calcutta.[73] Priests refused to perform religious ceremonies where European goods were used or worn. On the occasion of the Mahalaya on 28 September 1905, a *Mahapuja* was held at Kalighat, where the officiating Brahmin commanded the congregation to worship the mother-country above all other deities, to give up all sectarianism and religious differences, and devote their lives to the relief of her distress. The assembly then followed the Brahmin swearing:

in the holy presence of Kali Mata and at this holy Pitasthan that I will not use foreign-made goods as far as practicable, that I will not buy at foreign merchants' shops articles that are available at the shops of the people of this country, and I will not get anything done by a foreigner which can be done by a country man of mine.[74]

Throughout September schoolboys and students joined the campaign against the purchase of European goods. Students

on seeing any Bengali, or in fact any native, making purchase of British or other foreign-made goods, have accosted them and have attempted to, and in most cases induced him, either not to buy or to return the purchased articles. The inducement has been argument, not force. These lads or boys have been furnished with small printed or manuscript slips and these they tender to the purchaser or would-be purchaser. The slips set forth that any person buying imported goods, will drink the blood of his father and mother and will practically kill a *lac* of Brahmins.[75]

Some shop-keepers, especially dealers in leather and cloth, sustained heavy losses during September as a result of the boycott.[76] October 16, the day of partition, was observed by Bengalis as a day of mourning. The Chingrighata fish market was closed,[77]

[71] The most populous town in Nadia district, on the river Hooghly; a celebrated bathing place.

[72] Town in 24-Parganas, famous as a seat of Sanskrit learning.

[73] Kalighat was the largest Hindu temple in Calcutta, ' a place of great sanctity for Hindus, and numbers go there every day to bathe in Tolly's Nullah. The temple ... about 300 years old, has 194 acres of land assigned to its maintenance.' *Imperial Gazetteer of India*, Vol. IX, p. 274.

[74] Note by C. J. Stevenson-Moore, 2 December 1905. Notes, Home Public A, June 1906, 169–86, NAI.

[75] Chief of Police, Calcutta, to Govt. Bengal, 21 September 1905. Notes, Home Public B, October 1905, 114–15, NAI.

[76] *Ibid.*

[77] This was one of the largest fish markets. It was owned by Babu Jotindra Nath Chaudhuri. Note by H. A. Stuart, 10 November 1906. Notes, Home Public A, December 1906, 310–11, NAI.

Bengalees fasted and by an attempt to stop the supplies of fish, meat, vegetables, etc., in Calcutta tried to compel others to fast also. The cry of Bande Mataram (Hail O Mother), which is the watchword of the agitation was raised all over Calcutta and the Mofussil and the *Rakhi* ceremony, instructions for which had gone out from Calcutta and which consisted in binding a yellow thread on the left wrist, was performed wherever friends met.[78]

The spectacular protest meetings in Calcutta were matched by spontaneous demonstrations in other districts. Numerous instances of petty violence and picketing were reported. Yet they were confined to Bengal Proper. Outside the Bengali-speaking districts, and away from the localities where the literati lived, the movement against the partition met with apathy or open hostility. In Orissa, 'where Bengalis are cordially disliked by the Uriyas, there has been no attempt to compel either sellers or purchasers to confine themselves to swadeshi goods'.[79] In Bihar, the agitation was confined to expatriate Bengalis living in the cities. Surendranath Banerjea visited Bhagalpur at the end of September 1906, 'apparently with the intention of drawing the Biharis into the movement, but so far the only effect of his visit has been to create a split between the Biharis (both Hindus and Muhammadans) on the one side, and the Bengalis on the other'.[80] While in Patna division, 'the Bengali element has nowhere been strong enough to go beyond starting a few swadeshi stores for the sale of swadeshi articles which have mostly had a very short existence'.[81] At Deogarh, a favourite health resort in Santhal Parganas for Calcutta gentry, the swadeshi movement had some success, but 'the meetings which they hold are expressively described by the common people as "Babu *tamasha*" '.[82]

Within Bengal itself it soon became clear that the boycott of foreign goods was not working. The statistics given in the *Annual Reports on the Maritime Trade of Bengal* show that the decrease in imports of foreign goods through Calcutta was relatively small and of temporary duration.[83] Further, there is much to suggest that little of the decrease was

---

[78] *Ibid.*

[79] FR Bengal, 17 September 1906. Home Public B, October 1906, 13, NAI.

[80] FR Bengal, 8 October 1906. Home Public A, December 1906, 144, NAI.

[81] FR Bengal, 17 September 1906. Home Public B, October 1906, 13, NAI. In a marginal note H. H. Risley wrote 'the Biharis hate the Bengalis who for years have held many appointments in Bihar and had an undue share of the leading practice in the courts.'

[82] Note by H. A. Stuart, 10 November 1906. Notes, Home Public A, December 1906, 310–11, NAI.

[83] The value in crores of rupees of certain commodities imported through Calcutta 1903–04 to 1907–08:

due directly to the boycott agitation. The government called for a special report to investigate the possible influence of the political agitation on trade.[84] The agitators wished for a boycott of cotton piece-goods, salt, sugar, tobacco and footwear. Of these cotton was the most important, and the investigation showed that more cloth remained in Calcutta warehouses on 31 August 1906, and a greater proportion of it remained unsold than in any of the previous five years.[85]

However, the slackening of the sale of cotton piece-goods during the first year of partitioned Bengal, could be explained by several factors which were totally unconnected with the boycott. Heavy forward buying by Indian merchants had taken place during the winter of 1904–05, causing a glut in the market,[86] and it had been followed by a serious dispute between Indian Merchants and Lancashire manufacturers. This dispute led the Marwaris to support the political agitation for a while in order to increase their bargaining power with Lancashire.[87] There had been a marked rise in the price of food grains,

[83] (cont.)

	1903–04	1904–05	1905–06	1906–07	1907–08
Cotton goods	15.59	18.66	21.44	18.62	23.73
Apparel	0.47	0.57	0.51	0.42	0.55
Woollen goods	0.71	0.98	0.64	0.44	0.69
Salt	0.52	0.55	0.53	0.52	0.62
Sugar	1.83	2.09	2.53	3.34	3.78
Liquors	0.49	0.48	0.54	0.50	0.59
Tobacco	0.23	0.28	0.32	0.31	0.36

The figures show that between 1905–06 and 1906–07 there was a 13 per cent decline in imports of cotton manufactures, 41 per cent decline in imports of boots and shoes; 5 per cent decline in imports of tobacco; 14 per cent decline in imports of brandy; and 17 per cent decline in imports of whisky. The figures are quoted in S. Sarkar, 'Trends in Bengal's Swadeshi Movement (1903–1908)', Bengal Past and Present, Vol. LXXXIV, Part II, July–December 1965, p. 151.

[84] The reason why import figures alone offered no sure guide was that 'imports alone might show an apparently healthy growth, while an investigation of stocks might disclose the fact that the increment was not passing into commerce but was accumulating in the merchants' warehouses'. Director-General of Commercial Intelligence to Govt. India, 5 October 1906, para. 2. Home Public Deposit, December 1906, 38, NAI.

[85] The enquiry was carried out by investigating the stocks of the four largest importers. The figures obtained showed that on average for the years between 1901 and 1905 the total stock in hand on 31 August represented 29.42 per cent of the total arrivals over the previous twelve months, and that of these stocks the average percentage remaining unsold was 18.2 per cent. On 31 August 1906 the total stock in hand amounted to 34 per cent of the imports for the year, and the amount of this remaining unsold was 31.22 per cent. paras. 4–6, ibid.

[86] Para. 10, ibid.   [87] Paras. 10–24, ibid.

reducing the purchasing power of the community at large,[88] and there had been an even sharper rise in the price of English cloth.[89] These factors alone would have encouraged people to resort to cheaper, indigenous goods, yet the import and sale of foreign cloth continued to rise: the value of English cotton goods arriving in Calcutta increased 13.26 per cent during the first year of the boycott movement over the previous year.[90]

The rise of 24.75 per cent in the price of English cloth was matched by a smaller increase in the price of swadeshi cloth. The Bombay mill owners, to whom Bengali politicians looked to supersede Lancashire,[91] increased their prices 8.4 per cent over the same period.[92] The value of imported Indian cloth through Calcutta between 1904 and 1906 went

[88] For example, exports of rice, the staple for most of Bengal, shrank by 13 per cent in quantity, although only 4.9 per cent in value, the difference between these percentages indicating that there was no such decline in export price as would in itself account for the falling off. Imports of rice increased by 52.8 per cent during 1905–06 on the previous year, while production of rice in Bengal fell short by only 1 per cent on the figures of the previous year, a record year, but well in excess of the average production over the previous five years. Yet the retail price of rice was reckoned to have increased in 1906 by 23.1 per cent on the average for the previous five years. Paras. 32–44, *ibid.*

[89] The average price increase of seventeen different descriptions of imported foreign cottons between 1904–05 and 1905–06 was 24.75 per cent. Paras. 13, 30, *ibid.*

[90] Statement of value of imports arriving at Calcutta 1904–06

Quarter ending	Arrival of foreign piece-goods
1904 June	Rs 3,79,82,000
September	4,87,89,000
December	4,40,61,000
1905 March	4,34,02,000
June	4,52,56,000
September	5,32,32,000
December	4,73,50,000
1906 March	5,14,77,000

The percentage increase calculated by comparing the average of the first four quarters with that of the second four. Para. 29, *ibid.*

[91] 'Bombay has a great destiny before her in connection with the Swadeshi Movement. The inspiration may have come from Bengal, but the consummation lies with you, the people of Bombay. You can make or mar the fortunes of this movement.' Speech by Surendranath Banerjea, December 1906. S. N. Banerjea (ed.) *Speeches and Writings of Hon. Surendranath Banerjea* (Madras, no date), p. 291. He went on to chide the Bombay mill owners for having increased their prices in the autumn of 1905.

[92] Statement of monthly average variations in the maximum prices of eighteen descriptions of Indian fabric, the mean for the year ending August 1905 being taken as 100:

up 52.6 per cent,[93] and in 1907 the Bengal Government reported that
'as a result of the boycott Bombay *dhooties* are now established in the
market to an extent formerly unknown'.[94] But this did not mean that
Indian manufacturers had made any substantial inroads into the market
as a whole, or that the boycott accounted for any increase in swadeshi
sales. The Indian share of the market in 1904–05 was 4.8 per cent; in
1905–06 it had risen only to 6.3 per cent.[95] Indian mills had to make a
tremendous increase in production if they were to replace those of
Lancashire. Besides, even these figures did not present a clear picture,
for Indian and Lancashire cottons were not in direct competition with
each other, the former producing a coarse cloth and the latter a fine

[92] *(cont.)*

	1904–05	1905–06
September	92.9	109.1
October	96.2	106.5
November	96.2	109.1
December	101.0	109.1
January	101.0	110.5
February	98.3	110.5
March	98.0	110.5
April	101.0	108.0
May	101.0	108.0
June	101.0	108.0
July	104.2	105.9
August	109.1	105.9
Average	100.0	108.4

Para. 30, Home Public Deposit, December 1906, 38.
[93] Statement of value of imports arriving at Calcutta 1904–06.

Quarter ending	Arrival of Indian piece-goods
1904 June	Rs 16,65,000
September	22,58,000
December	31,57,000
1905 March	17,05,000
June	21,27,000
September	35,34,000
December	53,68,000
1906 March	23,78,000

The increase percentage calculated by comparing the average of the first four
quarters with that of the second four. Para. 29, *ibid.*
[94] FR Bengal, 6 September 1907. Home Political A, October 1907, 50, NAI.
[95] Para. 29, Home Public Deposit, December 1906, 38, NAI.

one. The matter was further complicated by the fact that some Lancashire firms exported their goods to Bombay, where they were marked
as swadeshi goods and then sent to Bengal.[96]

There was no marked change in the value or amount of salt and
sugar imported to Bengal.[97] These were the two commodities on the
boycotters' list which were consumed by Bengalis at large and against
which the most vigorous propaganda was carried. The failure to
enforce a boycott of salt and sugar was symptomatic of the failure to
bring mass support to the cause. On the other hand, imported tobacco
and footwear, which were bought almost entirely by the bhadralok,
showed the most dramatic decline. The Director of Commercial
Intelligence considered the drop in tobacco imports highly satisfactory
since it could easily be grown in India.[98] The trade in boots and shoes
was the only one he believed to have been directly affected by the
agitation.[99] The bhadralok were the only significant purchasers of
foreign leather, and the trade had the advantage of being in Muslim
hands 'so it is fair game to the Hindu, and the figures throw an interesting sidelight on that spirit of brotherhood which is supposed to unite all
Indian castes under one patriotic legend'.[100] Even here the boycott was
not effective for long. By July 1908 the Bengal Government reported
that 'Bengalis are not afraid to be seen wearing English-made *dhoties
chudders*, and shoes'.[101] The zeal with which some Bengalis implemented
a boycott of foreign goods[102] did not extend to all the inhabitants of the
province.

[96] 'A feature of the year's trade in Bombay has been the increase in the imports of
dhooties of the Bengal type. Taking the eight months January to August these imports
have amounted to 10,533 bales as against an average of 6,000 in the same period of
each of the previous three years. This suggests . . . that there is truth in the statement
that unstamped dhooties are imported at Bombay and there imprinted with Swadeshi
marks conducing to their sale as Indian goods.' Para. 55, *ibid.*

[97] Para. 47, *ibid.*

[98] '. . . the importation of a preparation of tobacco into a country where tobacco
can so well be grown represents an unnatural condition which it is not even
desirable to maintain.' Para, 47, *ibid.*

[99] Though even here there had been other influences. The leather trade the world
over had suffered from a rise in price. In 1905 Britain's imports of leather goods
increased in value by £29,000 while declining in quantity by 13,500 cwts. Further,
India was increasing her own production of leather goods, having plenty of her own
raw hide. 'It is in the nature of things that a country that exports raw hides and skins
to a value of Rs 1,000 lakhs and tanned hides and skins to a value of Rs 360 lakhs
should cease to take large quantities of leather goods from abroad.' Para. 47, *ibid.*

[100] Para. 47, *ibid.*

[101] FR Bengal, 4 July 1908. Home Political A, August 1908, 130, NAI.

[102] For example, in the fervour of the swadeshi movement students refused to write
examinations on foreign paper and Hindu gentry reverted to using the thicker, stuffier

The failure of the economic programme did not lead to the collapse of the agitation. The partition was too important a political issue for it to die away quietly. In west Bengal special efforts were made to observe the anniversaries of the 7 August and the 16 October, and in Calcutta, with its large student population, meetings continued to be held on a large scale. No gathering was complete without some reference to the partition; no meeting ended without those present being urged to boycott foreign goods and devote themselves to schemes of self-help. But in east Bengal, the agitation assumed a different form. For one thing, in the eastern districts activity continued throughout the year, except for the worst of the rainy season. While the government of Bengal often had to cast around for some small incident to put into its Fortnightly Report on the state of the agitation, the Eastern Bengal Secretariat had no difficulty in covering two or three pages. Not all the districts in the new province were equally active. Although each had its share of petty disturbances—picketing by schoolboys, a scuffle in the market, or a cart-load of Liverpool salt overturned—the names of two or three stand out: Dacca, Mymensingh, Faridpur, Tippera, Noakhali, and above all, Bakarganj.

The persistence of the agitation in these districts calls for explanation. They were all backward, deficient in communication and lacking urban centres. Their geographical position on the Ganges–Brahmaputra delta meant that there were virtually no roads or railways.[103] Communities on the shifting alluvial deposits were very simply structured. In 1911 the average population of each census village in this area was 379, although there is every evidence that the size of viable communities was much smaller.[104] In these villages only two to five castes were likely to live together, and there was little formal interaction between them in communal life.[105] There was no widespread religious organization; no well-established district officers and little government.[106] The sharpest division between people living on the delta was between the respectable classes who refused to perform manual work, who were mainly high-

native cloth for mosquito nets. S. N. Banerjea, *A Nation in Making*, p. 182; B. C. Allen, *Dacca District Gazetteer* (Allahabad, 1912), p. 86.

103 In Dacca waterways provided the main avenues of communication. In 1912 there were only eight and a half miles of metalled road outside municipal areas in the district. *Dacca District Gazetteer*, p. 135. Examination of a large-scale map of Bakarganj shows it laced with waterways. The district had no railway and by 1918 it had 387 miles of road, of which only twelve were metalled. *Bakarganj District Gazetteer*, p. 85.

104 M. Marriott, *Caste Ranking and Community Structure in Five Regions of India and Pakistan* (Reprint, Poona, 1965), p. 72.

105 *Ibid.*, p. 72–3.

106 *Ibid.*, p. 75.

caste Hindus, and the mass of labouring peasantry. The social structure
allowed for considerable mobility by single families and small groups.
Marriott describes settlement in these districts as

for the most part scattered homesteads and indefinite neighbourhoods. In
place of a closely knit economy of traditional exchanges among particular
members of different castes, one finds a relatively free economy of cash
transactions with itinerant traders, or at shifting market places . . . And other
economic activities seem less likely to place one local group beneath another
than to subordinate all local groups equally to the same absent landlord.[107]

The importance of this local structure for the swadeshi movement can
hardly be overestimated. The disjointed nature of society and the mobility of social and economic status it allowed, the lack of urban centres,
and poor communications made it virtually impossible to organize a
coordinated movement extending over several districts, particularly
when the political leadership came from a minority of a different
religion from most people. On the other hand the concentration of
high-caste Hindus in certain areas within these districts meant that at a
local level they were able to mount successful campaigns.

The bhadralok of east Bengal had particular reasons for being restless.
They were the main group to be adversely affected by partition, which,
cutting them off from Calcutta and west Bengal, left them an embattled
and embittered minority in a region where seven out of every eight
villages were Muslim[108] and where the administration was actively
encouraging the development of a Muslim counterweight to Hindu
superiority. The literate Hindus of eastern Bengal felt the competition
for employment and education more than other groups, and partition
could only increase their distress. Coupled with this was a rise in prices,
which, dating from the nineteenth century, was particularly sharp in the
immediate post-partition years, and which impinged most on those
non-cultivating classes who lived on small fixed incomes.[109]

---

[107] *Ibid.*, p. 74–5. J. C. Jack wrote: 'The most characteristic feature of Bakarganj
life is the absence of the gregarious instinct. The urban population shows no signs of
growing and lives in widely separated homesteads. The big bazaars and markets
outside the towns do not attract a residential population, while there is no such thing
as a village site in the whole of Bakarganj. Ordinarily each family lives on an ample
plot of land which is surrounded by a deep moat and by a thick belt of trees and
usually the homestead is not flanked by another homestead, but is further separated
by paddy land from the nearest habitation.' *Bakarganj District Gazetteer*, p. 37–8. For
Faridpur see J. C. Jack, *The Economic Life of a Bengal District: A Study* (Oxford, 1916),
p. 18–19.
[108] M. Marriott, *Caste Ranking and Community Structure in Five Regions of India and
Pakistan*, p. 72.
[109] The crops in Bengal were severely damaged by monsoon and flood in 1905 and

The anti-partition agitation acquired its particular features from circumstances in eastern Bengal. Zemindars and lessors of markets used their local power to force people to join the swadeshi-boycott movement. In the districts there were numerous ill-paid pleaders, *mukhtears*, *moharrirs*, and zemindari agents, who could be banded together as 'volunteers' and brought out to picket markets and to intimidate purchasers and sellers. The same bands of youths were swelled by the growing number of thwarted schoolboys and students whose idealism was matched by their poor prospects. In some parts the self-help movement became a way of life in itself; yet social sanctions might also be directed against those who refused to participate in it. The most desperate of the east Bengalis turned to religious fanaticism and a cult of physical fitness. For them the step to secret societies and terrorism was very short. Yet although the districts were roused, the campaign against the partition was in no sense a coherent movement. Each neighbourhood gave vent to its grievances in its own way, and each locality relied upon its own resources for its political protest. Perhaps it would be worth while considering a few specific examples before carrying further the arguments about the significance of the anti-partition agitation.

1906. *Prices and Wages in India*, 29th Issue (Calcutta, 1912), p. 2. In Dacca district between 1899 and 1904 the average price for rice was 15.26 seers for one rupee. In 1906 and 1907 the average price was 8.11 and 8.06 seers for one rupee. The highest previous price reached in Dacca was in 1897 when it was 9.6 seers for one rupee. *Dacca District Gazetteer*, p. 84. In Mymensingh prices of food showed a similar over-all rise:

Rice	Wheat	Ghee
1901	Rs 3–4–0 per maund	Rs 5–0–0 per maund	Rs 1–8–0 per seer
1915	Rs 6–4–0 per maund	Rs 8–4–0 per maund	Rs 2–4–0 per seer

Mymensingh District Gazetteer, p. 67. These figures should be taken simply as a rough indication of the rise of prices, and unrelated as they are to other economic data it is mpossible to interpret their real significance. The overall trend upward in the prices of foodstuffs was encouraged in Dacca by the increasing population, and the yield per acre fell during these years as poorer soil was brought under cultivation. The extension of jute growing also displaced areas previously used for rice. The success of jute brought a great amount of wealth into the district (in 1906 the Dacca crop brought in 450 lakhs of rupees—*Dacca District Gazetteer*, p. 96) and increased the power of the consumer to pay. *Ibid.*, p. 84. In 1906 in Faridpur 'the moneylender was sucked so dry that no money was available for loan to cultivators with even the best security'. J. C. Jack, *The Economic Life of a Bengal District*, p. 103–4.

R

IV. The anti-partition agitation: zemindari organization leads to rioting in Mymensingh

Against a background of long-standing zemindari oppression and outbreaks of peasant discontent, the call to boycott foreign goods by Hindu landlords was not likely to be well received by their tenants. But the zemindars in eastern Bengal also owned and controlled markets. On 16 October 1905, the day of partition, the agents of the Gauripore, Ramgopalpur and Nattore zemindars, notified by beat of drum at Jamalpur that no one was to take cooked food and that all shops were to close as a sign of mourning. The shopkeepers at Jamalpur thought the order unjustified, and disobeyed. They were picketed and sales prevented. One Muslim who hung a Partition Proclamation outside his shop was taken to his zemindar's cutcherry and beaten. All the shopkeepers who were tenants of the three zemindars were made to sign bonds undertaking not to buy British goods. The following year one disobeyed and his stocks of cloth were burnt. He was unable to take his case into court, because if he did he was threatened with eviction from his shop.[110]

Jamalpur was the focus for communal disturbances which occurred in the district of Mymensingh between 1906 and 1908.[111] The municipality lay 35 miles north-west of Mymensingh and covered an area of twelve square miles. The greater part of the area was rural, and 12,320 of the 17,965 people who lived there were Muslims. The small Hindu population, largely Government officials, zemindari agents, lawyers and medical practitioners were densely congregated in the urban core of the municipality. Most of the Muslims who lived in this part of Jamalpur were shopkeepers.[112] Apart from the permanent trading centre, Jamalpur was the site of one of the most important Bengali fairs. The *mela* lasted from February until April and was the distributing centre for cattle coming from Bihar going to the Garo Hills in the north and Tangail in the south.[113] This important centre for internal trade

[110] Note by the District Magistrate, Mymensingh on incidents at Jamalpur in connection with the Boycott, 17 June 1907. Enclosure 2 in Enclosure in Govt. EB & A to Govt. India, 17 August 1907. Home Political A, December 1907, 58, NAI.

[111] The whole problem of communal rioting in eastern Bengal generally has been very well treated by Sumit Sarkar, 'Hindu–Muslim relations in Swadeshi Bengal, 1903–1908,' in *Indian Economic and Social History Review*, Vol. IX, Part II (June 1972), pp. 161–216.

[112] Commissioner, Dacca to Govt. EB & A, — July 1907. Enclosure in Govt. EB & A to Govt. India, 17 August 1907. Home Political A, December 1907, 58, NAI.

[113] The Jamalpur *mela* was started in 1883 by Sub-divisional officer Nunda

was the headquarters of the Gauripore, Nattore and Ramgopalpur Zemindars.[114] The only influential Muslim residents were a registrar of marriages, his brother, and a few of the more substantial shopkeepers.

From partition onwards there had been recurrent quarrels between Hindus and Muslims arising out of endeavours of the zemindari agents to try to force the latter to make a common cause with them in agitating against the government and to join a boycott of foreign goods. The zemindari employees and the pleaders of Jamalpur organized processions and public meetings advocating swadeshi manufactures, but because Jamalpur was a relatively large centre of trade they had not met with great success. Consequently there had been a series of petty disturbances as the Hindu agitators tried to force their movement onto the shop-keepers and purchasers. During the spring of 1907 local 'volunteers' were formed under the captaincy of Prakash Chandra Dutta. The volunteers took to wearing uniform puggrees and to moving about in well-drilled groups.[115]

All over eastern Bengal the Bengali New Year was heralded with religious bathing festivals, often associated with *melas*. In 1907 these festivals passed off without incident at the principal centres of pilgrim-age, although there were many minor disturbances at other places. The rioting at Jamalpur in 1907 differed from these disturbances only in the degree of organized aggressiveness which the Hindus displayed and the length to which the Muslims carried their retaliation. The climax of the *mela* was a bathing festival held on 20 April. The day before groups of volunteers arrived at the *mela*, armed with sticks ostensibly to protect the pilgrims at the bathing festival. The festival went off without mishap although the volunteers picketed the approach to the *mela*. The

Krishna Bose. It drew cattle merchants because they crossed the river Jamuna on their trek from Bihar at a ferry just south of Dewanganj. A fine grove of mangoes made a splendid centre for the *mela*, while grassy *chars* north of the town provided cheap fodder. The income from the *mela* at 10 annas per animal could well exceed Rs 9,000, and between 1909 and 1914 the *mela* made an annual profit of between Rs 7,000 and Rs 10,460. *Mymensingh District Gazetteer*, p. 148 and pp. 89–90.

114 The most important of these estates was that of Gauripore. The estate yielded about 4 lakhs of revenue a year, and most of the land was situated in the Jamalpur and Sadar sub-divisions of Mymensingh. The zemindary was divided between Babu Brajendra Kishore Roy Choudhuri and his mother in the proportion 75 per cent to 25 per cent, expressed more commonly in Indian terms as a 12 anna share and a 4 anna share. The estate was not partitioned, but mother and son collected their rents separately. Both were absentees, the son living in Calcutta and the mother in the famous health resort, Deogarh, in Santhal Parganas. Commissioner, Dacca to Govt. EB & A, 13 October 1907. Enclosure in Govt. EB & A to Govt. India, 6 January 1908. Home Political A, December 1907, 58, NAI.

115 *Ibid.*

traders suffered and complained to the Sub-divisional Officer, who proclaimed by beat of drum that anyone could buy and sell freely. The zemindari Superintendents and the President of the Volunteers were warned not to picket the stalls, and they promised to agree. On the afternoon of 21 April, however, a hundred Hindus marched to the *mela* in four organized bands, the first three being students and volunteers, and the fourth being zemindari agents, pleaders and respectable Hindu residents. The demonstrators offered to take pilgrims to swadeshi stalls and they ruined trade for that day. The students overstepped the picketing and some destruction of property occurred, whereupon the Muslims took up bamboos and other weapons and attacked the processions in the *mela*. The volunteers, being out-numbered, fled and were pursued by the irate Muslims, who attacked swadeshi shops and the cutcherries. The Hindus were pursued to a *Durgabari* where the Muslims stopped. Some forty or fifty entered the *natchghir* and broke the lamps, while seven or eight of them went further and broke the clay images of the Goddess.[116]

The disturbances drew to the town Muslims from the surrounding villages and it was only due to the efforts of the respectable Muslim residents and the arrival on 22 April of forty Gurkhas that prevented further disturbances.[117] Four days later the Gurkhas were withdrawn, but simultaneously the volunteers were strengthened by a contingent from Mymensingh.[118] These youths then caused another breach of the peace. Their captain, Prakash Chandra Dutta, together with four Calcutta youths and some of the volunteers wandered about the town disguised as Muslims. They were discovered and pursued, and while escaping turned and fired revolvers at their pursuers, wounding one of them in the thigh. The Hindu youths took refuge in the cutcherries. An angry Muslim crowd gathered and the Hindus hid in temples and began a flight from the town that spread alarm over the whole area. In particular it encouraged the lower-caste Muslims in the countryside[119] to

[116] The festival at Jamalpur was the Vasanti Puja, in honour of the Goddess Durga. For a Hindu reaction to the news of the desecration, N. C. Chaudhuri, *Autobiography of an Unknown Indian*, p. 240.
[117] Commissioner Dacca to Govt. EB & A, — July 1907. Enclosure in Govt. EB & A to Govt. India, 17 August 1907. Home Political A, December 1907, 58, NAI.
[118] The people of Mymensingh had tried to get a special train to run volunteers to Jamalpur, but their request had been refused. When the magistrate went to Jamalpur on 22 April he stopped some twenty youths travelling in his train, but sixteen arrived in the town by the evening train. *Ibid.*
[119] To the north of the town the Muslim peasants were low-caste cultivators, called *shandars*, who were prone to acts of violence and dacoity. The Muslim peasants to the south and west of the town were of relatively higher caste and more peaceable. *Ibid.*

indulge in looting and dacoity at Bakshiganj and Dewanganj. The Commissioner returned to Jamalpur on 28 April and stayed until 2 May, after which the area quietened down.[120]

The disturbances at Jamalpur were typical of disturbances throughout the eastern Bengal districts, except that the outbreaks did not have such serious repercussions in other places. The breaches of the peace were

directly provoked by an attempt forcibly to impose the 'boycott' upon Mahomedan shop-keepers and the ryots who are their customers, and as to the other disturbances which followed, it has been shown that long persistence in a course of irritating interference to buy and sell, and in other private matter, has been the climax of a long list of agrarian and social grievances which had already worked up the ignorant and somewhat turbulent peasantry into a very dangerous condition.[121]

After the rioting on 21 April, twenty-one people were arrested and fifteen convicted. The Superintendents of the 12 annas and 4 annas Gauripore estates, and two of the principal pleaders of the town were each fined Rs 1,000. Among others convicted were the *naib* of the Nattore cutchcrry, another pleader, two *mukhtears*, Prakash Chandra Dutta, and seven volunteers. 'The most sinister feature of the occurrence,' wrote the Commissioner, 'is that the dangerous and oppressive violation of the law was organized by, and carried out under, the orders of the principal Hindu residents of the town.'[122] Eight Muslims were imprisoned for the damage done to the lamps and idols in the *Durgabari*. Prakash Chandra Dutta, who was the principal cause of the second outbreak had been a *muharrir* at the Ramgopalpur cutcherry, and was the son of a *mukhtear* who worked for the same estate.[123] The attempt by the Hindu residents of Jamalpur to extend the boycott of foreign goods and stimulate the anti-partition agitation, was construed by Muslim shopkeepers and tenantry as another instance of zemindar tyranny. At a time of high prices the agents of the Gauripore zemindars forbade their tenants or shopkeepers on their land, under pain of threats, fines and destruction of their property, to buy in the cheapest market. To encourage the population of Jamalpur to support the anti-partition agitation the bhadralok organized themselves into groups of volunteers who interfered with free buying and selling and eventually led to rioting. Inevi-

[120] *Ibid.*
[121] *Ibid.*
[122] *Ibid.*
[123] Prakash Chandra Dutta's brother-in-law was one of the respectable pleaders fined Rs 1,000 for his part in the disturbances of 21 April. *Ibid.*

tably the young, the less respectable, and the most desperate, carried the technique too far.

In this case, instead of attracting people into the anti-partition movement, the agitation had accentuated the fissures in Bengali society. In Mymensingh the zemindari agents gave the government an opportunity to step in and find ample evidence to justify the partition. Their activities also encouraged Muslim communal politics and pushed Muslim leaders into support of the new provincial arrangements. In the previous year, Muslim *moulvis* had been prominent in encouraging the tenantry to resist illegal enhancement of rent, and extra levies which went towards the upkeep of Hindu temples and idols. Maulvi Samiruddin and Maulvi Mohamad Ismail, two of the principal Muslim preachers, had at first opposed the partition of Bengal. They then decided more was to be gained from supporting the government than by opposing it, and since the creation of the new province, Maulvi Samiruddin had managed to secure election to a local Board. The Commissioner saw the swadeshi agitation as being a last straw for the Muslims, who were beginning to resent oppression by Hindu zemindars. 'Gradually with the increase of education the clever young men passed through schools and madrassas and come back to preach a movement for social and religious reform. The movement made apparently little progress until the new province came to assure the more intelligent men that Government would now have more leisure to attend to their wants and grievances.'[124]

V. The anti-partition agitation: the swadeshi-boycott movement in Bakarganj

The agitation in the district of Bakarganj has particular importance in any study of the unrest in Bengal. All the threads which made up the cloth of the swadeshi and boycott movement were woven together most systematically and successfully in this district. The agitation was controlled by Aswini Kumar Dutt, whose personal standing and strength of character were acknowledged by Indians and the government alike. The agitation was conducted in such a way as to give the government no real opportunity to interfere, and when in 1908 Aswini Kumar Dutt was finally deported, there was misgiving on the part of the British.[125] Similarly, of all the Bengali leaders, Aswini Kumar Dutt tried the

[124] Commissioner, Dacca to Govt. EB & A, 6 June 1906. Home Police B, September 1906, 67, NAI.

hardest to enlist the support of the Muslims and lower Hindu castes. In a few homesteads and villages in Bakarganj, the swadeshi movement became a living ideal.

On 7 November 1905, Aswini Kumar Dutt issued an appeal to the people of Barisal to support the swadeshi movement. He argued that ultimately swadeshi cloth would sell cheaper than foreign cloth, since the clothes worn by Indians were largely manufactured from cotton and jute grown in India. If the raw materials were made up in India, it would provide work for indigenous labour. The appeal recognized that Indians would have to make sacrifices before native and foreign goods could be displayed on open markets at competitive prices, and urged them to adhere faithfully to the swadeshi cause. Force was recognized as having no value in persuading the people to buy swadeshi goods. 'Our duty is not to force, but to persuade people on our knees.'[126] Until the passing of the Regulation of Meetings Ordinance in 1907, Aswini Kumar Dutt held regular weekly meetings at Barisal to advance swadeshi ideas.[127] He also urged the people to boycott British goods and Government officials, advised the young to take up gymnastic training, demanded the expulsion of the British from India, and begged the Muslims to join the movement.[128]

Aswini Kumar Dutt backed up his campaign with social and ritual sanctions. The appeal of 1905, after disclaiming the use of force, continued:

There is, however, one thing we may do. If there are men who refuse to listen to the voice of reason and are determined to act against the wishes and sentiments of all their neighbours, there is nothing to prevent us from excommunicating them. To fulfil this and other objects and for the good of our motherland, there should be a people's association in each village. And

[125] At the height of the agitation in 1907 the district magistrate wrote that Aswini Kumar Dutt was 'a very respectable man and has a great reputation for beneficent and unselfish work on behalf of the people'. Diary of the district magistrate, 3 August 1907. Enclosure in Govt. EB & A to Govt. India, 13 August 1907. Home Political B, August 1907, 242, NAI. A sympathetic portrait of A. K. Dutt is to be found in B. C. Pal, *Character Sketches* (Calcutta, 1957), p. 45 f.

[126] Quoted in H. & U. Mukherjee, *India's Fight for Freedom, or the Swadeshi Movement, 1905–1906* (Calcutta, 1958), pp. 112–13.

[127] Between September 1905 and May 1907 A. K. Dutt addressed 33 meetings in Barisal and 10 in the mofussil, that have been recorded in Police Abstracts. Enclosure 2 in Memorandum on A. K. Dutt, 20 June 1907. Enclosure in Govt. EB & A to Govt. India, 3 July 1907. Home Political A, August 1907, 106, NAI.

[128] *Ibid.* Aswini's speeches also drew attention because unlike those of other Bengal agitators they were not 'characterized by the same violence and virulent hatred'. It was never possible to attempt to prosecute him for seditious speech. Memorandum on A. K. Dutt, Section A, *ibid.*

our humble request is that the names of the secretaries to these associations
should be communicated to Aswini Kumar Dutt.[129]

In no other district of either Bengal was the technique of social boycott
so rigorously enforced, and in no other district was the local network of
associations so highly developed.

The *Swadesh Bandhab Samiti* was founded in August 1906 to try to
coordinate the activities of the village branches and to enforce the social
boycott. The members of the society were drawn from the densely
settled Hindu villages in Barisal, Bakarganj, and the north-eastern
thanas of the district. They numbered in all about 2,000, and when the
Government outlawed the *samiti* in 1908 there were 159 branches
throughout the district.[130] The headquarters of the *samiti* were at
Barisal at the Broja Mohan Institution, a private school and college of
high standing in Bengal, which had been founded by Aswini Kumar
Dutt's father.[131] Although the staff of both college and school were
active in the agitation, some effort was made to restrict the role played
by students, since Aswini had no desire to have the institution dis-
affiliated from Calcutta University.[132] Conditions were rather different
at Jhalakati where the branch of the *samiti* was practically the organization of the local high school.[133] The schoolmasters of the district were
'anti-Government to a man' and disseminated their views through the
schools.[134] Yet despite the prominence of schoolboys and students in the
agitation in other parts of Bengal, out of all the volunteers in Bakarganj
only 17 per cent were students.[135] The volunteers of the *samiti* used to
patrol *hats* and picket the bazaars, distributing leaflets urging support
for the swadeshi movement. But because of the precarious Hindu-
Muslim relationship in Bakarganj, neither volunteers nor zemindars
ever resorted to violent intimidation.[136]

[129] Quoted in H. & U. Mukherjee, *India's Fight for Freedom*, p. 113.
[130] Memorandum on the National Volunteer Movement, 11 September 1907. Home
Political Deposit, October 1907, 19, NAI.
[131] Babu Broja Mohan Dutt founded the school in 1884 and the institution became
a first-grade college in 1898. *Bakarganj District Gazetteer*, p. 117.
[132] Thus losing the right to send candidates for the matriculation examination
which was the minimum qualification for government servants at the English-
speaking level.
[133] Commissioner, Dacca to Govt. EB & A, 14 December 1908. Home Political A,
May 1909, 135, NAI.
[134] Diary of the district magistrate for January 1908. Enclosure in Govt. EB & A
to Govt. India, 24 February 1908. Home Political A, April 1908, 24, NAI.
[135] Memorandum on the National Volunteer Movement, 11 September 1907.
Home Political Deposit, October 1907, 19, NAI.
[136] Since there were no large zemindars in Bakarganj they did not exercise the
same importance in the agitation as in Mymensingh, but Upendra Nath Sen of

The most formidable weapon used by the *samiti* was that of social boycott, and its branches in the villages of the northern *thanas* helped to enforce social sanctions. The most spectacular case was when they were employed against four firms of Shaha merchants.[137] The four firms, based in Dacca, were the largest merchants in Barisal and they conducted an extensive trade in the mofussil of the district. In 1906 the managers were induced to take a vow not to import any English cloth between September and November, the briskest time of year for trade. One of the merchants broke the vow and imported Rs 20,000 worth of English cottons, and the other firms were compelled to follow suit. At a meeting held by the agitators it was resolved to fine the merchants and to have them boycotted. The offenders found 'their *Dhobies* and priests were induced not to attend them, and intending customers prevented from going to their shops.'[138] The *samiti* organization tried to check the trade of the Shahas in the mofussil. One of Aswini's lieutenants went to Galachipa and persuaded two traders there to return Rs 3,000 worth of cloth to the Shahas.

The merchants were also prevented from landing their goods at a *Ghat* in Galachipa, or rather they were offered the use of the ghat by the owners at the prohibitive price of Rs 50 *per diem*. This *Ghat* is a private one, partly owned by Aswini Kumar Dutt, the wellknown swadeshi leader of these parts, and the owners are presumably within their rights in permitting only such goods as they choose to be landed there.[139]

When the merchants complained to the police they were informed that they could land their goods at the *thana* ghat, but they maintained that this was of little use unless the passage of their stuff into the interior could be protected.

In Barisal the boycott of the Shahas was kept active by speeches in which they were denounced as traitors. They were

unable to celebrate the Sarasvati Puja, as local priests and musicians were forbidden to go to them. They thereupon procured two priests from Dacca ... who were threatened with assault and insult if they performed the ceremonies for the ostracized merchants. Some students of the Broja Mohan College, which is owned by Babu Aswini Kumar Dutt, met the priests as they landed from the steamer, and tried to coerce them, but were prevented by

Basanda and the Dasses of Bansburnia, and zemindars at Baufal and Kalaskati did employ their *amla* to enforce boycott of British goods. Diary of the district magistrate for January 1908. Enclosure in Govt. EB & A to Govt. India, 24 February 1908. Home Political A, April 1908, 24, NAI.

[137] Petition from Sri Brindaban Chandra, Krishan Chandra Shaha and others, Barisal, 18 February 1907. Home Public B, June 1907, 81, NAI.

[138] Magistrate Bakarganj to Commissioner, Dacca, 2 May 1907, *ibid*.

[139] *Ibid*.

the Town Head Constable. Police protection in the shape of 25 constables was given to the merchants, to allow them to celebrate their festival, which in spite of the peaceful efforts of the opposing party to prevent its success, passed off quietly.[140]

A *jatra* party held in the police lines, to which these merchants were invited, was boycotted by the Hindu community. One of the merchants, Madhu Sudham Shaha, was in the habit of celebrating the *Mahotshab* in his house in Dacca. Usually about 5,000 people attended, but in 1907, Aswini Kumar Dutt sent one of his agents to Dacca where, assisted by two local zemindars, he prevented more than 100 people attending. The boycott on the merchants was extended to the people who served them, and the local hotel keepers were forbidden to supply them with food.

On 15 March 1907 three of the merchants complained to the District Superintendent of Police that Sirish Chandra Rai had been sent out by Aswini Kumar Dutt to Kalaskati and elsewhere to instruct middlemen who bought from the Shahas not to pay them. The merchants claimed that some Rs 40,000 were outstanding. It was difficult, however, to reckon how much of this was the result of the social boycott, for in the cloth trade a large balance was necessarily always outstanding. The District Superintendent of Police interviewed three of the merchants on 10 April and was told that

(1) They are at present selling Manchester cloth in Barisal without any interference.
(2) Owing to the action of swadeshi zamindars in preventing them from selling their goods at some of the *hats* in the mofussil, their trade has decreased by about 50 per cent.
(3) They desire that Government should prevent these zamindars from interfering with them and hindering them from realizing their dues.[141]

But the magistrate also discovered that the merchants had not told the truth when they said their trade had fallen as a result of the oppression. Indeed by a comparison of figures for the months of September to March for the year 1905–06 and 1906–07, the District Magistrate, Hughes-Buller, discovered that between them the four firms had increased their imports of English cotton from Calcutta by 516 maunds.[142] His conclusions were that although the merchants had been

[140] *Ibid.*
[141] *Ibid.*
[142] Hughes-Buller does not disclose his source, but wrote about 'reliable figures I have obtained, enabling me to compare their imports of piece goods from Calcutta with those of the corresponding period last year'. The firms imported 3,093 maunds in the 6 months of the first period and 3,609 in the second period. *Ibid.*

the victims of a venomous social boycott, and that the action taken against them had been such as to preclude their having recourse to the law, they had had proper protection from the district authorities. The agitation in Bakarganj was the most persistent in eastern Bengal. Yet it depended for its success on the skills of Aswini Kumar Dutt, on the idealism of his followers, and on their use of social boycott against those who refused to join the cause. Aswini Kumar Dutt's tactics worked well within a relatively small face-to-face society. But they could not be transported easily to other districts, nor were they of much use in a more general context. Although social boycott could discipline men who were in close ritual relationships with each other, it had not brought to heel the low-caste Barisal cloth merchants. The strength of Aswini's movement was that it was firmly rooted in a particular society in north-eastern Bakarganj district; its limitation was that it could not easily be used beyond that locality.

VI. Secret societies and terrorism

The economic distress of the Hindu gentry in east Bengal gave substance to the anti-partition agitation which it might otherwise have lacked. But the partition was not the fundamental cause of the distress, nor did the agitation against it bring relief. In their despair some Bengali youths turned to clandestine violence. Beginning in 1906 with an unsuccessful robbery, the catalogue of Bengali terrorist crimes grew longer with each year that passed, ranging from petty theft to attempted and successful murder.[143] This method of political activity was confined, in the main, to eastern Bengal, especially the district of Dacca, although there were occasional outbreaks in the districts around Calcutta.[144] The participants in revolutionary crime were almost all young, and almost all drawn from the high-castes. Over 70 per cent of those convicted of specific crimes between 1907 and 1917 were in the age-group 16 to 25, and 88.5 per cent of them were Brahmins, Kayasths and Baidyas.[145]

[143] The Rowlatt Commission considered an attempted dacoity at Rangpur in August 1906 to be the first manifestation of Bengal terrorism. See the chronological statements of revolutionary crimes, *Sedition Committee 1918 Report* (Calcutta, 1918), *in passim*.

[144] Up to 1914 there were 28 incidents in Dacca, 17 in Mymensingh, 10 in Faridpur 10 in Tippera. There were 13 in 24-Parganas and 5 in Calcutta. *Ibid.*

[145] *Ibid.*, p. 226. The total number of convictions given comes to 176 in the table classifying by age, but 186 in that by caste. 68 of the 186 convicted or who were killed in commission of a revolution crime, were students.

The divisions in Bengal society made it impossible to contemplate a real mass movement. The terrorists were a romantic elite who sought to overthrow the government by armed insurrection. But their very method of working was subversive of all order, and the strong religious bent given to the secret societies and terrorist ideology precluded any further effort to bridge the divisions. The development of terrorism could not but cause consternation amongst the families from which the terrorists themselves were drawn. However much the bhadralok may have dreamt of ending British rule it realized that the young terrorists were an unnecessary and wasteful asset in an already violent society.[146] Terrorism drew support from those most alienated from society, and terrorists struck at traditional order wherever it was found.

The development of secret societies made more difficult the task of controlling any political movement even in a restricted locality. By the end of 1907 the Government of Eastern Bengal reported that of the agitators drawn from the legal profession 'the most persistent . . . are out of work juniors,'[147] while a report from Dacca remarked:

The most disturbing feature here, as elsewhere, is to be found in the number of undisciplined boys and young men, students or ex-students, who now appear to be completely beyond the control of their parents and guardians or of the more responsible political leaders.[148]

The mushroom growth of second-rate schools, whose teachers were ill-qualified and whose students never had any real chance of achieving the improvement in status they sought or release from the economic pressures upon their families, provided the raw material for the secret societies and brotherhoods, while the swing to Hindu revivalism pointed a path they might tread and win eternal renown.

The secret societies were run with an iron discipline. The most important in eastern Bengal was the *Anusilan Samiti* at Dacca, for not only did it begin the dacoities and murders which were to become a familiar part of the Bengal scene, but after it had been officially outlawed at the end of 1908 it went further underground and organized branches in other districts.[149] The *samiti* was founded in 1906 by Pulin Behari Das, and at first it had the good wishes of Bipin Chandra Pal and Ananda Chandra Chakravarty, a prominent pleader in Dacca. It

---

[146] See N. Chaudhuri, *Autobiography of an Unknown Indian*, p. 44f. Even in 1920 when staying at Kishorganj in Mymensingh, his birthplace, Nirad Chaudhuri 'went out for my evening walks with a hatchet under my shawl, and never felt ashamed of this act of stupidity'. *Ibid.*, p. 46.

[147] FR EB & A, 25 October 1907. Home Political A, November 1907, 18, NAI.

[148] *Ibid.*

[149] *Sedition Committee Report*, p. 219.

began as a club for the promotion of physical culture, self-help and self-dependence, boycott of British goods and institutions, the promulgation of swadeshi principles, and the ultimate aim of political freedom. It had between 300 and 400 members, 'sons of Hindu gentlemen and mostly students and young men.'[150] The drill followed the pattern of other physical culture societies, although the instruction seems to have been on a wider scale.[151]

The organization of the *samiti* was highly centralized. The secretary, Pulin Behari Das, kept a register of names, ensured attendance at meetings, and provided the sticks for exercises.[152] He was a complete despot at the *samiti's* headquarters where 'nothing can be done without Pulin's orders; all correspondence must be first read; guards posted day and night; and severe punishments inflicted for the least breach of the rules.'[153] By the end of 1908 there were 119 cells in Dacca district[154] each with its own definite chain of command,[155] and rigorously subordinated to headquarters.[156] The whole ethos of the *samiti* was that all the members should submit themselves body and soul to one leader for the good of their country.

To achieve their end, aspirants to the *samiti* went through a preparatory period of training and were required to take several oaths before they became full members. Young boys were encouraged to take an interest in the society, and many of its potential recruits came from the National School at Dacca.[157] Those under twelve years old were allowed to take part in the gymnastic exercises, and they had the vows of the *samiti* read over to them, but they remained an outer band of members.

[150] Sub-inspector of Police to Superintendent of Police Dacca, 12 October 1907. Enclosure A in Enclosure 2 in Govt. EB & A to Govt. India, 28 November 1907. Home Political A, February 1908, 70, NAI.

[151] There were twelve instructors in the *samiti* who taught drill, the use of *lathis*, daggers, knives, bamboo spears, swords and *gulailbash* (a kind of cross-bow for projecting a clay bullet baked in the sun). *Ibid.*

[152] *Ibid.*

[153] Commissioner Dacca to Govt. EB & A, 14 December 1908. Enclosure in Govt. EB & A to Govt. India, 19 December 1908. Home Political A, May 1909, 135, NAI.

[154] 16 branches were in Dacca city; 18 in Dacca Sadar; 21 in Narayanganj, 41 in Munshiganj and 23 in Manikganj sub-division. *Ibid.*

[155] Each cell had an *adhyaksha*, or chief; *sampadak*, or secretary; *dalpati*, who was leader of a *dal* or band of ten members; each *dal* had a *sikshak* or instructor and all full members were styled *sabhya*. Report by M. H. L. Salkeld on the Anusilan Samiti in Dacca, Vol. 1, p. 1. Home Political Deposit, August 1909, 21, NAI.

[156] A system of inspection was employed to keep up standards. *Ibid.*, p. 9. The *samiti* was notorious, however (as indeed were other terrorist organizations in Bengal), for its internal factionalism.

[157] Note by J. C. Ker, undated. Notes, Home Political Deposit, August 1909, 21, NAI.

Initiation was achieved by taking two oaths, the *Adhya Pratigna* and the *Antya Pratigna*. Between them they involved adherence to twenty-one separate promises of which thirteen were held to be unobjectionable,

even excellent. These may be summed up as promises to advance the object of the samiti, to improve the character and physical condition, to live in amity with fellow members, to help fellow members in danger or in difficulty, to do one's best for each other, the country, and, lastly, mankind, not to hate but forgive and bring backsliders into the right path, and to obey every call of duty.[158]

The other promises concerned the object of the *samiti*, and how the member must follow it. He must be completely subservient to the chief. If a member married, or fell ill, or moved to another part of the district (which under ordinary circumstances would have been a reasonable excuse for leaving a club) he remained a member of the *samiti*. Each member was set to watch the others, and had to report any breaking of rules.[159]

The final vow, taken before a man became fully initiated, imposed secrecy on the members. They also vowed that they would work for nothing else until the object of the society was attained.[160] They undertook not to smoke or drink, to remain celibate for as long as possible, not to have sex with a woman other than their own wife, not to masturbate or indulge in homosexual practices. The prominence given to the clauses relating to vice had particular relevance to the *samiti's* headquarters, where on an average some thirty-six young people lived:[161]

There is obviously great danger in removing from home-life and bringing together in one building a large number of young men and boys. The head of the institution recognized the danger and its pernicious influence upon the material which was destined to achieve the great object which he had placed before him, and therefore did his best to combat the evil.[162]

The regime at headquarters was very severe, in theory eighteen and a half hours a day being made over to religious and physical exercises and study, and five and a half hours being set aside for sleep. The main

[158] Report by M. H. L. Salkeld on the Anusilan Samiti in Dacca, Vol. I, p. 35. Home Political Deposit, August 1909, 21, NAI.
[159] *Ibid.*, p. 36.
[160] This was a special vow taken by the innermost core of members. *Ibid.*, p. 44.
[161] Note by J. C. Ker. Notes, Home Political Deposit, August 1909, 21, NAI.
[162] Report by M. H. L. Salkeld on the Anusilan Samiti at Dacca, Vol. I, p. 46. Home Political Deposit, August 1909, 21, NAI. 'That the evil was not merely feared but actually existed within the Samiti can be proved from papers found within its walls.' *Ibid.*, and see actual examples pp. 47–8.

doctrine of the *samiti* was revolution on a religious basis, the English being demons who would be driven out of the country by the Gods with the help of an incarnation of Kali. The members took their oaths in the presence of an image of Kali, and all political assassinations were a sacrifice to the Goddess.[163]

Inevitably the religious basis for action excluded any possibility of Muslims joining the secret societies. In his book *Pavidarahak* (The Visitor), Pulin Behari Das explained why Muslims could not participate:

The answer is that a careful perusal of Indian history must convince the readers that the Musalmans have always been treacherous to the Hindus on every occasion the latter placed confidence in the former.[164]

Against a background of increasing Hindu-Muslim tension, and militant Hindu revivalism, the Muslims were regarded as treacherous enemies who could not be entrusted with the work of securing political freedom. The terrorists did not have much use for low-caste Hindus either. Their ideals were based on *sakta* ritual and worship of the goddess Kali. They looked back to a golden age in Bengal and saw that the decline had come with Buddhism and the popular cults of medieval Hinduism like Vaishnavism. In the secret societies was an opportunity to restore Bengal to a Brahminical age. Consequently help from lower castes could be given only on certain conditions:

Where influential members such as zemindars have any influence over low-class men, they should be requisitioned to organize such low-class men. But it must always be seen that such low-class men are not allowed to act independently. Such men must be made to bind themselves by oath within the precinct of a temple, by touching copper, *tulshi* leaf, and the water of the Ganges, and made to work under the guidance of our associations.[165]

The halo of martyrdom was one not easily shared.

The murder in April 1908 of Mrs and Miss Kennedy at Muzaffarpur uncovered an anarchist school in Calcutta run by Barindra Kumar Ghose, the brother of Aurobindo. The police surrounded and searched a house in Maniktolla and seized a quantity of arms, explosives and

---

[163] Note by J. C. Ker. Notes, Home Political Deposit, August 1909, 21, NAI. Salkeld reported that the discipline 'enforced within the Samiti was extremely severe and calculated to ruin the constitution of young boys.' Report by M. H. L. Salkeld on the Anusilan Samiti at Dacca, Vol. I, p. 46. As an example he cited a case where for misconduct a boy had to take boiled rice without salt for 15 days without talking to anyone, and had to keep watch from 2 am to 5 am for 8 days and for the whole night for 7 days.

[164] WR DCI, 26 September 1908. Home Political B, October 1908, 7, NAI.

[165] *Ibid.*

manuals on how to manufacture them.[166] Like the Dacca Anusilan Samiti, the club run by Barindra Kumar Ghose aimed to free the country from a foreign yoke with moral and religious inspiration, tempered by acts of violence. Twenty-one youths had taken oaths of allegiance to the society[167] and had been recruited from the meetings held in College and Beadon Squares. Barindra 'addressed his appeal mainly to uncritical and emotional youths already stirred up to unwonted depths and enlisted in a popular political cause.'[168] The youths went to live in the house in Maniktolla where in complete obedience to Barindra Ghose they learnt how to manufacture and use explosives, and studied political history and religious philosophy.[169] The government of Bengal reported that

The boys connected with the society have been turned into religious maniacs, and are, one and all, thoroughly imbued with the idea that obedience to the orders of the wire-pullers is a sacred, religious duty, and that they are all simply acting as all faithful worshippers of the 'Mother' are bound to do.[170]

Members did not know one another's real identity, and were bound to keep the secrets of the society by oaths administered in Bengali and Sanskrit.[171]

[166] Memorandum on the discoveries made in Calcutta concerning the Anarchist society of Barindra Kumar Ghose. Notes, Home Political A, May 1908, 112–50, NAI.
[167] 5 came from Hooghly District, 4 from Jessore, 3 from Khulna, 2 from Nadia, and one each from Faridpur, Rajshahi, French Chandernagore, Tippera, Dacca, and Malda. Note by DCI, 18 May 1908. Home Political Deposit, May 1908, 17, NAI.
[168] *Sedition Committee Report*, pp. 19–20.
[169] The daily routine was: rise at 4 am, wash at 4.30 am, meditate until 5.30 am. 5.30 am–6 am physical exercises; 6 am–9 am study, 9 am–11 am target practice and cooking; 11–11.30, bath; meditation from 11.30 to noon, after which they ate and rested until 3 pm, when 1½ hours of study in class followed with more exercises and meditation. 6 pm–7 pm was spent in private study, and 7–9 pm was spent cooking. Supper was held at 9 pm followed by conversation and singing, and finally, at 10 pm, sleep. Note by the DCI, 18 May 1908. Home Political Deposit, 17, NAI.
[170] Govt. Bengal to Govt. India, 13 May 1908. Notes, Home Political A, May 1908, 112–50, NAI. The relations of religion and political action of the terrorist type was well illustrated by a speech of Aurobindo Ghose where he justified murder by Khatriyas, although not Brahmins, to further the happiness of mankind even if by so doing 'your duty to your family seems to conflict with your duty to society, that of society to the nation and that of the nation to mankind.' Aurobindo's exposition of the *Gita* was construed by the Government as 'provided a man works himself up into a sufficiently fanatical frame of mind he may commit without blame any crime including murder, and further that according to the Hindu religion it is Brahmins alone who are prohibited from taking life.' WR DCI, 10 July 1909. Home Political B, August 1909, 122, NAI.
[171] Note by DCI, 18 May 1908. Notes, Home Political Deposit, May 1908, 17, NAI.

Although the bhadralok in Bengal turned to gymnastic clubs and contemplated a military solution for their political woes[172] the activities of the secret societies caused consternation. Involved in several breaches of the peace during 1907 members of the Anusilan Samiti were responsible for a stabbing incident at Dacca which shocked the local community.[173] No serious politician could condone overt acts of violence. Even firebrands, like Babu Trailokya Nath Bose of Dacca, considered that the physical force movement had gone too far after the attempt on the life of B. C. Allen, the district magistrate, and 'shows some signs of modifying his intensely anti-Government attitude.'[174] Risley rather contemptuously noted 'The Bengali student is a curious mixture of sexuality and hysteria and playing at conspiracy appeals to him enormously.'[175] But the young, alienated, bhadralok were not content just to play. The Muzaffarpur murders on 30 April 1908 were the first political murders in Bengal, the bomb-throwers actually having for their target the Chief Presidency Magistrate of Calcutta, Mr Kingsford.[176] Others followed in their train, and despite reviving prosperity and reunification of Bengal in 1912, anarchist conspiracies, revolvers and bombs, remained a feature of Bengal politics.

VII. Partition, Agitation and Congress

The various, particular, and chronic grievances of Bengal's high-caste Hindus were all taken up into the anti-partition agitation. In those villages and towns where life was hard and where insecurity threatened hard-won positions of eminence, the agitation was vigorous and persistent. But as a broad provincial campaign it was less successful. The unanimity of protest which had greeted the news of the partition did not last for very long. Within Bengal different groups and districts soon came to hold opposing views about where their best interests lay. The

---

[172] 'From the outset we judged all political action by the criterion of insurrection. We took it as an axiom that only military power, actual or potential, could drive out the English. This idea obtained a lodgment not only in the minds of us, the young, but, fantastic as it may sound, in those of our elders as well.' N. Chaudhuri, *Autobiography of an Unknown Indian*, pp. 250–1.

[173] District Magistrate to Commissioner, Dacca, 21 October 1907. Enclosure 2 in Govt. EB & A to Govt. India, 28 November 1908. Home Political A, February 1908, 70, NAI.

[174] WR DCI, 7 March 1908. Home Political B, April 1908, 44, NAI.

[175] Note by H. H. Risley, 21 January 1908. Notes, Home Political A, February 1908, 70–1, NAI.

[176] *Sedition Committee Report*, p. 32.

Marwari merchants, having joined the protest to bolster their case for a revision in the small print on the trading contracts they signed with firms in Lancashire, defected during 1906, once they had made their point.[177] The large landholders were the next to go. The conjunction of the British Indian Association and the Indian Association, which had made the first anti-partition meetings in Calcutta so auspicious, did not survive many moons. It was more important for most zemindars to continue in association with the government and to maintain their hold over local institutions than to be involved with a noisy anti-government campaign. By August 1907, the British Indian Association had engineered a statement, signed by the principle zemindars of both Bengals, firmly dissociating itself from the more violent phases of the agitation.[178]

The partition of Bengal opened up new opportunities for leaders in Calcutta, but it also created difficulties for them. At first, Surendranath Banerjea and his colleagues in the Indian Association and the Bengal Congress, welcomed the issue in order to demonstrate to the government the extent of their support in Bengal. The early meetings, although planned and held in Calcutta, claimed to voice the unanimous opinion of the whole Bengali nation. But as more and more people began to accept the partition, and as the government found little difficulty in coping with the problems of disorder resulting from the agitation, the Calcutta leaders were in danger of being left out on a limb. The Indian Association realized the need to keep up the campaign, and to set itself firmly at the head of the movement. After the Secretary of State for India had announced the partition to be a 'settled fact',[179] more vigorous direction was called for. In April 1906 the Bengal Provincial Conference was invited to Barisal. The local people, led by Aswini Kumar Dutt, were in favour of having the conference, but disturbances in the district[180] led the magistrate to issue orders forbidding processions in the streets during the conference, especially if they were accompanied by shouts of '*Bande Mataram* or other cries known as exciting and likely to give offence to those who did not share the views of the demonstrators.'[181] This decision was communicated to Aswini Kumar Dutt, the President, and Rajani Kanta

[177] Paras. 10–24, Director-General of Commercial Intelligence to Govt. India, 5 October 1906. Home Public Deposit, December 1906, 38, NAI.

[178] WR DCI, 17 August 1907. Home Political B, August 1907, 141, NAI.

[179] In the House of Commons on 26 February 1906. *Parliamentary Debates, Fourth Series*, Vol. CLII, col. 844.

[180] Minor breaches of the peace in November 1905 had resulted in the stationing of Gurkas in Barisal. R. C. Majumdar, *History of the Freedom Movement in India* (Calcutta, 1962), Vol. II, p. 94f.

[181] Commissioner, Dacca to Govt. EB & A, 18 April 1906. Enclosure in Govt. EB & A, to Govt. India, 25 April 1906. Home Public A, June 1906, 165, NAI.

Das, the Secretary of the Reception Committee of the Conference, and they had no option but to obey the orders. The steamers carrying the delegates from Bengal arrived on the evening of 13 April. Some 3,500 people waited on the bank to meet them, but as a result of the agreement with the police they did not shout *'Bande Mataram'* in reply to those on board the steamer. Surendranath Banerjea wrote that as

the Barisal people were our hosts, and we were their guests . . . we should, if possible do nothing that would compromise their position. Their compact with the authorities should be respected, but it was equally binding upon the delegates to vindicate the legal right, which they undoubtedly possessed, of uttering the cry in the public streets against the arbitrary order of the Government of East Bengal. The agreement of the Barisal leaders was limited to not uttering the cry on the occasion of welcoming the delegates, it did not go further. It was therefore settled, with their full concurrence on board the steamer, that the understanding with the Barisal leaders should be respected, but that on all other occasions during the Conference we should utter the cry as if no Government order to the contrary had been issued.[182]

On 14 April the District Superintendent of Police, F. E. Kemp, learned that the Calcutta delegates were planning to march in procession from the Raja Bahadur's Haveli to the Conference Hall.[183] The decision to do this had been taken by Surendranath and the Calcutta people. The procession started at 2 pm. Surendranath led the way, accompanied by the President of the Conference Mr A. Rasool, with Motilal Ghose and Bhupendranath Basu. Behind came a procession of the members of the Anti-Circular Society. The Police moved in to stop the procession, using their sticks and allegedly tearing off the *Bande Mataram* badges worn by the youths. 'Some of them were badly hurt, and one of them Chittaranjan Guha . . . was thrown into a tank full of water, in which, if he had not been rescued, he would probably have found a watery grave.'[184] On hearing of the disturbances Surendranath turned back and claimed full responsibility for the procession, whereupon he was arrested, brought before the magistrate and fined Rs 200. The procession of 14 April showed that the

local leaders were simply pushed aside and superseded by the Calcutta delegates with Babu Surendranath Banerji at their head, and also that the organized procession was composed (wholly or in great part) of foreigners to the district, and especially of members of the Anti-Circular Society . . . members of which were brought down to disobey, as a means of bringing on

[182] S. N. Banerjea, *A Nation in Making*, pp. 204–5.
[183] Report on the Barisal Conference, 17 April 1906. Enclosure in Govt. EB & A to Govt. India, 25 April 1906. Home Public A, June 1906, 165, NAI.
[184] S. N. Banerjea, *A Nation in Making*, p. 206.

a 'test case', any order that might have been passed regulating the proceedings.[185]

On 15 April the Conference again planned to hold a monster procession. Kemp consulted the local leaders and was told that a procession was not on the programme of the Conference. As this was no assurance that the procession would not take place, he drew proceedings under section 144 of the Criminal Procedure Code, putting an end to all meetings in the town. He took this to the pandal and gave the Conference the opportunity of being allowed to continue, so long as an undertaking was given that there would be no noisy processions. As no undertaking was forthcoming Kemp ordered the meeting to disperse, which it did quietly. 'Since then the streets have been quiet, the only noise being the shouts of *Bande-Mataram* by delegates and others on board the river steamers as they left the ghat.'[186]

The Barisal Conference had been 'a splendid advertisement for Surendra Nath Banerji,'[187] but his triumph placed him in a difficult position. With the accession to power of a Liberal government in England, and with the near-certainty of constitutional and administrative reform in India, it became less clear that the best course for a serious Bengali politician to pursue was one of unmitigated hostility towards the government. As the reforms came nearer, the Indian Association began to tack towards moderation. Only eleven months after the Barisal conference, Surendranath called on the Viceroy, together with J. Chaudhuri, Narendranath Sen, the Maharaja of Darbhanga and three Muslim leaders. They told Minto that they were anxious to

put an end to unrest and bad feeling, and that they propose to organize associations throughout the country with a view to inducing Mahommedans and Hindus to work together for the control of their respective communities ... It was simply marvellous, with the troubles and anxieties of a few months ago still fresh in one's memory, to see the 'King of Bengal' sitting on my sofa with his Mahommedan opponents, asking for my assistance to moderate the evil passions of the Bengali, and inveighing against the extravagances of Bepin Chandra Pal.[188]

And in July Surendranath decided that '*swadeshi* and boycott were to be treated as an industrial and economic and not as a political movement,

[185] Commissioner, Dacca to Govt. EB & A 18 April 1906, Enclosure in Govt. EB & A to Govt. India, 25 April 1906. Home Public A, June 1906, 165, NAI. The Anti-Circular society was formed by students to protest against the Government of Bengal's circular forbidding the participation of students in politics.

[186] Report on the Barisal Conference, 17 April 1906. *Ibid.*

[187] Note by A. T. Arundel, 24 April 1906. Notes, Home Public A, June 1906, 152–68, NAI.

[188] Minto to Morley, 19 March 1907. Quoted in Mary, Countess of Minto, *India Minto and Morley, 1905–1910* (London, 1934), pp. 108–9.

so that there might be no objection to students and teachers taking part in it.'[189]

The fact of partition cramped the style of the Bengali leaders. The failure to prevent the change to the boundaries of the province had driven the minorities most affected by the alteration to adopt new and more vigorous techniques of agitation, and, having set their face against any compromise short of re-unification, the Bengali Congressmen found themselves painted into a corner. They were interested in reforms from the government, but to collaborate with the government unless the partition was annulled was to lose support from their own special following. To stand aloof from the government meant that other interests would steal a march on them. For not all the peoples of the province minded about the partition, and those who showed themselves to be cooperative naturally benefited from reform.[190] Moreover, while the bhadralok were wholeheartedly against the partition, less recognized politicians could be more extreme in their propaganda. The partition provided new material for the existing factional quarrels in Calcutta; it threw up new spokesmen for Bengal. Thus Motilal Ghose, the editor of the *Amrita Bazar Patrika*, had no difficulty in sniping at every move his old enemy Surendranath Banerjea made in the direction of a rapprochement with the government, while Bipin Chandra Pal and Aurobindo Ghose, previously without much standing in Bengal affairs, became experts at organizing student demonstrations in Calcutta, and at stirring up the districts of eastern Bengal, every time they detected signs of moderation in the established leadership. In their hands, the boycott of trade was developed into a more extreme programme, amounting to nothing less than non-cooperation and passive resistance.[191] Bengali leaders had to keep pace with the extremists in order to retain some support, but in so doing they further alienated the government[192] and, just as important, they lost the sympathy of their colleagues in the all-India Congress.

[189] DR DCI, 16 July 1907. Home Political B, August 1907, 59, NAI.

[190] The Indian Association, for example, split in 1909 over the question whether to stand for the new legislative councils. A majority, including Surendranath, agreed not to do so until the province was re-united. When they did enter the election campaigns in 1913, many of them were defeated by the sitting candidates. J. H. Broomfield, 'The vote and the Transfer of Power: a study of the Bengal General Election, 1912–1913', *Journal of Asian Studies*, vol. XXI, no. 2 (1962), pp. 172–3.

[191] H. & U. Mukherjee, *Sri Aurobindo and the New Thought in Indian Politics* (Calcutta, 1964), *in passim*; H. & U. Mukherjee, *Bipin Chandra Pal and India's Struggle for Swaraj* (Calcutta, 1958), *in passim*.

[192] See the disparaging remarks made by C. J. Stevenson-Moore, 15 October 1909. Notes, Home Political B, November 1909, 103–4, NAI.

Bengalis had been among the founding-fathers of the Indian National Congress. From its earliest days they had been among its most enthusiastic supporters and they had helped to draw up all-India demands. The Calcutta leaders now expected the national Congress to further their provincial case. To begin with, the Congress had been very solicitous about Bengal. In 1903, when the first hint of partition had been leaked, the Congress had passed a resolution condemning the proposal, and this had been repeated in 1904.[193] At Benares in December 1905, the Congress had gone so far as to give its blessing to the boycott movement in Bengal, arguing that a special grievance might warrant the use of special political techniques.[194] But most Congressmen from other provinces regarded the partition as a provincial matter which should not be allowed to intrude too much onto the all-India stage. The Congress leadership, based in Bombay, was particularly anxious to avoid too close a connection with Bengal extremism because it hoped for substantial reforms from the Liberal government. Gopal Krishna Gokhale, who had been in England during the summer of 1905, who had presided over the Congress at Benares, and who had then returned to England in 1906 for talks with the new Secretary of State for India, was convinced that the Liberals were serious in their plans for reform.[195] It was vitally important, therefore, to keep the Congress united, and to keep its politics moderate.

Unfortunately, at Benares, it had been agreed to hold the 1906 session of the Congress in Calcutta. Not unexpectedly the movement fell foul of the quarrels between the Bengali leaders[196] and its whole proceedings were overshadowed by Bengal's political problems. In July 1906, Surendranath Banerjea, as the leading Congressman of Bengal, had explained to Dadabhai Naoroji, by now one of the elder statesmen of the Congress, 'Mr Morley's inaction and his unwillingness to modify partition have produced deplorable results in Bengal. The party of constitutional agitation is losing ground; while the anti-constitutional party which has been opposed to the Congress is gaining in strength and numbers. People are fast losing confidence in the British Government; and a strong feeling of discontent is abroad.'[197] The fact was that no Bengali could be other than an extremist in his own province while it lay cut in two parts. As Satyananda Bose wrote to Gokhale just before the Con-

---

[193] Resolution IX of the 1903 Congress; Resolution XIV of the 1904 Congress.
[194] Resolution XII of the Congress.
[195] Gokhale to Natesan, 10 May 1906 and 6 July 1906. Gokhale Papers, Reel 4, NAI; Gokhale to Krishnaswami Iyer, 27 July 1906. *Ibid.*, Reel 5.
[196] Gokhale to Krishnaswami Iyer, 29 September 1906. *Ibid.*
[197] Banerjea to Naoroji, 12 July 1906. Naoroji Papers, NAI.

gress was convened 'You are well aware that Bengal is very keen about the swadeshi boycott Partition and National Education. The feeling is not confined to the Extremists but is shared by the Moderates also.'[198]

In fact, these were the four main planks to the Bengali platform. First of all, Bengalis wanted the Congress to condemn the partition of Bengal; related to this was a resolution, first passed in 1905, that the boycott movement practised in Bengal was a legitimate political technique. The boycott was primarily aimed at foreign goods, and the swadeshi movement to encourage indigenous industries was linked to it in the Bengali campaigns. After the tightening up of government educational facilities the Bengalis had also started a scheme for an independent structure of schools and colleges, and in these great emphasis was placed on scientific and technical learning. Of course all these issues were subject to a wide range of interpretation within Bengal—did boycott include government schools, offices and titles for example? Some of the resolutions bore different meanings outside Bengal—to a Punjabi or a man from the United Provinces the development of indigenous industries had been vigorously championed by both local governments and local politicians since the mid-nineteenth century. Quarrels developed over the phrasing and meaning of the resolutions put before the Congress—particularly those about the partition, the swadeshi movement, and, above all, boycott.

Conflicting interpretations of policies polarized around moderate and extremist factions whose quarrels threatened to split the Congress. In the disputes the radicals made the running. For, whereas the Bombay leaders, and those in whose interests it lay to keep the programme of the Congress moderate, had to rely on men like Surendranath Banerjea, who for provincial reasons could not afford to cool their ardour, Bengali extremists were able to link up with parties restive of Bombay's control of the Congress and who did not mind how keen they became in the defence of Bengal. Bal Gangadhar Tilak from Poona, G. S. Khaparde from Amraoti, and Lajpat Rai from Lahore found plenty to attract them in the programme put forward by Motilal Ghose and Bipin Chandra Pal. The result was that the Bengali radicals, already numerous, received weighty support from other provinces, much to the discomfort of the Congress leadership.

The Subjects Committee of the Congress divided first on the partition resolution. In draft, this resolution asked for an enquiry by the government into partition. Motilal Ghose argued that the time had come to

[198] Bose to Gokhale, 16 December 1906. Gokhale Papers, Reel 2, NAI.

give up petitioning for government enquiries and he moved that this clause be struck out. Dadabhai Naoroji decided that the feeling of the house was against the amendment, but wisely refused to put it to a vote.[199] In the end, Surendranath Banerjea decided to accept the amendment, and speaking in the open session he said that 'all reference to the commission of inquiry will be deleted' from the final wording of the resolution.[200]

After partition was discussed, the Committee turned to the swadeshi resolution. This too provoked heated exchanges. A poll was demanded, but Naoroji refused to grant it, saying that there was a majority against the Pal-Tilak party. Khaparde insisted that they had a right to divide the house. A procedural wrangle then ensued 'and the President showed an attitude of hostility and would not consent to divide the house.'[201] Thereupon, Khaparde and some two hundred followers left in a body. Tilak stayed to watch over further proceedings in the Committee while Khaparde drafted his party's amendments, sent them to the press, and gave notice that they would be taken up again the following day.[202] However, compromise was again reached. Ananda Charlu, who had been a constant supporter of Congress since 1885, moved the swadeshi resolution in the Congress:[203] it was seconded by Madan Mohan Malaviya from the United Provinces. He stressed, however, that the swadeshi movement had nothing to do with the agitation in Bengal: 'As you have been told, the Swadeshi movement is an *old* movement in this country. It is not born either of Partition or after Partition and it is extremely desirable that this should always be looked upon as entirely independent of any political considerations.'[204] Tilak, speaking after Malaviya, insisted that the swadeshi movement involved more than simply encouraging Indian industries: it also involved self-help, determination and sacrifice on the part of those who consumed foreign goods.[205] In plain words it involved boycott, and this was precisely what the Congress leadership disliked.

[199] G. S. Khaparde, Diary, 31 December 1906. Khaparde Papers, NAI.
[200] *Report of the . . . Indian National Congress . . . 1906 [INC 1906]*, p. 72.
[201] Khaparde, Diary, 31 December 1906, Khaparde Papers, NAI.
[202] *Ibid.*
[203] The resolution finally read: 'This Congress accords its most cordial support to the *Swadeshi* movement and calls upon the people of the country to labour for its success by making earnest and sustained efforts to promote the growth of indigenous industries and to stimulate the production of indigenous articles by giving them preference over imported commodities even at some sacrifice.' Resolution VIII, *INC 1906*.
[204] *Ibid.*, p. 107.
[205] *Ibid.*, p. 111.

The real conflict came on the wording of the boycott resolution itself. At the 1905 Congress, under pressure from Bengal, the Congress leaders had accepted that boycott of foreign goods was a legitimate and constitutional technique for use in Bengal. The Bengali extremists, emboldened by outside support, now attempted to widen the concept by arguing that boycott applied to everything British, not just manufactured goods, and that it was a perfectly acceptable form of agitation in any province at any time. The Congress leaders were particularly anxious to disown such an interpretation since it would inevitably be associated in England with Irish tactics and would consequently damage the Indian cause. The resolution passed at Benares had been quite limited and specific,[206] but as it emerged from the Calcutta Subjects Committee, the resolution laid before the Congress was capable of much wider interpretation.

A. C. Mazumdar, in a speech which managed to ignore any discussion of boycott,[207] moved in the open session of Congress that 'Having regard to the fact that the people of this country have little or no voice in its administration, and that their representations to the Government do not receive due consideration, this Congress is of opinion that the Boycott Movement inaugurated in Bengal by way of protest against the partition of that province was and is legitimate.'[208]

The Congress leaders had agreed to accept this formulation of the resolution in the hope that, like the one on swadeshi, it met the demands of the extremists without making them explicit. But if they expected to get the resolution through without a split, their hopes were rudely shattered when Bipin Chandra Pal rose to second it. He began by making pleasantries about Mazumdar, to whom he was usually opposed.[209] Then he began his speech in earnest: 'As regards the resolution that has already been read out to you, you will have observed that the word "boycott" is attached to the word "movement". The word "boycott" is left alone, left severely alone, and the only qualification that the authors of this resolution have attached to the word "boycott" is, that it shall move, move from point to point (hear, hear), move from

---

[206] 'That this Congress records its earnest and emphatic protest against the repressive measures which have been adopted by the authorities in Bengal after the people there had been compelled to resort to the boycott of foreign goods as a last protest and perhaps the only constitutional and effective means left to them of drawing the attention of the British public to the action of the Government of India in persisting in their determination to partition Bengal in utter disregard of the universal prayers and protests of the people.' Resolution XIII, 1905 Congress.

[207] *INC 1906*, pp. 81–3.

[208] Resolution VII, *INC 1906*.

[209] *Ibid.*, p. 83.

city to city (hear, hear), move from division to division, move, I hope you will allow me to add, from province to province (cheers and hear, hear) and the omission of any other qualifying expression in regard to this term is significant. It is not, you will observe, a mere boycott of *goods*. It is a boycott of something else. Do not be afraid. We have done that something in that part of Bengal which I have the honour in my humble way to represent. We, in eastern Bengal and Assam, have not only tried to boycott, so far as it has lain in our power, British goods, but all honorary offices and associations with the Government.'[210] The message was clear: 'boycott has come to remain and it will remain until every grievance, that we have, is redressed.'[211]

The Congress leaders were furious, and disputed Bipin Chandra Pal's interpretation. L. A. Govind Raghava Iyer from Madras was the first to speak. He warned that boycott must be used with caution and 'that while the necessities of Bengal do require the use of this weapon, such a necessity has not arisen elsewhere.'[212] Madras was sympathetic to Bengal, but, he argued, Madras delegates would have nothing to do with boycott as a regular political tactic.[213] Asutosh Chaudhuri then had the unenviable task of reassuring the other provinces that nothing more was intended than that the Congress should support the boycott in Bengal, without at the same time antagonizing the large number of Bengali supporters of Bipin Chandra Pal.[214] Pandit Madan Mohan Malaviya, however, was standing for no strained interpretations. He argued that the Congress did express its approval of the adoption of boycott in Bengal, for there all other political techniques had failed to move the government on the burning issue of the partition. So, as a last resort, Bengal had 'declared a boycott of British goods . . . to invite the attention of the English people to the grievances under which they [sic] laboured.' Congress endorsed this action, but within severe limits. There was no question of using boycott as a regular technique, and there

---

[210] *Ibid.*, p. 83.

[211] *Ibid.*, p. 84.

[212] *Ibid.*, p. 86.

[213] *Ibid.* At this point there were cries of 'no, no,' 'not all' from the Madras delegates. Raghava Iyer went on: 'Those of you who were in the Subjects Committee last night must have recognized that even in Madras there is difference of opinion (voices: "There is"). But he will be a bold man who will contradict me when I say that the general body of opinion in Madras is decidedly in favour of the view that I put forward. Gentlemen, I simply say that what we mean by this resolution, is, as I understand it, that is exactly the same as was done at last year's Congress in Benares.'

[214] He said, 'We want you to say that Bengal was right and we want you to adopt this resolution simply with regard to Bengal. We all express the pious hope, every one of us, that if and when circumstances make it necessary, the other Provinces in their own time will adopt it.' *Ibid.*, p. 87.

was no question of deploying it outside of Bengal. Therefore, 'the Congress does not, I am certain—speaking certainly for a large number of delegates of different Provinces—I declare emphatically that the Congress does not associate itself with the remarks of Mr Bipin Chandra Pal.'[215]

At this there were cries of 'yes, yes' and 'no, no' and 'great disorder prevailed.'[216] Malaviya however held his ground and in a running exchange with his audience affirmed on behalf of a large number of delegates present—not only from the United Provinces—that his interpretation was correct. Gokhale concluded the debate with a simple statement that whatever interpretation individuals put on specific resolutions, official Congress policy was that the boycott applied only to British goods, and it involved only Bengal.[217] The resolution was put to the Congress by the President and passed.[218]

The Calcutta session of 1906 was a notable landmark in the history of the Indian National Congress. The resolutions were more radical than ever before. The Congress had urged more activity in India, and more self-help. National education and swadeshi were endorsed by the delegates. The Congress had re-affirmed the legitimacy of boycott as a political weapon in Bengal, and the widely reported speeches of Bipin Chandra Pal and Tilak showed that to some delegates it meant much more. The Congress had also given a new twist to some of its old demands. The claims that the superior civil service examinations should be held in India as well as in England; that Indians should sit on the councils of the Secretary of State, the Viceroy and the Governors of Madras and Bombay; that the legislative councils be reformed; and that local government bodies should have more power, were now linked together to form a general demand that the system of government in in India be similar to that in other self-governing colonies.[219] Dadabhai Naoroji picked up the theme in his closing address. Congressmen now had before them 'a clear goal, a clear star, as Sir Henry Campbell-Bannerman would have called it, of Self-Government or Swaraj.'[220]

Of course there would be many definitions of 'self-government' in the

[215] *Ibid.*, pp. 87–8.
[216] *Ibid.*, p. 88.
[217] *Ibid.*, p. 89. Gokhale went on to say 'Beyond this, if any of you want to go, go by all means but do not go in the name of the Congress. You go forward as individuals; you have every right to do that; we do not question that by any means, but do not drag the rest who do not want to go with you.' *Ibid.*
[218] *Ibid.*, p. 89.
[219] *Ibid.*, Resolution IX. Most of these demands had, in some form or other, found a place in Congress resolutions from the very earliest meetings.
[220] *Ibid.*, p. 139.

debates that followed, but there was no doubt that the Congress had emerged from Calcutta 'triumphant and rejuvenated.'[221] During the anti-partition agitation Bengalis had experimented with new political tactics and they had refurbished their political vocabulary. In December 1906 the concepts refined in the heat of the Bengal campaign became part and parcel of national thinking. But Bengal's articles of faith were to be honoured by the nation more in their breach than in their observance. The wording of the Calcutta resolutions became regarded by many as sacrosanct, but Bengal's shibboleths could not be allowed to fetter the national organization. The Congress had already become an open, accommodating party, housing many interests and reconciling many opinions. It fulfilled too important an all-India role to be pulled permanently off-course by a programme occasioned by the special needs and dilemmas of partitioned Bengal. During the next few months the events of Calcutta were put into a longer perspective. Although the radicalism of Bengal haunted the disputes between Congress workers in Nagpur and at Surat during 1907, the spectre gradually became less forbidding. At Allahabad in April 1908, the Congress leaders devised a new constitution for the national movement. They accepted most of the detailed proposals that were presented by delegates from Bengal, but they set their face against embodying in the Congress creed the articles passed at Calcutta in 1906.[222] The Congress, by setting out again in its old direction, had slipped its moorings in Bengal.

[221] *Mahratta*, 6 January 1907.

[222] G. Johnson, *Provincial Politics and Indian Nationalism: Bombay and the Indian National Congress 1880 to 1915* (Cambridge, 1973), Chapter IV.

Congress in Decline: Bengal, 1930 to 1939*

JOHN GALLAGHER

I

DURING the twenty years after the First World War, Indian politics were moulded by two main forces, each of which drew strength from the other. Important constitutional changes devolved a range of powers to Indians. But the British did not plan these reforms of 1919 and 1935 as stages by which they would quit India, bag and baggage, but rather as adjustments in the methods of keeping their Indian connection while retaining intact most of its fundamental advantages. At the centre of government in India, the powers of the Raj were increased; in the provinces more and more authority was entrusted to Indians. This system canalized much of Indian political action into the provinces. Moreover, by placing the new provincial administrations upon greatly widened electorates, it gave the Raj a further range of collaborators, selected now for their mastery of vote-gathering. The reforms of 1919 provoked another seminal development. By widening the functions of local government bodies in municipalities and the rural areas, which were to be chosen by the same voters who elected the new provincial councils, they linked the politics of the localities more closely to the politics of the province.

The second main development arose out of these changes, since constitutional initiatives by the British prompted political responses by the Indians, cooperators or non-cooperators alike. Whether they chose to work the reforms or preferred to press for further concessions, the politicians in nearly all provinces of India had to take account of the new electoral system. Those interested in forming ministries had to secure their bases in local constituencies; those attracted by the greater patronage and influence which local bodies now possessed, were anxious to sink their teeth into them. Those who were active in building movements capable of challenging their rivals and of putting pressure on the Raj, also needed local bastions from which to extend their influence.[1]

* Castigated and emended by Dr Anil Seal, to whom I am most grateful.

[1] Thus Gandhi's programme in 1920 for non-cooperation allowed his followers to continue cooperating on local bodies.

Government impulse had linked much more closely the local and the provincial arenas of politics; and the general trend among Indian politicians, constitutionalist or not, was to react to this initiative by copying it.

In so doing, they altered the working of Indian politics. Politics, electoral and agitational alike, were now built upon organizations with broader constituencies, whether these were defined by the reforms or laid down by Gandhi. Provincial issues were less easily settled by a caucus; parties were harder to control by bosses in city chambers. Central leadership had to be more responsive to local needs; and there were more people to voice them. That is not to say that Indian politics had been tidied up into parties with programmes, tailored to fit the needs of coherent social groups. The main elements were still the links between patrons and clients, the connections in localities and the shifting alliances between factions; these continued to cut across the spurious unities which now seemed to have emerged. Nevertheless, there had been an important change: more localities had to be bonded together, and they had to be related to the politics of larger arenas. The lessons of these electoral systems followed the logic of administrative change. This had already begun to link province and district so that neither could ignore the other. For administrative and electoral reasons alike, leaders in the province had now to cultivate connections in the locality, and local interests needed a say in larger arenas.

Bengal fitted awkwardly into this pattern, and it was to remain out of joint until the province was finally repartitioned. Since the days of the Nawab, the administration of Bengal had been strikingly decentralized, particularly in its eastern districts. The Permanent Settlement in 1793 had ratified this state of affairs. It was a system of transferring many of the functions of government to those men in rural society who were ready to assume the tasks of collecting the land revenue and shouldering much of the administration of their neighbourhoods. To some extent the British had leased out franchises of this sort in many other parts of India, but elsewhere they had avoided the error of giving away as much as they had in Bengal. By the later nineteenth century government was coming to intervene with more determination in the affairs of the localities. But this bureaucratic counter-attack was bound to be less successful in Bengal than in other provinces. Consequently, the districts of Bengal, and especially those in the east, went on enjoying a good deal of immunity from the interference which was becoming normal elsewhere. Even when they were equipped with elective institutions of local self-government, some of this immunity survived, and so, district politicians lacked the incentive to link locality with province. Conversely, politicians at the centre of Bengali affairs could afford to leave the districts pretty much on their own. It looked as though the new trends did not apply to Bengal as much as to other parts of India. The politicians' base was Calcutta; by comparison with the power of the metropolis, the mofussil seemed to matter little. Moreover, in the eastern hinterland, combinations between one district and another were almost out of the question. The lay of the land and the water was enough to make this so.

This helps to explain why Bengali politicians concentrated upon their city and ignored the districts. During the nineteen-twenties, when they could still feel insulated from hinterland opinion, they enjoyed the luxury of quarrelling among themselves over the spoils of the city. But even if they had wanted stronger links with the localities, there were other reasons why these would have been hard to forge. The reversal of partition in 1911 had been the one resounding success of political Bengal. But in that success lay desperate complications for the future. Undivided Bengal kept together regions and peoples whose interests were hard to reconcile. In the east, Muslims were a majority, in the west, Hindus. In both regions, the socially dominant, Hindu in the main, had lines into the political leadership of Calcutta. But in both regions their local dominance was being challenged by other interests which did not possess links of that sort. Congress in Bengal was thus based on the great city. It was also the spokesman of interests which were now on the defensive. Therefore vigorous agitation in the districts was the last thing it wanted, since this might spill over into a demand for social levelling. In other provinces, Congress might become a champion of underlying forces and a coordinator of agitation. It would find it much harder to be so in Bengal. As the defender of interests vulnerable to social change and a wider franchise, the Bengal Congress needed to make a quick bargain with the British. But this neither the British nor the Congress outside Bengal was ready to permit.

The difficulties which the Bengali politicians faced in the nineteen-twenties are more apparent to the historian than they were to Chittaranjan Das and his successors. Since Bengal had been less affected by the reforms of 1919 than most other provinces, its politicians still enjoyed many of the luxuries and freedoms of the past. But by 1929 further constitutional reform was on its way. It was to turn these freedoms into servitudes. Government had no intention of picking and choosing between regions; the new reforms would have to operate throughout the Indian empire in a uniform way. In their search for new collaborators the British chose to leap in the dark by extending the franchise to thirty-five million voters, of whom eight millions were to be in Bengal. A self-governing Bengal shaped by these voters might well lead to the ruin of the Bengal Congress. The Communal Award of 1932 turned these fears into near certainties. Consequently, the Bengal Congressmen needed the support of the all-India Congress as never before. For all their scorn of Gandhism and for the simplicities of Hindustan, they were now beggars and could not be choosers.

But there lay further dilemmas. The all-India purposes of the Congress centre did not match the interests of the Bengal Congress. Preoccupied with the struggle against the British, with the desire to hold Muslim support, with the need to satisfy other provinces where the party worked with securer social bases and better electoral prospects than it had in Bengal, the centre took decision after decision which further weakened the Congress in Bengal. Gandhi forced civil disobedience upon the province and reactivated its districts. The high command prevented the Bengal Congress from campaigning against the Communal Award and made matters even worse by forcing it to accept the Poona Pact. One by one, these external directives stripped away the prestige and sapped the strength of the Bengal Congress. It had need of outside support, either from the British or from the Congress centre; but as matters turned out, neither of these had need of the Bengal Congress. It is with such melancholy themes that this essay is concerned.

II

These new trends were in the end to prove deadly for the political leaders in Bengal and for the unity of the province itself. In retrospect it might seem that the nineteen-twenties were their decade of lost opportunities; but it is hard to see how they could have staved off the troubles to come. For the time being, the skills of Das seemed to have steered the Bengal Congress through the reforms. At the height of its influence, non-cooperation had apparently galvanized the politics of Bengal. Once Das and his supporters had expelled Surendranath Banerjea, they set out to exploit, and at the same time to control, the new wave of discontents which followed the war. The hartals in Calcutta, the agitations among the railway-workers and tea-coolies, the peasant demands in east Bengal, the campaigns against union boards in Midnapore, were a series of local discontents combined into what looked like a unified political aim. At the same time, the movement was strengthened by the growth of agitation among the Muslims; indeed, in

Bengal as elsewhere in India, the Khilafat issue acted as supercharger to the whole non-cooperation campaign.

But what Das wanted was to bring the British to terms in a tidy, a precise, an un-Gandhian way. The opportunists of the Presidency did not share the same aims as the zealots of the centre, for Das and his lieutenants worked a system of non-cooperation with limited liability.[2] He was striving not to achieve Ramraj in India, but to squeeze the British into making constitutional concessions in Bengal without unleashing a levelling movement inside his own province. When non-cooperation failed, Das and his faction judged that the best way of bringing the British to terms was by entering the Legislative Council. From their conservative point of view, these were sensible tactics. The reforms had enfranchised about 1,330,000 voters in Bengal, many of them Muslims and the richer Hindu peasants of east and west. When the logic of these changes came to work its way into electoral results, it would harm the interests of the Hindu leadership which viewed itself as the political nation of Bengal. Its best course lay in exploiting what was left of its electoral advantage while the going was good. The Bengal Congress was still a powerful body. While the policy of organizing the Congress into linguistic provinces had divided Madras and Bombay into three and five Provincial Congresses respectively, the Bengal Congress had retained all thirty-two of its districts.[3] Moreover, it still enjoyed great intellectual prestige. Bengalis delighted to remind the rest of India that their province had provided the most sophisticated spokesmen for the nationalist cause. This passion for advanced thinking was to become all the more ardent as their options for political practice grew narrower.

At first Das's tactics seemed correct for Bengal. In 1923 his Swarajists did so well in the elections that they could dominate the Legislative Council. Das also won the first election to the new Calcutta Corporation, with its greatly extended powers. Once he became mayor, he had gained for the party what was to become the poisoned crown of controlling the metropolis. But Das's success in swinging the party towards electoral politics, and his growing preoccupation with the affairs of Calcutta, drained the militant spirit out of the districts. When the issue was no longer how to challenge the state, but how to enter its councils, few of

[2] For Das's attitude towards the decision to boycott the councils, taken by the Calcutta Congress in September 1920 and ratified at Nagpur in December, see R. A. Gordon, 'Non-Cooperation and Council Entry, 1919–20', above.

[3] The Bengal Provincial Congress Committee [PCC] controlled District Congress Committees [DCCs] in each of the twenty-six districts of the Presidency. In addition, Calcutta was divided into four DCCs, and the two Bengali-speaking districts of Cachar and Sylhet in Assam had committees under the jurisdiction of the PCC.

T

the party workers in the districts thought this cause was worth a broken head. For those veterans in the wars of non-violence, it was a matter of once non-cooperative, twice shy. The price of bidding for collaboration was local torpor.

Except for electoral purposes, the leadership now neglected the districts in east and in west Bengal alike. During non-cooperation, local enthusiasm had set up some 170 National Schools throughout Bengal, as a way of evading British control over education. By 1924 there were only seventy of them, and they were scraping along with meagre support.[4] But it was the fate of Das's Village Reconstruction Fund which showed where his priorities lay. The Fund was to bring tidings of great joy to the peasants, announcing to Muslims and Hindus alike that the Swarajya Party was their friend. Nearly two and a half lakhs of rupees were collected. But one and a half lakhs of the Fund were spent in buying the *Indian Daily News* and turning it into the *Forward*, a Calcutta daily, committed to the policies of Das. As the Government of Bengal reported with mordant pleasure, no more than Rs. 2,000 of the Fund seem to have been used on work in the villages.[5]

Already by 1923 Congress organization in the districts was plainly running down.[6] More and more the political activists became obsessed with winning control over the provincial machine in Calcutta, and they reduced the local organizations into mere vote-gatherers for electing their own supporters to the PCC.[7] Das's very success in guiding the

[4] Bengal fortnightly report [FR Bengal] for the second half of April 1924 [henceforth the first and second halves of the month will be indicated by (1) and (2)]; Home Poll file 112 of 1924, National Archives of India, New Delhi [NAI].

[5] FR Bengal September (2) 1924, *ibid.*

[6] The decline of the Dacca DCC illustrates this. Dacca, the second city of the province, was the strongest outpost of the Hindu bhadralok enisled amid the Muslim masses of east Bengal. Das and several of his lieutenants had strong connections with the district. It had been active in non-cooperation, and it was one of Das's chief bases during his struggle to recapture the Bengal Congress in 1923. Das was president of the DCC. Like the president, its two secretaries lived in Calcutta, one of them being Kiren Shankar Roy, an aide of Das's. By October 1923 the organization in Dacca was moribund, its only signs of life being 'a nice building with a sign board over the door and a few so-called volunteers residing therein', and its only function being to help the supporters and hinder the opponents of its masters in Calcutta. *Amrita Bazar Patrika*, 1 July, 6 October, 17 October 1923.

[7] During this period and until 1934 the Bengal PCC was composed as follows:

elected by DCCs on proportion of population   268
co-opted by these elected members,
  one for each DCC   32
Muslims   14
Women   10
Total   324

Bengal Congress into a policy of potential collaboration made it hard to reconcile the interests of the party as a legislative group with its interests as spokesman for the districts. In order to dominate the Legislative Council, the party had to attract some Muslim support; but its local members in the east Bengal districts detested any concession to Muslim pressures, especially over tenancy legislation. In order to placate its supporters in the districts, the party in council had to oppose tenancy legislation; and this endangered its Muslim alliance. Thus there was always the risk that the legislative wing of the party in Calcutta would fly apart from its membership in the mofussil. As a way of preventing this, Das himself held the offices of president of the PCC and Swarajist leader in the Legislative Council, roles which even he found hard to combine. On 16 June 1925, the death of Das removed the most brilliant opportunist in Indian politics, virtuoso of agitation, broker between irreconcilables, gambler for glittering stakes. Das was the last chance of the old system.

The end of his political adventure left his successor, J. M. Sen Gupta, with an impossible inheritance. Sen Gupta had talent and charm; he had the support of Gandhi; he controlled the PCC.[8] But he simply could not bend Das's bow, and in 1927 he was dislodged by the group led by Subhas Bose, who had been another of Das's would-be Dauphins. From then, until the outbreak of civil disobedience, the Bengal Congress was distracted by the efforts of rival bands of Calcutta politicians to dish each other. From time to time, the disgruntled leaders of the mofussil would have their little hour upon a larger stage. But local politics were still dominated by Calcutta, and back-biting in the mofussil was seasoned by vendettas imported from the metropolis. In 1925 the Atma Sakti group had denounced Das; in 1926–27 Sen Gupta was harshly attacked by the Karmi Sangha. Both these groups claimed to speak for the party workers in the districts. In each case the complaints were the same: Calcutta was corrupting the leaders. They were neglecting the countryside. They were pandering to the Muslims. At face value, these protests came from the sons of the soil, unpolluted by urban trickery; in fact they were encouraged by those camarillas which were out of power in Calcutta. The Atma Sakti demands were orchestrated by Calcutta politicians hostile to Das; the Karmi Sangha found backers in the Big Five, Calcutta politicians and businessmen hostile to Sen Gupta.

The political importance which the districts had won during the

---

[8] There is an account of Sen Gupta which stresses the charm, if not the talent, in M. Collis, *Trials in Burma* (London, 1945, second edition), pp. 84–137.

agitation of 1919–22 had itself been encouraged by the city politicians for their own ends. Now that they were preoccupied with electoral politics and the patronage of Calcutta, they had little time to waste on the affairs of the districts. In their thinking, they had no need to do so. The Bengal Congress was Hindu nationalism. Therefore Hindus of east and west Bengal would vote for it. The purpose of district branches was to bring out the votes which would give it control of the Provincial Council. There the city politicians could settle the future of the province before a widening of the franchise brought millions of fractious Muslims within the pale of the constitution. Local politicians then, might sigh, but they had to obey.

Nearly all these plans, as we shall see, were to be ruined. But during the nineteen-twenties they were still credible. Local politics had become enervated, but this was true in most provinces, where the downfall of non-cooperation had led to a slump in membership and an enfeebling of the party machine. In Bengal, it still seemed rational to run politics from the metropolis. No other Indian city dominated its hinterland as completely as Calcutta dominated Bengal. More than one million and a quarter persons lived in Calcutta during the nineteen-twenties; outside it, only 4 per cent of the population of Bengal were urban-dwellers, and indeed twelve and a half million Bengalis lived in hamlets with fewer than 500 inhabitants apiece.[9] The metropolis was the centre of almost all the higher education in Bengal; and so its cultural style was stamped upon the professional classes in all the districts. Equally, the city's economic predominance was manifest. Nearly 80 per cent of Bengal's income tax in 1918–19 was paid by Calcutta.[10] The city was a stronghold of the bhadralok; in 1921, half the Bengali Hindus in the city were Brahmins, Kayasths or Baidyas. Calcutta was pre-eminently their city. Just as they dominated its social life, so too they dominated its politics, and they had no intention of making Calcutta politics a career open to the talents of rustics without the right connections. When B. N. Sasmal became secretary of the PCC in 1927, the combined efforts of the four Calcutta DCCs quickly pushed him out of office;[11] not only was he an

[9] *Report of the Indian Statutory Commission* (London, 1930), I, 61–62.

[10] *Statistical Returns of the Income Tax Department, Bengal* (Calcutta, 1919), p. ii. Peasants in even the remotest hinterland felt the powerful influence of Calcutta. Jute, Bengal's most important cash crop, was grown in twenty-four districts; prices of jute in up-country markets were settled by Calcutta, and often artificially depressed by gambling in jute futures at Calcutta's Bhitar Bazar. *Royal Commission on Agriculture in India*, Volume IV, *Evidence Taken in the Bengal Presidency* (Calcutta, 1927), qq. 21498, 21599–606, 21644–47, 21716–18.

[11] *Forward*, 12 February 1927. Another reason for their hostility was their desire to keep Sasmal from gaining any of the patronage of Calcutta Corporation.

up-country man from Midnapore, he was also a Mahisya. The true heirs of Das were more presentable men, such as Subhas Bose, J. M. Sen Gupta, K. S. Roy (all three educated at Oxford or Cambridge), Anil Baran Ray and P. C. Guha Roy.

But the most revealing of the party's links in Calcutta was with men of great possessions. Das's newspaper, *Forward*, was backed by the group who later became celebrated in Bengal as the Big Five, and as supporters of Subhas Bose. Tulsi Charan Goswami was a great zemindar with rich interests in jute; Sarat Chandra Bose, brother of Subhas, was a leader of the Calcutta Bar; Nirmal Chandra Chunder was a wealthy solicitor who had become one of the leaders of Kayasth society in the city; Bidhan Chandra Roy was one of its most successful physicians and a man with industrial connections; while Nalini Ranjan Sarkar was first and foremost a businessman who had made his pile in insurance.

The most notorious result of the party's preoccupation with Calcutta was its shady role in the affairs of the Corporation. Once the Calcutta Municipal Act had been passed by Surendranath Banerjea in 1923, most of the workings of the city government came under the control of eighty-five councillors, five aldermen and the mayor they elected. When Congress candidates won the first election in 1924, they took command of an institution with an annual revenue of two crores of rupees and with large patronage to spread among businessmen, contractors, shop-keepers, municipal employees and ratepayers. With the severity of youth, Subhas Bose could jeer at old Surendranath as 'Tammany Banerjea';[12] but his own group soon picked up the same way of making friends. As the first mayor of Calcutta under the new system, Das made it plain that the spoils belonged to the victors, an understanding which held good throughout the nineteen-twenties (and long after) when Congressmen usually controlled the Corporation.[13]

Municipal patronage was too agreeable a perquisite to be shared with country cousins. When the PCC as a whole put up candidates for the Corporation in 1927, all five Calcutta DCCs protested, saying that the right of nomination was theirs. But even they could not bear to share it among themselves: in 1930 three of them were denouncing the other two as the puppets of the Big Five who were grinding down the faces of

[12] Subhas Bose to Sarat Bose, 17 July 1925, in *Subhas Chandra Bose: Correspondence, 1924–1932* (Calcutta, 1967), p. 59.
[13] The tone of municipal corruption was clearly set as early as 1924. Calcutta gossip was soon alleging that the party had made Rs. 50,000 by placing a waterworks con-tract with an understanding firm; and the shopkeepers in the Municipal Market were soon being squeezed into contributing to party funds. FR Bengal July (1) 1924 and December (1) 1924, Home Poll file 25 of 1924, NAI.

the poor.[14] But whichever of the Calcutta factions came to power, it did not usher the rule of the saints into the government of the city. One era of corruption succeeded another, and the victory of one faction merely spurred the other into making a new bid for control of these fruits of office. So obsessed were the politicians of Calcutta with their intrigues over the Corporation that in March 1930 they seemed oblivious of the larger events which were unfolding in India. On the eve of Gandhi's campaign, Jawaharlal Nehru was writing:

When everyone is thinking and talking of civil disobedience, in Calcutta people quarrel over the Municipal election.[15]

Here was a poor outlook for civil disobedience in Bengal. It was all the worse because of the party's decay as a link between the leadership and opinion in the districts. The districts of Bengal contained 150 sub-divisions; by 1928 only sixty of these sub-divisions possessed any Congress committees. At most, the total membership of the party in the province was about 25,000, a figure compiled from DCC returns which the PCC, perhaps prudently, did not try to check.[16] Moreover, the organization had lost its precarious footing in the villages: '... as far as I know', the secretary of the PCC had to report, 'there are very few Village Congress Committees: mostly the members are in the towns'.[17]

But the province was slowly coming under the influence of forces that were to change politics beyond the calculations of the Bengal Congress. In west and east Bengal alike, rural tranquillity had long depended on a smooth relationship between landlords and rich peasants or *jotedars*. In west Bengal many of these rich peasants were Mahisyas, a low caste which had been actively organizing since the late nineteenth century into caste sabhas, whose leaders deeply distrusted Calcutta.[18] In east Bengal the most conspicuous of the rich peasants were Namasudras, Hindu tenants who had more and more moved into opposition against their Hindu landlords,[19] and who were to use the new political rules

[14] *Liberty*, 19 February, 26 February and 1 March 1930; *Amrita Bazar Patrika*, 25 February, 1 March and 5 March 1930. For the purposes of this campaign the Twenty-Four Parganas DCC claimed itself as one of the Calcutta DCCs, in addition to North, South, Central Calcutta and Burra Bazar DCCs.

[15] J. Nehru to Secretary, Bengal PCC, 7 March 1930, file G120/186 of 1930 of the records of the All-India Congress Committee [AICC], Nehru Memorial Museum and Library, New Delhi.

[16] J. Nehru, 'Notes of Inspection, Bengal PCC', 14 March 1929, file P 28(i)/151, AICC.

[17] Kiran Shankar Roy to Secretary, AICC, 14 February 1929, file P24/148 of 1929, AICC.

[18] Their political role during the nineteen-thirties will be discussed below.

[19] For the earlier history of Mahisyas and Namasudras see B. B. Chaudhuri, 'Agrarian Economy and Agrarian Relations in Bengal, 1859–1885' (Oxford University,

after 1920 to make common cause with their Muslim fellow tenants. These new forces, more portentous for the future of Bengal than the log-rolling of the PCC, arose from the social changes which were slowly transforming the province. By the beginning of the twentieth century many of the districts of west and central Bengal were in agricultural decay, growing markedly less jute and fine grain than the districts of the east.[20] There the vitality of agriculture helped to raise the aspirations of the more substantial peasants, who pressed for firmer tenurial rights. By the Bengal Tenancy Amendment Act of 1928 these 'occupancy raiyats' were given full rights of transferring land; while many of the under-raiyats who in some districts were already exercising many of the rights of occupancy raiyats,[21] now formally obtained all the rights of their superiors except the right to transfer land.

The 1928 Act is a striking illustration of the constraints under which the Bengal Congress was labouring by this time. In the eastern districts its supporters were the class of rent-receivers. To them tenant-right was landlord-wrong, and the party was therefore bound to oppose the legislation; but in doing so it furnished unanswerable proof to the have-nots that it was the party of the haves. The grievances of the upper tenants ensured that there was no dearth of discontent in east Bengal. In 1923 tenants were restive in Tippera, in 1924 in Mymensingh and Dacca, in 1926 in Tippera, Mymensingh, Pabna and Jessore.[22] But both the Muslims and the less well-to-do Hindus had other grievances as well. Educational spending in Bengal was notoriously concentrated on the higher levels—only Assam had a smaller proportion of its boys proceeding upwards from Class IV; only the Punjab spent a smaller proportion of its educational expenditure on primary education; of the scandalously small sums spent on primary education in Bengal, more than one-third came from fees.[23] The politics of education in Bengal had a very seamy side. If the cost of higher education was out of all propor-tion to that of primary education, this was because of the selfishness of upper-class opinion and the ineffectiveness of the new voters enfran-

D.Phil. thesis, 1968); R. K. Ray, 'Social Conflict and Political Unrest in Bengal, 1875–1908' (Cambridge University, Ph.D. thesis, 1973).

[20] *Report of the Land Revenue Commission, Bengal* (Alipore, 1940), III, evidence of the British Indian Association, 279–96.

[21] *Ibid.*, I, final report of the Commission, 29.

[22] FR Bengal September (2) 1923, Home Poll file 25 of 1923; FR Bengal January (2) 1924, Home Poll file 25 of 1924; FR Bengal January (2) 1926, March (2) 1926, Home Poll file 112 of 1926, NAI.

[23] *Indian Statutory Commission. Interim Report. (Review of growth of Education in British India by the Auxiliary Committee appointed by the Commission) September 1929* (London, 1929), pp. 46, 258, 260.

chised by the Reforms. Government raised the bulk of its revenue from
the agriculturists but spent only one-third upon them. Part of the
reason for this lay in 'a certain fear among the upper classes in this
country of the lower classes being educated'.[24]

There was nothing new about these grievances. But the progress of
the eastern districts during the twentieth century gradually turned old
complaints into political counters. The Montagu-Chelmsford reforms
gave the aggrieved the chance to defend themselves. Before 1919 there
had been five Muslims among the twenty-eight elected members of the
Legislative Council, and they had been chosen by 6,346 Muslim voters.[25]
The Act of 1919 gave the Muslims thirty-nine out of eighty-five territorial constituencies; thirty-three of these Muslim seats were for rural
areas, mainly in the Dacca, Chittagong and Rajshahi divisions of east
Bengal. Of the million and a quarter new voters in the province, more
than four hundred thousand were in the Muslim rural constituencies.[26]
With their 45 per cent of the territorial constituencies in the Legislative
Council, the Muslims had the means to defend the community's interests in the districts. But they failed to make the most of this opportunity. Clumsy, naive and self-seeking, the Muslim members of the
Council were easily split by Das and Sen Gupta. Faction was as rife
among them as it was among Congressmen, and the passing of the
Tenancy Act of 1928 owed more to the British than to the members
whose constituents it was intended to protect.

In the Council the aggrieved got little protection. But they got rather
more at lower levels where the union boards, local boards and district
boards formed an ascending hierarchy of local government. The Bengal
Village Self-Government Act of 1919 had confirmed union boards as
village authorities and allowed them an elected chairman. By 1926,
2,419 of these boards had been set up, and they were elected by
881,773 voters.[27] Above these boards were the local boards, concerned
with the affairs of a sub-division, and elected by the same franchise. In
1926 there were eighty-two of them, elected by 1,691,333 voters. At the

[24] *Royal Commission on Agriculture*, IV, evidence of Director of Public Instruction,
Bengal, qq. 23509–10, 23549, 23555.

[25] *East India (Constitutional Reforms . . .) vol. I, Report of the Committee . . . to enquire into
questions connected with the Franchise. . . . Cmd.* 141 (London, 1919), p. 38.

[26] *Ibid.*, p. 44. The Franchise Committee estimated that the total number of voters
would be 1,228,000, and that the Muslim rural voters would amount to 422,000. At
the first election held under the new constitution, 1,021,418 persons voted, of whom
449,382 voted in Muslim rural constituencies. *PP*, 1921, XXVI [*Cmd.* 1261], 10–13.

[27] The vote was given to persons paying Rs 1 as a cess or a chaukidari tax. The
figure is for those who actually voted in 1926, and not the larger number who were
entitled to vote.

top of the system were the district boards, most of whose members were elected by the local boards. By 1926, twenty-six district boards had been set up. The powers of district boards were quite extensive. They appointed almost all the petty officials of their districts, controlled road-building and water-supply and had some powers in the administration of vernacular education. District boards had the power to levy a cess in their districts, and together with their subordinate bodies they were responsible for substantial sums of money: in 1925–26 they spent Rs 10,237,988.[28] This position they intended to expand. Their powers over education in the districts were less than those in some other provinces, but by the later nineteen-twenties they were working to establish district education boards.

This was a situation full of hopeful possibilities for the enemies of privilege in the eastern districts, Hindu and Muslim alike. The number of voters for these bodies of rural self-government was much the same as the number who could vote in the rural constituencies for the Legislative Council. But there was a vital difference between the two systems of representation. Voting for the Council was done by separate electorates, but the members of the rural boards were chosen by joint electorates. By taking to organization in the eastern districts, and by winning the support of lower-caste Hindu voters there, the Muslims now had the opportunity of winning control of the local boards, and so of most of the district boards. Here at last was their chance to wrest the control of local patronage and perhaps of local education from the zemindars and their clients. Their progress towards these goals is traced in Tables 1 and 2.

[28] *Government of India: Memorandum on the Development and Working of Representative Institutions in the Sphere of Local Self-Government, February 1928*, pp. 31–64, 74–5, 83. This may seem a substantial sum, but it should be compared with expenditure in other provinces.

Expenditure of district boards and municipalities, 1920–21 and 1929–30, in lakhs of Rs

| | 1920–21 | | 1929–30 | |
	district boards	municipalities	district boards	municipalities
Bengal	113.32	62.37	140.51	92.45
Bombay	129.81	165.97	198.91	235.90
Madras	221.44	100.29	410.18	167.00
UP	152.13	125.24	199.71	175.47

Source: Gyan Chand, *Local Finance in India* (Allahabad, 1947), pp. 312, 314, 317, 319.
These comparisons help to explain why politicians in some other provinces took a livelier interest in the institutions of local self-government.

TABLE 1*

Muslim membership of Local Boards

	Total population	Muslim population	Percentage		1920–21	1921–22	1922–23
			Exceeds 50%	Less than 50%			
BENGAL	47,592,462	25,486,124	*53.55*		37.13	37.3	38.1
Burdwan Division	8,050,642	1,082,122		13.44	14.6		12.6
Burdwan	1,438,926	266,281		18.51	19.0		19.05
Birbhum	847,570	212,460		25.07	25.0		25.0
Bankura	1,019,941	46,601		4.57	18.18		13.3
Midnapore	2,666,660	180,672		6.78	7.69		5.9
Hooghly	1,080,142	173,633		16.08	18.0		15.38
Howrah	997,403	202,475		20.30	12.5		12.5
Presidency Division	9,461,395	4,476,741		47.32	33.3		36.5
24-Parganas	2,628,205	909,786		34.62	27.7		33.8
Calcutta	907,851	209,066		23.03			
Nadia	1,487,572	895,190	*60.18*		31.3		28.79
Murshidabad	1,262,514	676,257	*53.56*		39.6		49.2
Jessore	1,722,219	1,063,555	*61.75*		33.3		33.3
Khulna	1,453,034	722,887		49.75	35.8		37.9
Rajshahi Division	10,345,664	6,349,689	*61.38*		49.29		44.7
Rajshahi	1,489,675	1,140,256	*76.54*		65.0		66.6
Dinajpur	1,705,353	836,803		49.07	35.1		40.0
Jalpaiguri	936,269	231,683		24.75	Nil		11.1
Rangpur	2,507,854	1,706,177	*68.03*		*54.54*		*53.7*
Bogra	1,048,606	864,998	*82.49*				*59.25*
Pabna	1,389,494	1,053,571	*75.82*		50.0		47.2
Malda	985,665	507,685	*51.51*				
Darjeeling	282,748	8,516		3.01			5.26
Dacca Division	12,837,311	8,946,043	*69.69*		49.5		*50.0*
Dacca	3,125,967	2,043,246	*65.36*		29.7		*29.8*
Mymensingh	4,837,730	3,623,719	*74.91*		62.0		*61.0*
Faridpur	2,249,858	1,427,839	*63.46*		42.2		*45.4*
Bakarganj	2,623,756	1,851,239	*70.56*		54.7		*56.4*
Chittagong Division	6,000,524	4,356,207	*72.60*		*60.32*		*64.22*
Tippera	2,743,073	2,033,242	*74.12*		*52.77*		*65.96*
Noakhali	1,472,786	1,142,468	*77.57*		*70.37*		*68.75*
Chittagong	1,611,422	1,173,205	*72.81*				*56.66*

Source: calculated from *1921 Census, Bengal*, V, part II, 464–99 and *Government of Working of the District Boards in Bengal* [after 1930, *District and Local Boards*, on title-

* I am indebted to the SSRC Modern Indian History project and Mr. C. Emery

in all Bengal districts, 1920–35

1923–24	1924–25	1925–26	1926–27	1927–28	1928–29	1929–30	1930–31	1931–32	1932–33	1933–34	1934–35
36.2	38.3	40.9	40.45	46.0	43.3	43.7	45.4	45.6	46.51	47.14	47.0
11.8	12.16	12.5	13.6	14.53	14.65	14.32	15.1	15.4	17.3	16.85	17.2
19.05	19.05	19.4	19.75	20.98	20.98	19.75	20.98	22.22	22.22	22.22	23.45
25.0	25.0	25.0	25.0	30.0	29.16	29.16	33.3	33.3	33.3	33.33	33.3
13.3	13.3	6.6	6.6	6.6	6.6	3.3	3.3	3.3	10.0	10.0	10.0
5.1	5.1	5.98	8.5	8.5	8.5	8.5	8.5	8.5	12.3	11.1	11.1
13.8	13.8	13.8	13.8	15.2	15.2	15.2	16.6	16.6	16.6	17.0	17.1
12.5	16.6	16.66	16.66	16.66	16.66	17.9	17.9	17.9	17.9	17.9	18.4
38.83	38.46	42.3	41.1	44.82	43.9	44.2	44.8	45.4	47.7	48.02	48.02
33.8	32.4	32.3	30.8	29.41	29.4	27.9	27.9	27.9	35.2	35.3	35.3
28.79	30.15	46.9	43.9	40.99	40.9	45.45	45.4	45.45	45.45	46.9	46.9
49.2	49.2	49.2	50.79	50.79	50.79	50.57	50.7	50.79	50.0	50.0	50.0
43.83	42.46	43.8	43.83	64.38	60.27	58.9	61.6	61.64	65.75	65.7	65.7
37.93	37.93	39.6	36.2	36.2	36.2	36.2	36.1	39.65	39.65	39.6	39.6
44.7	44.6	48.6	47.47	50.2	53.3	54.0	55.2	54.9	51.7	53.8	52.8
68.7	68.7	68.7	68.7	70.8	75.0	75.0	75.0	75.0	62.5	66.6	64.5
37.8	51.1	51.1	51.1	60.0	62.2	62.2	62.2	57.7	57.7	57.7	57.7
11.1	13.3	22.2	22.1	22.22	11.1	11.1	38.8	33.3	22.2	22.2	22.2
53.7	53.7	51.85	51.85	51.85	53.7	57.4	57.4	59.2	59.26	66.66	64.8
59.25	59.25	59.25	59.25	59.25	59.2	59.2	74.0	74.07	74.07	74.0	74.0
47.2	47.2	58.3	50.0	55.5	66.6	66.6	66.6	66.6	66.6	66.6	63.8
							44.4	50.0	50.0	50.0	50.0
5.26	5.3	5.2	5.3	5.3	7.8	7.8	7.8	7.8	5.2	5.2	5.2
51.5	51.2	50.5	53.2	58.4	58.1	58.4	59.5	63.5	63.9	66.5	66.5
31.5	29.8	28.07	24.5	44.8	44.8	44.8	44.8	44.8	50.0	58.6	60.3
65.5	65.5	64.5	67.7	65.5	65.5	66.6	66.6	73.4	71.3	73.4	72.3
43.4	43.4	43.4	52.2	52.2	52.2	52.2	57.9	60.8	60.8	62.3	62.3
56.4	56.4	56.4	57.7	65.4	64.2	64.1	62.9	67.9	67.9	67.9	67.9
63.3	70.0	70.64	71.55	68.8	68.8	74.3	74.3	73.39	75.22	74.52	73.59
63.8	63.83	68.09	70.21	64.0	65.96	70.21	70.2	68.08	70.21	69.56	67.36
68.8		68.75	68.75	70.0	70.0	81.25	81.25	81.25	81.25	83.33	83.33
56.6	76.66	76.66	76.66	76.6	73.33	73.33	73.3	73.33	76.66	73.33	73.33

Bengal. Local Self-Government Department. [Annual] *Resolution reviewing the Reports on the* page] *during the year 1920–1 to 1934–35* (Calcutta, 1922–37), Appendix G. for help with this and subsequent tables.

TABLE 2

Muslim Membership of District Boards

	Total population	Muslim population	Percentage Exceeds 50%	Percentage Less than 50%	1920–21	1921–22	1922–23
BENGAL	47,592,462	25,486,124	53.55			31.78	34.4	32.1
Burdwan							
Division	8,050,642	1,082,122		13.44	13.56	11.11
Burdwan	1,438,926	266,281		18.51	11.11	11.11
Birbhum	847,570	212,460		25.07	18.75	18.7
Bankura	1,019,941	46,601		4.57	18.75	8.3
Midnapore	2,666,660	180,672		6.78	12.5	8.3
Hooghly	1,080,142	173,633		16.08	15.3	15.3
Howrah	997,403	202,475		20.30	5.55	5.55
Presidency						
Division	9,461,395	4,476,741		47.32	22.01	25.19
24-Parganas	2,628,205	909,786		34.62	20.8	23.3
Calcutta	907,851	209,066		23.03		
Nadia	1,487,572	895,190	60.18		20.8	20.0
Marshidabad	1,262,514	676,257	53.56		33.3	44.4
Jessore	1,722,219	1,063,555	61.75		16.6	16.6
Khulna	1,453,034	722,887		49.75	18.7	18.7
Rajshahi						
Division	10,345,664	6,349,689	61.38		41.73	35.6
Rajshahi	1,489,675	1,140,256	76.54		63.6	54.5
Dinajpur	1,705,353	836,803		49.07	31.8	33.3
Jalpaiguri	936,269	231,683		24.75	11.7	14.3
Rangpur	2,507,854	1,706,177	68.03		45.09	44.44
Bogra	1,048,606	864,998	82.49		43.7	50.0
Pabna	1,389,494	1,053,571	75.82		46.65	41.6
Malda	985,665	507,685	51.51		46.6	33.3
Darjeeling	282,748	8,516		3.01		10.0
Dacca						
Division	12,837,311	8,946,043	69.69		43.0	40.0
Dacca	3,125,967	2,043,246	65.36		32.1	27.2
Mymensingh	4,837,730	3,623,719	74.91		50.0	45.8
Faridpur	2,249,858	1,427,839	63.46		45.8	41.6
Bakarganj	2,623,756	1,851,239	70.56		45.8	50.0
Chittagong						
Division	6,000,524	4,356,207	72.60		46.42	57.14
Tippera	2,743,073	2,033,242	74.12		44.44	53.33
Noakhali	1,472,786	1,142,468	77.57		57.9	70.83
Chittagong	1,611,422	1,173,205	72.81		36.84	50.0

Source: as in Table 1.

in all Bengal Districts, 1920–35

1923–24	1924–25	1925–26	1926–27	1927–28	1928–29	1929–30	1930–31	1931–32	1932–33	1933–34	1934–35
33.8	35.5	35.5	36.89	38.0	40.8	42.4	42.3	42.4	41.73	41.87	41.8
10.07	10.2	10.8	11.1	13.07	13.07	13.07	14.9	14.9	14.28	14.28	14.84
11.11	11.11	11.11	16.66	16.66	16.66	16.66	16.66	16.66	16.66	16.66	20.9
18.7	16.66	16.6	16.66	20.8	20.8	20.8	25.0	25.0	25.0	20.9	20.9
8.3	8.3	4.2	4.2	4.2	4.2	4.16	4.16	4.16	4.16	4.16	4.0
6.06	6.06	6.06	6.06	6.06	6.06	6.06	8.82	8.82	8.82	11.76	11.76
13.3	13.3	13.3	13.3	16.6	16.6	16.6	16.6	16.6	13.3	13.3	13.3
5.55	5.55	16.66	16.66	16.66	16.66	16.66	22.22	22.22	22.22	22.22	22.22
27.4	28.57	27.6	29.07	28.3	38.29	41.8	41.1	40.81	37.41	37.41	37.4
23.3	23.3	23.3	23.3	23.3	23.3	30.0	26.6	26.66	30.0	26.6	26.6
23.33	20.69	20.0	23.3	23.3	23.3	33.33	33.33	33.33	33.33	33.3	33.3
44.44	44.44	44.4	40.74	40.74	40.74	40.74	44.44	44.44	33.33	33.3	33.3
20.83	30.0	26.66	33.33	30.0	70.0	70.0	66.6	66.66	56.6	60.0	60.0
25.0	25.0	25.0	25.0	25.0	33.3	33.33	33.3	33.33	33.3	33.3	33.3
37.4	40.22	43.2	45.81	46.36	45.8	46.3	46.3	44.5	43.2	42.7	43.2
66.6	66.6	66.6	70.3	66.6	51.8	48.1	48.1	48.1	44.4	44.4	44.4
37.03	44.4	51.9	51.9	51.85	55.5	55.5	55.5	48.1	48.1	48.1	48.1
14.3	14.3	14.3	19.05	19.05	19.0	14.2	14.2	14.29	12.5	12.5	12.5
40.74	48.15	48.15	48.15	48.15	51.8	51.8	51.8	44.44	44.44	48.15	55.5
44.44	44.44	44.44	66.66	66.66	66.6	61.11	61.1	61.11	61.11	61.11	61.11
41.6	41.6	54.2	54.2	54.2	54.2	75.0	75.0	75.0	75.0	62.5	62.5
33.3	40.0	40.0	33.3	46.6	46.6	46.6	46.6	50.0	50.0	50.0	50.0
10.0	10.0	10.0	10.0	10.0	15.0	10.0	10.0	10.0	10.0	15.0	10.0
46.8	48.4	45.6	47.6	53.1	57.1	57.1	56.3	55.5	58.4	59.5	58.7
27.2	27.2	24.2	24.2	18.2	33.3	33.3	33.3	33.3	34.3	45.4	45.4
63.6	66.6	66.6	66.6	75.7	75.7	75.7	72.7	66.6	66.6	66.6	63.63
46.6	46.6	41.3	53.3	56.6	56.6	63.3	66.6	66.6	66.6	60.0	60.0
50.0	53.3	50.0	46.6	63.3	63.3	56.6	53.3	56.6	66.6	66.6	66.6
55.95	61.90	60.71	60.71	58.3	60.7	66.6	65.43	71.42	71.42	72.28	71.08
53.33	56.66	56.66	56.66	53.3	53.33	56.66	53.57	66.66	63.33	63.3	63.33
66.66	62.5	58.33	58.33	54.16	58.33	75.0	75.0	75.0	75.0	78.25	78.25
50.0	66.66	66.66	66.66	66.66	70.0	70.0	68.96	73.33	76.66	76.66	73.33

TABLE 3

Elections to Local Boards in all

	Total population	Muslim population	Percentage Exceeds 50%	Less than 50%	1920–21	1921–22	1922–23
DACCA Sadar	3,125,967	2,043,246	*65.36*		29.7		29.8
Subdivision Narayanganj	1,079,723	662,201	*61.33*		25.0		22.2
Subdivision Munshiganj	869,961	675,977	*77.70*		40.0		41.6
Subdivision Manikganj	683,876	374,390	*54.75*		37.5		33.3
Subdivision	492,407	330,678	*67.16*		11.1		22.2

Source: as in Table 1.

The course of elections to the local bodies, with their active electorate of more than one and a half millions, reveals the history of the voters' choice. In twelve of the fifteen districts of Rajshahi, Dacca and Chittagong divisions, the Muslims were a majority of the population. In 1920–21 they controlled more than half the local boards in six of these districts. By 1934–35, they controlled that many in twelve of these districts. Apart from Jessore district in the Presidency division, the electoral swing was greatest in Dacca district, where the Muslim share of local boards increased from 29.7 per cent to 60.3 per cent. This result is all the more striking because of the concentration of bhadralok in Dacca and the importance of their connections with education and politics in Calcutta. Nevertheless the trend is quite clear throughout the district, as Table 3 shows. The course of the district board elections shown in Table 2 says less about the popular choice, since not all members of district boards were elected. The Hindus' local influence and the importance of their interests worked in their favour. It is noticeable that throughout the period they kept control of the Dacca district board. Nevertheless, the Muslim upsurge was remarkable. In 1920–21 Muslims controlled two of the district boards in the Rajshahi, Dacca and Chittagong divisions; by 1934–35 they controlled nine.

In the short run, these changes had little immediate effect. Just as the incompetence and faction of Muslim members let their case go by default in the Legislative Council, so too the Muslim members of rural boards were often at sixes and sevens. After the local elections in Mymensingh in 1927, the District Magistrate reported:

Subdivisions of Dacca District, 1920–35

1923–24	1924–25	1925–26	1926–27	1927–28	1928–29	1929–30	1930–31	1931–32	1932–33	1933–34	1934–35
31.5	29.8	2807	24.5	44.8	44.8	44.8	44.8	44.8	50.0	58.6	60.3
22.2	22.2	22.2	16.6	44.4	44.4	44.4	44.4	44.4	61.1	61.1	61.1
50.0	50.0	50.0	41.6	50.0	50.0	50.0	50.0	50.0	50.0	66.6	66.6
33.3	27.7	22.2	22.2	44.4	44.4	44.4	44.4	44.4	44.4	44.4	50.0
22.2	22.2	22.2	22.2	40.0	40.0	40.0	40.0	40.0	40.0	70.0	70.0

Not a Hindu has been elected. Yet . . . never was intrigue and faction more alive in the District and Local Boards than at present.[29]

But experience together with communal rancour soon put this right, and by the nineteen-thirties the Hindu politicians of east Bengal faced the cheerless prospect of losing control of the districts they had dominated for so long.

The longer-term implications of these changes were more important. Since elections to local boards were by joint electorates, their results allowed both Hindus and Muslims to measure the likely consequences of abandoning the separate electorates which had been in force in conciliar elections since 1909. It was now clear that in east Bengal the Muslims had nothing to fear from joint electorates; in west Bengal on the other hand, where they were generally in small minorities, separate electorates would be their only hope of winning any representation at all. For the Hindus, it was the other way round. In west Bengal they would gain from joint electorates, but in the east they would lose badly and might find their social dominance in ruins. Consequently, any demand for joint electorates would accurately divide the interests of Hindus and Muslims in the eastern and western districts alike.

III

Thus did the Bengal Congress, obsessed with Calcutta, neglectful of the

[29] FR Bengal March (2) 1927, Home Poll file 32 of 1927, NAI.

localities, weakening in the eastern districts, devoid of mass support, enter the nineteen-thirties. At the start of that decade the civil disobedience movement was to drag into the open the internal constraints which were to cripple the Congress in Bengal. Later the initiatives of the British Government, and the responses of the Congress centre to those initiatives, were to reveal the external constraints upon the politics of the province.

Civil disobedience was forced upon Gandhi (who had his own constraints) by a rising militancy in some of the provinces and by his failure to bring Irwin to terms in 1929. The strategy to which he had to turn in 1930 was meant to exert an increasing pressure on the British by unifying a series of regional resistances against them. To the Bengal politicians (and some others) this was a distasteful prospect, only too likely to upset their provincial applecarts. When Gandhi opened the campaign on 12 March 1930 they had to fall in line; but with one of their finer touches they did so by forming two rival civil disobedience councils. In the event, none of the Calcutta factions had much influence on the course of the movement. The Bengal PCC, controlled by Subhas Bose, claimed to have organized eleven centres of civil disobedience; but ten of them were in the district of Twenty-Four Parganas, only next door to Calcutta.[30]

In the districts it soon turned out that civil disobedience could succeed only where there were local grievances which the agitators could exploit. Its disasters in east Bengal showed how impotent the movement was when local grievances were of the wrong sort. There the Gandhians had been working among the people for a decade. Now the time had come to collect the political dividend. Members of the Nawabganj ashram tried to ignite Dacca district; the Khalispur ashram preached civil disobedience in Khulna; khadi workers in Faridpur and members of the national school in Dinajpur called for resistance, while satyagrahis from the Vidyasram in Sylhet agitated in that district and in Noakhali.[31] But instead of attracting mass support, the campaign provoked wide opposition. In Dacca, Faridpur, Bakarganj and Mymensingh, the Muslims asserted themselves against civil disobedience; while the vast majority of the Namasudras either remained aloof from the movement or, as they did in Faridpur and Bakarganj, actively worked in

[30] Six DCCs controlled by Bose's faction also set up such centres. But those in Khulna, Noakhali, Tippera, Bakarganj and Howrah were ineffective, and the success of the sixth (Mahisbathar, in Twenty-Four Parganas) owed more to the Gandhians. The claims of the Bengal PCC are set out in *Liberty*, 17 April 1930.

[31] Bengal Council of Civil Disobedience to AICC, 6 November 1930, file G 86/186 F, 177 N of 1930, AICC.

Government's favour.[32] The contrast with the non-cooperation movement is striking: from the end of 1921 until March 1922, many eastern districts, conspicuously Tippera, Rangpur and Noakhali, had refused to pay taxes.[33] But those days had gone, and now the Government of Bengal could report with relief that:

The movement is generally confined to volunteers of the bhadralok class, and generally speaking, few of the villagers have so far taken part in it.[34]

Some of the western districts showed what could be done by exploiting local grievances. The Mahisbathar sub-division of Twenty-Four Parganas was successfully aroused—but less by the Congress volunteers than by the lucky chance that a local zemindar was at odds with Government; the Arambagh sub-division of Hooghly also responded well—but once again because of local circumstances. Arambagh had large numbers of discontented Mahisya *jotedars*; in any case it was contiguous to Midnapore. There the movement was so effective that when he contemplated civil disobedience over the whole of India, the Secretary of the Home Department in Simla concluded:

. . . I would put Midnapore as the district where the prestige of Government has fallen more than in any other.[35]

Gandhi's negotiations with Irwin ended the first phase of civil disobedience in March 1931. The campaign had much increased the prestige of the Congress centre. Gandhi had decided when the movement was to begin. Twelve months later it was Gandhi who brought it to an end. Admittedly, while the campaign was being fought, with the Working Committee in gaol and the provincial movements harried by the police, there was no chance of day-to-day control from the centre. Nevertheless the trend was there. Not even the Bengal PCC could stand aloof from civil disobedience, however much they disliked its leadership and tactics. Moreover, in regaining the initiative he had possessed in 1921, Gandhi now enjoyed once more the great political advantage which it brought. Civil disobedience had mobilized Indians into politics on a scale which had been unknown for nearly a decade. It was to the centre, to the Mahatma, that they looked, not to their local leadership. This gave the all-India centre the chance to settle accounts with the Bengal Congress.

[32] FR Bengal June (2) 1930, Home Poll file 18/7 of 1930, NAI.
[33] Note on Movements for the Non-Payment of Revenue, Taxes or Rent, n.d., Home Poll file 168 of 1929, NAI.
[34] FR Bengal April (1) 1930, Home Poll file 18/5 of 1930, NAI.
[35] Minute by H. W. Emerson, 20 June, 1931, on Government of Bengal to Home Department, Government of India, 11 June, 1931, Home Poll file 14/8 of 1931, NAI.

U

Within a month of Gandhi's pact with Irwin, the leaders of the PCC were embarrassed by the charge that they were out of line with his policy.[36] By stages the Mahatma moved into the role of the supreme authority, whose rulings came to Bengal Congressmen over the heads of their own leaders, and whose attitude towards these leaders could make or break them.[37] Seeing which way the wind was blowing, B. C. Roy, who was now mayor of Calcutta, began to move away from Subhas taking on the role of the centre's candid correspondent from Bengal. Soon there was fresh trouble over Calcutta Corporation, with Sen Gupta calling for purifications. 'I know', B. C. Roy told Vallabhbhai Patel, 'what purity there was during the four years that Mr Sen Gupta was the Mayor. . . .'[38] Evidently the soul of Tammany Banerjea went marching on.

This new outburst of intrigue gave the centre its chance. In August Vallabhbhai Patel directed M. R. Aney of Berar to enquire rigorously into Bengal affairs. Earlier enquirers from the centre had restricted themselves to tossing olive branches to both factions and then jumping thankfully into the train at Howrah. Aney's intervention was far more decisive and far more partisan. As usual, the Corporation was blamed for much of the mischief, but Aney came down heavily against the Subhas group, removing them from office and installing the Sen Gupta faction as the rulers of the PCC.[39] Nirmal Chandra Chunder, one of the Big Five, previously the patron of Subhas, agreed to become its acting president—another mark of the latter's decline.

A further result of civil disobedience was that political life was reviving in the districts. The campaign had shown that the leaders were lagging behind their followers. As the Bengal Council of Civil Disobedience had found: 'The people as also the workers . . . wanted a more forward programme.'[40] In Bengal that meant that they had to construct it for themselves. During the campaign, unhampered by

---

[36] On 14 April 1931, *Liberty*, Subhas's paper, deplored and denied attacks of this sort which were appearing in Sen Gupta's *Advance* 'and its supporters in the Calcutta gutter press'.

[37] The episode of the Bengal floods in 1931 illustrates this change. Naturally, both factions formed relief committees. To combat the general belief that Gandhi was supporting Sen Gupta's committee against his own, Subhas found it worth his while to send a telegram to the Mahatma (by then on his way to London) asking for impartial support for both relief funds. *Advance*, 19 August 1931; *Liberty*, 8 September 1931.

[38] B. C. Roy to Vallabhbhai Patel, 7 September 1931, file P 15/379 of 1931, AICC.

[39] Report by M. R. Aney on Bengal Congress Disputes, 25 September 1931, file G 25/506 of 1934–35, AICC.

[40] 'The Bengal Council of Civil Disobedience, a Brief Account of its Work', n.d. (*circa* 30 September 1930), file G 86/186 E of 1930, AICC.

leadership from Calcutta, they were bound to go their own ways; and this unusual experience of freedom left them very touchy about metropolitan control once the campaign was over. By June 1931, Sen Gupta and his municipal purifiers had been able to persuade twenty-two of the thirty-two DCCs to rebel against the dominant faction on the PCC; by July, twenty-six had come out in opposition.[41]

Once the Congress centre had restored the Sen Gupta faction to power, Subhas could now play tit-for-tat by poking the fires in the districts. This proved easy to do. After Gandhi had failed at the Second Round Table negotiations, a Bengal Political Conference was held at Berhampore in December 1931. Its members resolved 'that Government has practically ended the Gandhi-Irwin Pact', and 'that the time has arrived for resumption of the Satyagraha campaign for attainment of independence'. Until it was resumed, not only British goods, but also those banks, insurance companies, steamships and newspapers controlled by the British, should be boycotted.[42] This sounded so much like fighting talk that Nirmal Chandra Chunder resigned as president of the PCC.[43]

Admittedly, tempers at Berhampore had been inflamed by fresh Government ordinances against terrorism, but the violence of district representatives at the conference is plain. When Bankim Mukherjee (later to become a Communist leader in Bengal) called for a 'country-wide no-rent and no-tax campaign', his motion was narrowly beaten by 189 votes against 143.[44] But the best evidence about district opinion is that even the PCC, now dominated by the centre's men, did not risk rebutting it. They held back as long as they dared, hoping that 'Bengal will not precipitate matters until she has heard what Mahatmaji has to say'.[45] But Mahatmaji was still at sea, too far away to save them from the pressure of local opinion; and on 19 December they surrendered to it by accepting the boycott resolution.[46] Bengal's slide into militancy, together with a similar development in the UP, were among the chief reasons why the Government of India suddenly struck at the Congress in the first week of January 1932 and thus precipitated the second campaign of civil disobedience.

In its second phase, civil disobedience worked under much greater difficulties than in the first. This time authority was well prepared, and the Bengal Government immediately locked up the entire Congress leadership in the province. At once the connection between the Congress

[41] *Liberty*, 4 June 1931; *Advance*, 17 July 1931.   [42] *Liberty*, 7 December 1931.
[43] *Ibid.*, 13 and 14 December 1931.   [44] *Advance*, 8 December 1931.
[45] *Advance*, 15 December 1931.   [46] *Liberty*, 18, 20 and 25 December 1931.

and the districts was snapped; while the districts themselves, bereft of
the local men who had led them in the first campaign, had now to
depend on their ability to generate mass movements. Nearly everywhere, that was an impossibility, for it took more than dire threats
against British banks and insurance to bring the peasants out of the
fields. Once again everything depended upon the presence or absence
of local grievances for which the British could be blamed. The slump in
crop prices might have seemed a promising issue.[47] But this did no good
in east Bengal. Here the economic crisis caused agitation in the districts,
but it was against the Congress, since the troubles of the tenants were
blamed on the landlords and their party. In these districts the cry could
now be heard that the peasants would never prosper until '. . . the control over the Government was transferred to the people',[48] when money-
lenders and landlords (often the same persons) would get their deserts.
But it was not only among the Muslims that the Hindu gentry was
running out of credit. At its meeting on 20 December 1931, the Bengal
Backward Classes Association, voicing the opposition of the Namasudras, noted a '. . . want of faith in Congress professions of sympathy
for the Backward classes and . . . signs of revolt against the Congress.
. . .'[49] Consequently, civil disobedience in the eastern districts was easily

[47] *Jute Prices in Calcutta, Rs per 400 lb. bale.*

1929	71–4
1930	50–4
1931	37–5
1932	31–12

Source: *Statistical Abstract for British India,*
Cmd. 4835 of 1935, p. 760.

Common Rice Prices, Rs per maund.

	Calcutta	Dacca	Midnapore
1929	8–8	6–9	5–4
1930	7–7	6–4	4–9
1931	5–5	4–5	3–0
1932	4–2	3–2	2–7

Source: *ibid.*, p. 765.

[48] *Liberty*, 2 November 1931. This affair is a good example of the way in which the
Muslim political ferment had reached the village level, where it was organized with
the help of the district towns. At meetings of tenants in villages of Madhupur,
Mymensingh district, '. . . the discussions practically centred round the question of
payment of rent and of the dues of the Mahajans [moneylenders]'. The meetings were
addressed by three Muslim members of the district bar.

[49] *Liberty*, 27 December 1931.

snuffed out; deprived of mass support, the young bhadralok had to console themselves with terrorism, the second to last throw of a privileged class near the end of its tether.[50]

The efficient repression of 1932 also crimped the movement in most of the districts of western Bengal. There, militancy was not absent, and there were games of tip-and-run in Calcutta, where the young sparks organized a Congress Postal Service and, more durably, their underground newspaper, *The Challenge*.[51] In some areas of west Bengal a mass resistance was successfully organized. In April 1932 Government identified Bishnapur in Bankura, Arambagh in Hooghly, and the entire Midnapore district as the most recalcitrant areas of Bengal;[52] and Arambagh and Midnapore were to persist in civil disobedience almost until the end of 1933, long after it had petered out in the rest of the province.[53]

Once more, local grievance gave the leverage. In November 1931 a new revenue settlement had been imposed upon Arambagh 'to the utter dismay and surprise of the distressed peasantry',[54] but to the advantage of the agitators.[55] In Midnapore the resumption of civil disobedience was the signal for reviving the agitation against the chaukidari tax which had been active in the district in 1930. Both these issues were especially important to the richer peasantry who dominated Arambagh and Midnapore alike. It was their domination which gave the resistance the flavour of a mass movement in those areas, so that Imperial Chemical Industries (India) glumly reported about Midnapore: 'There appears to be a network of volunteers, and passive assistance to the movement is given by the villages and merchants.'[56] And that was why during the second civil disobedience movement sixty-four of the seventy-six union boards in Contai sub-division took part in the agitation against chaukidari taxes. Between January and the end

[50] The last was to be Marxism.

[51] Postmaster-General, Bengal, to Director-General, Posts and Telegraphs, 13 February 1932, Home Poll file 21/7 of 1932, NAI. *The Challenge* was a pert and rather charming cyclostyled paper. There are a few copies in the AICC files.

[52] FR Bengal April (1) 1932, Home Poll file 18/7 of 1932, NAI.

[53] Until October 1933, numerous telegrams from Bengal to Delhi continued to report resistance in Arambagh and Midnapore. Home Poll file 3/1 of 1933, NAI.

[54] *Liberty*, 12 November 1931, letter from Profulla Chandra Sen (a future Chief Minister of west Bengal).

[55] 'Arambagh War Council: Report from January to June 1932', file 4/406 of 1932, AICC.

[56] Imperial Chemical Industries (India) to Bengal Chamber of Commerce, 5 September 1932, enclosed in Bengal Chamber of Commerce to Commerce Department, Government of India, 27 September 1932, Home Poll file 195 of 1932, NAI.

of June 1932, 5,900 persons were arrested in Tamluk, 4,343 in Contai.[57]

In Arambagh and Midnapore alike, the power of the rich peasants, Kaibarttas transmuted into Mahisyas, could turn civil disobedience into a mass movement. In Tamluk, where almost the entire population consisted of Kaibarttas, the threat of boycott by the caste saw to it that no one came to the rescue of the persecuted chaukidars.[58] As he grappled with Midnapore, the Commissioner of the Burdwan division recognized that the root of his difficulties lay in '. . . the solidarity of the opposition due to the fact that most of the inhabitants are Mahisyas'.[59] The result was that political activity went deeper than elsewhere, affecting many unlettered men. Many of those imprisoned in Midnapore for civil disobedience were of lower social standing than in the other districts of Bengal.[60] That is why the movement was so strong.

Midnapore was the only counterpart in Bengal to such districts as Kaira and Surat in Gujarat, or Guntur and Nellore in Andhra: where local leaderships took up issues popular with the richer peasants, confidently relying on their solidarity. But what was good for other provinces was not good for the Bengal Congress. The old firm did not welcome a lower class of customer. As the ardent editors of *The Challenge* had to note with regret:

Of the 32 Congress districts, the fringe of the mass has been touched in only a few of them, but in the majority of the districts, the so-called middle-class gentry and educated young men have been drawn into the movement.[61]

The only district of Bengal which did exploit local grievance took care to keep out of the control of its PCC:

Midnapur [*sic*] D.C.C. has been trying to work with as little outside control as possible . . . the whole of Midnapore have all along being trying to keep themselves aloof . . . from the quagmire of Bengal party politics.[62]

[57] 'Tamluk Sub-Divisional War Council: Report on Civil Disobedience Movement in Tamluk from January to June 1932', n.d. (*circa* August 1932), 'Statistical Report of the Civil Disobedience at Contai, Midnapore, from January to July 1932', 24 August 1932, file 4/406 of 1932, AICC.
[58] Narendra Nath Das, *History of Midnapur, Part-Two* (Calcutta, 1962), p. 164.
[59] FR Bengal July (2) 1930, Home Poll file 18/8, NAI.
[60] By the end of 1932, Hijli gaol had housed some 2,957 prisoners convicted during the second civil disobedience movement. Nearly all of them came from Midnapore and Bankura. They were described as 'corner boys' or 'village youths' whose level of literacy was much lower than that of the other civil disobedience prisoners in Bengal, who were predominantly bhadralok. Report on Types of Civil Disobedience Prisoners in Bengal, n.d., enclosed in Government of Bengal to Home Department, Government of India, no. 5394, PJ, 26 November 1932, Home Poll file 23/66 of 1932, NAI.
[61] *The Challenge*, 11 July 1932.
[62] 'Civil Disobedience in Tamluk', a report by G. Singh, Director of Tamluk

All that was left under the control of the Bengal Congress were the sectors of stagnation; all that was dynamic in the eastern and western districts was slipping out of its control. Civil disobedience had exposed the underlying trend of politics:[63] in the east, local power was dribbling through the fingers of the landed supporters of the Congress; in the west, the rich peasants resisted the British and Calcutta alike. Both in the eastern districts, where its allies were being knocked off their perches, and in the western districts, where its nominal supporters kept it at bay, the internal constraints upon the Calcutta clique were growing apace. Sapped by these weaknesses, it had now to face a tightening of external constraints from British political initiatives and the responses to these initiatives from the all-India centre of nationalist politics.

IV

The Communal Award, announced by the British Government in August 1932, was a new sign of its determination to warp the Indian question towards electoral politics. During the late nineteen-twenties there had been many discussions about revising the Montagu-Chelmsford Act so as to put provincial government into Indian hands. All of them had smashed against the question how the communities were to be represented in the new provincial legislatures. Should they be represented by separate electorates as Muslims had been since 1909? In what proportions? And by what franchise? When he went to London for the second session of the Round Table Conference in 1931 Gandhi had hoped to cut through these controversies by insisting that Indian control of the central government must precede communal settlements in the provinces.[64] At the conference, the Minorities Committee would not hear of this. A self-governing India would mean a central government dominated by Hindus. But once the issue of provincial self-government was compounded by a demand for *purna*

Civil Disobedience Council, no date [early 1931], file G 86/186 E, 177N, of 1930, AICC.

[63] During the first half of 1932, some 16,383 persons were arrested in the province, most of them for picketting. The total compares poorly with the 11,025 arrests in Gujarat, a region with only one-sixth of Bengal's population, *The Challenge*, 25 July 1932.

[64] When challenged to be more precise, all he would suggest were joint electorates and a reservation of seats for both Hindus and Muslims on the basis of their populations in those provinces where either community was less than 25 per cent of the population. *Indian Round Table Conference (Second Session), Proceedings of the Minorities Committee*, Appendix I.

swaraj, everyone wanted to see where he stood. Before coming to that point, minorities meant to entrench their own positions. This brought about a deadlock, and towards the end of the conference, MacDonald, the British Prime Minister, announced that since there could be no constitutional progress without settling the issue of communal representation, he would decide between the competing claims.

It was in Bengal and the Punjab that the most vexing problems lay. In most of the provinces of British India the Hindus stood in unchallengeable majorities, and there the only task was to get the best possible terms for the minorities. The North-West Frontier Province was a special case: while possessing a Muslim majority of more than 90 per cent, it was still without a council. Sind was not yet a province. But Bengal and the Punjab were provinces of the first importance, and in both of them the Muslims were a majority, in Bengal of nearly 55 per cent, in the Punjab of nearly 57 per cent. Unless the new constitution ensured their hold on these provinces, the Muslim politicians could not afford to accept it. On the other hand, a British acceptance of their claims would bring bitter protests from the most vociferous Hindu politicians of Bengal and the Punjab, not to mention Sikhs who were 13 per cent of the population of the latter.

In so thorny a question the British were not quick to move.[65] What set them to work on their decision were all-India considerations, in the form of a warning from Willingdon, the Viceroy, 'that the Muslim position is extremely shaky . . . their leaders cannot control them. . . .'[66] Hoare, the Secretary of State for India, reported to the Cabinet that 'unless an undertaking to issue a decision was made before the Mohammadan Conference at Lahore on March 21st, the Mohammadan communities would probably not co-operate further in the work of the Round Table Conference Committees. . . .'[67]

When Hoare first set his mind to drafting the terms of the Award, he was clear that British interests would be served by bettering the existing Muslim position in Bengal and the Punjab; but he believed that in each province, Hindus and Muslims ought to get seats in proportion to their shares of the population. In principle, the Governors of the two pro-

---

[65] There were, however, good technical reasons for delay. The question was bound up with whatever extensions might be made to the franchise; the Indian Franchise Committee did not report until May 1932. Moreover, the Cabinet was still uncertain whether to put its plans for provincial self-government and for federating India into one and the same Bill; indeed it was not yet committed to producing any Bill at all.

[66] Willingdon to Hoare, private, 21 March 1932, Templewood Papers, vol. 5, Mss Eur E 240, India Office Library, London [IOL].

[67] Cabinet Minute, 23 March 1932, file 49 of Private Office Papers [L/PO], IOL.

vinces agreed with this view.[68] From Calcutta, Anderson advised that out of a Council of 250 for Bengal, the Muslims should have 111 seats or 44.4 per cent of the whole, and the Hindus 107 or 42.8 per cent; the rest were to go to special interests, especially those of the Europeans. But the Government of India felt scant concern for holding a communal balance in Bengal; they proposed to give 121 seats to the Muslims, or 48.4 per cent of the total, and to the Hindus ninety-six, or 39.2 per cent of the total.[69]

Hoare thought that New Delhi was being unfair to the Bengal Hindus. But when he pressed the Government of India to reconsider, the Viceroy came out with his political reasons for turning down Anderson's plan:

Governor naturally has approached problem solely in its provincial aspect in the light exclusively of Bengal conditions. Our own responsibilities compel us to take a wider view. We cannot afford to ignore reactions outside Bengal. ... Governor's proposals ... will alienate from us Moslem support not merely in Bengal but throughout India. ... No words that I can use ... can overstate the importance which I and my colleagues ... attach to a decision by His Majesty's Government accepting our proposals in preference to Governor's. ...[70]

With some reluctance, Hoare accepted the Viceroy's case, and the Cabinet settled the matter on 4 August. Previously, the Hindus had forty-six seats to the Muslims' thirty-nine in the Bengal Council; the Award gave them eighty General seats to the Muslims' 119.[71] This was a stunning blow to the Hindu politicians and their patrons. But when they struck it, the British did so for reasons that in the main were not connected with the province at all, but with averting 'reactions outside Bengal', or in other words to satisfy the Muslim politicians of the UP and the Punjab.

Having been smitten by the British, the Bengal Hindus were now

[68] Hoare to Willingdon, telegram, secret, 22 March 1932; de Montmorency to Willingdon, private, 29 April 1932; Anderson to Willingdon, private, 5 May 1932, *ibid.*

[69] Anderson to Hoare, secret, 7 June 1932; Willingdon to Hoare, telegram 438-S, 14 June 1932, *ibid.* At the same time the Viceroy and his Council thought that the seats to be allotted to the Depressed Classes—then estimated at about ten—should come from the Hindus' ninety-six.

[70] Willingdon to Hoare, telegram 493-S, 9 July 1932, *ibid.* One member of the Viceroy's Council dissented. This was the Law Member, Sir B. L. Mitter. He was a Bengali.

[71] Annexure to *East India (Constitutional Reforms): Communal Decision*, Cmd. 4147 of 1932, in fact, Hoare was harder on the caste Hindus than Willingdon had been, since some of the General seats were meant for the Depressed. Of course, caste Hindus could expect to pick up a few more from the special constituencies.

squeezed by the Congress. The Award had prolonged the system of separate electorates for Hindus, Muslims and Sikhs, and it had extended the system to those whom the draftsmen ambiguously described as the Depressed Classes. At the same time the fourth paragraph of the Award stated that the British Government would not take part in any negotiation to amend the decision, but that it might agree to any 'practicable alternative' which the Indian communities might settle for between themselves. This easement left still darker the prospects of the Bengal Congress. When Gandhi's fast led to the Poona Pact, this meant that the Congress centre bought up the separate electorates awarded to the Depressed Classes; the price it had to pay was to reserve for them a share of the Hindu seats in every province. Generosity on this scale was all very well for the Congress leaders in provinces where, on any assumptions, there would be a copper-bottomed Hindu majority. But in Bengal the caste Hindus had nothing to spare. Matters were all the worse for them because of the obscurity of the term 'Depressed Classes' in the province. In the event it was defined so widely that almost all the non-bhadralok castes were able to get themselves included in the category. At first, Government had intended that the Depressed Classes in Bengal should obtain ten seats. The intervention by the Congress centre raised this number to thirty, and these came from the seventy-eight in the Hindu quota, shrinking it still further.[72]

V

But at first Hindus and Muslims in Bengal were able to work out their attitudes to the Award without much prompting from their all-India patrons. The Congress centre had become a victim of the Ordinance Raj and was closed down; the Muslim League and the Muslim Conference were neither of them credible spokesmen for the all-India interests of the community. The first reaction among politically minded Hindus was one of united commination. Over this issue, at least, there was no disagreement between the factions of the PCC. *Liberty*, which was still writing in the Subhas interest, denounced the terms of the Award as:

... insulting and positively mischievous. ... The Hindus are rendered politically impotent, and the reactions of this process on the cultural, economic and political life of the province will be disastrous.[73]

[72] The Bengal Congress could reasonably hope to win some of these thirty seats.
[73] *Liberty*, 17 August 1932.

Advance, which spoke for Sen Gupta, repeated these indictments:

... the award has sacrificed the province to the Moslem and European communities and has left no real autonomy to the children of the soil.[74]

When Government ruled that eighty-seven Bengal castes were to be included in the Depressed Classes, both newspapers protested again. *Liberty* wrote that this was tantamount to saying that '. . . the Bhadralogs of Bengal are the only undepressed class', whereas they had merely acted for the good of all the rest:

The political interests of socially inferior classes never suffered for reasons of their social inferiority.[75]

Advance took the same line, blaming the Namasudras and Rajbansis for allowing themselves to be classed as Depressed. In any case:

... there does not exist in Bengal any caste or castes which may perpetually come under the definition of 'depressed'.[76]

Whatever their dissension over other issues, when the Bengal factions did agree, their unanimity was wonderful. It is easy to see behind this concord their anxiety for the safety of the Permanent Settlement, if the Award were to give the Muslims control of a self-governing Bengal. Further tenancy legislation would really hurt 'the children of the soil'. Since both groups were candidly devoted to the landholder interest,[77] this initial unity was natural. But it was not to last. Towards the end of the year a Unity Conference at Allahabad considered the communal question in India as a whole. For Bengal they proposed that the Muslims should be given an absolute majority of seats (127) in the Legislative Council. In return for this assurance of control, the Muslims were to agree that representation of the Hindus should be increased to 112. More important, the Muslims were to agree to joint electorates. Now there were many Indian politicians who specialized in Unity

---

[74] *Advance,* 18 August 1932.

[75] *Liberty,* 22 January 1933. Although the Poona Pact was made on 25 September 1932, it was not until the following January that the Government of Bengal ruled which castes in Bengal were to be included under its arrangements for the Depressed Classes. By defining some substantial peasants as Depressed, the Government showed once more how British administrative categories rode rough-shod over Indian social facts.

[76] *Advance,* 22 January 1933.

[77] During the civil disobedience movement, *Advance* took the opportunity of describing a Muslim motion in Council for further amendment of the Tenancy Amendment Act of 1928 as 'grotesque'. *Advance,* 23 November 1932. Its rival wrote that 'The better type of landholder[s] in Bengal . . . have inspired the best of our cultural movements and financed every public endeavour that has had for its object the accomplishment of something great and good.' *Liberty,* 1 March 1933.

Conferences, where they turned real conflicts into bland unrealities.
So we need not take the Allahabad proposals very seriously. But what is
interesting about them is their reception in Bengal. Some Congressmen
were firmly against them, but others wobbled. None of them liked the
notion of an absolute Muslim majority, but they were divided over the
notion of joint electorates. In the western districts, with their Hindu
majorities, Congressmen had nothing to fear from joint electorates. But
in the eastern districts, the trend of the district board elections had
shown how much they had to lose. In the event, the scheme came to
nothing, but the divisions it opened were a portent of greater trouble
to come.[78]

Even in the short run the Award was managing to divide the Bengal
Muslims as well. When news of its terms first reached Calcutta, the
Bengal Government telegraphed its impression that 'Muslims are satisfied but are determined to continue demand for statutory majority,
more as offset to Hindu demands than as demand in itself sustainable.'[79]
All the Muslim political groups complained that their 48 per cent of
representation in the council would leave any Muslim ministry dependent on the good will of others. Their demand for the elusive 51 per
cent was voiced by Fazl-Huq, the Bengal Muslim League and the Bengal section of the Muslim Conference; but it was also expressed by the
few Muslims who belonged to the Congress. With the whole community
jubilant at the prospect of becoming the masters, no Muslim party
could flout that mood by not pressing for an absolute majority. But in
every other respect, the Award divided these parties. Predictably, the
Congress Muslims, following the party's line, attacked separate electorates. So too did the Bengal wing of the Muslim League, whose
members were close enough to the populist roots of east Bengal to
realize that they had nothing to fear from joint electorates. On the other
hand, the old-fashioned Central National Muhammadan Association,
which derived its strength from Calcutta and the western districts,
where the community was weaker, held strongly to separate electorates.

---

[78] For brevity, this account neglects the role of the Hindu Mahasabha. During the
1920s Bengal had rejected the Mahasabha. After the failure of Das's Pact, the temper of
the Bengal Congress was sufficiently anti-Muslim for it to perform the Mahasabha's
work without acknowledgement. But the Award gave the Mahasabha a fresh chance
in Bengal. It was active in protest (e.g. *Advance*, 21 August 1932; *Liberty*, 5 September
1932). It strongly opposed the Allahabad scheme, making impossible stipulations
and finally inducing Congressmen to make them as well. For the negotiations over the
proposals see *Advance*, 29 November 1932, and *Liberty*, 12, 26, 28 and 29 December
1932.

[79] Government of Bengal to Secretary of State, telegram, 22 August 1932, Home Poll
file 41/4 of 1932, NAI.

This was also the view of the Bengal section of the Muslim Conference which was dominated by wealthy men such as Sir A. K. Ghaznavi and Nazimuddin, who had no wish to see Muslim radicalism encouraged by campaigns fought in joint electorates.[80] All these preliminary divisions among Hindus and Muslims in Bengal were to be widened once the issue of the Award came to be examined on the stage of all-India politics.

In devising their attitudes to the Award, the spokesmen of all-India interests, Muslim and Hindu alike, were aware of its enormous implications for electoral politics. From their all-India standpoints, the root problem was that the Award affected both communities in different ways in different provinces. In Bombay, Madras, the Central Provinces, Bihar and the United Provinces, it was not contentious, since there the Hindus were bound to win in any case. In Sind, if Sind were to become a separate province, Muslims of some sort were bound to win, and so they were in the North-West Frontier Province, although here the winners were likely to be unsympathetic to the Muslim centre. The rub came in Bengal and the Punjab, where the composition of the new legislature was likely to strip the Hindus of much of their previous political importance. Here was an apple of discord for the Congress. Its claim to be spokesman for the entire Indian nation rested on its carrying a Muslim wing of its own. For these Congress Muslims there was no choice but to accept the Award in Bengal and the Punjab. Opposing it would have meant their political extinction. This would also have extinguished the credibility of Congress claims to represent Indians of all communities. On the other hand, for the Congress to acquiesce in the Award would enrage its Hindu members in Bengal and the Punjab.

At first, civil disobedience postponed the dilemma for the Congress centre. Gandhi and the other leaders were in gaol; the police broke up the annual sessions; and anyway, with nothing precisely known about the new constitution, there was nothing immediately to decide. From his prison, Gandhi advised his followers to keep mum;[81] and for seven months after his release in August 1933, he was able to bottle up discussion of the awkward issue. But it was bound to spill out. Early in 1933 a White Paper outlined the British Government's suggestions about the shape of the reforms.[82] Here was a powerful stimulus to electoral poli-

---

[80] Ghaznavi and Nazimuddin told the Governor of Bengal that the Muslims should be given an absolute majority of seats for otherwise 'the strong section which has always favoured joint electorates without reservation of seats would again assert itself. . . .', enclosed in Anderson to Hoare, 22 July 1932, file 49 of L/PO, IOL.

[81] Gandhi to Birla, 21 January 1933, G. D. Birla, In the Shadow of the Mahatma (new edition, Bombay, 1968), p. 87.

[82] Proposals for Indian Constitutional Reform, Cmd. 4268 of 1933.

tics, for now it was reasonably plain that under the new constitution the provinces would practically govern themselves. For many Congressmen this was a much more glowing prospect than sticking in the dead end of civil disobedience; moreover, the approach of the interim elections to the Delhi Assembly provided an excuse for reviving the Swarajist Party. Here, as usual, calculations of provincial interest were everything. In provinces with a majority of Hindus, the chances of Congress-Swarajist candidates for the Assembly would be bright; but brighter by far would be the chances of these candidates for provincial elections under the new constitution, when there would be everything to play for, and when there would be Hindu majorities guaranteed by the Award. Men of that sort, ready to rush for nomination, did not share Gandhi's anxiety about snapping the unity of the movement. There was no gainsaying them; and at a meeting of the All-India Congress Committee at Patna, between 18 and 20 May 1934, the bargain was struck. On his side, Gandi agreed to abandon civil disobedience and to sanction a programme of fighting the elections to the Assembly. For their part, the new Swarajists swallowed the argument that since Congress was totally opposed to the reforms which were taking shape in London, the question of its attitude to the Award simply did not arise. Therefore, Congress, it was announced, neither accepted nor rejected the Award.[83] So sybilline a statement warded off trouble, but the trouble was bound to return. To fight the elections meant setting up a Parliamentary Board to supervise nominations and expound the party's views, including its views on the most vexed issue in Indian politics—the Award.

What were these views? Gandhi still hoped he would not have to say. But when the Working Committee met members of the Parliamentary Board in June, the clash of interests showed that the cat could not be kept in the bag. Malaviya and Aney, with their Mahasabha connections, thought it scandalous that Congress should not candidly denounce the Award, and they threatened to resign unless it was rejected. On their side, the Congress Muslims, Khaliquzzaman, Asaf Ali and Dr Syed Mahmud, protested that such a rejection would finish their influence with their own supporters. If the Award was denounced, they too threatened to resign, and their leader, Dr Ansari, would go with them. Harassed by both sides, Gandhi improvised a new resolution.

[83] For new evidence about the evolution of this decision, see K. M. Munshi, *Indian Constitutional Documents*, vol. I (Bombay, 1967), pp. 357–82. There is an illuminating account in 'The Communal Award', a memorandum prepared by Chandrashankar Shukla, Vallabhbhai Patel Papers. Shukla had acted as one of Gandhi's secretaries in 1934. There is further information in Rajendra Prasad, *Autobiography* (Bombay, 1957), pp. 378–9.

Congress rejected the White Paper. Only a constituent assembly could settle the communal problem. 'The White Paper lapsing', he continued in a daring *petitio principii*, 'the Communal Award lapses automatically'. Nevertheless,

Since, however, the different communities in the country are sharply divided on the question of the Communal Award, it is necessary to define the Congress attitude on it. The Congress claims to represent equally all the communities composing the Indian nation and therefore, in view of the division of opinion, can neither accept nor reject the Communal Award as long as the division of opinion lasts. . . . Judged by the national standard the Communal Award is wholly unsatisfactory, besides being open to serious objections on other grounds.[84]

So it had come to this. On one of the most crucial of issues before the country, the divisions inside Indian society forced Congress to move from one tongue-tied position to another. First, the self-styled spokesmen for India could not speak. Then, when they were driven into speaking, they had nothing to say. This was good enough for the Congress Muslims, who were too beggared of support to be choosers; but for the Mahasabha wing of the Congress, who were not short of other options, it was merely a word game. Gandhi did his best:

The more I think about it, the clearer I become that the Working Committee . . . resolution is faultless. . . . Non-committal is the only position the Congress can take up. We must not tease the communal boil. The more we tease it, the worse it becomes. In my opinion it is a fatal blunder to turn our opinion from the White Paper. If the reforms are not killed, the Award will stand in spite of agitation. The reforms can be killed by sustained effort.[85]

By July 1934, this was a sanguine statement. It did not convince Malaviya and Aney. They quit the Parliamentary Board and went on to organize a new Congress Nationalist Party, designed to cripple the Swarajists at the elections by dilating on the wrongs of Bengali and Punjabi Hindus. When they began marshalling their forces at the All-India Communal Award Conference held on 25 October, most of the old faces from the Mahasabha breakaway of 1926 were to be seen. Their conference was attended by Kelkar, Moonjee and Aney, veterans from the Tilak school of politics, by Bhai Parmanand and

---

[84] The text of the resolution, as it was approved by the Working Committee, is printed in *The Indian National Congress, Resolutions 1934–6* (Allahabad, n.d.), pp. 19–20. Gandhi's draft, which differs in unimportant ways, is in Appendix 2 to the memorandum by Chandrashankar Shukla, *loc. cit.* The account of these discussions in June by Chaudhry Khaliquzzaman, *Pathway to Pakistan* (Lahore, 1961), pp. 123–26, differs in some details, and also in some dates.

[85] Gandhi to Aney, 12 July 1934, quoted in Shukla, 'The Command Award', Vallabhbhai Patel Papers.

Radha Kumud Mukerji, also of the Mahasabha persuasion, and by Raja Narendranath and Master Tara Singh, a couple brought into startling and short-lived agreement by the grievances of Hindus and Sikhs in the Punjab. The conference castigated the Congress attitude to the Award as 'a virtual acquiescence in the decision'.[86] Of course it was. The point was taken in Bengal as well. Objurgations and appeals from the province poured into the AICC, most of them from east Bengal, conspicuously from Dinajpur, Barisal, Chittagong, Khulna, Dacca, Pabna, Jessore, Mymensingh and Brahmanbaria.[87]

These complex events were now enlivened by another round of quarrelling inside the Bengal PCC. By now the old paladins were no longer there, for Subhas had gone to Europe and Sen Gupta had died, and their factions had passed into the hands of B. C. Roy and J. C. Gupta respectively. The latter group had been alarmed that the new Swarajist machine for fighting elections in Bengal would fall under the control of their rivals;[88] after this quarrel had been patched up, there was another struggle for control of the Corporation, and for a while Calcutta was graced by the presence of two rival mayors. It was not that the factions differed in their attitude to the Award; all that separated them over this issue was that B. C. Roy, now leader of the majority in the PCC, had tacked so close to Gandhi that he had to accept the Working Party's ambiguous statements about the Award; J. C. Gupta, on the other hand, with the freedom of leading the outs, kept on demanding that the Congress centre should permit open agitation in Bengal against it.[89] But these were no more than tactical

---

[86] Resolution of the first session of the All-Indian Communal Award Conference, enclosed in Ramanand Chatterjee to Rajendra Prasad, 27 October 1934, file G/24 of 1934–36, AICC.

[87] Here are some of the messages of protest from east Bengal all addressed to Vallabhbhai Patel, President of the Congress: Joginchandra Chakravarty [Dinajpur], telegram, 7 September 1934; Saratchaira Guha, telegram, 7 September 1934; Mohin Das, 7 September 1934; Mymensingh conference, 7 September 1934; Khulna Congress Committee, telegram, 6 September 1934; Pabna Congress Committee, 8 August 1934; Jhenida Congress Committee [Jessore], 12 August 1934; statement by President, Dacca DCC, enclosed in Secretary, Congress Nationalist Party, Bengal, to AICC, 6 August 1934. There were also protests from Hooghly, Burdwan, Calcutta and Birbhum in west Bengal, file G 24 of 1934–36, AICC.

[88] For the development and the temporary settlement of this devious affair see K. M. Munshi to Gandhi, n.d. [circa 8 April 1934], in Munshi, Indian Constitutional Documents, I, 369; Bhulabhai Desai to unnamed correspondent, 10 May 1934, in M. C. Setalvad, Bhulabhai Desai (New Delhi, 1968), pp. 120–1; J. C. Gupta, Amarendranath Chatterjee, D. C. Chakravarti and others to AICC, 11 May 1934, file G 25/506 of 1934–35, AICC; Munshi to Gandhi, 23 May 1934, in Munshi, Indian Constitutional Documents, I, 374.

[89] J. C. Gupta to Gandhi, 16 August 1934, Vallabhbhai Patel Papers.

differences; their inwardness was expressed by the Gandhian workers of
Bengal, who were without any hope of power in the PCC, and so could
afford to play the role of impartial observers:

'Amrita Bazar Patrika' is communal. The vernacular 'Basumati' is frankly
sanatanist. 'Ananda Bazar Patrika' . . . is a vehement supporter of the Hindu
Sabha. . . . 'Advance' is a close ally of the 'Ananda Bazar Patrika'. These
two papers seized the opportunity of the resignations of Panditji [Malaviya]
and Sj. Aney . . . to make their party strong by damning the Parliamentary
Board and the Working Committee as having played into their hands. . . .
'Forward'[90] has no love for the Working Committee or for you either. But it
supports because it has to.[91]

The communalism of Bengal Hindus, which seemed so deplorable to
the Congress centre, seemed indispensable to the PCC in Calcutta, if
they were to make headway against the Nationalists in the forthcoming
elections. B. C. Roy pleaded with Gandhi to permit the Bengal Congress to come out against the Award. Would he allow them to announce
that their candidates for the Assembly would vote against any move to
support the Award there? Gandhi would not. Nor would he allow these
candidates to be dispensed on conscientious grounds from obeying the
Working Committee resolution: 'Those . . . who want dispensation have
simply to belong to the Nationalist Party.'[92] At the same time, the all-
India interests, for whose sake he was hobbling the Bengal Congress,
were driving him to try for an electoral pact with the Nationalists. But
Malaviya and Aney pitched their price too high.[93] Their party per-
sisted with its campaign against the Congress, and when the Assembly
elections took place in Bengal, they carried all seven seats in the General
constituencies: Congress won none. The new policy of strictly
subordinating Bengal to the centre had produced another ominous
result.

[90] *Forward* was *Liberty* under a new name.
[91] Birendra Nath Gupta to Gandhi, 21 August 1934, Vallabhbhai Patel Papers.
Like everyone else in Bengal, the Gandhians had their factions. B. N. Gupta belonged
to the group led by Suresh Chandra Banerji.
[92] B. C. Roy to Gandhi, 22 August 1934; Gandhi to B. C. Roy, 25 August 1934;
Gandhi to B. C. Roy, 30 August 1934; Vallabhbhai Patel Papers. In fact, Gandhi
had offered a version of the conscience clause to Malaviya. He proposed to apply it in
individual cases. Malaviya demanded that it must apply to all candidates.
[93] Malaviya and Aney demanded twenty seats. Gandhi and Vallabhbhai then
proposed local arrangements in which the 'demonstrably weaker party' should retire.
Forwarding this second scheme, Gandhi commented: 'I do not know what view the
Parliamentary Board will take but Sardar [Patel] accepts it in substance.' Gandhi to
Malaviya, 3 September 1934, Vallabhbhai Patel Papers. This is an interesting com-
mentary on the powers of the Board.

VI

At this point Bengal was whirled into the vortex of the all-India problem, for reasons of which its politicians knew little, and by agencies of
which they disapproved. Once again, the initiative came not from
India but from Westminster. When the Joint Select Committee reported in October 1934, the lines of the imminent Government of
India Act became clear. In the long term, India was to be federated,
although the shape of the federation was still up in the air. In the short
term, the provinces were to receive self-government, although the imperial safeguards were somewhat fussier than they had been in the
White Paper. In its decadence, British imperialism was swinging
between the concessions of 1933 and the safeguards of 1934. But the
Congress leaders could now be sure that they were dealing with a power
which knew it must give way in the provinces.

For the right-wing men who dominated the Congress leadership,
men such as Vallabhbhai Patel, Rajendra Prasad and Rajagopalachari,
this initiative in British policy underwrote their own choice in favour of
electoral politics. During the nineteen-twenties they had argued for no-
change against the Swarajists of those days. Das and Motilal Nehru,
those frustrated collaborators, had entered the Councils. But they had
never controlled the ministries. Now the survivors could do so. Provincial power was in sight for the Congress right wing. They had waited
long for it. They meant to take it. Better still, the British were on the
run; so the independence of all-India might be within grasp, especially
if the Muslims could be brought into a nationalist coalition. How then
were the Muslims to be paid? Obviously by tactical concessions in
Bengal and the Punjab. In Wardha and Ahmedabad and Madras this
seemed a fair price to pay.

But which Muslims were to be squared? The Award, it is true, dealt
the community high cards to play against Congress, if the latter needed
a joint opposition against the British. One obvious way of playing the
hand would be by a long, slow game, cashing its immediate winnings
from the Award, and ultimately settling for an independent India with
a weak centre and strong provinces—a United States of India where the
Muslims would be entrenched in their own majority regions. The argument for the waiting game was well expressed by the Aga Khan, one of
the leaders of the Muslim Conference:

The Conf[erence], the League or any other body, if it is to meet & discuss,
will open the door to the other elements to counter-attack the Com[munal]

Award, and by making, thanks to the Hindu press, all powerful, such a noise as to frighten the B[ritish] Gov[ernment] to go back & say 'as important Muslims are opposed to it, they are not prepared to push it through Parliament'. . . . By all means let us have . . . our Unity conferences . . . but *only after the Com[munal] award is law of the land & Act of Parliament a reality.*[94]

The community should stand pat. It should eschew negotiation. It should be wary of schemes of self-government at the centre. As for the Muslim League, it was in disarray until Jinnah returned to take the lead, but it was clear that Muslims must hold on to 'those rights which have already been conceded to them'.[95]

But this was the view from Delhi or the Ritz Hotel. In fact there was no more a general interest for all Muslims than there was for all Hindus. In their majority provinces, what preoccupied Muslim leaders were the interests of their followers in those provinces, and in different districts of those provinces. In the Punjab, Sind and Bengal, where the Award had rendered their majorities secure, some of them were ready to flirt with joint electorates.[96] Without an effective centre, with the Muslim Conference a network of notables and the Muslim League a cockpit of rivals, the position of the community was chaotic. Some Muslims wanted the Award and wanted the reforms as a way of buttressing it. Others wanted the Award but would not hear of the reforms. Some worked for joint electorates, others worked against them. Some glimpsed provincial power moving into their grasp; others saw it vanishing for ever.

But after March 1934, when Jinnah was back in power in the Muslim League, the position became a little simpler. His rivals, Fazl-i-Husain and the Aga Khan, had placed the Muslim Conference firmly behind the Award, but many Muslims from east Bengal were ready to bargain about it. This gave Jinnah an alternative way of playing the hand which the British had dealt: he could offer the Congress the League's co-operation over joint electorates if in return the Congress would accept

[94] Aga Khan to Fazl-i-Husain, Private, 21 January 1934, Fazl-i-Husain Papers [italics in original].

[95] Resolutions of the Muslim League on the Communal Award, 25–6 November 1933, *All-India Muslim League Resolutions, 1924–36* [n.d.], pp. 57–8.

[96] In 1933 the Muslim leaders of the Punjab calculated that by conceding joint electorates they could turn their representation of 49 per cent, guaranteed by the Award, into an absolute majority. But the plan cleft the Muslims of west Punjab, where the majority was large, and the Muslims of east Punjab, where the Hindus had the majority in the Ambala division. Moreover, the plan exposed the split of interests between the rural Muslims of the west, and the urban Muslims whose chance of representation in Lahore and Amritsar would be much reduced. Fazl-i-Husain to Zafrullah Khan, 8 May 1933; to Shafat Ahmad Khan, 19 June 1933, Fazl-i-Husain Papers. For Sind, see Fazl-i-Husain to Abdulla Haroun, 16 December 1932, *ibid.*

Muslim majorities in Bengal and the Punjab. Jinnah had sound reasons for seeking agreement with Congress. If he was to beat the Conference, then he had to broaden the basis of the League. An agreement with Congress would be helpful and might be possible, since he was as opposed to safeguards as they were, and his Bengal followers would accept joint electorates. This would mean trouble in the Punjab, where Muslim politics were controlled by Fazl-i-Husain, but he had little to lose there.[97]

Twelve months earlier, the Congress high command had been aware that they might buy Jinnah's support against the British, at the cost of selling out the Hindus in Bengal and the Punjab.[98] Now in January 1935, when the Joint Select Committee's report gave them a solid incentive to do so, Jinnah made his offer in plain terms:

I have nothing in common with the Aga Khan. He is a British agent. I am devoted to my old policy and programme. . . . If the Congress can support the Muslims on the question of the Communal Award, I would be able to get all the Muslim members except 7 or 8.

I . . . take the view that the J.P.C. [Joint Select Committee] Provincial constitution would be acceptable if the powers of the Governor and the legislative independence of the police department were removed. . . .

I am for the complete rejection of the proposals relating to Central Government. . . .

As things stand, the practical way would be for just a few leaders of political thought to combine for the purpose of preparing a formula which both the communities might accept. The Congress I admit would have to change its attitude in some respects, but looking to the great interests at stake Congress leaders should not flinch. I think that the future is with the Congress Party and not with me or the Aga Khan.[99]

[97] In any case, Jinnah still saw himself less as a party leader than as a go-between whose role lay in the central Assembly (to which he had been re-elected in October 1934). There the support of the Congress members would strengthen his claim to be a national leader.

[98] In January 1934 Jinnah had suggested a combined attack against the proposals of the White Paper, if Congressmen would accept the Communal Award; Munshi to Gandhi, 27 January 1934, in Munshi, *Indian Constitutional Documents*, I, 360, 361.

[99] 'Summary of conversation between Mr. Jinnah and myself', Vallabhbhai Patel Papers. This document is unsigned and undated. It is uncertain who made the summary, since copies of many documents circulating among the Congress high command found their way into Vallabhbhai's papers. But its date is fairly clear. The report had been published in December 1934. Jinnah returned to India in January 1935. The Aga Khan was also in India during that month. Jinnah's unknown interlocutor suggested that if there were to be conversations, they 'should take place before the Muslim League met'. The Council of the League met on 25–6 January. We may therefore conclude that the date of the conversation must have been very shortly before 23 January, when the talks between Jinnah and Rajendra Prasad did, in fact, begin.

On 23 January 1935, Rajendra Prasad, now president of the Congress, opened negotiations. He soon found that Jinnah was ready to bargain about the Award; for a price he would agree to joint electorates.[100] The Congress right wing had now to settle how much they were ready to pay. On the evening of 30 January, the Congress president, together with Vallabhbhai, Malaviya and Bhulabhai Desai agreed on the price: they would give the Muslims 51 per cent of the seats in Bengal and in the Punjab—more than the British had awarded them.[101] When this was put to Jinnah on the following day, he asked for more, observing 'that he was unable just yet to see any way to induce the Punjab although he felt that he had good grounds for recommending joint electorates to Bengal'; the Muslims would be more readily persuaded, if they were granted a differential franchise as well.[102]

At that point the talks were adjourned for twelve days, so that both sides might sound their followers. It says much for the anxiety of the Congress leadership to clinch the agreement that they made no immediate difficulties over Jinnah's higher terms; and still more, that they deliberately let the bulk of Bengal Congress opinion go by default, even when their province was coming up for auction. The only Bengal politician consulted by the Congress centre seems to have been B. C. Roy, who could speak convincingly for the rich men of Calcutta but not for the opinion of the districts.

On 13–14 February, Prasad and Jinnah finally nerved themselves to

[100] 'Substance of conversation ... on the 23rd January 1935', Rajendra Prasad Papers [RPP] XI/35/1/2; 'Notes on conversation on 28 January 1935', RPP XI/35/1/6.
[101] 'Notes of conversation between ... Malaviya ... Patel ... Desai ... and ... Prasad ... on the 30th of January 1935', RPP XI/35/1/9. This meeting ratified the agreement reached earlier that day between Prasad and Jinnah, that in all provinces other than Bengal, the Punjab and Assam, the weightage given to minorities under the communal decision should stand; and that in Bengal both Hindus and Muslims should try to persuade the Europeans to surrender some of their seats. These were then to be divided between the two communities.
[102] 'Notes of conversation ... on 31st January, 1935', RPP XI/35/1/10. If a given percentage of seats was to be reserved for either Hindus or Muslims under a system of separate electorates, this could be contrived by allotting to each community that percentage of constituencies which were bound to elect Hindu or Muslim members. In the Punjab the Sikhs possessed separate constituencies as well. This system had existed under the Montagu–Chelmsford constitution. But if separate electorates were to be replaced by joint electorates, then seats might still effectively be reserved by altering the terms of the franchise. Such schemes for a differential franchise implied altering British proposals by readjusting the franchise so that the electoral rolls reflected the proportion of population formed by Hindus and Muslims in Bengal and the proportion of Hindus, Muslims and Sikhs in the Punjab.

agree on a formula 'as a basis for further discussion'. Joint electorates were to replace separate electorates in the voting for the central and provincial legislatures. Bengal and the Punjab apart, in all the other provinces of British India the number of seats reserved to the Muslims under the Communal Award was to stand. In Bengal and the Punjab, the franchise was to be adjusted on a differential basis. In Bengal, 'the seats allotted to the Muslims under the award are to remain reserved for them', and if the Europeans surrendered any of their seats, these were to be divided between Hindus and Muslims in proportion to their population in the province—which would give the Muslims an absolute majority.[103]

The drafting of this 'basis for further discussion' was very cautious; its inwardness lay in generally accepting, although not in so many words, the Communal Award. Congress had bought out the Muslim asset of separate electorates at the cost of acquiescing in the certainty of Muslim control of the Punjab and the likelihood of Muslim control of Bengal. From his all-India point of view, Rajendra Prasad was satisfied with the bargain. The loss of Bengal and the Punjab was regrettable, but there was the compensation, as he reminded Vallabhbhai Patel, that:

Joint electorates are in themselves important as opening a way for joint action which has great possibilities for the future. Hindus have always attached great value to them and if they can be had they should be prepared to pay some price.[104]

From the summit of the Congress high command (as of the Government of India) it was easy to assume the existence of some solid mass defined as 'Hindus'; but that assumption slid over the awkward local facts. It was not the Hindus as a whole who would have to pay the price, but some Hindus in some districts of some provinces. In the Ambala division of Punjab, and the Presidency and Burdwan divisions of Bengal, the Hindu majorities had nothing to fear from joint electorates; just as on the other side of the hill, the Muslim majorities in west Punjab and east Bengal stood to gain from them. But where the shoe pinched was in areas where socially powerful minorities of Muslims and Hindus would be trapped in constituencies which they could never hope to capture. The Jinnah-Prasad proposals could expect no support from the urban Muslims of the Lahore division or from the

---

[103] 'Notes on conversations . . . on the 13th and 14th February, 1935', RPP XI/35/1/17. The Muslims were also to keep the one-third share of seats in the new central legislature which Hoare had allotted them.

[104] Rajendra Prasad to Vallabhbhai Patel, 14 February 1935, Vallabhbhai Patel Papers.

upper-caste Hindus of the Dacca, Rajshahi and Chittagong divisions. As for the Sikhs, they had already blocked an earlier scheme of differential franchise for the Punjab, and it was hard to see how any variant could secure them their 18 per cent of seats under the Award. These were not hopeful signs.

The combined efforts of Bhulabhai Desai, Patel and Prasad gradually won over the Hindus of the Punjab, but this was to be their only success. At first, the Congress president hoped to carry Hindu opinion in Bengal; apparently B. C. Roy and his coterie in Calcutta persuaded him that the formula 'may be accepted by other influential Bengalis also'.[105] But the time had gone when influential Bengalis could credibly speak for the Hindus of their province. So far as the Congress politicians in the districts were concerned, the issue cut too near the bone for them to leave their case in the hands of a few Congress notables. Other troubles were mounting as well. The Sikhs would not hear of the Punjab formula. The Hindu Mahasabha denounced the Bengal formula.[106] So did Malaviya, the voice of Hindu orthodoxy.[107] But Jinnah was now stipulating that Sikhs, Mahasabha and Malaviya must all agree before he would risk trying to push the scheme through the Muslim League.[108] Sceptics were coming to wonder whether the negotiations were more than a charade, a view expressed by Sir N. N. Sarcar, the Law Member of the Government of India: 'I feel . . . that the peace talk is pure moonshine. Jinnah is humbugging the Congress and the latter know that they are being humbugged'.[109]

Whatever Jinnah's motives may have been, his conditions gave the Bengal Congress a way out of its isolation. Now it could band together with the disgruntled from other provinces against the Congress centre. With Malaviya and the spokesmen for the Sikhs and the Mahasabha milling around him in Delhi, Prasad had enough difficulties. His troubles were compounded by the arrival of emissaries from the Bengal Congress, those pastmasters of faction. They brought their own splits

---

[105] Rajendra Prasad to Vallabhbhai Patel, 14 February 1935, Vallabhbhai Patel Papers.

[106] The Mahasabha were demanding that no seats should be reserved for either community in Bengal; Hindu Sabha to Prasad, telegram, 16 February 1935; Ramanand Chatterji, H. N. Dutt, J. N. Basu, Rajendra Dev, B. N. Majumdar and Indra Narayan Sen to Prasad, telegram, n.d. (?16 February 1935); Secretary, All-Bengal Hindu Conference to Prasad, 16 February 1935, RPP XI/35/1/21.

[107] Malaviya also opposed the scheme for giving the Muslims too much in the new central legislature.

[108] 'Daily Notes', 20 and 22 February 1935, RPP XI/35/30.

[109] Sarcar to R. M. Chatterji, 18 February 1935, N. N. Sarcar Papers, Nehru Memorial Museum and Library, New Delhi.

with them. The division between Hindu interests in east and in west
Bengal had been dragged into the open by the Prasad-Jinnah plan.
East Bengalis were prominent among the root and branch group who
wanted to knock the Bengal formula to pieces by scrapping the differential franchise, limiting the reservation of seats to ten years, pulling
down the Muslim share of seats from 119 to 110, and pushing up the
Hindu share to about ninety. Pitted against them was a more moderate
view, expressed by the west Bengal leaders, P. N. Bannerji and Amarendranath Chatterji, who supported the first two demands but who were
prepared to leave the distribution of seats alone.[110]

When Prasad confronted the Bengalis and the all-India leaders of the
Mahasabha on 25 February, he was both perplexed and irritated by
the demands of the Bengal opposition. Expounded by Sarkendranath
Roy, Indra Narayan Sen, Dinesh Chakravarty and Makhen Lall Sen,
these had a pronounced flavour both of the Hindu Sabha and of east
Bengal. The Congress president's own notes describe the clash:

I told the gentlemen present that so far as I could see there was no chance of
these proposals being accepted by Mr. Jinnah and I took it that their instruction was that I should break off negotiations. . . . Some Bengal friends said
that sooner the negotiations were broken off the better, but Dr. Bannerji
[West Bengal] said that there was a sharp difference of opinion and I should
not take that as the Bengal opinion. . . . Dr. Bannerji asked Malaviyajee to
take the question in his hand, accept anything he considered fair and
reasonable and they would all accept it. Mr Anney [Mahasabha] said that
he would not give that authority to Malviyajee alone. Dr. Moonjey [Maha-
sabha] said that they should all assist Malaviyajee in finding a formula.
Pandit Malaviyajee said that seeing that there was such sharp difference of
opinion he would not take any such responsibility on himself. . . . I said . . .
I would show their demands to Mr. Jinnah but I had no hopes of their being
accepted. I pointed out that we were losing a great opportunity of getting
Joint Electorates about which we had been speaking so much.[111]

Clearly there was no hope of meeting Jinnah's conditions. But so
anxious were Prasad and Vallabhbhai Patel to save their bargain that
when the Congress president met Jinnah on 27 February he suggested
confining the agreement to the Congress and the League, leaving aside
the more intransigent bodies. Jinnah refused. That was the end of the
affair.[112] Another all-India leader of the Congress, a man eager for
electoral victory in his own province, commiserated with Prasad:
'It is very tragic'.[113]

[110] 'Daily Notes', 25 February 1935, RPP XI/35/30.
[111] Ibid.
[112] 'Daily Notes', 27 February 1935, RPP XI/35/30.
[113] Rajagopalachari to Rajendra Prasad, 2 March 1935, RPP XI/35/40.

Perhaps the odds had always been against success; but the history of the negotiations is revealing. Prasad's account shows that in his view it was the Bengal Hindus who used Jinnah's conditions to upset the bargain. Ever since 1932, they had been alarmed by the new electoral arithmetic. From the British India Association to the University, from the zemindars to the literary men, from chairmen of district boards to members of the Legislative Council, they had shouted their hatred of the Communal Award from the housetops. It had been in the interest of Hindu politicians in all districts to do so.

But their general solidarity was dividing into regional interests of east and west. At one time they had rightly seen that from one end of Bengal to another, their advantage lay in pressing for joint electorates; even where they were outnumbered by Muslims, as in the districts of east Bengal, their local influence could win seats for them. But these calculations dated from the golden days of Hindu predominance. By the nineteen-thirties they had everything to lose in the eastern districts by joint electorates. In west Bengal, where joint electorates were in the interest of the political oligarchy, the Jinnah-Prasad formula would rescue something from the Award. But in east Bengal, where their last hope now lay in preserving separate electorates, the formula would ruin them completely. Rajendra Prasad had been misled by his Calcutta advisers, for as he ruefully admitted:

When we came to discuss the merits of the proposed formula it appeared that there was difference of opinion as regards the value of joint electorates some friends saying that separate electorates would suit Hindus in Eastern Bengal better.[114]

Birla put the point more bitingly when he reported to Gandhi that

Among the Bengal Hindus those who come from West Bengal are favourably disposed towards joint electorates. On the other hand, East Bengal is simply frightened of it.[115]

This glaring division of interests put a further strain upon the Bengal Congress. The all-India leadership had already brought it to heel. Every fresh act of control by the centre added to the difficulties under which the Bengal Congress had to work. The centre had unleashed civil disobedience and unsettled the preponderance of Calcutta. It had demolished the power of the majority faction. It had surrendered thirty seats to the lower castes. Now it had clearly shown that in the pursuit of its wider interests it meant to abandon Bengal to the Muslims.

[114] 'Daily Notes', 26 February 1935, RPP XI/35/30.
[115] Birla to Mahadev Desai, 28 February 1935, Birla, *In the Shadow of the Mahatma*, p. 150.

Y

VII

By their strategy of concentrating on the greatest good of the greatest number of Hindus in other provinces, Prasad and Patel had shown how little value they placed on Bengal. When the Congress president visited Calcutta in March 1935, he found Congressmen still full of resentment about the negotiations with Jinnah and fearful of new encroachments from the centre. Central agencies such as the All-India Village Industrial Association which Gandhi had recently set up, were regarded with suspicion, in case the high command intended them to supplant the PCC.[116] But for all its rodomontades, the Bengal Congress could not evade the power of the centre. Even without Subhas and Sen Gupta, their followers still jockeyed for position, since the lure of controlling Calcutta Corporation was still strong. Now Sarat Bose and Suresh Majumdar were pitted against B. C. Roy and K. S. Roy, and when the former group won a majority, the opposition appealed again to the centre, alleging that many of the membership lists were bogus. One of Rajendra Prasad's tasks in Bengal was to enquire into this shady affair. Rather contemptuously, he confirmed the Bose-Majumdar group in power.

These internal quarrels meant more external intervention. But the high command now held a better surety for the good behaviour of the provincial Congress. The elections which were due in January 1937 would decide who were to be the masters of the province. Whoever they might be, they could hardly be the Bengal Congress, but it was important for the PCC to do as well as possible. After all, other parties in Bengal had their factions as well, and a sizeable bloc of votes in the new Assembly would be a useful bargaining factor. But under the new constitution many more Bengalis would have the vote. One and a third million of them had been enfranchised in 1920; now eight millions were to receive the vote. After its cold-shouldering of the districts, most of these persons were outside the influence of the PCC.

How unrepresentative was the Bengal Congress, how etiolated its condition becomes plain from its own returns to the Mass Contact Committee in 1936. At first sight its membership still seemed fairly high:

[116] 'Summary Report of informal talks held . . . at Bengal P.C.C., 19-3-35'; 'At Dr. B. C. Roy's residence, 19-3-35'; 'Conference with Congress Workers . . . outside the present Bengal Executive, 20-3-35', RPP IV/36/1.

TABLE 4

Strength of the Bengal Congress by Districts, 1936

District	No. of members	No. of Primary Committees
Twenty-Four Parganas	1765	31
Jessore	1529	22
South Calcutta	1018	3
Central Calcutta	1087	6
Rajshahi	1913	5
Jalpaiguri	1015	3
Howrah	4790	27
Burdwan	792	16
North Calcutta	1844	6
Bankura	1545	11
Midnapore	nil*	nil*
Murshidabad	819	16
Dinajpur	1932	8
Nadia	1350	55
Sylhet	2831	15
Dacca	798	17
Noakhali	1436	21
Khulna	1296	40
Burra Bazar	1565	1
Hooghly	797	18
Birbhum	606	2
Rangpur	1161	12
Malda	1014	5
Bogra	1154	15
Pabna	1314	10
Mymensingh	2737	18
Faridpur	726	7
Barisal	661	29
Chittagong	71	2
Tippera	8958	19
Cachar	516	3
Total	49040	443

* The Congress was still banned in Midnapore.

Source: DCC answers to question 1/1 of questionnaire, Report of Congress and Mass Contact Sub-Committee, Bengal PCC, enclosed in Bengal PCC to Congress Mass Contact Committee, 16 August 1936, RPP IX/36/31. An earlier version of this table is enclosed in Bengal PCC to AICC, 10 July 1936, file P6/707 of 1936, AICC. This is a more optimistic and a less reliable estimate: e.g. it credits Midnapore with eighty-six Congress Committees.

But even the Bengal PCC did not believe their own figures about the number of primary committees:

The committees cannot all be said to be actually functioning today.[117]

Their estimates of total membership deserve a similar scepticism.[118] But in any case, whatever the nominal strength of the Bengal Congress may have been, the effective influence of its workers was small. Even on their own estimates, the popular appeal of the DCCs did not spread far:

TABLE 5

Mass contacts established by the DCCs

	Constructive Programme
Twenty-Four Parganas	'unsatisfactory'
Jessore	'to a little extent'
South Calcutta	'practically nothing'
Central Calcutta	'little opportunity'
Rajshahi	'no real constructive work'
Jalpaiguri	'we could do nothing'
Howrah	'constructive work did not help towards the contact with masses'
Burdwan	'some extent'
North Calcutta	'not . . . sufficiently worked to elicit effect'
Bankura	'libraries, schools, dispensaries, village industries'
Midnapore	'National School, Khadi work, health and industrial exhibition and arbitration work'
Murshidabad	No answer
Dinajpur	'No attempt made'
Nadia	'educational works among depressed classes'
Sylhet	'during last thirteen years Khadi, untouchability and other constructive works failed to create any consciousness of enthusiasm'
Hooghly	'in Arambagh Sub-Division whole-time workers running primary schools, doing Khadi work, by medical work and other constructive activities have been able to develop contact with the masses effectively'
Pabna	'flood relief'
Dacca	'to a small extent'
Noakhali	'no serious attempt made except through Khadi work'
Faridpur	'no constructive work'

Source: DCC answers to question 1/5 of questionnaire, Report of Congress and Mass Contact Sub-Committee, Bengal PCC, enclosed in Bengal PCC to Congress Mass Contact Committee, 16 August 1936, RPP, IX/36/31.

Only twenty of the thirty-two Congress DCCs in the Bengal province bothered to report, but the general position is clear.

[117] Bengal PCC to AICC, 10 July 1936 file P6/707 of 1936, AICC.

[118] At first, the Bengal Congress claimed that its membership was 56,750; after checking the lists, the AICC reduced the figures to 42,385. Rajendra Prasad to Bengal PCC, 8 March 1936, RPP IV/36/21. The PCC accepted the correction; the higher figures given in Table 4 were alleged to have been the result of later recruitment.

The same picture emerges from the reports of the DCCs about the nature of their membership. When they estimated the number of 'peasants' and 'workers' among their members they tied themselves into knots, just as the British census commissioners did with their own unreal categories. Nevertheless, the returns are revealing, especially when they are read with the returns about the presence or absence of peasant organizations in the districts.

TABLE 6

Reported Percentages of 'Peasants' and 'Workers' in Bengal DCCs, and Peasant Organizations in those Districts

	Percentages of 'Peasants' or 'Workers'	Peasant Organizations
Twenty-Four Parganas	Peasants 5 Workers 5	'The particulars are not known'
Jessore	Peasants + Workers = 5	Nil
South Calcutta	Both 'negligible'	No answer
Central Calcutta	Peasants nil; Workers 'hardly any'	Nil
Rajshahi	No answer	No information
Jalpaiguri	'50% are peasants and landless labourers'	Nil
Howrah	Peasants 50 Workers 10	Nil
Burdwan	'75% cultivators, i.e. those who live upon land.'	District Kisan Samiti
	'Actual tillers and workers form a small fraction'	District Ryot Association
North Calcutta	Nil	Nil
Bankura	'actual tillers nil'	Nil
Midnapore	'Question does not arise'	Nil
Murshidabad	No answer	Nil
Dinajpur	Peasants + Workers = 16.5	District Praja Samiti
Nadia	Peasants 75 Workers 5	Nil
Sylhet	Peasants 6 Workers 'negligible'	Surma Valley Peasant Association
Dacca	'nothing worth mentioning'	District Praja Samiti
Noakhali	Peasants 1	District Krishak Samiti
Hooghly	Peasants 50 Workers 10	'We are not aware of any'
Faridpur	'Negligible'	Nil
Pabna	Peasants 'hardly any' Workers nil	Nil

Source: DCC answers to question 1/7 and 2/1 of questionnaire, Report of Congress and Mass Contact Sub-Committee, Bengal PCC, encl. in Bengal PCC to Congress Mass Contact Committee, 16 August 1936, RPP IX/36/31.

When Tables 4 and 5 are read together, there is a plain correspondence between the districts which had been militant during civil disobedience and those which in 1936 were reporting strong membership or useful mass contacts. The Mahisyas in Midnapore, in parts of Bankura and in the Arambagh sub-division of Hooghly remained active. In east Bengal, Mymensingh, Noakhali and Rajshahi still claimed large memberships,[119] but here some of the traditional centres of Congress strength, such as Dacca, Chittagong and Barisal, were clearly in decline. But apart from these crude (and probably exaggerated) figures of membership, Tables 5 and 6 show how few were the districts where Congress possessed any influence whatever among the new electors. This isolation from the people was most marked in the east Bengal districts, where the new electors were mostly Muslims or lower-caste Hindus.

Consequently, for many of the new voters there would be little charm in the appeals of the Bengal Congress. But if they would not vote for a caucus in Calcutta, they might vote for a Mahatma in Wardha. The prestige of the Congress centre, the impact of its all-India agencies, its new financial strength, its apparent denial of caste distinctions, all worked to make the centre a greater electoral asset than the PCC. Here was the surety which bound the Bengal Congress to the high command. But in the meantime the Bengal Congress was hampered by the demands of its own constituents. After all, the new electors were birds in the bush; the old supporters were birds in the hand. On the one side, the Congress centre forbade them to denounce the Award; on the other, their old supporters insisted that they should do so. The final period before the elections left the Bengal Congress hopelessly caught in the nut-crackers.

When the Government of India Act reached the statute book in 1935, the Communal Award became law. By 1936, with the elections drawing near, the beleaguered Hindu notables of Bengal made one last effort to press London into amending it by Order in Council.[120] To this end they drew up a memorial, signed by all Hindu members of the Legislative Council, by twenty-three chairmen of municipalities, by eight chairmen of district boards, and by thirty-six 'representative Hindu leaders'. Here is the roll-call of Hindu eminence in Bengal, for they included members of the Council of State, great zemindars, the

[119] The huge membership figures returned from Tippera are an obvious overstatement. Nevertheless, membership may have been quite high, since Congress had benefited from the disputes between the Raja and his tenants.

[120] They argued that the Act of 1935 empowered the British Government to amend its terms by Order in Council, subject to the approval of both Houses of Parliament.

mayor of Calcutta, the vice-chancellor of Calcutta University, Sarat Chandra Chatterji, the novelist, Sir P. C. Ray, the chemist, Ramanand Chatterji, editor of the *Modern Review*, Sir Nilratan Sircar, the eminent doctor, Rabindranath Tagore and Sir Brajendranath Seal.[121] Out of this memorial came a last campaign in which the thwarted collaborators of Bengal repeated their grievances in Calcutta, Dacca, Barisal, Howrah and elsewhere.[122] The Indian Association was active in the movement; so was the Hindu Sabha. By July, the political implications of the campaign were brought into the open by the Mahasabha who now threatened to contest the Bengal elections as Congress Nationalists;[123] the following month they gave Congress their terms for standing down. The terms were simple: unqualified rejection of the Communal Award.[124]

Majumdar and Sarat Bose did their best to make the Congress Working Committee relent. Once the Lucknow session of Congress had gone through the motions of rejecting the new constitution and had installed as president Jawaharlal Nehru, still regarded as the hammer of the Congress Right, they begged for a harder line against the Award, '. . . with a view . . . to bring about the much needed United front in the Congress ranks in Bengal . . . so far as this province is concerned, the only difference between the two groups centres round the issue of non-rejection by the Congress of the Award'.[125] But Nehru replied that: '. . . the question has to be tackled on an all-India basis',[126] it was an answer that might have been written by Prasad or Patel.

The next move from the PCC was one of its ritual gestures. K. S. Roy of the minority faction, hopefully cast bread on the waters by denouncing Majumdar and Bose to the centre as enemies of official Congress policy.[127] Nothing floated back from Allahabad. Both factions in the PCC had failed. But by now they understood their electoral dangers. At last the factions preferred unity to acrimony and agreed to share power in the Bengal PCC. Elections had joined together those whom the Corporation had put asunder.

Indeed, the need for unity between these oligarchs was urgent. In its

[121] Memorial enclosed in Maharaja of Burdwan to Zetland, 4 June 1936, *Bengal Anti-Communal Award Movement; a Report* (Calcutta, 1939), pp. 3–9.

[122] *Ibid.*, pp. 11–35.

[123] *Advance*, 8 July 1936.

[124] Statement by Indra Narayan Sen Gupta, General Secretary, Congress Nationalist Party, *Amrita Bazar Patrika*, 22 November 1936.

[125] Suresh Chandra Majumdar to Jawaharlal Nehru, 18 July 1936, file P6/707 of 1936, AICC; cf. Sarat Bose to Nehru, 11 August 1936, *ibid.*

[126] Jawaharlal Nehru to Suresh Chandra Majumdar, 6 August 1936, *ibid.*

[127] K. S. Roy to Jawaharlal Nehru, 6 August 1936, RPP IV/36/83.

election manifesto, the AICC rejected the new constitution but refused to sanction agitation against the Communal Award, on the gnostic ground that such an agitation would be one-sided. The Congress Nationalists of Bengal pounced on this statement,[128] and on 2 September they decided to run their own candidates. To level the bidding, on the same day Sarat Bose moved a resolution before the new Executive Council of the Bengal PCC:

That inasmuch as the Communal decision, apart from being an All-India problem, is one of the gravest and most vital problems affecting the province of Bengal . . . it is the duty of the provincial Congress organisation . . . to carry on agitation both in and outside the legislature for the rejection of the Communal decision. . . . [129]

Since these were now the days of unity, the resolution was carried unanimously. The PCC prudently failed to report it to the Working Committee, but there were other friends who did so. When Nehru protested, Sarat Bose was unrepentant:

You are well aware of the volume of popular feeling in our province against the communal decision. . . . The electorates . . . are not willing to tolerate any uncertain or equivocal attitude towards the communal decision. To ignore that fact would be to court defeat at the coming elections; and we shudder to think what the effect of such a defeat would be on the Congress organisation as a whole.[130]

Nehru found it best to confront this challenge in ideological terms, complaining that, as he had predicted, the Bengal Congress was losing its doctrinal purity:

It seemed to me that they were gradually converting themselves into the Nationalist Party. That fear seems to me even more justified now after the last decision of the B. [engal] P.C.C.[131]

That was true enough. But a problem which jeopardized the Congress in the all-India elections could not be solved by doctrinal definitions. At this time Nehru was acutely dependent on the support of the conservatives in the Working Committee. In July they had protested that his socialist turns of phrase would do the party electoral damage, and

---

[128] Statement by Akhil Chandra Dutta, President of the Bengal Congress Nationalist Party, *Amrita Bazar Patrika*, 27 August 1936.

[129] Resolution enclosed in Sarat Bose to Jawaharlal Nehru, 19 September 1936, file G 24/710 of 1936, AICC.

[130] Sarat Bose to Jawaharlal Nehru, 19 September 1936, *ibid.* He went on, maliciously, to quote Nehru's own judgement: 'The Congress attitude to the Communal Award was extraordinary. . . . It was the inevitable outcome of the past neutral and feeble policy'. J. Nehru, *An Autobiography* (London, 1936), p. 575.

[131] Jawaharlal Nehru to Sarat Bose, 4 October 1936, file G 24/710 of 1936, AICC.

their threat of resignation had curbed his experiments with truth. During the confrontation with Bengal in September and October it was they, and not the Congress president, who shaped the tactics of the centre. What moved Patel and Prasad were not ideological niceties but electoral needs, and these demanded a hard line against Bengal. They needed to cow the province. Now they had the ideal weapon at hand.

One of the first tasks of the newly united PCC had been to appoint a Provincial Parliamentary Committee, to scrutinize candidates nominated by the DCCs for the forthcoming elections. Once they had approved the list, the Bengal Committee wanted to publish it quickly, partly so that it might appear before 20 October, when the Puja holidays would bring politics to a standstill,[132] and partly, perhaps, because half the candidates they had approved were members of the Congress Nationalist Party.[133] But the list had also to be approved by the All-India Parliamentary Committee. With India standing on the brink of the elections, this body was one of the most powerful organizations in the entire Congress. Its president was Vallabhbhai Patel and its secretary was Rajendra Prasad.

Vallabhbhai had an old dislike of the Bengal Congress and of the Bose brothers. Now he seized the chance to use the full powers of the centre against provincial indiscipline:

The interpretation that has been put by the Bengal Executive Committee on the A.I.C.C. electoral statement about the Communal Decision is entirely wrong and unless the candidates whose recommendations are forwarded by you agree to accept the policy and programme of the [AICC] Manifesto, it would not be possible for the Central Parliamentary Committee to accept the recommendations, and there would be consequently considerable delay in getting a decision from authoritative sources afterwards.[134]

The leaders of the Bengal Congress might be united in detesting the Award; but they were no less united in desiring to contest the elections. So there was nothing for it except to surrender. On 8 November, the offending resolution was replaced by another which said nothing about destroying the Award; and this time the PCC punctiliously informed all members of the Working Committee that it had changed its mind.[135]

[132] B. C. Roy to Rajendra Prasad, 4 October 1936, *ibid*.
[133] Statement by Indra Narayan Sen Gupta, Secretary, Bengal Congress Nationalist Party, *Amrita Bazar Patrika*, 22 November 1936.
[134] Vallabhbhai Patel to B. C. Roy, 9 October 1936, file G 24/710 of 1936, AICC.
[135] Secretary, Bengal PCC to all members of the Working Committee, 13 November 1936, *ibid*.

The centre had disciplined a united Bengal. Bengal retaliated by embarrassing a divided centre. Sarat Bose appealed to Nehru as one advanced thinker to another:

... pro-ministry wallahs like Patel ... & others will sidetrack the main issue but Bengal will always stand by you in the fight for independence.[136]

But there was nothing to be gained by declaiming long-term slogans to a Congress president who was trapped in a Working Committee obsessed with a short-term aim. Nehru could not help. In any case Vallabhbhai had not finished with the Bengal PCC. On 8 November that body had transferred all the powers of its Parliamentary Committee to Sarat Bose and B. C. Roy. When Bose's list of candidates came before the All-India Parliamentary Committee, a number of them were rejected. He resigned from the task, leaving it to an apprehensive B. C. Roy,[137] who then received this encouragement from Nehru:

I do not know what you expect from me in the way of inspiration and guidance, but if I may venture to offer a suggestion—why not arrange for some of the Gilbert and Sullivan operas to be shown in Calcutta for the free entertainment and instruction of our over-worked and over-worried colleagues. Of course there is that other sovereign remedy of standing on one's head which the Bengal Parliamentary Board and the B.P.C.C. might indulge in with advantage. I can commend this method from personal experience. . . .[138]

Roy found no pleasure in this advice. Next the All-India Parliamentary Committee began to reject his nominees as well. It was now his turn to resign.[139] When the Bengal Congress fought the elections in January 1937, it was as the captive of the centre.

These low affairs have to be placed in a larger setting. All over India the provincial Congress parties were now squarely facing the demands of electoral politics; and most of them saw the need for integrating themselves into local centres of power. This they did, in the United Provinces, the Central Provinces and Bihar; after some difficulty they did so in Berar and Maharashtra;[140] and most conspicuously of all, they did so in Madras.[141] In that province Congress won 74 per cent of seats in the elections to the new provincial Assemblies under the new fran-

---

[136] Sarat Bose to Jawaharlal Nehru, 18 November 1936, *ibid.*
[137] B. C. Roy to G. B. Pant, 30 November 1936, file P 6/707 of 1936, AICC.
[138] Jawaharlal Nehru to B. C. Roy, 3 December 1936, *ibid.*
[139] B. C. Roy to G. B. Pant, 17 December 1936, *ibid.*
[140] Now that important powers were at stake, provincial politicians were compelled to woo the localities.
[141] C. J. Baker, 'Political Change in South India' (Cambridge University, Ph.D. thesis, 1972), Chapter IX.

chise; in Bihar it won 65 per cent, in the Central Provinces 62.5 per cent, in the United Provinces 59 per cent, and in Bombay 49 per cent. In the elections in Bengal, Congress won 21.6 per cent.[142] This was a feeble result. The best that could be said of it was that no party did well in Bengal. Hence for a while, members of all the factions, such as J. C. Gupta, B. C. Roy, K. S. Roy, Sarat Bose and T. C. Goswami, could hope to take office in alliance with the Muslim-Namasudra party of Fazl-Huq.[143] But the Working Committee would not hear of it.[144] Reluctantly Bengal Congressmen had to watch portfolios floating away from them:

The Proja party members headed by Moulvi Fazul Huq begged of the Congress members to form a coalition with them. . . . Due to Congress decision we were unable to accede to their request. . . .[145]

As it turned out, there was never to be a Congress ministry in an undivided Bengal. But its disappointed Hindu politicians had one last fling. In provinces with Congress ministries there were other disappointed politicians. They might be recruited into a foray against those in possession. In 1937 Subhas Bose had returned to India, and he became president of the all-India Congress the following year. He was soon at odds with the right wing at the centre, because of his dislike of the Congress ministries and his outright opposition to federation. Stands of that sort were meat and drink to his supporters in Bengal, and they also won over the aggrieved factions in other provinces. This coalition forced through his re-election in January, 1939.[146] Not that it mattered. The opposition of the right wing, led by Gandhi himself,

---

[142] Congress candidates in Bengal won forty-three of the forty-eight General Seats, six of the seats reserved for the Depressed Classes and five of the seats reserved for Labour. Of the 250 seats in the new Assembly they won fifty-four.

[143] Nalinaksha Sanyal to Nehru, 20 February 1937; file E 5/840 of 1937, AICC.

[144] On 18 March the Working Committee agreed in principle that in provinces where Congress held a majority of Assembly seats, they might consider forming ministries. Of course, this did not apply to Bengal. On 29 April this permission was withdrawn. On 8 July, after a great deal of negotiating with Government, the Working Committee again granted permission for accepting office, but Nehru directed that in Bengal the Congress should not negotiate for membership of any coalition.

[145] J. C. Gupta to Jawaharlal Nehru, 14 August 1937, file P 5/868 of 1937, AICC.

[146] Bose won support from the Punjab and Bengal, provinces without Congress ministries. He also won support from the UP, where some sections of the provincial Congress were opposed to the tenancy legislation of the Pant ministry; from Madras, where the Rajagopalachari ministry had alienated a number of supporters; and from Karnatak, where there was dislike of the tenancy legislation of the Kher ministry in Bombay. For details of this coalition I am indebted to the work of Mr B. R. Tomlinson of Trinity College, Cambridge.

forced Subhas to resign in April, 1939.[147] He retaliated by founding the Forward Bloc and the Left-Consolidation Committee, efforts to give organized form to his inter-provincial alliance of the aggrieved. These picked up little support except from men who had been tossed and gored by Vallabhbhai. In August the Working Committee removed Subhas from all his positions in the Congress. The coalition vanished. Deserted by the M. N. Roy group, by the Trade Unionists, by the Congress Socialists and by the National Front,[148] Subhas was now a general without an army, reduced to demonstrating in front of British statues on the Calcutta maidan. In January 1941, he fled from India, disguised as a Muslim insurance agent.

It was the misfortune of Bengal that the history and social structure of the province made a jigsaw which no longer could be teased into a solution. Perhaps the best friend of the old politicians had been the proconsul whose partition of Bengal would have cut away their troubles in the eastern districts. But they had rejected the surgery of George Nathaniel Curzon. By the nineteen-twenties their options inside undivided Bengal were closing. By the time of the Communal Award and the wider franchise, self-government for Bengal could only mean the rule of others. No one would permit Bengal to contract out of the empire on Burmese lines; and in any case the province lacked the internal solidarity to pull the Bengali peoples out of India. Inside the province the balance had tilted against the Hindu politicians, so radical in style, so conservative in practice. Inside India as a whole, it had tilted against Bengal. Only a new partition could salvage something from the wreck.

The modern history of Bengal has often been taken as the exemplar of Indian nationalism. In fact, Bengal more and more deviated from it. In the nineteenth century the province had done much to establish the trends in the national movement; by the nineteen-thirties it was struggling against them. By their failure to link province with locality, its politicians were bound to lose in the great game of the last days of the Raj. No province had done as much to develop theories and programmes for the national movement. Yet this narrative should have shown how irrelevant ideology turned out to be in this most ideologically minded of Indian provinces. It also demonstrates the need to reintegrate the study of Indian history. Bengal's fate had been largely determined by national and imperial considerations which were outside its control. Locality and

---

[147] For the moves and counter-moves between Subhas and Gandhi, see S. C. Bose, *Crossroads* (London, 1962), pp. 126–70.

[148] This was the Communist Party of India in sheep's clothing.

province cannot be studied in isolation from the nation and the empire to which they belonged.

There was a tragic sense to the struggles of the Bengal Congress as it tried to hold its own against the unsentimental calculations of the British and the Congress centre. Those Bengalis who once had gained so much by their enthusiastic acceptance of British rule and culture, were finally cast aside by the Raj. The province which had inspired Indian nationalism was sacrificed for its sake. Imperialism devours its own children. Nationalism destroys its own parents.